Logic Design

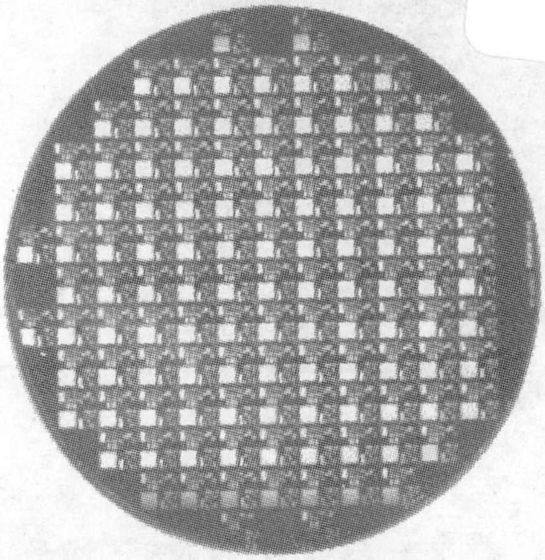

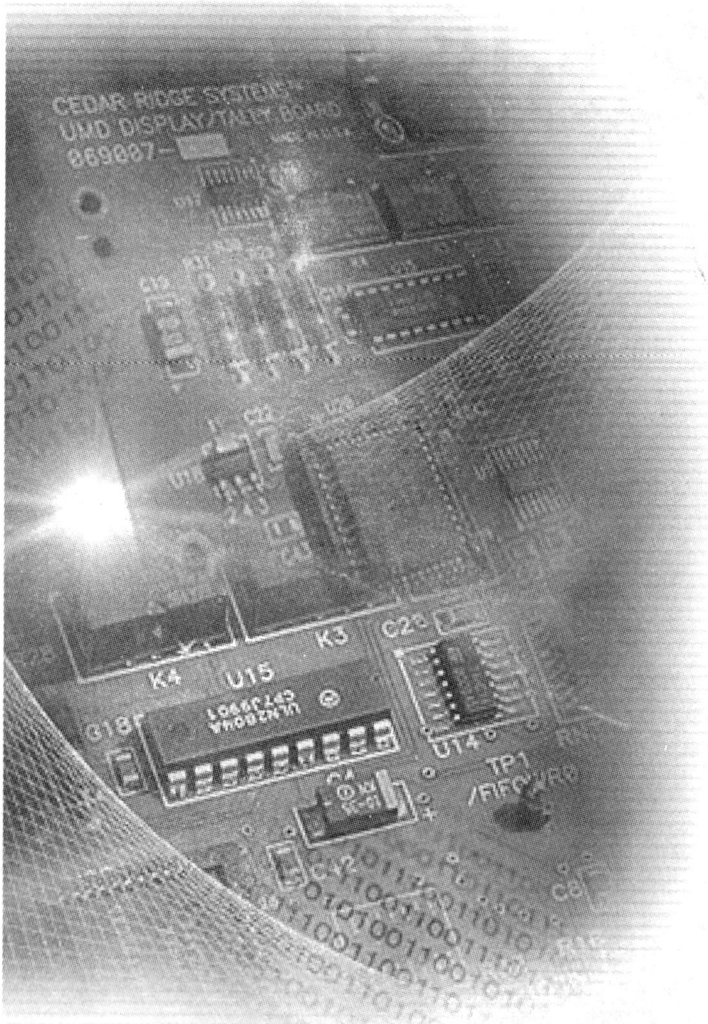
K3
K4
U15
U14
TP1

Logic Design

R. S. Allurkar

Assistant Professor
Department of Instrumentation Technology
Basaveshwar Engineering College
Bagalkot (Karnataka)

With contributions from

Renuka Allurkar

Formerly Lecturer, NES Polytechnic
Gulbarga (Karnataka)

CBS PUBLISHERS & DISTRIBUTORS PVT. LTD.

NEW DELHI • BENGALURU • CHENNAI • KOCHI • MUMBAI • PUNE

ISBN : 978-81-239-1705-4

First Edition : 2009
Reprint : 2014

Published by Satish Kumar Jain for
CBS Publishers & Distributors Pvt. Ltd.,
CBS Plaza, 4819/XI Prahlad Street, 24 Ansari Road, Daryaganj,
New Delhi - 110002, India. • Website: www.cbspd.com
e-mail: delhi@cbspd.com, cbspubs@airtelmail.in
Ph.: 23289259, 23266861, 23266867 • Fax: 011-23243014

Branches:

- ***Bengaluru:*** Seema House, 2975, 17th Cross, K.R. Road, Bansankari 2nd Stage, Bengaluru - 560070
  • Ph.: +91-80-26771678/79 • Fax: +91-80-26771680
  • E-mail: cbsbng@gmail.com, bangalore@cbspd.com
- ***Pune:*** Bhuruk Prestige, Sr. No. 52/12/2+1+3/2, Narhe, Haveli (Near Katraj-Dehu Road By-pass), Pune - 411041
  • Ph.: +91-20-64704058/59, 020-32392277 • E-mail: pune@cbspd.com
- ***Kochi:*** 36/14, Kalluvilakam, Lissie Hospital Road, Kochi - 682018, Kerala • Ph.: +91-484-4059061-65
  • Fax: +91-484-4059065 • E-mail: cochin@cbspd.com
- ***Chennai:*** 20, West Park Road, Shenoy Nagar, Chennai - 600030
  Ph.: +91-44-26260666, 26208620 • Fax: +91-44-42032115
  • E-mail: chennai@cbspd.com
- ***Mumbai:*** 83-C, Ist Floor, Dr. E. Moses Road, Worli, Mumbai-400 018, Maharashtra Ph.: +91-9833017933, 022-24902340/24902341
  • E-mail: mumbai@cbspd.com

Printed at :
India Binding House, Noida (UP)

to
our
beloved parents

Preface

There are several books in the area of logic design. No doubt the present book is different in the ways it is presented. It is written especially to cater to the needs of the students of electrical engineering, electronics and communication engineering, computer science and engineering, and several other electrical and electronics related disciplines at the degree level. It aims to serve as a textbook suitable for a semester. The objective of this textbook is to provide students the basics of digital electronics with emphasis on the fundamental concepts of logic design through a simple and understandable approach.

Efforts have been made to include examples with step-by-step procedure wherever necessary. Varieties of solved problems are given in each chapter to make the students familiar with the solution methods. Exercises are given at the end of each chapter for practice. Answers to these exercises are provided at the end of the book for the students to verify the results.

Valuable suggestions and corrections for the improvement of the book will be highly appreciated.

R. S. Allurkar
rsa_bgk@yahoo.co.in

Acknowledgements

This book has been possible with the support of many people. It has gained from the constructive criticism and suggestions of many reviewers. Thanks to Mr S. M. Iddalagi, Mr K. Bhat, Mr Shridhar S. K. and Mr S. G. Kambalimath (Basaveshwar Engineering College, Bagalkot).

It is my pleasure to thank the following whose words and wishes were a great encouragement to me in writing this book: Dr H. K. Verma (SGSITS, Indore), Dr S. R. Mahadeva Prasanna (IIT, Guwahati), Mr Baburao Khadakbhavi (MBE Society's College of Engineering, Ambajogai), Dr R. N. Herkal, Dr G. B. Mukartihal, Dr S. S. Balli, Mr P. N. Kulkarni, Mr S. G. Koolagudi, Mrs C. L. Chayalakshmi, H. R. Patil, Mr P. L. Timmanagoudar, Mr B. Veeresh, my colleagues in the Department of Instrumentation Technology (Basaveshwar Engineering College, Bagalkot), and my brother Siddharaj Allurkar (GND Engineering College, Bidar).

I would like to thank Mr Basavaraj Patil Sedam, Mr V. C. Charantimath, and the management of BVV Sangha, Bagalkot, for their moral support and encouragement.

I am grateful to my wife Mrs Renuka as without her contribution and sacrifice this book would not have been possible. Special thanks to my daughter Prithvi who helped me in proof-correction of the figures.

My special tribute to Mr H. S. Poplai in encouraging me to write this book. I am grateful to Mr Y. N. Arjuna, Senior Director, CBS Publishers & Distributors, and the entire CBS team for their cooperation and help in bringing out this book. I also thank the typesetters for their wonderful effort.

Finally, I offer thanks to my students for pointing out necessary corrections.

R. S. Allurkar
rsa_bgk@yahoo.co.in

Contents

Logic Gates

1

1.1 INTRODUCTION

Digital techniques play a very important role in modern electronics. Most of us when we hear the term 'digital', think of digital device like 'digital calculator' or 'digital voltmeter', but it is only a part of the main story. The more important thing is that the internal workings of digital components depend on electrical effects which can be described by the so called 'binary digits' 0 and 1. These often corresponds to two voltage levels LOW and HIGH in positive logic and HIGH and LOW in negative logic. Both logics are used in digital systems, but positive logic is common.

Today, digital techniques are applied in many areas, such as telephony, radar, medical instruments, process control and consumer products. The digital computer is one of the best-known example of a digital system. The building blocks of any simple or complex digital system are logic gates.

Digital logic design is concerned with the interconnections among digital components and modules and is a term used to denote the design and analysis of digital systems.

The digital components are manufactured in the form of integrated circuits (ICs). These integrated circuits contain a large number of interconnected digital circuits within a small package. The logic designer should be familiar with the various digital components in integrated circuit form.

Digital circuits are designed for two-state operation, which means that the signal voltages are either at a LOW level or a HIGH level.

Digital circuits are called logic circuits because they simulate some of our mental processes. It is to be noted that four different names have been used for the same type of circuits; digital circuits, switching circuits, logic circuits and logic gates or simply gates. The most basic gates are the NOT gate, the AND gate, and the OR gate. By using these gates in different ways, we can build more complex logic circuits such as counters, registers, decoders, and memories. Such circuits are then combined to form complete digital systems designed to perform a specific task.

It is known that in the world of electronics analog signals have continuous variations in voltage or current while digital signal consists of a train of pulses for the voltage or current. So it is clear that these pulses are involved in the operation of digital circuits. Figure 1.1 shows the ideal positive and negative pulses.

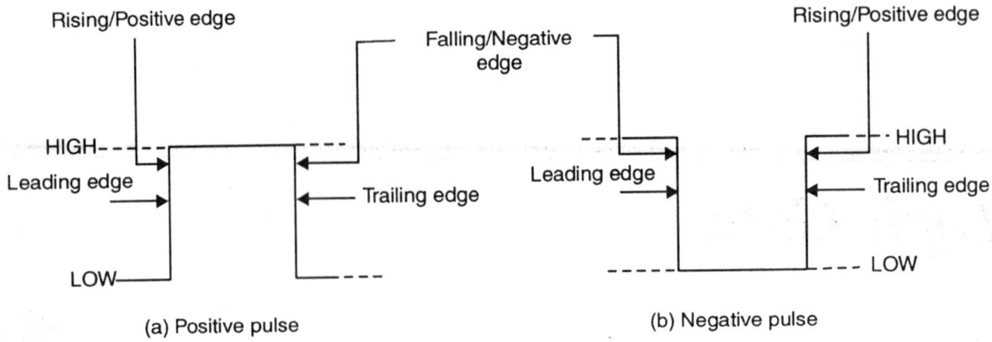

Fig. 1.1 Pulses

1.2 THE INVERTER (NOT GATE)

An inverter is a circuit with only a single input and a single output. The inverter performs basic logic function called inversion or complementation.

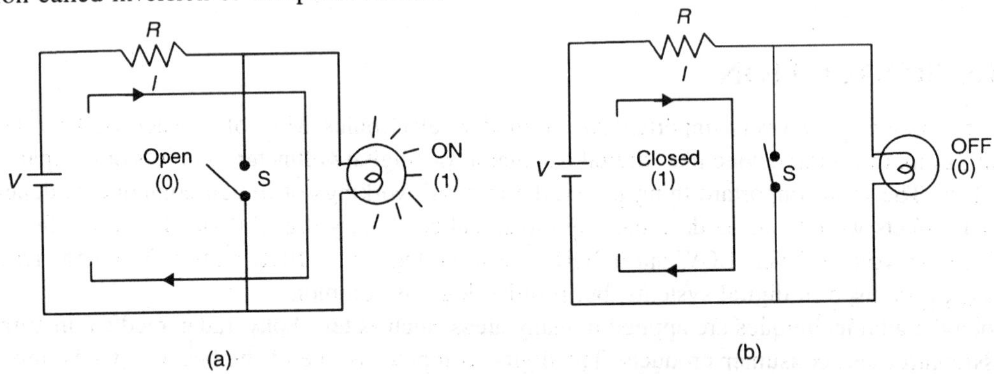

Fig. 1.2 A switch in parallel with the lamp-logic NOT

The operation of the inverter is such that the output is HIGH when the input is LOW and the output is LOW when the input is HIGH.

The logic function of the inverter can be illustrated by the analogy shown in Fig. 1.2.

The lamp is ON, when the switch is OPEN (0) and the lamp is OFF, when the switch is closed (1).

The standard logic symbols for the inverter are shown in Fig. 1.3. The operation of the inverter is summarized in Table 1.1, commonly known as a *truth table,* which shows all the input–output possibilities of a logic circuit. The pulsed operation of the inverter is as shown in Fig. 1.4.

Fig. 1.3 Standard logic symbols for the inverter

* Symbol developed by the Institute of Electrical and Electronic Engineers (IEEE) together with the American National Standards Institute (ANSI).

Table 1.1 Inverter truth tables

Input	Output
LOW	HIGH
HIGH	LOW

≡

Input	Output
0	1
1	0

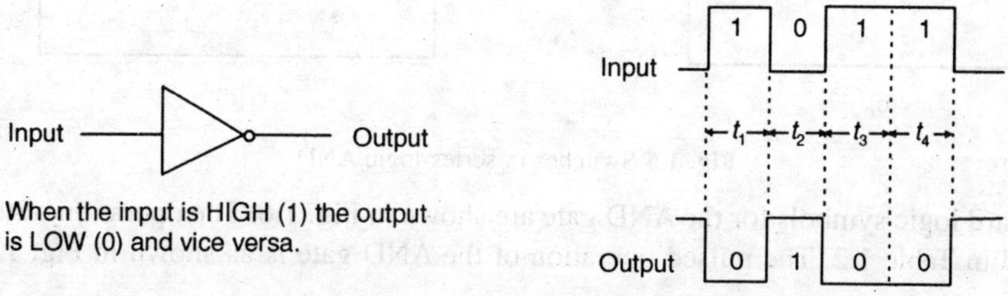

Fig. 1.4 Pulsed operation of the inverter

Note: There is one isolating gate called *buffer*, used to provide isolation between two parts of a circuit. The buffer produces the output same as the input. The logic symbol and the buffer truth table are shown below.

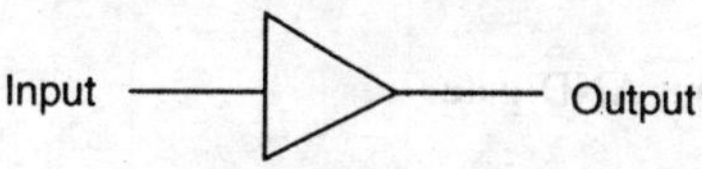

Input	Output
0	0
1	1

1.3 THE AND GATE

An AND gate is a circuit with two or more inputs and a single output. The AND gate performs the logical multiplication, more commonly known as AND function.

The operation of the AND gate is such that the output is HIGH only when all of the inputs are HIGH. When any of the inputs is LOW, the output is LOW.

The logic function of the AND gate can be illustrated by the analogy shown in Fig. 1.5.

The lamp is OFF (0) if any one of the switches is open (0) and the lamp is ON (1) only if all the switches are closed (1).

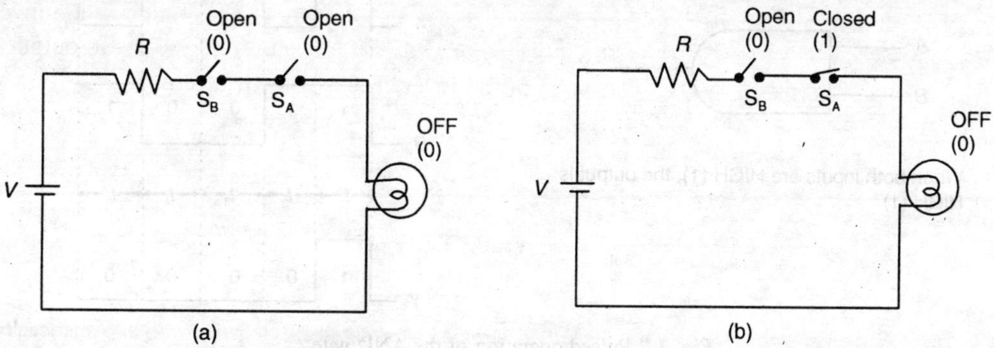

Fig. 1.5 Switches in series-logic AND

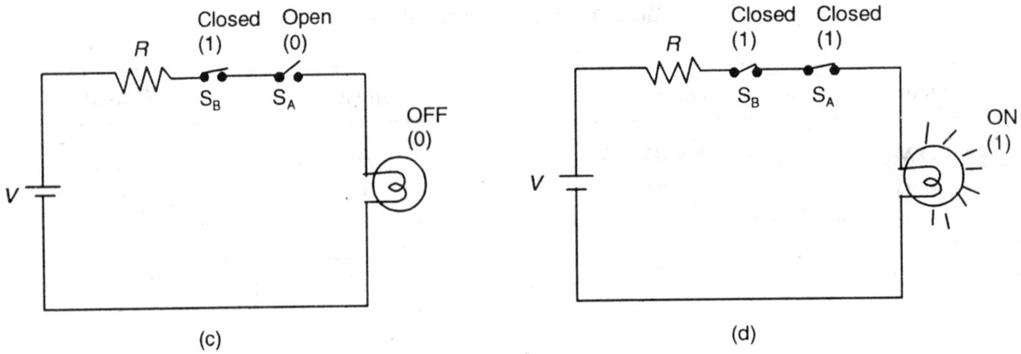

Fig. 1.5 Switches in series-logic AND

The standard logic symbols for the AND gate are shown in Fig. 1.6. The operation of the AND gate is summarized in Table 1.2. The pulsed operation of the AND gate is as shown in Fig. 1.7.

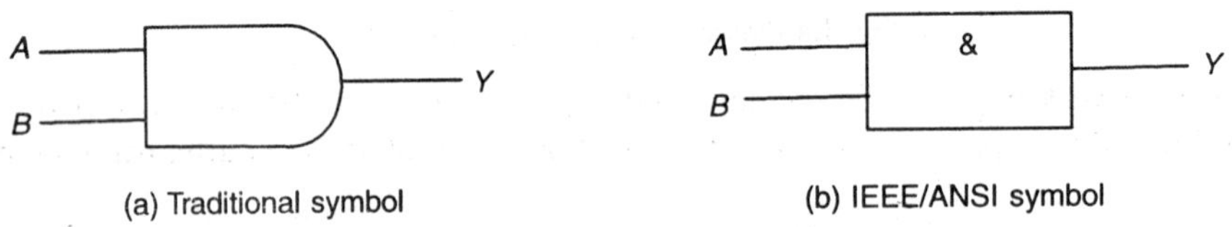

Fig. 1.6 Standard logic symbols for the two-input AND gate

Table 1.2 Truth table for a two-input AND gate

Inputs		Output
A	*B*	*Y*
0	0	0
0	1	0
1	0	0
1	1	1

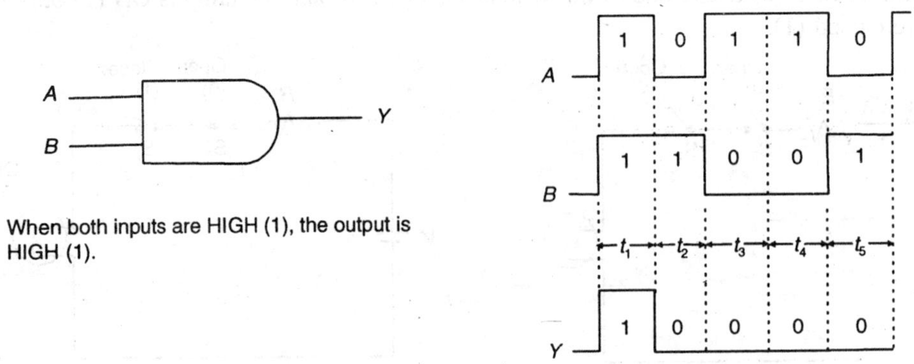

Fig. 1.7 Pulsed operation of the AND gate

Note: The total number of possible combinations of binary inputs is determined by the formula: $N = 2^n$, where n is the number of inputs. For example a 3-input AND gate has a truth table with $2^3 = 8$ possible combinations.

1.4 THE OR GATE

An OR gate is a circuit with two or more inputs and a single output. The OR gate performs the logical addition, more commonly known as OR function. The operation of the OR gate is such that the output is HIGH when any of the inputs is HIGH. The output is LOW only when all of the inputs are LOW.

The logic function of the OR gate can be illustrated by the analogy shown in Fig. 1.8.

The lamp is OFF (0), only if all the switches are open (0) and the lamp is ON(1), if any one of the switches is closed (1).

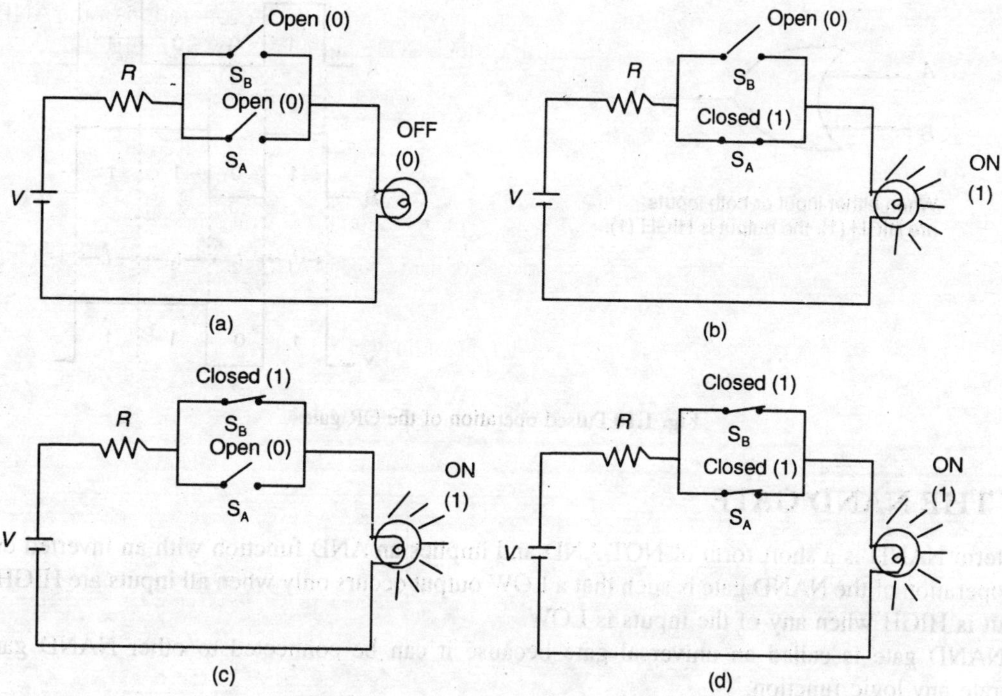

Fig. 1.8 Switches in parallel-logic OR

The standard logic symbols for the OR gate are shown in Fig. 1.9. The operation of the OR gate is summarized in Table 1.3. The pulsed operation of the OR gate is as shown in Fig. 1.10.

Fig. 1.9 Standard logic symbols for the two-input OR gate

Table 1.3 Truth table for a two–input OR gate

Inputs		Output
A	*B*	*Y*
0	0	0
0	1	1
1	0	1
1	1	1

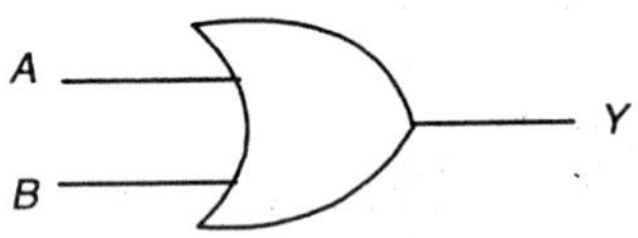

When either input or both inputs are HIGH (1), the output is HIGH (1).

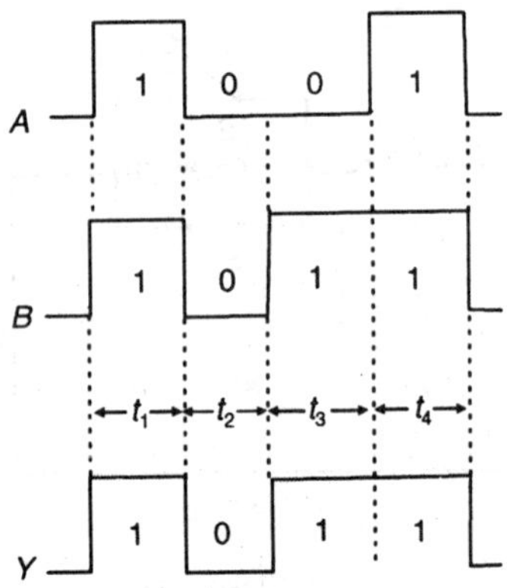

Fig. 1.10 Pulsed operation of the OR gate

1.5 THE NAND GATE

The term NAND is a short form of NOT-AND and implies an AND function with an inverted output. The operation of the NAND gate is such that a LOW output occurs only when all inputs are HIGH. The output is HIGH when any of the inputs is LOW.

NAND gate is called an universal gate because it can be connected to other NAND gates to generate any logic function.

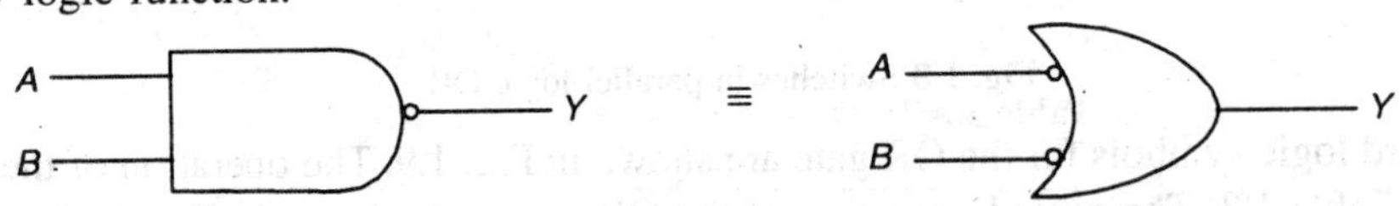

(a) Traditional symbols

(b) IEEE/ANSI symbols

Fig. 1.11 Standard logic symbols for the two-input NAND gate

NAND can be seen either as AND followed by NOT, or as NOT for each input followed by OR. The two alternative symbols for the NAND gate both in traditional and IEEE/ANSI representations are shown in Fig. 1.11. The operation of the NAND gate is summarized in Table 1.4.

Table 1.4 Truth table for a two-input NAND gate

Inputs		Output
A	*B*	*Y*
0	0	1
0	1	1
1	0	1
1	1	0

1.6 THE NOR GATE

The term NOR is a short form of NOT-OR and implies an OR function with an inverted output. The operation of the NOR gate is such that a LOW output occurs when any of its inputs are HIGH. The output is HIGH only when all of its inputs are LOW.

NOR gate is called an universal gate because it can be connected to other NOR gates to generate any logic function.

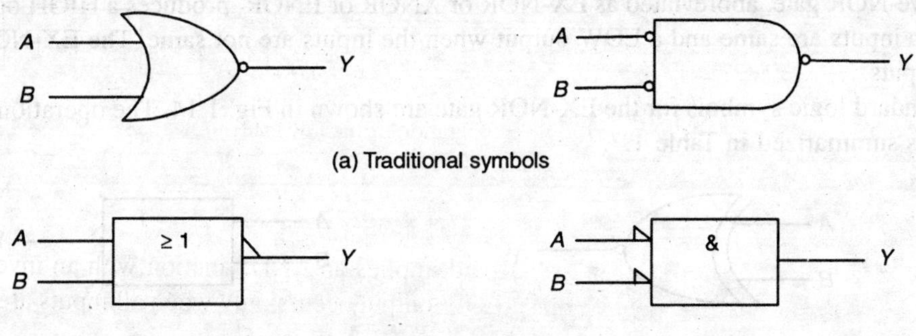

Fig. 1.12 Standard logic symbols for the two-input NOR gate

Table 1.5 Truth table for a two-input NOR gate

Inputs		Output
A	*B*	*Y*
0	0	1
0	1	0
1	0	0
1	1	0

NOR can be seen either as OR followed by NOT, or as NOT for each input followed by AND. The two alternative symbols for the NOR gate both in traditional and IEEE/ANSI representations are shown in Fig. 1.12. The operation of the NOR gate is summarized in Table 1.5.

1.7 THE EXCLUSIVE-OR GATE

An Exclusive-OR gate, abbreviated as EX-OR or XOR or EOR, produces a HIGH output whenever the two inputs are not same and a LOW output when the inputs are same. The EX-OR gate has only two inputs.

The standard logic symbols for the EX-OR gate are shown in Fig. 1.13. The operation of the EX-OR gate is summarized in Table 1.6.

(a) Traditional symbol (b) IEEE/ANSI symbol

Fig. 1.13 Standard logic symbols for the EX-OR gate

1.8 THE EXCLUSIVE-NOR GATE

An Exclusive-NOR gate, abbreviated as EX-NOR or XNOR or ENOR, produces a HIGH output whenever the two inputs are same and a LOW output when the inputs are not same. The EX-NOR gate has only two inputs.

The standard logic symbols for the EX-NOR gate are shown in Fig. 1.14. The operation of the EX-NOR gate is summarized in Table 1.7.

(a) Traditional symbol (b) IEEE/ANSI symbol

Fig. 1.14 Standard logic symbols for the EX-NOR gate

Table 1.6 Truth table for an EX-OR gate

Inputs		Output
A	*B*	*Y*
0	0	0
0	1	1
1	0	1
1	1	0

Table 1.7 Truth table for an EX-NOR gate

Inputs		Output
A	*B*	*Y*
0	0	1
0	1	0
1	0	0
1	1	1

1.9 DIGITAL INTEGRATED CIRCUITS

To reduce the size of electronic circuit, miniature circuit can be fabricated on a single silicon chip. Such a circuit is called *integrated circuit (IC)* because the components are an integral part of the chip. In terms of their function, ICs are classified as digital ICs and linear ICs. Digital ICs process digital signals, whereas linear ICs process analog signals.

Digital ICs are classified according to the complexity of their circuitry. Texas Instruments defines an SSI (Small-scale integration) chip as one that contain circuitry with less than 12 gates. MSI (medium-scale integration) chip contains circuitry equal to 12 to 100 gates. An LSI (large-scale integration) chip contains circuitry equal to 100 to 1000 gates, while VLSI (very large scale integration) chip contains more than 1000 gates. These definitions do slightly vary from manufacturer to manufacturer.

It is important that the terms used in digital IC technology be clearly understood. Some useful terms are therefore defined and discussed below.

Fan-Out

The *fan-out* of a gate is defined as the maximum number of other gate inputs of the same IC family that the gate can drive from its output while maintaining its output levels within specified limits.

For example, a logic gate has a fan-out of 20 can reliably drive 20 inputs to gates in the same IC family.

Propagation Delay

The *propagation delay* of a gate is the time interval between the leading edge of the input pulse to the leading edge of the output pulse or the time interval between the trailing edge of the input pulse to the trailing edge of the output pulse. The terms low speed and high speed, when applied to logic gates, refer to the propagation delays.

Power Dissipation

The *power dissipation* is the amount of power required to operate the gate. This parameter is expressed in milliwatts and represents the actual power dissipated in the gate.

Noise Margin

The *noise margin* is the maximum noise voltage added to the input signal of the gate that does not cause an undesirable change in the gate output.

1.10 DIGITAL IC LOGIC FAMILIES

Digital integrated circuits (ICs) operate with binary signals (0 and 1). The most common families of digital ICs are the TTL (transistor-transistor logic) and CMOS (complementary metal-oxide semiconductor). TTL ICs are based on the bipolar technology where CMOS ICs are based on the MOS technology. The other popular logic families of digital ICs are ECL (emitter-coupled logic) and I^2L (integrated-injection logic).

Pinout diagrams of some typical IC gates and their corresponding IEEE/ ANSI symbols are shown in Fig. 1.15. TTL gates of the 7400 series are shown in Fig. 1.15(a). The terminals marked V_{CC} requires a power supply voltage of +5 Volts, while GND is grounded.

CMOS gates of the 4000 series are shown in Fig.1.15(b). The terminal marked V_{DD} requires a power supply voltage from 3 to 15 Volts, while V_{DD} is usually connected to ground.

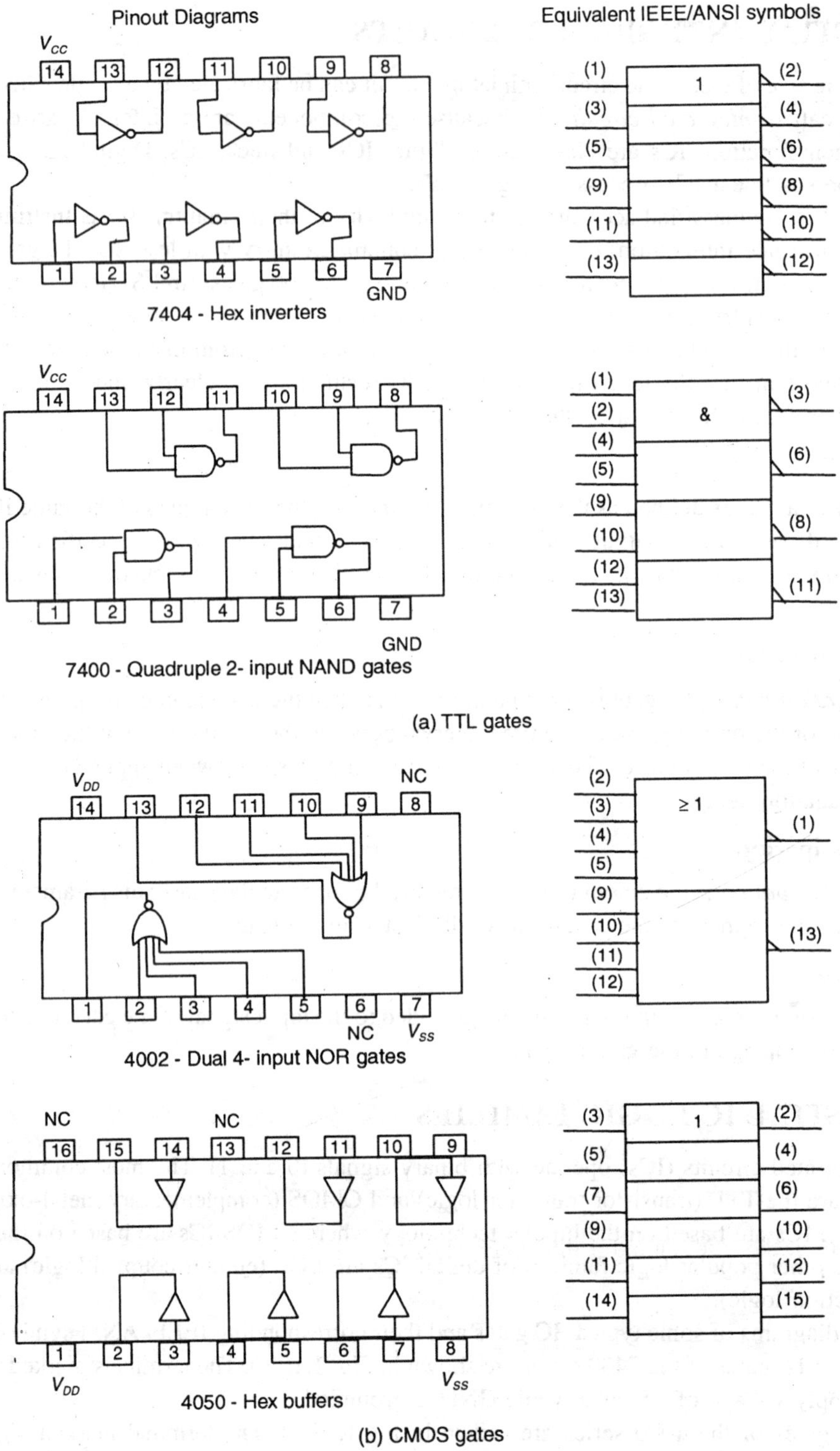

Fig. 1.15 Some typical IC gates

SOLVED PROBLEMS

1.1 Two input signals *A* and *B* are applied to a NAND gate as shown in Fig.P1.1. Draw the resulting output waveform.

SOLUTION:

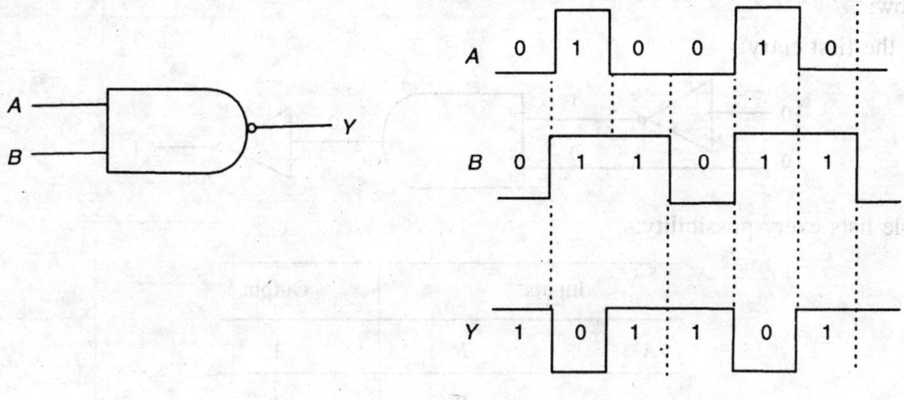

Fig. P1.1

1.2 Three inputs *A*, *B* and *C* to NOR gate are shown in the following Fig. P1.2. Sketch the output waveform.

SOLUTION:

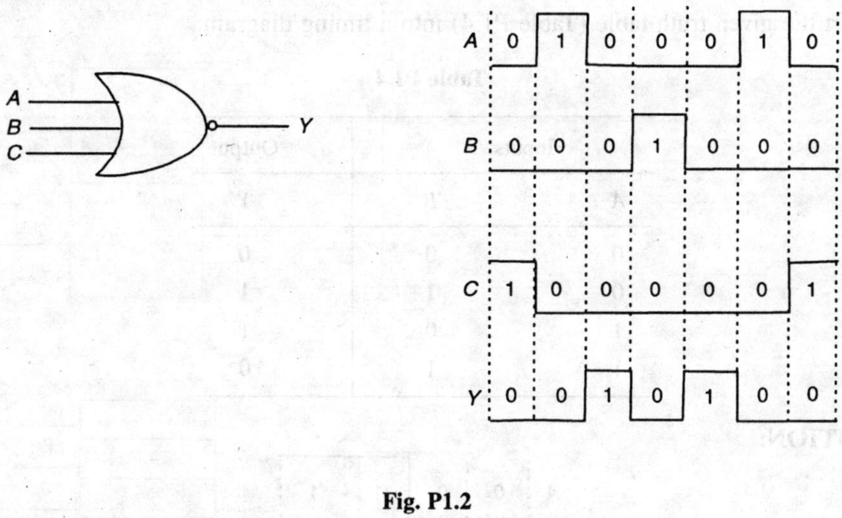

Fig. P1.2

1.3 Construct the truth table for the circuit shown in Fig. P1.3.

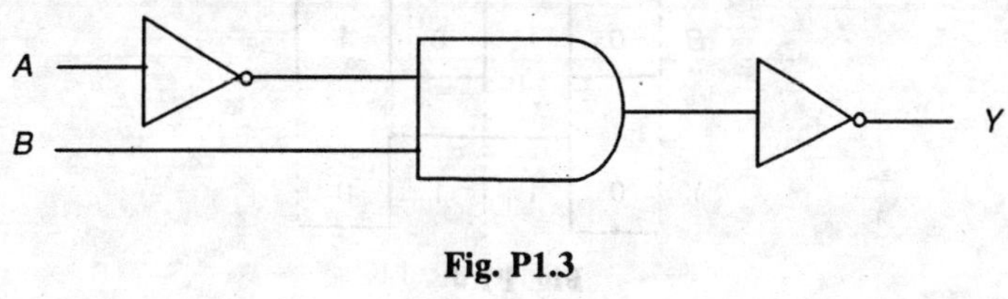

Fig. P1.3

SOLUTION: We know that the total number of rows in a truth table (possible input combinations) i.e., $N = 2^n$, where n is the number of inputs to a gate.

$\therefore \quad N = 2^2 = 4$

By analysing each input possibility, we can determine the output as described by the figure below:

For the first entry:

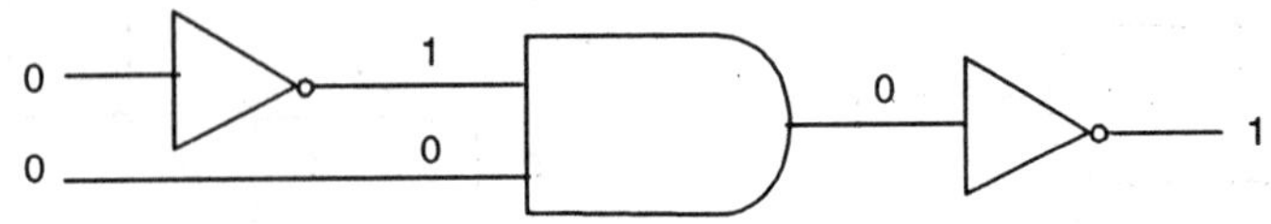

Table lists every possibility:

Inputs		Output
A	*B*	*Y*
0	0	1
0	1	0
1	0	1
1	1	1

1.4 Convert the given truth table (Table P1.4) into a timing diagram.

Table P1.4

Inputs		Output
A	*B*	*Y*
0	0	0
0	1	1
1	0	1
1	1	0

SOLUTION:

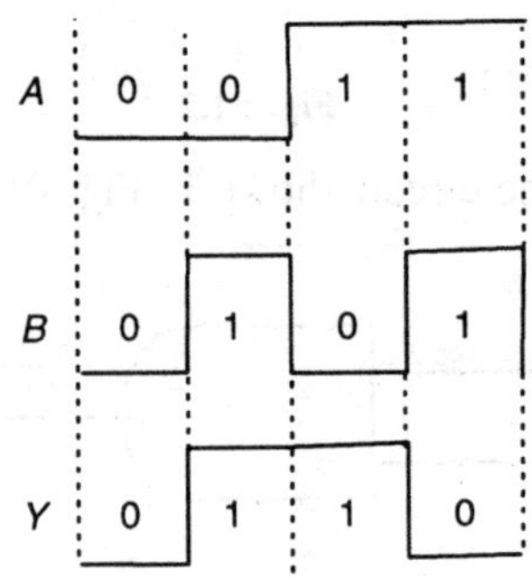

Fig. P1.4

EXERCISES

1.1 Three input signals *A*, *B* and *C* are applied to an AND gate as shown in Fig. E1.1. Determine the output waveform.

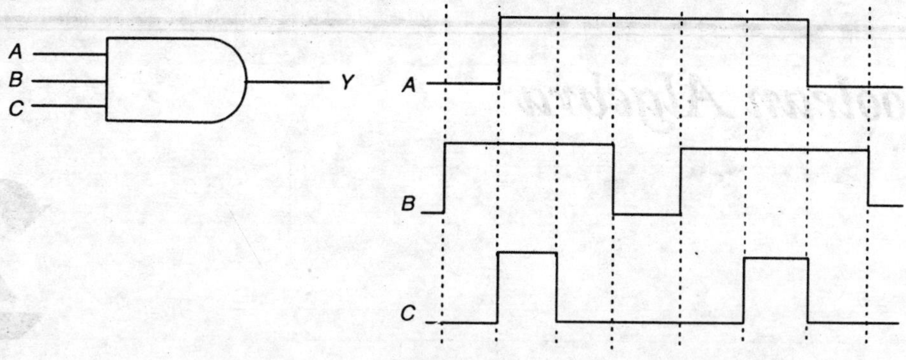

Fig. E1.1

1.2 Draw the output waveform for the NOTed OR gate with the given input signals as shown in Fig. E1.2.

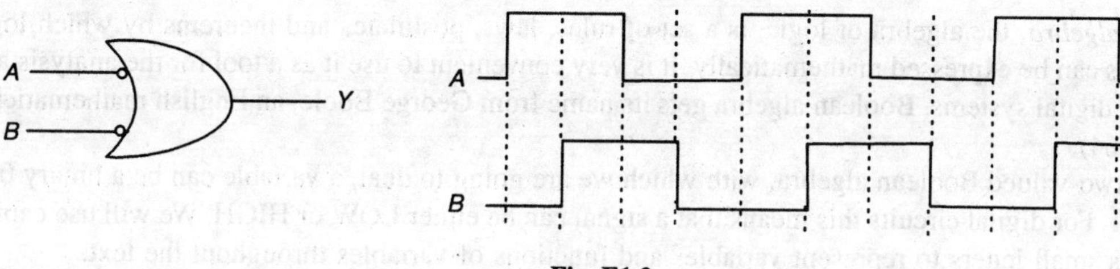

Fig. E1.2

1.3 Construct the truth table for the circuit shown in Fig. E1.3.

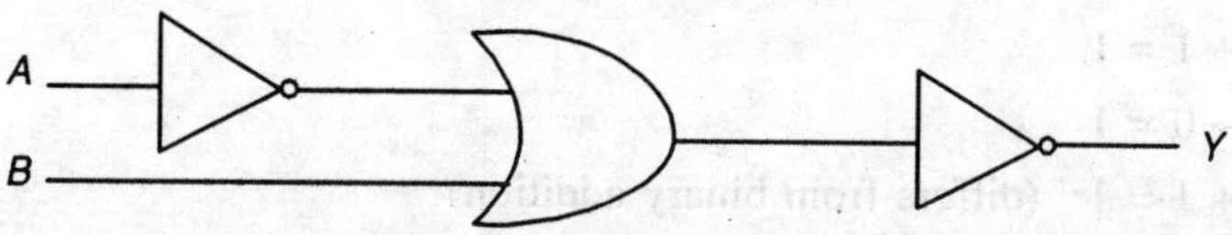

Fig. E1.3

1.4 Construct the truth table for the timing diagram shown in Fig. E1.4 where *A* and *B* are the inputs and *Y* is the output. Also identify the gate which obeys the given input output relation.

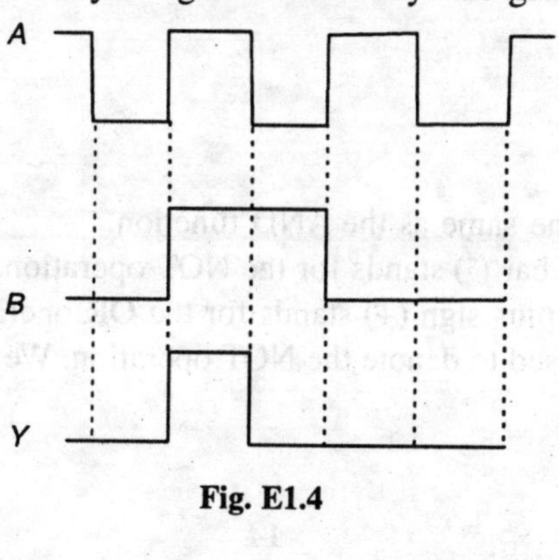

Fig. E1.4

Boolean Algebra

2

Boolean algebra, the algebra of logic, is a set of rules, laws, postulates and theorems by which logic operations can be expressed mathematically. It is very convenient to use it as a tool for the analysis and design of digital systems. Boolean algebra gets its name from George Boole, an English mathematician (1815-1864).

In a two-valued Boolean algebra, with which we are going to deal, a variable can be a binary 0 or a binary 1. For digital circuits this means that a signal can be either LOW or HIGH. We will use capital as well as small letters to represent variables and functions of variables throughout the text.

The basic rules for Boolean addition are as follows:

$$0 + 0 = 0$$

$$0 + 1 = 1$$

$$1 + 0 = 1$$

$$1 + 1 = 1 \quad \text{(differs from binary addition)}$$

Boolean addition is the same as the OR function.

The basic rules for Boolean multiplication are as follows:

$$0 \cdot 0 = 0$$

$$0 \cdot 1 = 0$$

$$1 \cdot 0 = 0$$

$$1 \cdot 1 = 1$$

Boolean multiplication is the same as the AND function.

In Boolean algebra the overbar (¯) stands for the NOT operation, the multiplication sign (·) stands for the AND operation and the plus sign (+) stands for the OR operation. Sometimes a prime symbol (′) or an asterisk symbol (∗) is used to denote the NOT operation. We can write logic expressions using these Boolean operators.

2.1 LOGIC EXPRESSIONS

NOT

A logic expression to symbolize the action of NOT gate (Fig. 2.1) can be written as $Y = \bar{A}$. This expression states that the output is the complement of the input.

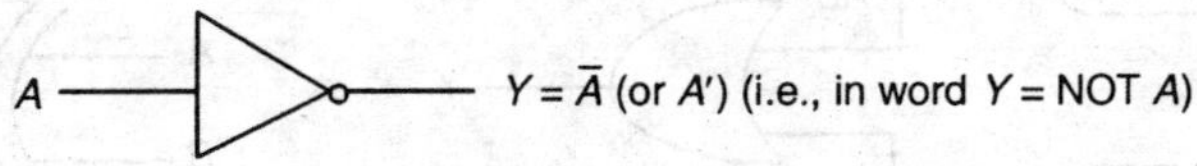

Fig. 2.1 NOT gate

AND

A logic expression to symbolize the action of two-input AND gate (Fig. 2.2) can be written as $Y = AB$, by omitting the dot.

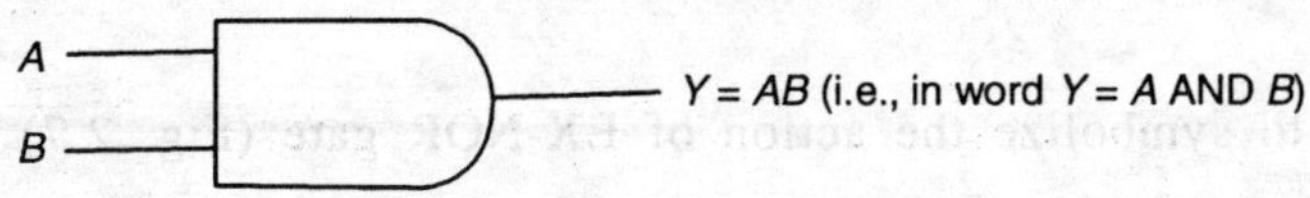

Fig. 2.2 Two-input AND gate

OR

A logic expression to symbolize the action of two-input OR gate (Fig. 2.3) can be written as $Y = A + B$.

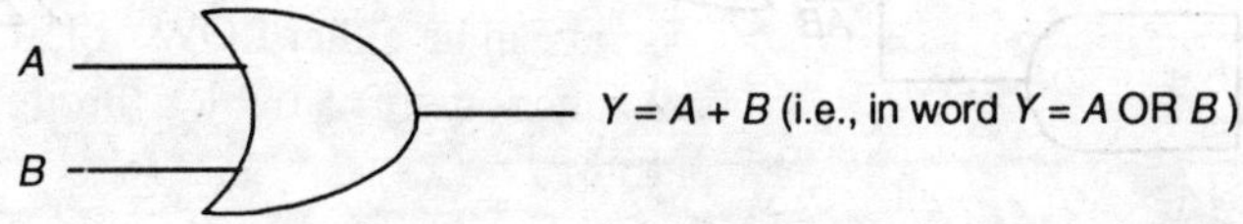

Fig. 2.3 Two-input OR gate

NAND

A logic expression to symbolize the action of two-input NAND gate (Fig. 2.4) can be written as $Y = \overline{AB}$.

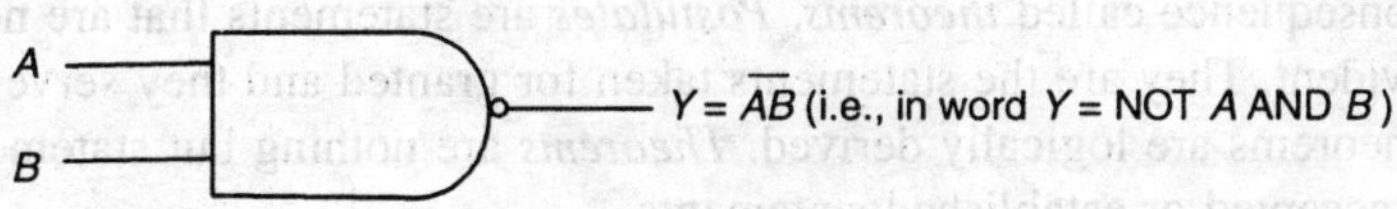

Fig. 2.4 Two-input NAND gate

NOR

A logic expression to symbolize the action of two-input NOR gate (Fig. 2.5) can be written as $Y = \overline{A + B}$.

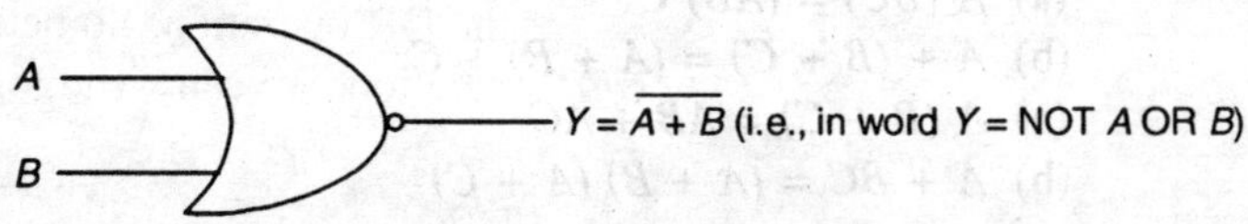

Fig. 2.5 Two-input NOR gate

EX-OR

A logic expression to symbolize the action of EX-OR gate (Fig. 2.6) can be written as $Y = A\overline{B} + \overline{A}B = A \oplus B$.

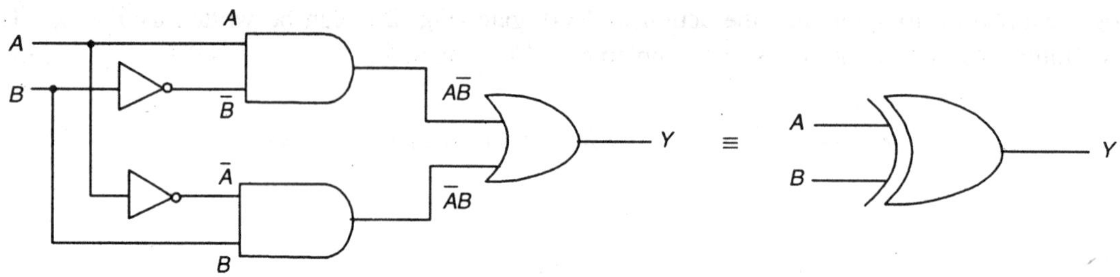

(a) Circuit (b) Symbol

Fig. 2.6 EX-OR gate

EX-NOR

A logic expression to symbolize the action of EX-NOR gate (Fig. 2.7) can be written as $Y = AB + \overline{A}\overline{B} = A \odot B$.

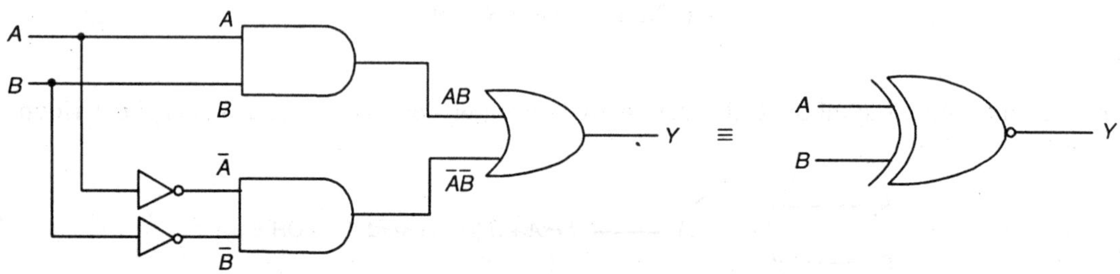

(a) Circuit (b) Symbol

Fig. 2.7 EX-NOR gate

2.2 LAWS, POSTULATES AND THEOREMS

The *laws* of Boolean algebra can be defined as certain equations called *postulates* (or *axioms*) together with their logical consequence called *theorems. Postulates* are statements that are not proved but considered to be self-evident. They are the statements taken for granted and they serve as a starting point from which other theorems are logically derived. *Theorems* are nothing but statements proven on the basis of previously accepted or established statements.

Basic Laws

Three of the basic laws of Boolean algebra are the same as in ordinary algebra.

Commutative Law: (a) $AB = BA$

(b) $A + B = B + A$

Associative Law: (a) $A(BC) = (AB)C$

(b) $A + (B + C) = (A + B) + C$

Distributive Law: (a) $A(B + C) = AB + AC$

(b) $A + BC = (A + B)(A + C)$

Note : Distributive Law (b) is valid only for Boolean algebra.

Postulates

1. (a) $A = 1$ if $A \neq 0$
   (b) $A = 0$ if $A \neq 1$
2. (a) $0 \cdot 0 = 0$
   (b) $1 + 1 = 1$
3. (a) $1 \cdot 1 = 1$
   (b) $0 + 0 = 0$
4. (a) $1 \cdot 0 = 0$
   (b) $0 + 1 = 1$
5. (a) $\overline{0} = 1$
   (b) $\overline{1} = 0$

Theorems

1. (a) $A + 0 = A$
   (b) $A \cdot 1 = A$
2. (a) $A + 1 = 1$
   (b) $A \cdot 0 = 0$
3. (a) $A + A = A$
   (b) $A \cdot A = A$
4. (a) $(\overline{A}) = \overline{A}$
   (b) $(\overline{\overline{A}}) = A$
5. (a) $A + \overline{A} = 1$
   (b) $A \cdot \overline{A} = 0$
6. (a) $\overline{A + B + C + \ldots\ldots} = \overline{A} \cdot \overline{B} \cdot \overline{C} \ldots\ldots$
   (b) $\overline{A \cdot B \cdot C \cdot \ldots\ldots} = \overline{A} + \overline{B} + \overline{C} \ldots\ldots$ } De Morgan's theorem
7. (a) $A(A + B) = A$
   (b) $A + AB = A$ } Absorption theorem

Note: The postulates and theorems indicated with (a) are the duals of the postulates and theorems indicated with (b). *Duality* is defined as the changing of all AND signs to OR signs, all OR signs to AND signs, all 1s to 0s, and all 0s to 1s. Thus starting with a Boolean relation using duality, we can derive another Boolean relation. The duality is a very useful tool in logic design.

2.3 DE MORGAN'S THEOREMS

De Morgan contributed two important theorems. These theorems are very useful in simplifying Boolean expressions. They are stated as follows:

First Theorem

$\overline{A + B} = \overline{A}\ \overline{B}$

That is, complement of a sum is equal to the product of the complements.

Second Theorem

$\overline{AB} = \overline{A} + \overline{B}$

That is, the complement of a product is equal to the sum of the complements.

Although we stated the theorems in terms of single variables A and B, they are equally valid even if A and/or B are expressions.

Figures 2.8 and 2.9 illustrate the above two theorems.

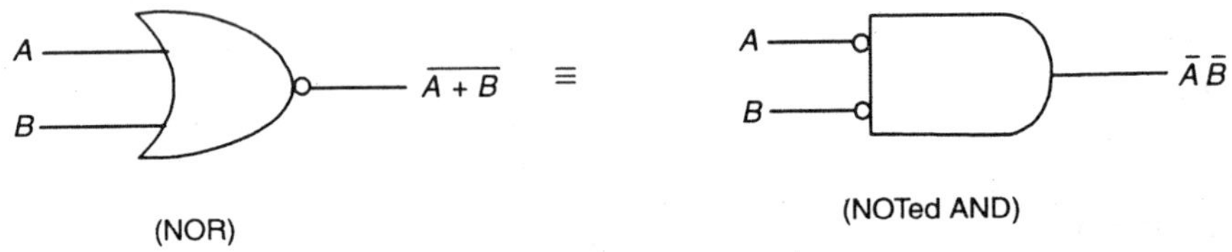

Fig. 2.8 De Morgan's first theorem

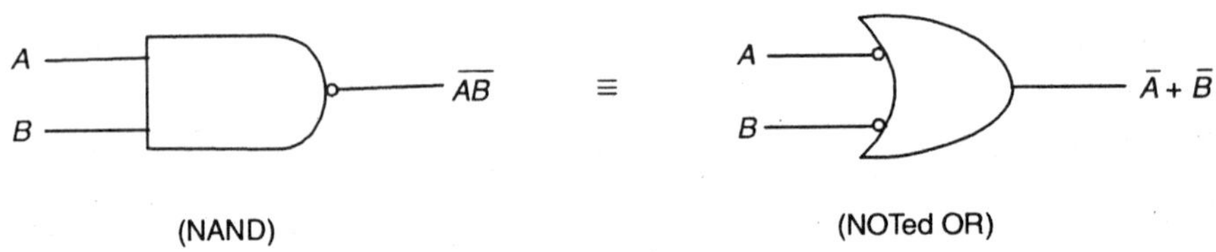

Fig. 2.9 De Morgan's second theorem

2.4 BOOLEAN FUNCTIONS

A Boolean function is an expression formed with binary variables, the two binary operators, OR and AND, the unary operator NOT, parentheses, and equal sign. For a given value of the variables, the function can be either 0 or 1.

A Boolean function can be represented as an algebraic expression or in a truth table form and it can be transformed into a logic diagram with combination of logic gates. When a Boolean function is implemented with logic gates, each literal in the function designates an input to a gate, and each term is implemented with a gate. A *literal* is nothing but a complemented or uncomplemented variable. Consider an example to illustrate this.

EXAMPLE 2.1: Obtain the truth table of the function $F = (A + B)(\overline{B} + C)$ and implement it with logic gates.

SOLUTION: $F = (A + B)(\overline{B} + C)$................ An algebraic expression.

The above function can be represented in a truth table (Table 2.1). The number of rows in a truth table is equal to 2^n, where n is the number of binary variables. Since there are 3 binary variables, the number of rows in the table = $2^3 = 8$. The possible combinations of binary inputs for each row can be easily obtained from the binary numbers by counting from 0 to $2^n - 1$.

Table 2.1 Truth table for $F = (A + B)(\overline{B} + C)$

A	B	C	$\overline{B}$	$A + B$	$\overline{B} + C$	F
0	0	0	1	0	1	0
0	0	1	1	0	1	0
0	1	0	0	1	0	0
0	1	1	0	1	1	1
1	0	0	1	1	1	1
1	0	1	1	1	1	1
1	1	0	0	1	0	0
1	1	1	0	1	1	1

The function F is implemented using logic gates as shown in Fig. 2.10.

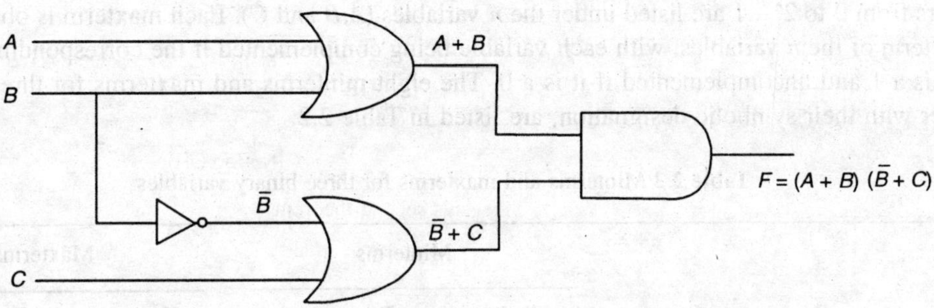

Fig. 2.10 Implementation of the Boolean function $F = (A + B)(\overline{B} + C)$

Complement of a Function

The complement of a function is obtained by interchanging AND and OR operators and complementing each literal as stated by De Morgan's theorem.

EXAMPLE 2.2: Find the complement of the function $F = ABC + \overline{A}\overline{B}\overline{C}$

SOLUTION: $F = ABC + \overline{A}\,\overline{B}\,\overline{C}$

$$\therefore \quad \overline{F} = \overline{ABC + \overline{A}\,\overline{B}\,\overline{C}}$$

$$= \left(\overline{ABC}\right)\left(\overline{\overline{A}\,\overline{B}\,\overline{C}}\right) \text{ by De Morgan's theorem}$$

$$= \left(\overline{A} + \overline{B} + \overline{C}\right)(A + B + C) \text{ by De Morgan's theorem}$$

Note: The complement of a function can also be obtained simply by taking the dual of the function and complementing each literal.

2.5 CANONICAL FORMS

Any Boolean function can be expressed in the following two general forms:

1. Minterm canonical form (sum of minterms)
2. Maxterm canonical form (product of maxterms).

Let us know what are these minterms and maxterms in the discussion followed.

Consider the two binary variables A and B combined with an AND operation. Since each variable may appear either in complemented or uncomplemented form, there are four possible combinations: $\bar{A}\,\bar{B}$, $\bar{A}B$, $A\bar{B}$ and AB. Each of these four AND terms is usually called a *minterm* or a standard product. In a similar way n variables provide 2^n possible minterms. The binary numbers from 0 to $2^n - 1$ are listed under the n variables (A, B and C). Each minterm is obtained from an AND term of the n variables, with each variable being complemented if the corresponding bit of the binary number is a 0 and uncomplemented if it is a 1.

Now if we consider two binary variables A and B combined with an OR operation, the four possible combinations are: $(\bar{A}+\bar{B})$, $(\bar{A}+B)$, $(A+\bar{B})$ and $(A+B)$. Each of these four OR terms is usually called a *maxterm* or a standard sum. In a similar way n variables provide 2^n possible maxterms. The binary numbers from 0 to $2^n - 1$ are listed under the n variables (A,B and C). Each maxterm is obtained from an OR term of the n variables, with each variable being complemented if the corresponding bit of the binary is a 1 and uncomplemented if it is a 0. The eight minterms and maxterms for three variables, together with their symbolic designation, are listed in Table 2.2.

Table 2.2 Minterms and maxterms for three binary variables

			Minterms		Maxterms	
A	B	C	Term	Designation	Term	Designation
0	0	0	$\bar{A}\bar{B}\bar{C}$	m_0	$A+B+C$	M_0
0	0	1	$\bar{A}\bar{B}C$	m_1	$A+B+\bar{C}$	M_1
0	1	0	$\bar{A}B\bar{C}$	m_2	$A+\bar{B}+C$	M_2
0	1	1	$\bar{A}BC$	m_3	$A+\bar{B}+\bar{C}$	M_3
1	0	0	$A\bar{B}\bar{C}$	m_4	$\bar{A}+B+C$	M_4
1	0	1	$A\bar{B}C$	m_5	$\bar{A}+B+\bar{C}$	M_5
1	1	0	$AB\bar{C}$	m_6	$\bar{A}+\bar{B}+C$	M_6
1	1	1	ABC	m_7	$\bar{A}+\bar{B}+\bar{C}$	M_7

Note: (i) $m_j \Rightarrow$ Minterm and $M_j \Rightarrow$ Maxterm, where subscript j denotes the decimal equivalent of the binary number of the term designated.

(ii) The maxterm with subscript j is a complement of the minterm with the same subcript j, and vice versa (i.e. $M_j = \overline{m}_j$ and vice versa).

Minterm Canonical Form (Sum of Minterms)

Expression in this form consists of two or more AND terms, each term being combinations of all variables involved, that are ORed together. Some examples of this form are :

1. $F_1 = AB + A\overline{B} + \overline{A}\,\overline{B}$
2. $F_2 = ABC + A\overline{B}\,\overline{C}$
3. $F_3 = \overline{A}BC\overline{D} + AB\overline{C}\overline{D} + AB\overline{C}\overline{D} + ABC\overline{D}$

Any Boolean function can be expanded to obtain a minterm canonical form. The following example illustrates this.

The minterm canonical form is sometimes called as a canonical SOP form.

EXAMPLE 2.3: Express the Boolean function $F = AB + AC + \overline{B}C$ in a sum of minterms.

SOLUTION: Each term in the given expression is inspected and if any term misses one or more variables, it is ANDed with an expression such as $A + \overline{A}$ $(\because A + \overline{A} = 1)$, where A is one of the missing variables.

$$F = AB + AC + \overline{B}C$$

$$= AB \cdot 1 + AC \cdot 1 + \overline{B}C \cdot 1$$

$$= AB(C + \overline{C}) + AC(B + \overline{B}) + \overline{B}C(A + \overline{A})$$

$$= ABC + AB\overline{C} + ABC + A\overline{B}C + A\overline{B}C + \overline{A}\overline{B}C \text{ by Distributive law}$$

$$= (ABC + ABC) + AB\overline{C} + (A\overline{B}C + A\overline{B}C) + \overline{A}\overline{B}C$$

$$= ABC + AB\overline{C} + A\overline{B}C + \overline{A}\overline{B}C \quad (\because A + A = 1)$$

Rearranging the minterms in ascending order, we get:

$$F = \overline{A}\overline{B}C + A\overline{B}C + AB\overline{C} + ABC$$

$$= m_1 + m_5 + m_6 + m_7$$

This function can be expressed conveniently in the following shorthand notation.

$$F(A, B, C) = \Sigma(1, 5, 6, 7)$$

The summation symbol Σ stands for the ORing of minterms; the numbers following it are the minterms of the function.

Maxterm Canonical Form (Product of Maxterms)

Expression in this form consists of two or more OR terms, each term being combinations of all variables involved, that are ANDed together. Some examples of this form are:

1. $F_1 = (A+B)(\bar{A}+B)(\bar{A}+\bar{B})$

2. $F_2 = (\bar{A}+\bar{B}+\bar{C})(A+\bar{B}+\bar{C})(A+\bar{B}+C)$

3. $F_3 = (A+B+C+\bar{D})(\bar{A}+\bar{B}+C+D)(A+B+\bar{C}+D)$

Any Boolean function can be expanded to obtain a maxterm canonical form. The following example illustrates this.

The maxterm canonical form is sometimes called as a canonical POS form.

EXAMPLE 2.4: Express the Boolean function $F = (A+\bar{B})(B+C)(A+\bar{C})$ in a product of maxterms.

SOLUTION: Each term in the given expression is inspected and if any term misses one or more variables, it is ORed with an expression such as $A\bar{A}$ $(\because A\bar{A}=0)$, where A is one of the missing variables.

$$F = (A+\bar{B})(B+C)(A+\bar{C})$$

$$= (A+\bar{B}+0)(B+C+0)(A+\bar{C}+0)$$

$$= (A+\bar{B}+C\bar{C})(B+C+A\bar{A})(A+\bar{C}+B\bar{B})$$

$$= (A+\bar{B}+C)(A+\bar{B}+\bar{C})(A+B+C)(\bar{A}+B+C)$$

$(A+B+\bar{C})(A+\bar{B}+\bar{C})$ by Distributive law

$$= (A+\bar{B}+C)\{(A+\bar{B}+\bar{C})(A+\bar{B}+\bar{C})\}(A+B+C)$$

$$(\bar{A}+B+C)(A+B+\bar{C})$$

$$= (A+\bar{B}+C)(A+\bar{B}+\bar{C})(A+B+C)(\bar{A}+B+C)(A+B+\bar{C}) \qquad (\because AA = A)$$

Rearranging the maxterms in ascending order, we get,

$$F = (\bar{A}+B+C)(A+\bar{B}+\bar{C})(A+\bar{B}+C)(A+B+\bar{C})(A+B+C)$$

$$= M_3 M_4 M_5 M_6 M_7$$

This function can be expressed conveniently in the following shorthand notation.

$F(A, B, C) = \pi\,(3,4,5,6,7)$

The product symbol π stands for the ANDing of maxterms; the numbers following it are the maxterms of the function.

Conversion between Canonical Forms

One canonical form can be converted into another canonical form. The following example demonstrates this. Consider the function which is in minterm canonical form:

$F(A, B, C) = \Sigma\,(1, 5, 6, 7)$

The complement of F can be expressed as:

$\bar{F}(A, B, C) = \Sigma\,(0, 2, 3, 4).$

$\overline{F} = m_0 + m_2 + m_3 + m_4$

Now, if we take the complement of $\overline{F}$, we get

$$F = \left(\overline{m_0 + m_2 + m_3 + m_4}\right)$$

$$= \overline{m}_0\, \overline{m}_2\, \overline{m}_3\, \overline{m}_4 \text{ by De Morgan's Theorem}$$

$$= M_0\, M_2\, M_3\, M_4 \qquad \left(\because \overline{m}_j = M_j\right)$$

$$F(A, B, C) = \pi(0, 2, 3, 4) \qquad ...(2.2)$$

In a similar way, a maxterm canonical form can be converted into a minterm canonical form.

In general we can state that to convert one canonical form into another canonical form, interchange the symbols Σ and π and list those numbers missing from the original form. That is,

If the function $F = \Sigma$ (set of *minterm* numbers)
then $F = \pi$ (set of *maxterm* numbers that are not included in the minterm list)
and vice versa.

Equations (2.1) and (2.2) clarify the above conclusion.

Conversion of a Truth Table to Canonical Forms

A Boolean function may be expressed in a minterm canonical form from a given truth table by forming a minterm for each combinations of the variables which produces output 1 in the truth table, and then ORing these terms.

A Boolean function may be expressed in a maxterm canonical form from a given truth table by forming a maxterm for each combinations of the variables which produces output 0 in the truth table, and then ANDing these terms.

The following example illustrates the conversion of a truth table into canonical forms.

EXAMPLE 2.5: Convert the given truth table (Table 2.3) into canonical forms.

Table 2.3

Input Variables			Output
A	B	C	F
0	0	0	0 → $A + B + C = M_0$
0	0	1	1 → $\overline{A}\,\overline{B}\,C = m_1$
0	1	0	0 → $A + \overline{B} + C = M_2$
0	1	1	0 → $A + \overline{B} + \overline{C} = M_3$
1	0	0	0 → $\overline{A} + B + C = M_4$
1	0	1	1 → $A\,\overline{B}\,C = m_5$
1	1	0	1 → $A\,B\,\overline{C} = m_6$
1	1	1	1 → $A\,B\,C = m_7$

SOLUTION: Consider the given truth table and forming the minterms and maxterms corresponding to 1 and 0 of the output.

Now, by ORing the minterms, we obtain:

$$F = m_1 + m_5 + m_6 + m_7$$

$F(A, B, C) = \Sigma(1, 5, 6, 7)$, which is in minterm canonical form.

Similarly, by ANDing the maxterms, we obtain:

$$F = M_0 M_2 M_3 M_4$$

$F(A, B, C) = \pi(0, 2, 3, 4)$, which is in maxterm canonical form.

2.6 STANDARD FORMS

It is desirable sometimes to write Boolean function in an easily examinable form. Such a form of the Boolean function is known as a *standard form*. There are two types of standard forms:

1. A Sum-of-Products (SOP) form
2. A Product-of-Sums (POS) form.

1. Sum-of-Products Form

Boolean function in this form consists of two or more AND terms (products) that are ORed together. Each AND term consists of one or more variables appearing in either complemented or uncomplemented form. Some examples of this form are:

1. $AB + AC + \bar{B}C$
2. $A + BCD + \bar{C}D$
3. $A\bar{B}C + ABCD + BC\bar{D}$

2. Product-of-Sums Form

Boolean function in this form consists of two or more OR terms (sums) that are ANDed together. Each OR term consists of one or more variables appearing in either complemented or uncomplemented form. Some examples of this form are:

1. $(A + \bar{B})(B + C)(A + \bar{C})$
2. $A(B + \bar{C} + D)(\bar{C} + D)$
3. $(A + \bar{B} + C)(A + B + C + \bar{D})(B + C + \bar{D})$

Note: A Boolean function which is expressed in a non-standard form can be changed to a standard form.

For example, $F = (AB + CD)(B + C)$ is not in a standard form. By applying the distributive law, we obtain $F = AB + ABC + BCD + CD$ which is in standard form.

SOLVED PROBLEMS

2.1 Simplify the following Boolean functions to a minimum number of literals.

(a) $F = \overline{\overline{X} + Y} + \overline{\overline{X} + \overline{Y}}$

(b) $F = ABC + \overline{A}B + AB\overline{C}$

(c) $F = C(AD + A\overline{D}) + BC$

SOLUTION:

(a) $F = \overline{\overline{X} + Y} + \overline{\overline{X} + \overline{Y}}$ given

$= \overline{\overline{X}}\overline{Y} + \overline{\overline{X}}\,\overline{\overline{Y}}$ De Morgan's theorem

$= X\overline{Y} + XY$ $(\because \overline{\overline{A}} = A)$

$= X(\overline{Y} + Y)$

$= X$ $(\because A + \overline{A} = 1)$

(b) $F = ABC + \overline{A}B + AB\overline{C}$ given

$= ABC + AB\overline{C} + \overline{A}B$ rearranged

$= AB(C + \overline{C}) + \overline{A}B$

$= AB + \overline{A}B$ $(\because A + \overline{A} = 1)$

$= B(A + \overline{A})$

$= B$ $(\because A + \overline{A} = 1)$

(c) $F = C(AD + A\overline{D}) + BC$ given

$= CA(D + \overline{D}) + BC$

$= CA + BC$ $(\because A + \overline{A} = 1)$

$= C(A + B)$

2.2 Using Boolean algebra techniques, prove that:

(a) $AB + AC + B\overline{C} = AC + B\overline{C}$

(b) $(A + B)(B + C)(C + A) = AB + BC + CA$

(c) $(x + y)(\overline{x} + z)(y + z) = (x + y)(\overline{x} + z)$

SOLUTION:

(a) LHS $= AB + AC + B\overline{C}$

$= AB(C + \overline{C}) + AC + B\overline{C}$ term AB is multipled with $C + \overline{C}$

$= ABC + AB\overline{C} + AC + B\overline{C}$ $\quad (\because C + \overline{C} = 1)$

$= ABC + AC + AB\overline{C} + B\overline{C}$ $\quad$ rearranged

$= AC(B+1) + B\overline{C}(A+1)$

$= AC + B\overline{C}$ $\quad (\because A + 1 = 1)$

= RHS

(b) LHS = $(A + B)(B + C)(C + A)$

$= (A + B)(A + C)(B + C)$ $\quad$ rearranged

$= (A + BC)(B + C)$ $\quad$ distributive law

$= A(B + C) + BC(B + C)$

$= AB + AC + BBC + BCC$ $\quad$ distributive law

$= AB + AC + BC + BC$

$(\because AA = A)$

$= AB + AC + BC$

$(\because A + A = A)$

$= AB + BC + CA$ $\quad$ rearranged

= RHS

(c) LHS $= (x + y)(\overline{x} + z)(y + z)$

$= (y + x)(y + z)(\overline{x} + z)$ $\quad$ rearranged

$= (y + xz)(\overline{x} + z)$ $\quad$ distributive law

$= y(\overline{x} + z) + xz(\overline{x} + z)$

$= y\overline{x} + yz + x\overline{x}z + xzz$ $\quad$ distributive law

$= y\overline{x} + yz + xz$ $\quad (\because A\overline{A} = 0 \;\&\; AA = A)$

$= y\overline{x} + yz + xz + x\overline{x}$ $\quad$ $x\overline{x}$ is added $(\because x\overline{x} = 0)$

$= y(\overline{x} + z) + x(\overline{x} + z)$

$= (x + y)(\overline{x} + z)$

= RHS

2.3 Determine the Boolean expression for the logic circuit shown in Fig. P2.3

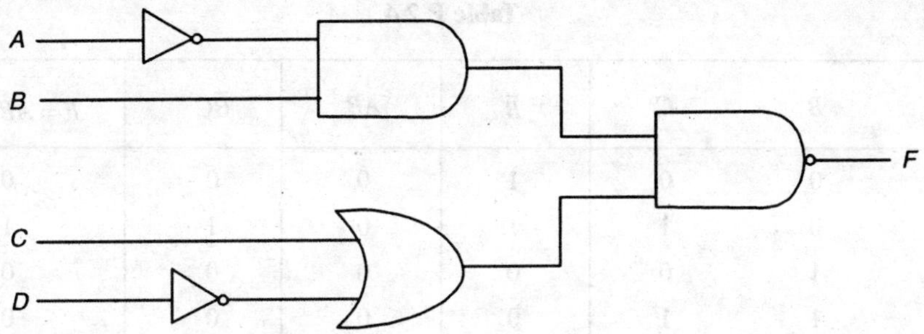

Fig. P2.3

SOLUTION:

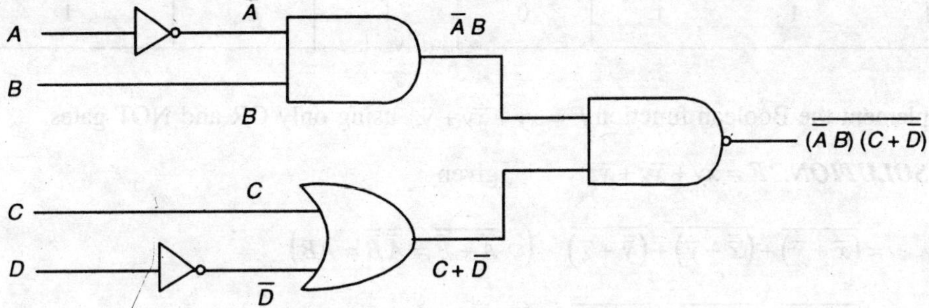

Thus,

$$F = \overline{(\overline{A}B)(C+\overline{D})}$$

$$= \overline{(\overline{A}B)} + \overline{(C+\overline{D})}$$

$$= (\overline{\overline{A}} + \overline{B}) + (\overline{C}\overline{\overline{D}})$$

} De Morgan's theorem

$$= A + \overline{B} + \overline{C}D \qquad (\because \overline{\overline{A}} = A)$$

2.4 Draw the circuit diagram that implements the expression $F = AB + \overline{B}C$ and obtain the truth table.

SOLUTION:

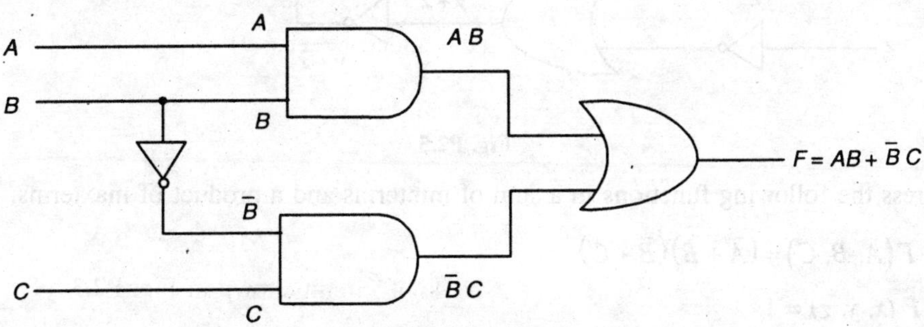

Fig. P2.4

Table P 2.4

A	B	C	$\overline{B}$	AB	$\overline{B}C$	$F = AB + \overline{B}C$
0	0	0	1	0	0	0
0	0	1	1	0	1	1
0	1	0	0	0	0	0
0	1	1	0	0	0	0
1	0	0	1	0	0	0
1	0	1	1	0	1	1
1	1	0	0	1	0	1
1	1	1	0	1	0	1

2.5 Implement the Boolean function $F = xy + \overline{x}y + \overline{y}z$ using only OR and NOT gates.

SOLUTION: $F = xy + \overline{x}y + \overline{y}z$ given

$$= \overline{(\overline{x}+\overline{y})} + \overline{(\overline{\overline{x}}+\overline{y})} + \overline{(\overline{\overline{y}}+\overline{z})} \quad \left(\because\ \overline{\overline{A}+\overline{B}} = \overline{\overline{A}}\,\overline{\overline{B}} = AB\right)$$

$$= \overline{(\overline{x}+\overline{y})} + \overline{(x+\overline{y})} + \overline{(y+\overline{z})} \quad \left(\because\ \overline{\overline{A}} = A\right)$$

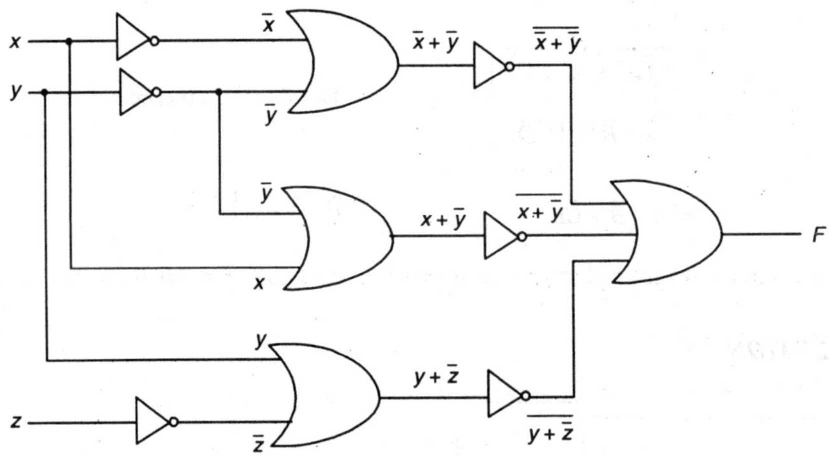

Fig. P2.5

2.6 Express the following functions in a sum of minterms and a product of maxterms.

(a) $F(A, B, C) = (\overline{A} + B)(\overline{B} + C)$

(b) $F\ (x, y, z) = 1$

SOLUTION:

(a) $F(A, B, C) = (\bar{A} + B)(\bar{B} + C)$

$= \bar{A}\bar{B} + \bar{A}C + B\bar{B} + BC$

$= \bar{A}\bar{B} + \bar{A}C + BC \qquad (\because B\bar{B} = 0)$

$= \bar{A}\bar{B}\cdot 1 + \bar{A}C\cdot 1 + BC\cdot 1 \qquad (\because A\cdot 1 = A)$

$= \bar{A}\bar{B}(C + \bar{C}) + \bar{A}C(B + \bar{B}) + BC(A + \bar{A}) \qquad (\because A + \bar{A} = 1)$

$= \bar{A}\bar{B}C + \bar{A}\bar{B}\bar{C} + \bar{A}BC + \bar{A}\bar{B}C + ABC + \bar{A}BC$

$= \underbrace{\bar{A}\bar{B}C}_{001} + \underbrace{\bar{A}\bar{B}\bar{C}}_{000} + \underbrace{\bar{A}BC}_{011} + \underbrace{ABC}_{111}$

$= m_1 + m_0 + m_3 + m_7$

$= m_0 + m_1 + m_3 + m_7$

$= \Sigma$ (0, 1, 3, 7) sum of minterms

The complement of F can be expressed as:

$\bar{F}(A, B, C) = \Sigma(2, 4, 5, 6)$

$= m_2 + m_4 + m_5 + m_6$

Now, taking the complement of $\bar{F}$, we get

$F(A, B, C) = \overline{m_2 + m_4 + m_5 + m_6}$

$= \bar{m}_2 \cdot \bar{m}_4 \cdot \bar{m}_5 \cdot \bar{m}_6$ by De Morgan's theorem

$= M_2\, M_4\, M_5\, M_6 \quad (\because \bar{m}_j = M_j)$

$= \pi(2, 4, 5, 6)$, product of maxterms

Alternative method to obtain product of maxterms:

$F(A, B, C) = (\bar{A} + B)(\bar{B} + C)$

$= (\bar{A} + B + C\bar{C})(A\bar{A} + \bar{B} + C) \qquad (\because A\bar{A} = 0)$

$= \underbrace{(\bar{A} + B + C)}_{100}\underbrace{(\bar{A} + B + \bar{C})}_{101}\underbrace{(A + \bar{B} + C)}_{010}\underbrace{(\bar{A} + \bar{B} + C)}_{110}$ by distributive law

$= M_4\, M_5\, M_2\, M_6$

$= M_2\, M_4\, M_5\, M_6$

$= \pi(2, 4, 5, 6)$, product of maxterms

(b) $F(A, B, C) = 1$

$$= (A+\bar{A})(B+\bar{B})(C+\bar{C}) \quad (\because A+\bar{A}=1 \;\&\; 1\cdot 1=1)$$

$$= \underbrace{\bar{A}\bar{B}\bar{C}}_{000} + \underbrace{\bar{A}\bar{B}C}_{001} + \underbrace{\bar{A}B\bar{C}}_{010} + \underbrace{\bar{A}BC}_{011} + \underbrace{A\bar{B}\bar{C}}_{100} + \underbrace{A\bar{B}C}_{101} + \underbrace{AB\bar{C}}_{110} + \underbrace{ABC}_{111}$$

$$= m_0 + m_1 + m_2 + m_3 + m_4 + m_5 + m_6 + m_7$$

$$= \Sigma(0, 1, 2, 3, 4, 5, 6, 7), \text{ sum of minterms.}$$

There are no maxterms.

2.7 Express the following truth table (Table P2.7) in terms of the Σ notation:

Table P2.7

A	B	C	F
0	0	0	0
0	0	1	1
0	1	0	0
0	1	1	0
1	0	0	1
1	0	1	1
1	1	0	0
1	1	1	1

SOLUTION: We can observe from the given truth table that there are four 1s in the output column. So the resulting Boolean function will have four minterms, which are:

$$001 : \bar{A}\bar{B}C = m_1$$

$$100 : A\bar{B}\bar{C} = m_4$$

$$101 : A\bar{B}C = m_5$$

$$111 : ABC = m_7$$

$$\therefore \quad F(A, B, C) = \bar{A}\bar{B}C + A\bar{B}\bar{C} + A\bar{B}C + ABC$$

$$= m_1 + m_4 + m_5 + m_7$$

$$= \Sigma(1, 4, 5, 7)$$

Note: Each variable of the minterm is complemented when the corresponding input variable is 0 and is uncomplemented when the corresponding input variable is 1.

2.8 Express the following truth table (Table P2.8) in terms of the π notation:

Table P2.8

A	B	C	F
0	0	0	0
0	0	1	0
0	1	0	0
0	1	1	1
1	0	0	0
1	0	1	1
1	1	0	1
1	1	1	1

SOLUTION: We can observe from the given truth table that there are four 0s in the output column. So the resulting Boolean function will have four maxterms, which are :

$$000 : (A + B + C) = M_0$$

$$001 : (A + B + \bar{C}) = M_1$$

$$010 : (A + \bar{B} + C) = M_2$$

$$100 : (\bar{A} + B + C) = M_4$$

$$\therefore F(A, B, C) = (A + B + C)(A + B + \bar{C})(A + \bar{B} + C)(\bar{A} + B + C)$$

$$= M_0 M_1 M_2 M_4$$

$$= \pi (0, 1, 2, 4)$$

Note: Each variable of the maxterm is uncomplemented when the corresponding input variable is 0 and is complemented when the corresponding input variable is 1.

EXERCISES

2.1 Simplify the following Boolean functions to a minimum number of literals.

(a) $F = (\bar{P} + Q)(P + Q + R)\bar{R}$

(b) $F = \overline{(\overline{CD} + A)} + A + CD + AB$

(c) $F = ABCD + AB\overline{(CD)} + \overline{(AB)}CD$

2.2 Using Boolean algebra, verify that

(a) $AB + \bar{B}\bar{C} + A\bar{C} = AB + \bar{B}\bar{C}$ (Hint: Multiply $A\bar{C}$ with $B + \bar{B}$)

(b) $\overline{AB + BC + CA} = \bar{A}\bar{B} + \bar{B}\bar{C} + \bar{C}\bar{A}$

(c) $(A + B)(\bar{A} + C) = AC + \bar{A}B$

2.3 Obtain the Boolean expression for the logic circuit shown in Fig. E2.3.

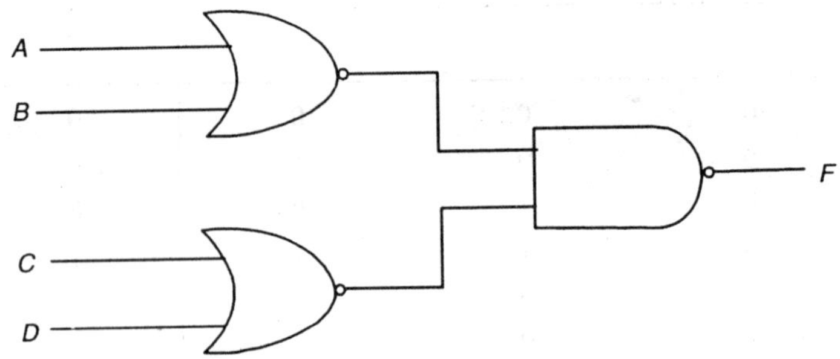

Fig. E2.3

2.4 Implement the Boolean function $F = AB + B\overline{C} + C\overline{A}$ using logic gates and obtain the truth table.

2.5 Implement the Boolean function $F = xy + \overline{x}y + \overline{y}z$ using only AND and NOT gates.

2.6 Express the following functions in a minterm canonical form and a maxterm canonical form.

(a) $F(x, y, z) = z$ (Hint: Multiply z with $(x+\overline{x})(y+\overline{y})$)

(b) $F(A, B, C, D) = D(\overline{A}+B)+\overline{B}D$

2.7 Express the following truth table (Table E2.7) in terms of the π notation.

Table E2.7

A	B	C	F
0	0	0	0
0	0	1	0
0	1	0	0
0	1	1	1
1	0	0	0
1	0	1	1
1	1	0	1
1	1	1	1

2.8 Express the following truth table (Table E2.8) in terms of π notation.

Table E2.8

A	B	C	F
0	0	0	0
0	0	1	1
0	1	0	0
0	1	1	0
1	0	0	1
1	0	1	1
1	1	0	0
1	1	1	1

Simplification of Boolean Functions

3

We have learnt how to simplify Boolean functions using Boolean laws and theorems. However, the way we have followed is not systematic and unique. A K-map, developed by Karnaugh, is another method for simplifying Boolean functions. It provides a very simple and ordered process for minimizing Boolean functions.

3.1 THE K-MAP METHOD

The K-map, like a truth table, is a means of representing Boolean function. It is made up of squares. Each square is to represent one minterm. Since the total number of minterms is 2^n for n binary variables, the K-map consists of 2^n squares. For example, for two variables (A and B) there are $2^2 = 4$ minterms $(\bar{A}\bar{B}, \bar{A}B, A\bar{B}$ and $AB)$ and hence K-map must have 4 squares.

Although K-map can be used to simplify Boolean functions consisting of any number of input variables, its practical usefulness is limited to six variables. We shall discuss the application of K-map method up to 4-variables only. For higher number of variables Quine-McCluskey method is used.

K-map formats to two, three and four variables are shown in Fig 3.1 and Fig 3.2.

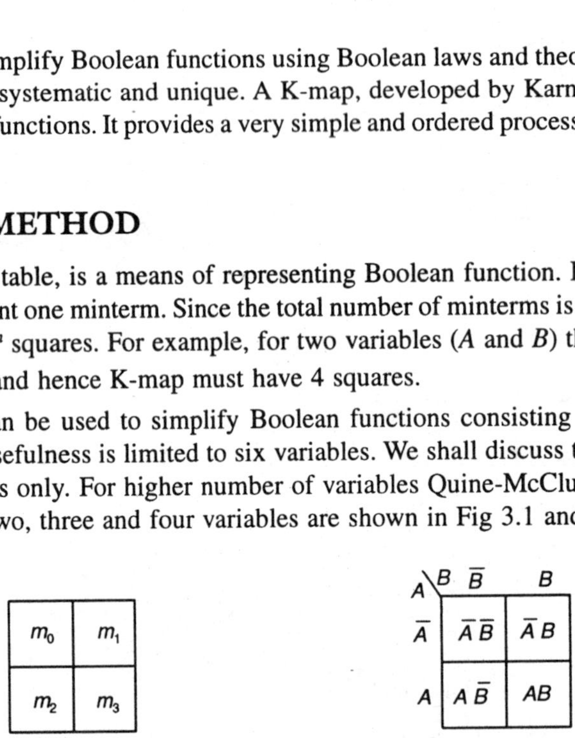

(a) Two-variable map

Fig. 3.1 Formats of K-maps

m_0	m_1	m_3	m_2
m_4	m_5	m_7	m_6

A \ BC	$\bar{B}\bar{C}$	$\bar{B}C$	BC	$B\bar{C}$
$\bar{A}$	$\bar{A}\bar{B}\bar{C}$	$\bar{A}\bar{B}C$	$\bar{A}BC$	$\bar{A}B\bar{C}$
A	$A\bar{B}\bar{C}$	$A\bar{B}C$	ABC	$AB\bar{C}$

(b) Three-variable map

m_0	m_1	m_3	m_2
m_4	m_5	m_7	m_6
m_{12}	m_{13}	m_{15}	m_{14}
m_8	m_9	m_{11}	m_{10}

AB \ CD	$\bar{C}\bar{D}$	$\bar{C}D$	CD	$C\bar{D}$
$\bar{A}\bar{B}$	$\bar{A}\bar{B}\bar{C}\bar{D}$	$\bar{A}\bar{B}\bar{C}D$	$\bar{A}\bar{B}CD$	$\bar{A}\bar{B}C\bar{D}$
$\bar{A}B$	$\bar{A}B\bar{C}\bar{D}$	$\bar{A}B\bar{C}D$	$\bar{A}BCD$	$\bar{A}BC\bar{D}$
AB	$AB\bar{C}\bar{D}$	$AB\bar{C}D$	$ABCD$	$ABC\bar{D}$
$A\bar{B}$	$A\bar{B}\bar{C}\bar{D}$	$A\bar{B}\bar{C}D$	$A\bar{B}CD$	$A\bar{B}C\bar{D}$

(c) Four-variable map

Fig. 3.1 Formats of K-maps

A \ B	0	1
0	0	1
1	2	3

(a) Two-variable map

A \ BC	00	01	11	10
0	0	1	3	2
1	4	5	7	6

(b) Three-variable map

AB \ CD	00	01	11	10
00	0	1	3	2
01	4	5	7	6
11	12	13	15	14
10	8	9	11	10

Minterm number

Note: 0 → Complemented variable

1 → Uncomplemented variable

(c) Four-variable map

Fig. 3.2 Modified formats of K-maps

The map is organised such that there is only a single variable change between any adjacent squares. The square in each map is to represent a minterm corresponding to row and column designations.

It is noted that the rows of the three-variable map and the rows and columns of the four variable map are numbered in a reflected code sequence.

Plotting a K-map

We know that the K-map simply provides a graphical display of the minterms involved in any canonical SOP form expression. Therefore a logic expression is plotted by entering a 1 in the squares representing minterms that are contained in the expression, whereas a 0 is entered in the other squares. Plotting can also be done directly from the truth table.

The following example illustrates map plotting when the given function is in different forms.

EXAMPLE 3.1: Plot the following Boolean functions on K-map.

(a) $F = \bar{A}\bar{B}\bar{C}D + \bar{A}BC\bar{D} + ABC\bar{D} + \bar{A}\bar{B}CD$

(b) $F(A,B,C) = \Sigma(0, 2, 4, 7)$

(c) $F(x, y, z) = \pi(0, 1, 5, 6)$

(d)

A	B	C	F
0	0	0	1
0	0	1	0
0	1	0	1
0	1	1	0
1	0	0	1
1	0	1	1
1	1	0	0
1	1	1	0

(e) $F = A\bar{C} + BC + ABC$

SOLUTION: (a) $F = \bar{A}\bar{B}\bar{C}D + \bar{A}BC\bar{D} + ABC\bar{D} + \bar{A}\bar{B}CD$

The term $\bar{A}\bar{B}\bar{C}D$ contained in the expression tells us to enter a 1 in a square which corresponds to row $\bar{A}\bar{B}$ (00) and column $\bar{C}D$ (01) and hence 1 is entered in the squares as shown in Fig. 3.3. In this way the blank map is filled with four 1s corresponding to four minterms contained in the expression and the remaining squares are filled with 0.

AB \ CD	$\bar{C}\bar{D}$ 00	$\bar{C}D$ 01	CD 11	$C\bar{D}$ 10
$\bar{A}\bar{B}$ 00	0	1	1	0
$\bar{A}B$ 01	0	0	0	1
AB 11	0	0	0	1
$A\bar{B}$ 10	0	0	0	0

Fig. 3.3

(b) $F(A, B, C) = \Sigma(0, 2, 4, 7)$

$A \backslash BC$	$\overline{B}\overline{C}$ 00	$\overline{B}C$ 01	BC 11	$B\overline{C}$ 10
$\overline{A}$ 0	1 (0)	0 (1)	0 (3)	1 (2)
A 1	1 (4)	0 (5)	1 (7)	0 (6)

Fig. 3.4

The given function is in the sum of minterms form. Hence 1 is entered in the squares corresponding to minterms numbered 0, 2, 4 and 7 and 0 is entered in the remaining squares as shown in Fig. 3.4.

(c) $F(x, y, z) = \pi\ (0,1, 5, 6)$

$x \backslash yz$	$\overline{y}\overline{z}$ 00	$\overline{y}z$ 01	yz 11	$y\overline{z}$ 10
$\overline{x}$ 0	0 (0)	0 (1)	1 (3)	1 (2)
x 1	1 (4)	0 (5)	1 (7)	0 (6)

Fig. 3.5

The given function is in the product of maxterms form. We can interpret this function as $\overline{F} = \Sigma$ (0, 1, 5, 6), which gives the minterms not included in the function F. Hence 0 is entered in the squares corresponding to these minterms showing their absence in the function F. The remaining squares are then filled with 1 (Fig. 3.5).

(d)

A	B	C	F
0	0	0	$1 \rightarrow m_0$
0	0	1	0
0	1	0	$1 \rightarrow m_2$
0	1	1	0
1	0	0	$1 \rightarrow m_4$
1	0	1	$1 \rightarrow m_5$
1	1	0	0
1	1	1	0

$A \backslash BC$	$\overline{B}\overline{C}$ 00	$\overline{B}C$ 01	BC 11	$B\overline{C}$ 10
$\overline{A}$ 0	1 (0)	0 (1)	0 (3)	1 (2)
A 1	1 (4)	1 (5)	0 (7)	0 (6)

Fig. 3.6

There are four combinations which produce output 1 in the truth table. Hence there will be four minterms as shown. 1 is entered in the squares corresponding to these minterms and 0 is entered in the remaining squares (Fig. 3.6).

(e) $F = A\overline{C} + BC + ABC$

$A \backslash BC$	$\overline{B}\overline{C}$ 00	$\overline{B}C$ 01	BC 11	$B\overline{C}$ 10
$\overline{A}$ 0	0	0	1	0
A 1	1	0	1	1

Fig. 3.7

The given function is not in minterm canonical form, because the terms $A\overline{C}$ and BC have less than three literals. These terms are represented in the map by more than one square. The squares corresponding to $A\overline{C}$ are obtained from the coincidence of A (row designated as A) and $\overline{C}$ (columns designated as $\overline{B}\overline{C}$ and $B\overline{C}$) as $A\overline{B}\overline{C}$ and $AB\overline{C}$ and 1 is entered in these squares. The squares corresponding to BC, which are the squares under the column BC, are $\overline{A}BC$ and ABC and 1 is entered in these squares. A 1 is also to be entered in the square ABC corresponding to the remaining term ABC in the expression, but 1 is already placed there by a preceding term. Note that 1 is placed only once in such common squares. The remaining squares are filled with 0 (Fig. 3.7).

Grouping

Boolean expression plotted on a K-map can be simplified by grouping 1s in adjacent squares according to the following rules by drawing a loop. The grouping of 1s in adjacent squares serves the purpose to eliminate the variable that appears both in complemented and uncomplemented form by applying logic adjacency theorem. It is interesting to note that K-map simplification by grouping 0s gives $\overline{F}$ in simplified form.

Rules:

1. Adjacent squares are squares that differ by only a single variable.
2. Grouping of 1s in adjacent squares must be done in groups of 1, 2, 4, 8, 16, and so on (refer Fig. 3.8 for examples).
3. Each group of 1s should be maximized to include the largest number of adjacent squares keeping rule 2 in mind.
4. Every 1 on the map must be included in at least one group. Groups can be overlapped.

Simplification

After grouping all the 1s on K-map, we go for simplification. Each group of 1s generates a product term which contains all variables that appear in only one form (i.e., either in uncomplemented or complemented) within the group and eliminates the variables that appear both in uncomplemented and complemented form. The final simplified expression is obtained by ORing the product terms generated by all the groups.

(a) Grouping of two 1s (pairs)

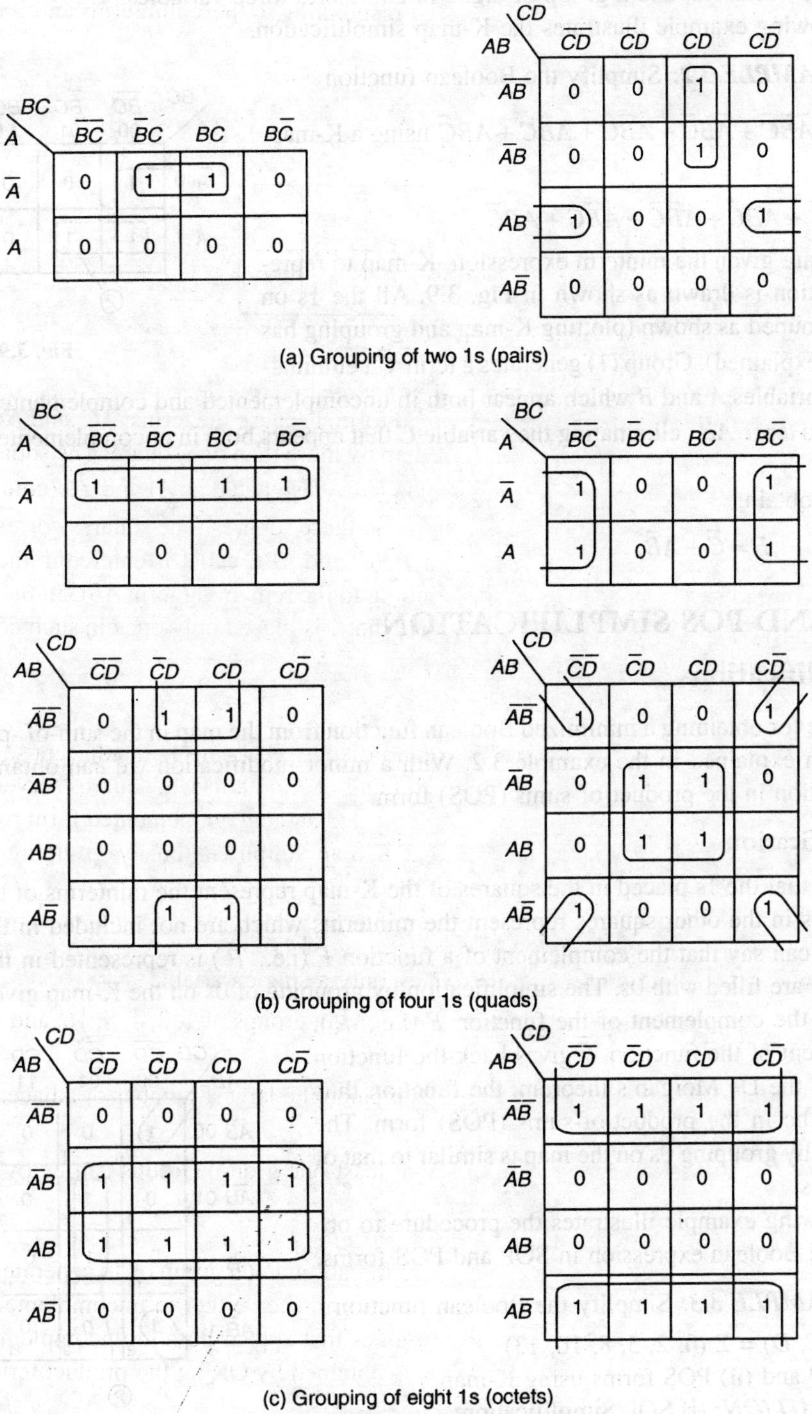

Fig. 3.8 Examples of grouping

While simplification notice that, a group of two 1s eliminates one variable, a group of four 1s eliminates two variables, and a group of eight 1s eliminates three variables.

The following example illustrates the K-map simplification.

EXAMPLE 3.2: Simplify the Boolean function

$F = \overline{A}\overline{B}\overline{C} + \overline{A}B\overline{C} + A\overline{B}\overline{C} + A\overline{B}C + AB\overline{C}$ using a K-map.

SOLUTION:

$$F = \overline{A}\overline{B}\overline{C} + \overline{A}B\overline{C} + A\overline{B}\overline{C} + A\overline{B}C + AB\overline{C}$$

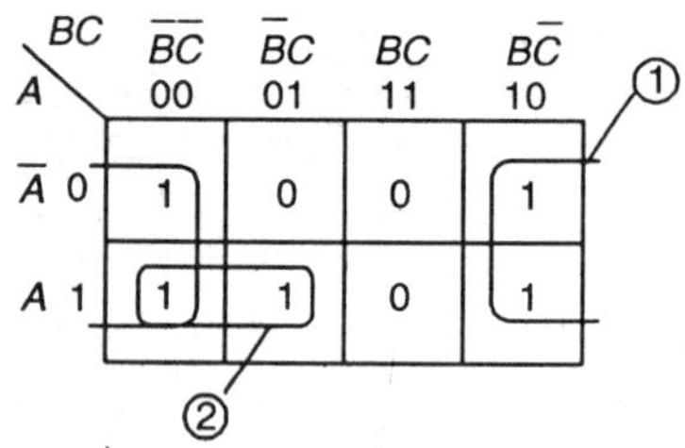

Fig. 3.9

Here we are given the minterm expression. K-map to represent the function is drawn as shown in Fig. 3.9. All the 1s on K-map are grouped as shown (plotting K-map and grouping has been already explained). Group (1) generates a term $\overline{C}$, eliminating the two variables A and B which appear both in uncomplemented and complemented form. Group (2) generates a term $A\overline{B}$, eliminating the variable C that appears both in uncomplemented and complemented form.

Thus we obtain:

$$F = \overline{C} + A\overline{B}$$

3.2 SOP AND POS SIMPLIFICATION

SOP Simplification

The procedure for obtaining a minimized Boolean function from the map in the sum-of -products (SOP) form has been explained in the example 3.2. With a minor modification we can obtain a minimised Boolean function in the product-of-sums (POS) form.

POS Simplification

We have seen that the 1s placed in the squares of the K-map represent the minterms of the function F, whereas the 0s in the other squares represent the minterms which are not included in the function F. From this we can say that the complement of a function F (i.e., $\overline{F}$) is represented in the map by the squares which are filled with 0s. The simplification by grouping of 0s on the K-map gives a simplified expression of the complement of the function F (i.e., $\overline{F}$). The complement of the function $\overline{F}$ gives back the function F. Because of the De Morgan's theorem, the function thus obtained will be in the product-of-sums (POS) form. The simplification by grouping 0s on the map is similar to that of by grouping 1s.

The following example illustrates the procedure to obtain simplified Boolean expression in SOP and POS forms.

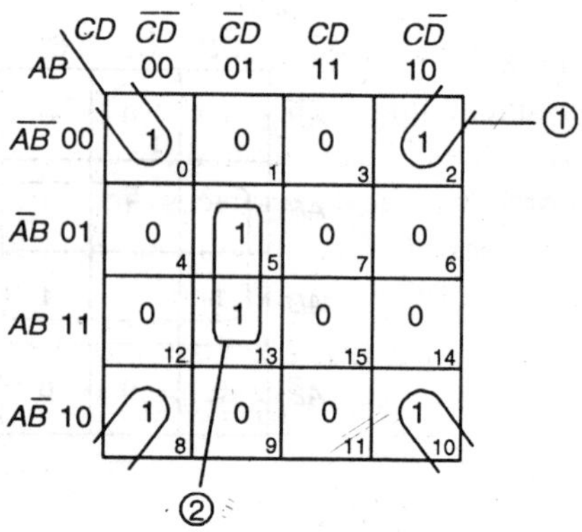

Fig. 3.10

EXAMPLE 3.3: Simplify the Boolean function

$F(A, B, C, D) = \Sigma\ (0, 2, 5, 8, 10, 13)$

in (i) SOP and (ii) POS forms using K-map.

SOLUTION: (i) SOP Simplification:

$$F(A, B, C, D) = \Sigma(0, 2, 5, 8, 10, 13)$$

Plotting and grouping is done (as shown in Fig. 3.10) as per the procedure explained in section 3.1. The simplification is as follows. Group (1) generates a term $\overline{B}\overline{D}$, eliminating the two variables A and C which appear both in uncomplemented and complemented form. Group (2) generates a term $B\overline{C}D$, eliminating the variable A that appears both in uncomplemented and complemented form. Thus we obtain:

$$F = \overline{B}\overline{D} + B\overline{C}D$$

(ii) POS Simplification:

Plotting and grouping (of 0s) is done (as shown in Fig 3.11) as per the procedure explained in section 3.1. The simplification is as follows. Group (1) generates a term $B\overline{D}$, eliminating the two variables A and C which appear both in uncomplemented and complemented form. Group (2) generates a term $\overline{B}D$, eliminating the variables A and C which appear both in uncomplemented and complemented form. Similarly group (3) generates a term CD. Thus we obtain:

$$\overline{F} = B\overline{D} + \overline{B}D + CD$$

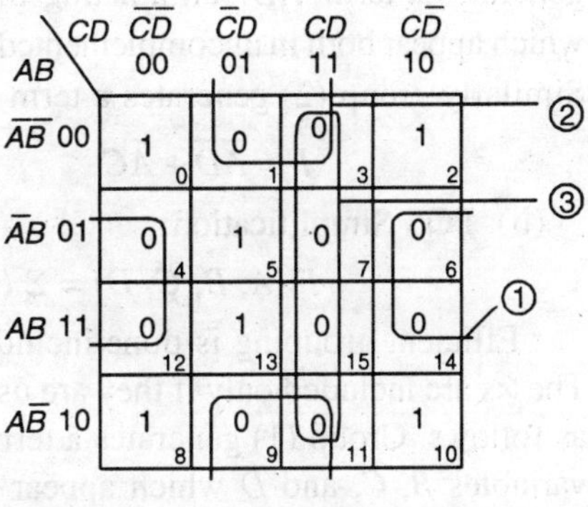

Fig. 3.11

Taking the complement of $\overline{F}$, we have:

$$\overline{\overline{F}} = \overline{(B\overline{D} + \overline{B}D + CD)}$$

$$\left.\begin{aligned} F &= \overline{B\overline{D}}\;\overline{\overline{B}D}\;\overline{CD} \\ &= (\overline{B} + D)(B + \overline{D})(\overline{C} + \overline{D}) \end{aligned}\right\} \text{by De Morgan's theorem.}$$

3.3 DON'T CARE CONDITIONS

Many times in digital system design, certain combinations of input variables never occur during normal operation; therefore, the corresponding output never appears. Since the output never appears, it is indicated by '×' or '*d*' or 'ϕ' in the truth table. In case of a four-bit decimal code, for example, six combinations (1010, 1011, 1100, 1101, 1110 and 1111) are not used. Any digital circuit using this code operates under the assumption that these unused combinations will never occur as long as the system is functioning properly. Hence, we don't care the function output for these combinations. Therefore, when the logic expression is being simplified, these don't care conditions may be assumed to be either 0 or 1, whichever produces the simplest expression. The don't care conditions need not be used at all if it does not contribute in efficient grouping.

The following example illustrates the K-map simplification when don't care conditions are given.

EXAMPLE 3.4: Simplify the function:

$$F(A, B, C, D) = \Sigma(0, 2, 3, 6, 7) + \Sigma_{\phi}(4, 5, 8, 10, 11, 15)$$

using don't care (ϕ) conditions in (i) SOP and (ii) POS forms.

SOLUTION:

(i) SOP Simplification:

$F(A, B, C, D) = \Sigma(0, 2, 3, 6, 7) + \Sigma_\phi(4, 5, 8, 10, 11, 15)$

1 is entered in the squares corresponding to minterms numbered 0, 2, 3, 6 and 7 and × is entered in the squares corresponding to minterms numbered 4, 5, 8, 10, 11, and 15 and the remaining squares are filled with 0s. And efficient grouping is done including 1s and ×s (Fig.3.12). The ×s are included only if they are useful. The simplification is as follows. Group (1) generates a term $\bar{A}\bar{D}$, eliminating the two variables B and C which appear both in uncomplemented and complemented form. Similarly group (2) generates a term $\bar{A}C$. Thus we obtain:

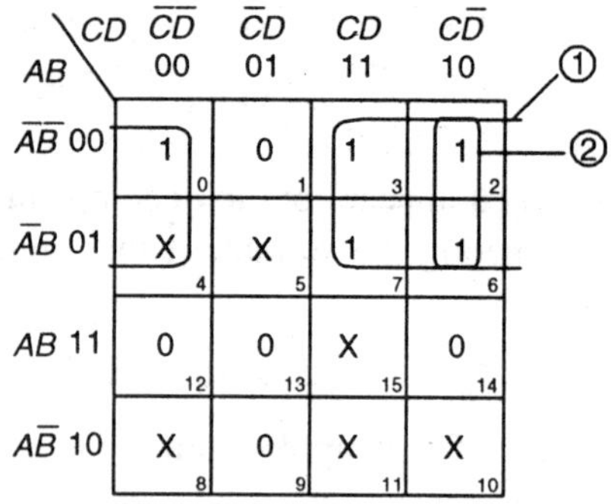

Fig. 3.12

$$F = \bar{A}\bar{D} + \bar{A}C$$

(ii) POS Simplification:

$$F(A, B, C, D) = \Sigma(0, 2, 3, 6, 7) + \Sigma_\phi(4, 5, 8, 10, 11, 15)$$

Efficient grouping is done including 0s and ×s (Fig.3.13). The ×s are included only if they are useful. The simplification is as follows. Group (1) generates a term A, eliminating the three variables *B*, *C*, and *D* which appear both in uncomplemented and complemented form. Similarly group (2) generates a term $\bar{C}D$. Thus we obtain:

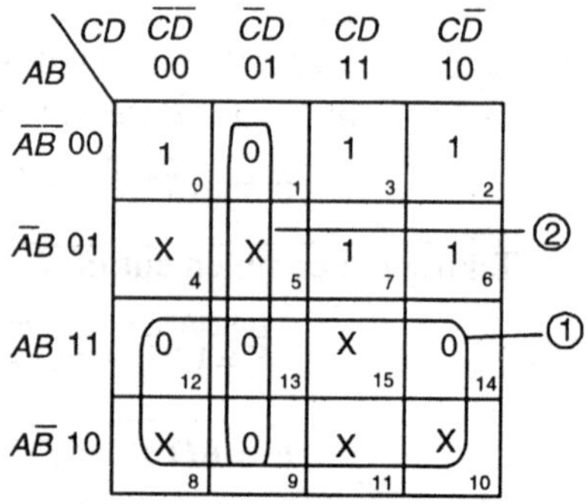

Fig. 3.13

$$\bar{F} = A + \bar{C}D$$

Taking the complement of $\bar{F}$, we have:

$$\bar{\bar{F}} = \overline{A + \bar{C}D}$$

$$\left.\begin{aligned} F &= \bar{A}\,\overline{\bar{C}D} \\ &= \bar{A}(C + \bar{D}) \end{aligned}\right\} \text{by De Morgan's theorem}$$

3.4 NAND AND NOR IMPLEMENTATION

The NAND and NOR gates are such devices that can be used to perform all the three logic functions: AND, OR, and NOT. That is why, they are called as *universal gates.* A complex digital system can be constructed using only NAND gates or NOR gates.. The NAND and NOR gates, being easier to fabricate, play a prominent role in digital circuit design. And hence the procedure for implementation of a Boolean function with these gates are discussed in this section.

As discussed earlier, we are familier with the function and symbols of NAND and NOR gates (refer section 1.5, 1.6 and 2.3). In addition to that we should note that a one-input NAND or NOR gate behaves like an inverter.

NAND Implementation

NAND implementation of a Boolean function requires that the function be simplified in the SOP form. Let us illustrate the implementation of the function $F = AB + C\bar{D} + E$ as shown in Fig. 3.14.

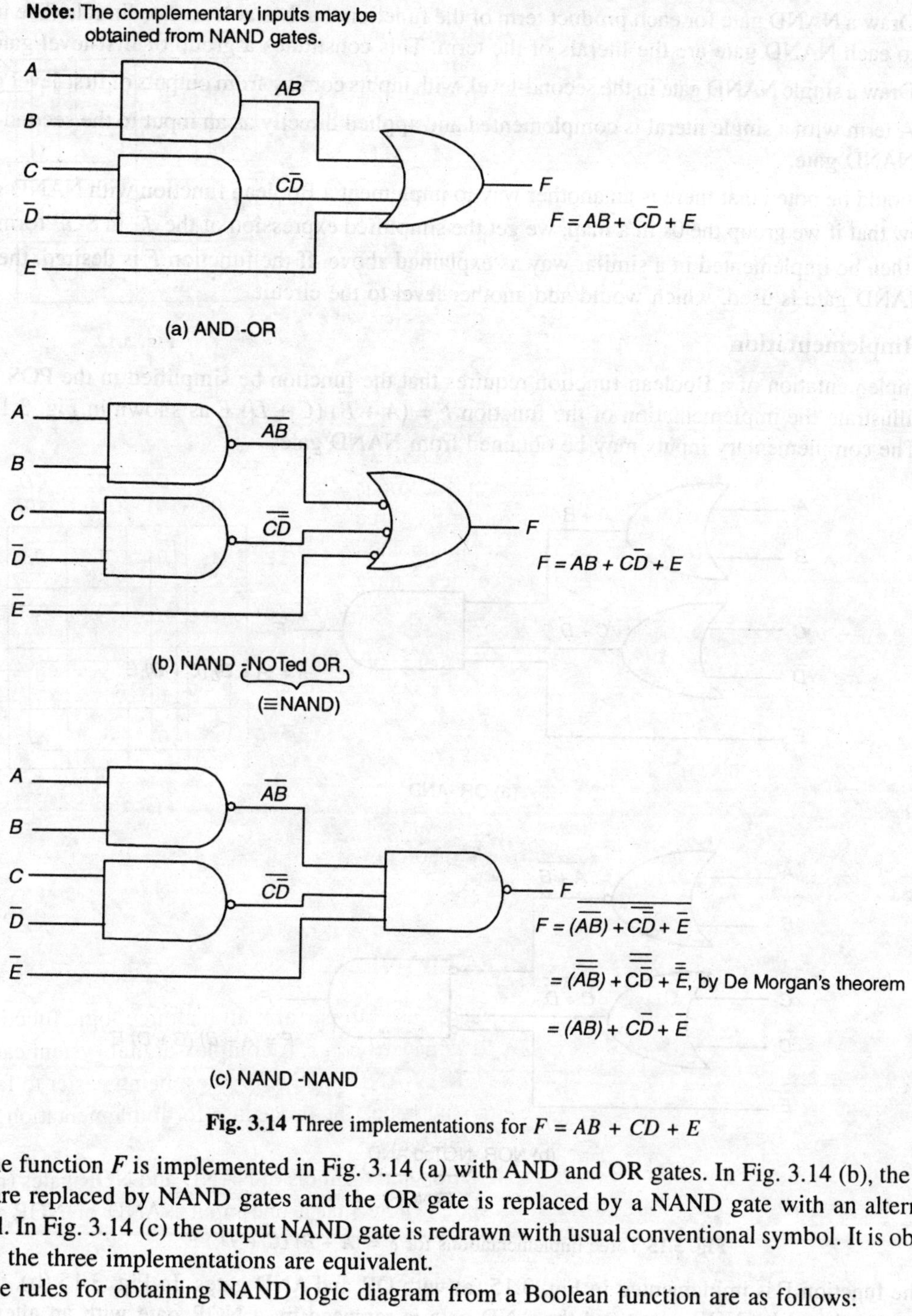

Fig. 3.14 Three implementations for $F = AB + CD + E$

The function F is implemented in Fig. 3.14 (a) with AND and OR gates. In Fig. 3.14 (b), the AND gates are replaced by NAND gates and the OR gate is replaced by a NAND gate with an alternative symbol. In Fig. 3.14 (c) the output NAND gate is redrawn with usual conventional symbol. It is obvious that all the three implementations are equivalent.

The rules for obtaining NAND logic diagram from a Boolean function are as follows:

Rules:

(1) Simplify the given function and express it in SOP form.

(2) Draw a NAND gate for each product term of the function that has at least two literals. The inputs to each NAND gate are the literals of the term. This constitutes a group of first-level gates.

(3) Draw a single NAND gate in the second-level, with inputs coming from outputs of first-level gates.

(4) A term with a single literal is complemented and applied directly as an input to the second-level NAND gate.

It should be noted that there is an another way to implement a Boolean function with NAND gates. We know that if we group the 0s in a map, we get the simplified expression of the $\overline{F}$ in SOP form. The $\overline{F}$ can then be implemented in a similar way as explained above. If the function F is desired, the one-input NAND gate is used, which would add another level to the circuit.

NOR Implementation

NOR implementation of a Boolean function requires that the function be simplified in the POS form. Let us illustrate the implementation of the function $F = (A + B)\ (C + D)\ E$ as shown in Fig. 3.15.
Note: The complementary inputs may be obtained from NAND gates.

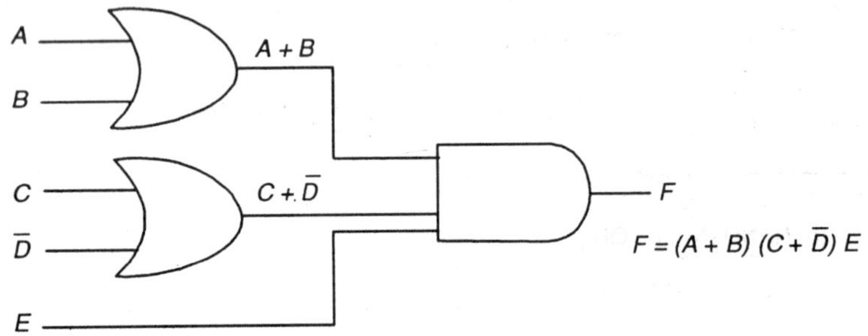

(a) OR -AND

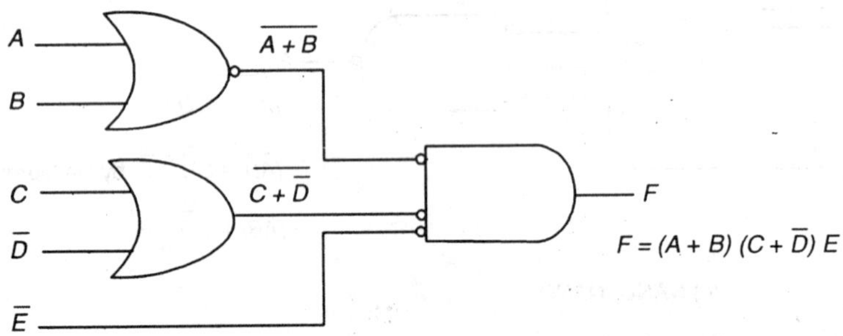

(b) NOR -NOTed AND
(≡NOR)

Fig. 3.15 Three implementations for $F = (A + B)\ (C + \overline{D}\ )\ E$

The function F is implemented in Fig. 3.15 (a) with OR and AND gates. In Fig. 3.15 (b), the OR gates are replaced by NOR gates and the AND gate is replaced by a NOR gate with an alternative symbol. In Fig. 3.15 (c), the output NOR gate is redrawn with usual conventional symbol. It is obvious that all the three implementations are equivalent.

The rules for obtaining NOR logic diagram from a Boolean function are as follows:

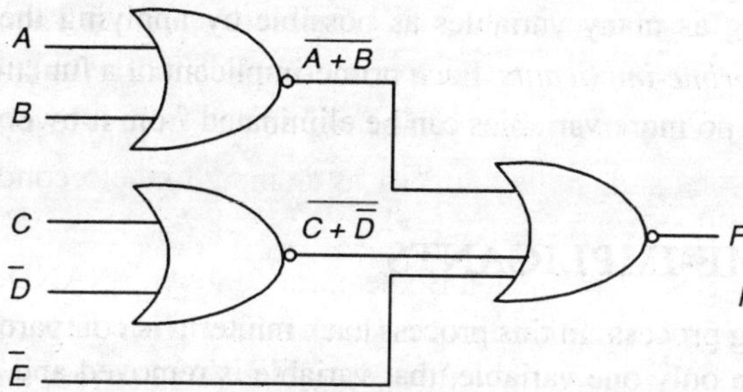

$$F = \overline{\overline{(A+B)} + \overline{(C+\bar{D})} + \bar{E}}$$

$$= \overline{\overline{(A+B)}}\ \overline{\overline{(C+\bar{D})}}\ \overline{\overline{E}}, \text{ by De Morgan's theorem}$$

$$= (A+B)\,(C+\bar{D})\,E$$

(c) NOR-NOR

Fig. 3.15 Three implementations for $F = (A + B)\,(C + \bar{D})\,E$

Rules:

(1) Simplify the given function and express it in POS form.

(2) Draw a NOR gate for each sum term of the function that has at least two literals. The inputs to each NOR gate are the literals of the term. This constitutes a group of first-level gates.

(3) Draw a single NOR gate in the second-level, with inputs coming from outputs of first-level gates.

(4) A term with a single literal is complemented and applied directly as an input to the second-level NOR gate.

An another way to implement a function F with NOR gate would be to use the expression for $\bar{F}$.

3.5 QUINE-MCCLUSKEY METHOD (The Tabulation Method)

The Karnaugh map method is a very useful simplifying technique in logic design. But it is not convenient to simplify functions involving a large (greater than 6) number of variables. Hence a more suitable simplifying technique for such functions is Quine-McCluskey method.

In mapping, we observed that adjacent minterms can be reduced. The reason for this reduction is that they differ by only one variable. For example, $\bar{A}B\bar{C}D$ and $\bar{A}BCD$ can be reduced because only the C variable differs. If we consider the binary designators of these minterms, which are : $01\underline{0}1$, and $01\underline{1}1$, it is worth to note that the 2's place in the minterm binary designators indicates precisely the same information that the variable C is the only variable that differs. That is why we combine minterms whose binary designators differ only in one place. This is the fundamental principle of the Quine-McCluskey method.

The Quine-McCluskey method reduces the logic expression to a minimum SOP form. Note that in order to apply Quine-McCluskey method, the function must be in sum-of-minterms form. If the function is not in this form, it must be converted.

The Quine-McCluskey method of simplification consists of two parts:

(1) The determination of prime-implicants.

(2) The selection of prime-implicants.

A minimum SOP form of expression for a given function can be obtained by summing some (but not necessarily all) of the prime-implicants of that function.

Note: The terms which we get by eliminating as many variables as possible by applying the logic adjacency theorem $(AB + A\overline{B} = A)$ are called *prime-implicants*. Each prime-implicant of a function has a minimum number of literals in the sense that no more variables can be eliminated from it by combining it with the other terms.

3.6 DETERMINATION OF PRIME-IMPLICANTS

The prime-implicants are obtained by matching process. In this process each minterm is compared with every other minterm. If two minterms differ in only one variable, that variable is removed and a term with one less literal is found. This process is repeated for every minterm until the exhaustive search is completed. The similar matching process cycle is repeated for those new terms just found. These cycles are continued until a single pass through a cycle yields no further elimination of variables. The remaining terms and all the terms that did not match during the process form the prime-implicants.

Let us go through an example in detail to understand the procedure.

EXAMPLE 3.5: Determine the prime-implicants of the function:

$F(A, B, C, D) = \Sigma\,(0, 2, 6, 8, 10, 14, 15)$ by Quine-McCluskey method, using (i) binary notation (ii) decimal notation.

SOLUTION:

Using binary notation

A method using binary notations involves comparing and matching of binary numbers. In the process the manipulation is quite tedious but easily understandable.

Table 3.1 Determination of prime-implicants of example 3.5 (using binary notation)

(a)						(b)						(c)					
	A	*B*	*C*	*D*			*A*	*B*	*C*	*D*			*A*	*B*	*C*	*D*	
0	0	0	0	0	✓	0, 2	0	0	–	0	✓	0, 2, 8, 10	–	0	–	0	
2	0	0	1	0	✓	0, 8	–	0	0	0	✓	0, 8, 2, 10	–	0	–	0	*D*
8	1	0	0	0	✓	2, 6	0	–	1	0	✓	2, 6, 10, 14	–	–	1	0	
6	0	1	1	0	✓	2, 10	–	0	1	0	✓	2, 10, 6, 14	–	–	1	0	*D*
10	1	0	1	0	✓	8, 10	1	0	–	0	✓						
14	1	1	1	0	✓	6, 14	–	1	1	0	✓						
15	1	1	1	1	✓	10, 14	1	–	1	0	✓						
						14, 15	1	1	1	–		*D* ⇒ Discarded term					

Step 1: Consider the binary form of all the minterm designators and arrange them in groups according to the number of 1s contained to make sections as shown in Table 3.1, column (a). Note that the first section contains the number with no 1s, the second section contains those numbers with only one 1, the third section contains those numbers with only two 1s. And it continues so on.

Step 2: Compare each binary number in one section with every term in the next section down only, and if they differ by only one position, place a ✓(check) mark to the right of both minterms. The resulting term, together with the decimal equivalents, is listed in column (b) of the table. For example minterms $\overline{A}\overline{B}\overline{C}\overline{D}$ (⇒ 0000) and $\overline{A}\overline{B}C\overline{D}$ ⇒ 0010) can be compared and combined to yield $\overline{A}\overline{B}\overline{D}$ (⇒ 0 0_0), removing the variable C. The variable elimination is shown by a '_' (underscore) in its original position. Hence we can say that two minterms fit into this category if they both have the same bit value in all positions except one.

Step 3: Now the terms of column (b) have only three variables. A '1' represents the uncomplemented variable, a '0' represents the complemented variable and a '_' (underscore) represents the eliminated variable. The searching and comparing process is repeated for the terms in column (b) to form the two-variable terms of column (c). Again, terms in each section need to be compared only if they have dashes in the same position. Note that the decimal equivalents are written on the left-hand side of each entry for identification purposes. The comparing process should be carried out again in column (c) and in subsequent columns as long as proper matching is encountered.

Step 4: The terms in the table without ✓ (check) mark form the prime-implicants. Note that each term in column (c) appears twice in the table, and as long as the term forms a prime-implicant, it is unnecessary to use the same term more than once. And hence additional terms are discarded.

Using decimal notation

A method using decimal notations involves comparing of decimal numbers. We know that each 1 in a binary number represents the co-efficient multiplied by a power of 2. If we consider two minterms which are the same in every position except one, the minterm with the extra 1 must be larger than the number of the other minterm by a power of 2. For example, the minterm 14 (binary 1110 which contains three 1s) is larger than the minterm 6 (binary 0110 which contains two ls) by 8, which is a power of 2. Therefore, two minterms can be combined together if the corresponding decimal numbers differ by a power of 2.

Step 1: Arrange the minterm numbers sectionwise as before. Here we actually start with only decimal equivalents of the minterms. The binary equivalent of the minterm is included in the first column only for the purpose of making sections according to number of 1s contained in binary number.

Step 2: Compare each decimal number in one section with every decimal number in the next section down only, and if the number in the section below is greater than the number in the section above by a power of 2 (i.e, 1, 2, 4, 8......), place a ✓ mark to the right of both minterms. Form a pair

Table 3.2 Determination of prime-implicants of example 3.5 (using decimal notation)

(a)		(b)		(c)	
0000	0 ✓	0, 2, (2)	✓	0, 2, 8, 10 (2, 8)	
0010	2 ✓	0, 8 (8)	✓	0, 8, 2, 10 (8, 2)	$\mathcal{D}$
1000	8 ✓	2, 6 (4)	✓	2, 6, 10, 14 (4, 8)	
0110	6 ✓	2, 10 (8)	✓	2, 10, 6, 14 (8, 4)	$\mathcal{D}$
1010	10 ✓	8, 10 (2)	✓		
1110	14 ✓	6, 14 (8)	✓		
1111	15 ✓	10, 14 (4)	✓		
		14, 15 (1)		$\mathcal{D}$ ⇒ Discarded term	

of these two numbers and transfer them to column (b) along with the difference number in parentheses. For example decimal equivalents of the minterms say 6 and 14 can be compared to result the term of column (b), i.e., 6, 14(8). All the sections of column (a) are similarly compared and subsequent sections formed in column (b).

Table 3.3 Prime-implicants of example 3.5

Decimal	Binary $A\ B\ C\ D$	Term
14, 15 (1)	1 1 1 _	ABC
0, 2, 8, 10 (2, 8)	_ 0 _ 0	$\overline{B}\overline{D}$
2, 6, 10, 14 (4, 8)	_ _ 1 0	$C\overline{D}$

Step 3: The comparison process in column (b) is carried out in a similar way as before, except that only those terms with the same number in parentheses are compared. A match is found, if the pair of numbers in one section differ by a power of 2 from the pair of numbers in the next adjacent section and if and only if these numbers are greater than the pair of numbers in the previous section. Now the resulted terms with two numbers in parentheses, which actually designate the position of dashes (see Table 3.1) shows the differences which have got while comparing the numbers from one section to the next adjacent section in column (a) and column (b). For example consider the terms:

$$\left.\begin{array}{r} 2, 6, (4) \\ 10, 14\ (4) \end{array}\right\} \text{ which results in 2, 6, 10, 14 (4, 8).}$$

4 in the parentheses shows the difference got while comparing 2 and 6 or 10 and 14 in column (a). 8 in the parantheses shows the difference got while comparing 2, 6 with 10, 14 in column (b), because 2 ~ 10 = 6 ~ 44 = 8.

Step 4: The terms in the column without ✓ mark form the *prime-implicants.* Since these terms are in decimal notation, conversion is done to have equivalent binary notation and dash is inserted in those positions designated by the numbers in parentheses. For example, 14, 15(1) is converted to binary as 1110, 1111 and a dash is inserted in the first position to get 111 _. The prime-implicants thus obtained are listed in Table 3.3.

3.7 SELECTION OF PRIME-IMPLICANTS

It is important to note that the sum of the prime-implicants gives us a simply SOP form of expression for the function but not necessarily the minimum one. That is why it is necessary to go for the selection of prime-implicants that give the minimized function.

The selection of prime-implicants is done through the prime-implicant selection chart. In this chart, all the prime-implicants are listed along the left side and all the minterms along the top side as shown in Table 3.6. A minimum set of prime-implicants is then selected. The procedure of selection is illustrated in the following example.

EXAMPLE 3.6: Simplify the function:

$$F\ (A, B, C, D) = \Sigma\ (0, 1, 2, 3, 7, 9, 12, 14, 15).$$

Using the tabulation method.

SOLUTION: **First part:** Determination of prime-implicants.

As we are already familiar with this part, we shall explain only the second part.

Table 3.4 Determination of prime-implicants of example 3.6 (using decimal notation)

(a)		(b)	(c)
0 0 0 0	0 ✓	0, 1 (1) ✓	0, 1, 2, 3 (1, 2)
0 0 0 1	1 ✓	0, 2 (2) ✓	0, 2, 1, 3 (2, 1) 𝒟
0 0 1 0	2 ✓	1, 3 (2) ✓	
0 0 1 1	3 ✓	1, 9 (8)	
1 0 0 1	9 ✓	2, 3 (1)	
1 1 0 0	12 ✓	3, 7 (4)	
0 1 1 1	7 ✓	12, 14 (2)	
1 1 1 0	14 ✓	7, 15 (8)	
1 1 1 1	15 ✓	14, 15 (1)	𝒟 ⇒ Discarded term

Table 3.5 Prime-implicants of example 3.6

Decimal	Binary A B C D	Term
1, 9 (8)	– 0 0 1	$\overline{B}\,\overline{C}D$
3, 7 (4)	0 – 1 1	$\overline{A}CD$
12, 14 (2)	1 1 – 0	$AB\overline{D}$
7, 15 (8)	– 1 1 1	BCD
14, 15 (1)	1 1 1 –	ABC
0, 1, 2, 3 (1, 2)	0 0 – –	$\overline{A}\,\overline{B}$

Second part: Selection of prime-implicants.

The prime-implicant selection chart is prepared first by making six rows to represent six prime-implicants and nine columns to represent nine minterms of the function as shown in Table 3.6.

Table 3.6 Prime-implicant selection chart of example 3.6

		0	1	2	3	7	9	12	14	15
✓ $\overline{B}\,\overline{C}D$	1, 9 (8)		×				×			
$\overline{A}CD$	3, 7 (4)				×	×				
✓ $AB\overline{D}$	12, 14 (2)							×	×	
BCD	7, 15 (8)					×				×
ABC	14, 15 (1)								×	×
✓ $\overline{A}\,\overline{B}$	0, 1, 2, 3 (1, 2)	×	×	×	×					
		✓	✓	✓	✓		✓	✓	✓	

The procedure of selection of prime-implicants is as follows. Crosses (×s) are placed in each row to indicate the minterms contained in the prime-implicant of that row. For example, the two ×s are placed in the first row as shown to indicate that minterms 1 and 9 are contained in the prime-implicant $\overline{B}\overline{C}D$. After this process we go for the selection of a minimum set of prime-implicants.

First we search for columns in Table 3.6 containing only a single ×. Here we find four such columns: 0, 2, 9 and 12. Note that prime-implicant $\overline{B}\overline{C}D$ covers the minterm 9, $AB\overline{D}$ covers the minterm 12 and $\overline{A}\overline{B}$ covers the minterms 0 and 2. These prime-implicants must be included in the minimum SOP form of expression for the function. That is why these prime-implicants are called *essential prime-implicants.* We can define *essential prime-implicants* as prime-implicants that cover minterms with a single × in their column. The essential prime-implicants are shown ahead with ✓ mark to indicate that they have been selected.

After this, we check each column whose minterm is covered by the essential prime-implicants. For example, the essential prime-implicant $\overline{B}\overline{C}D$ covers minterms 1 and 9. A ✓ mark is placed in the bottom of such columns. The resulting chart shows that the essential prime-implicants cover all the minterms of the function except 7 and 15. These two minterms must be included by the selection of one or more prime-implicants. It is clear from the table that prime-implicant BCD covers both minterms and is therefore the one to be included in the minimum set of prime-implicants.

Thus we have, the minimum set of prime-implicants:

$$S = \{\overline{B}\overline{C}D,\ AB\overline{D},\ \overline{A}\overline{B},\ BCD\}$$

and the minimised function:

$$F = \overline{B}\overline{C}D + AB\overline{D} + \overline{A}\overline{B} + BCD$$

The same expression can be obtained by mapping. We shall check it:

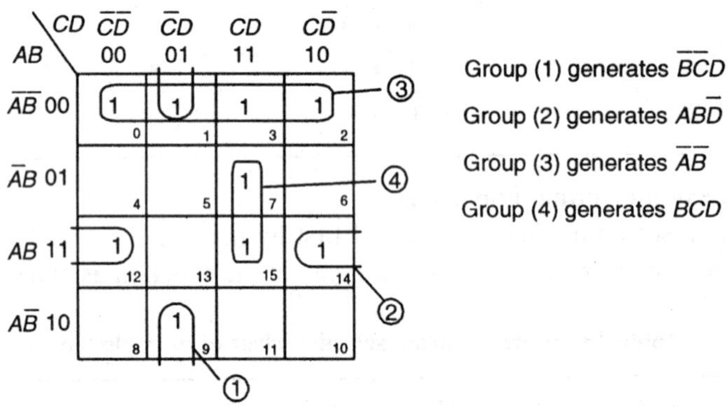

Fig. 3.16

From K-map (Fig. 3.16) also we get,

$$F = \overline{B}\overline{C}D + AB\overline{D} + \overline{A}\overline{B} + BCD$$

3.8 QUINE-MCCLUSKEY METHOD FOR 'Don't care' PROBLEMS

If a function is given with 'don't care' conditions for simplification, the Quine-McCluskey method can be used in the same way as before with slight modifications. Thing is that the don't care terms are included in the list of minterms while determining the prime-implicants but are omitted while forming the prime-implicant selection chart. The method is illustrated with the following example.

EXAMPLE 3.7: Minimize the following function using the tabulation method. $f(w, x, y, z) = m\,(1, 3, 7, 11, 15) + d\,(0, 2, 5)$

SOLUTION:

Table 3.7 Determination of prime-implicants of example 3.7

(a)		(b)	(c)
0 0 0 0	0 ✓	0, 1 (1) ✓	0, 1, 2, 3 (1, 2)
0 0 0 1	1 ✓	0, 2 (2) ✓	0, 2, 1, 3 (2, 1) $\mathcal{D}$
0 0 1 0	2 ✓	1, 3 (2) ✓	1, 3, 5, 7 (2, 4)
0 0 1 1	3 ✓	1, 5 (4) ✓	1, 5, 3, 7 (4, 2) $\mathcal{D}$
0 1 0 1	5 ✓	2, 3 (1) ✓	3, 7, 11, 15 (4, 8)
0 1 1 1	7 ✓	3, 7 (4) ✓	3, 11, 7, 15 (8, 4) $\mathcal{D}$
1 0 1 1	11 ✓	3, 11 (8) ✓	
1 1 1 1	15 ✓	5, 7 (2) ✓	
		7, 15 (8) ✓	
		11, 15 (4) ✓	

Table 3.8 Prime-implicants of example 3.7

Decimal	Binary w x y z	Term
0, 1, 2, 3 (1, 2)	0 0 _ _	$\overline{w}\,\overline{x}$
1, 3, 5, 7 (2, 4)	0 _ _ 1	$\overline{w}z$
3, 7, 11, 15 (4, 8)	_ _ 1 1	yz

Table 3.9 Prime-implicant selection chart of example 3.7

		1	3	7	11	15
$\overline{w}\,\overline{x}$	0, 1, 2, 3	×	×			
$\overline{w}z$	1, 3, 5, 7	×	×	×		
✓ yz	3, 7, 11, 15		×	×	×	×
			✓	✓	✓	✓

Note: The don't care terms are omitted while forming the prime-implicant selection chart.

Thus, we have the simplified function:

$$f(w, x, y, z) = yz + \bar{w}\bar{x}$$

or

$$f(w, x, y, z) = yz + \bar{w}z$$

Check:

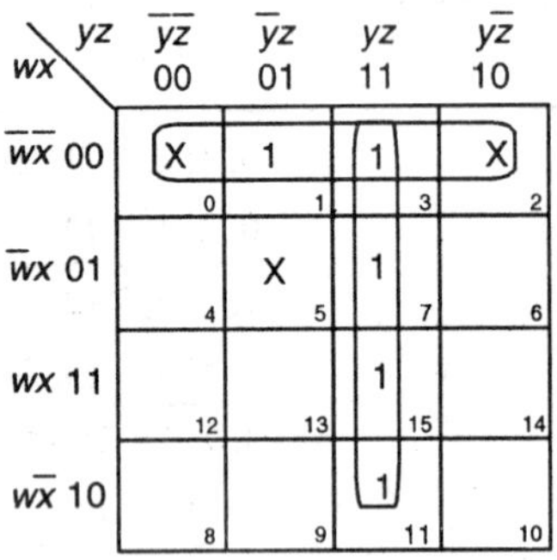

$f = yz + \overline{wx}$

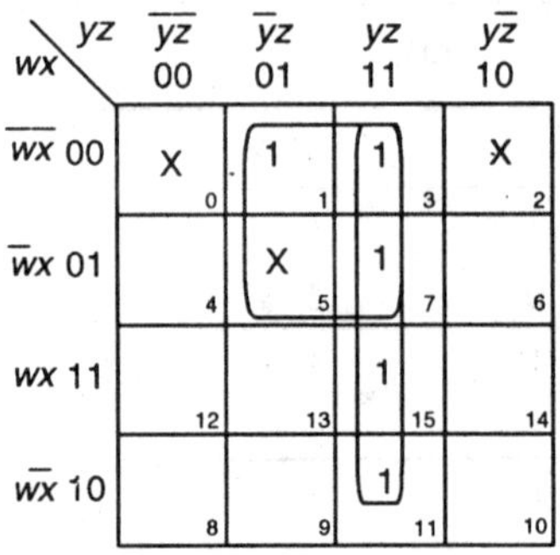

$f = yz + \bar{w}x$

3.9 COMPARISON OF K-MAP AND QUINE-MCCLUSKEY METHODS

K-map method	Quine-McCluskey method
(1) The method is very simple.	The method is very tedious.
(2) It is easy to understand.	It is difficult to follow.
(3) It is not suitable for simplification of functions which involve large number (greater than 6) of variables.	It is well suited for simplification of functions even if the functions involve large number of variables.
(4) Since the procedure relies on human ability to recognise certain patterns, it is difficult to be sure that the best simplified expression has been found.	It's systematic step-by-step procedure that guarantees to produce a simplified standard form expression for a function.
(5) The procedure is not suitable to computerize.	The procedure is suitable to computerize.

SOLVED PROBLEMS

3.1 Minimize the expression $X = \left(\bar{A}\bar{B} + A\bar{B}\right)\left(CD + C\bar{D}\right)$ using the K-map.

SOLUTION: Using the distributive law the given expression can be changed to standard form as:

$$X = \bar{A}\bar{B}CD + \bar{A}\bar{B}C\bar{D} + A\bar{B}CD + A\bar{B}C\bar{D}$$

Now, plotting of K-map is done by entering 1 in the squares corresponding to the minterms contained in the given expression. The remaining squares are then filled with 0. The grouping of 1s is done to get the simplified expression in SOP form.

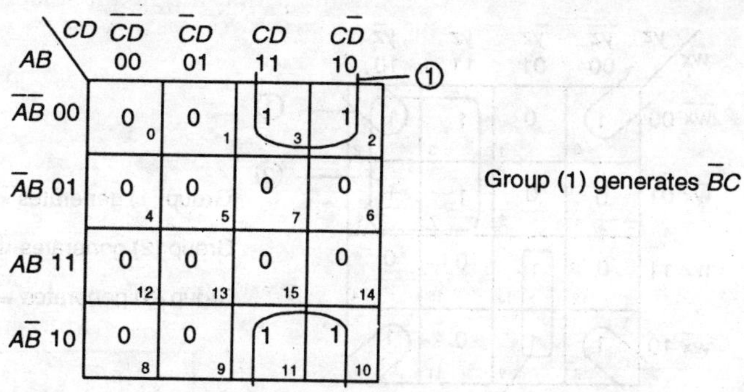

Fig. P3.1

Thus from K-map, we obtain:

$$X = \bar{B}C$$

3.2 Using the K-map method, reduce the function

$$f(A, B, C, D) = \Sigma\ (0, 2, 3, 4, 6, 8, 10, 11, 12, 14)$$

to its minimum sum-of-products form.

SOLUTION: Plotting is done by entering 1 in the squares corresponding to the minterms given. Grouping of 1s is done to reduce the function to its minimum SOP form as follows.

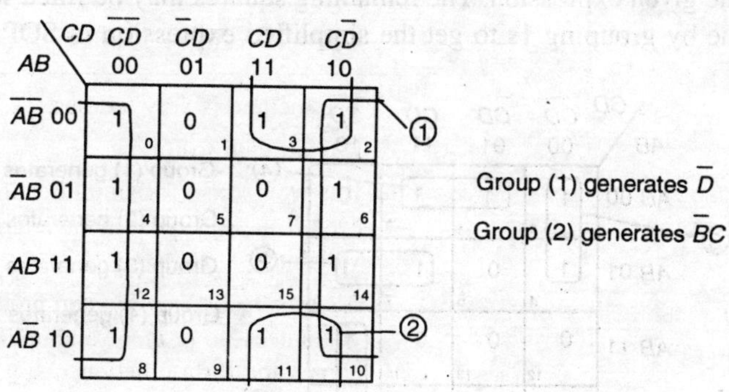

Fig. P3.2

From K-map, we get the minimum SOP form of the given function as:

$$f = \bar{D} + \bar{B}C$$

3.3 Using the K-map, reduce the function

$f(w, x, y, z) = \pi\ (1, 4, 5, 11, 12, 14, 15)$ to its minimum sum-of-products form.

SOLUTION: The given function is in the products of maxterms form. We can interpret the given function as:

$$\bar{f} = \Sigma(1, 4, 5, 11, 12, 14, 15)$$

which gives the minterms not included in the function *f*. Hence 0 is entered in the squares corresponding to these minterms showing their absence in the function *f*. The remaining squares are then filled with 1. Now grouping of 1s is done to reduce the function to its minimum SOP form as follows:

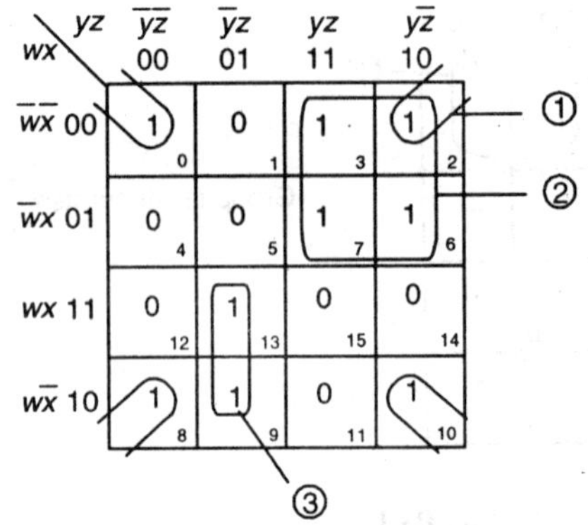

Group (1) generates $\bar{x}\bar{z}$

Group (2) generates $\bar{w}y$

Group (3) generates $w\bar{y}z$

Fig. P3.3

The K-map simplification reduces the given function to:

$$f = \bar{x}\,\bar{z} + \bar{w}\,y + w\,\bar{y}\,z$$

which is in SOP form.

3.4 Reduce the expression $Y = \Sigma\ (0, 1, 3, 4, 6, 7, 10, 14)$ to its simplest SOP form and implement in NAND logic.

SOLUTION: The K-map is plotted first by entering 1 in the squares corresponding to the minterms of the given expression. The remaining squares may be filled with 0. The map simplification is done by grouping 1s to get the simplified expression in SOP form.

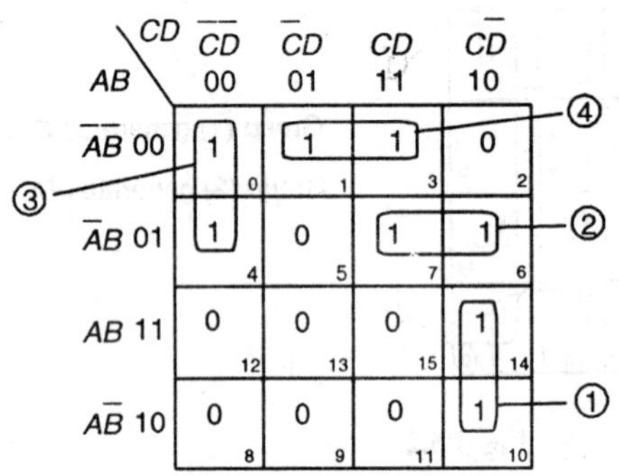

Group (1) generates $AC\bar{D}$

Group (2) generates $\bar{A}BC$

Group (3) generates $\bar{A}\bar{C}\bar{D}$

Group (4) generates $\bar{A}\bar{B}D$

Fig. P3.4 (a)

Thus we obtain:

$$Y = AC\bar{D} + \bar{A}BC + \bar{A}\bar{C}\bar{D} + \bar{A}\bar{B}D$$

NAND Implementation (refer section 3.4)

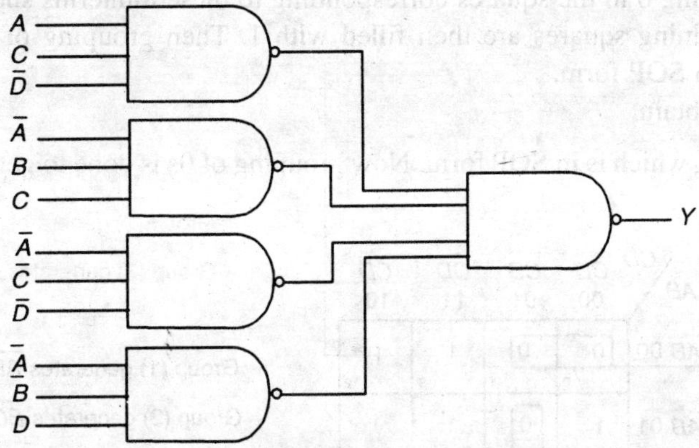

Fig. P3.4 (b)

The complementary inputs $\overline{A}, \overline{B}, \overline{C}$ and $\overline{D}$ can be obtained from NAND gates, for which another 4 NAND gates will be required.

3.5 Using K-map obtain the simplified expression in (i) sum-of-products and (ii) product-of-sums form of the function:

$$f(A, B, C, D) = (\overline{A}+\overline{B}+\overline{C}+\overline{D})(\overline{A}+\overline{B}+C+\overline{D})(A+\overline{B}+C+\overline{D})$$
$$(A+B+C+\overline{D})(A+B+C+D)$$

SOLUTION:

Consider the given function:

$$f(A, B, C, D) = (\overline{A}+\overline{B}+\overline{C}+\overline{D})(\overline{A}+\overline{B}+C+\overline{D})(A+\overline{B}+C+\overline{D})$$
$$(A+B+C+\overline{D})(A+B+C+D)$$

The complement of this function yields:

$$\overline{f} = ABCD + AB\overline{C}D + \overline{A}B\overline{C}D + \overline{A}\overline{B}\overline{C}D + \overline{A}\overline{B}\overline{C}\overline{D}$$

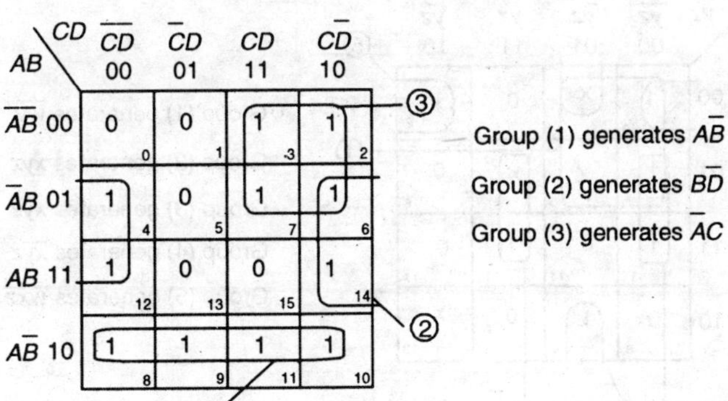

Fig. P3.5 (a)

We can interpret the terms of $\overline{f}$ as the minterms not included in the function f. Hence plotting of K-map is done by entering 0 in the squares corresponding to these minterms showing their absence in the function. The remaining squares are then filled with 1. Then grouping of 1s is done to get the simplified expression in SOP form.

From K-map, we obtain:

$f = A\overline{B} + B\overline{D} + \overline{A}C$, which is in SOP form. Now grouping of 0s is done to get the simplified expression in POS form.

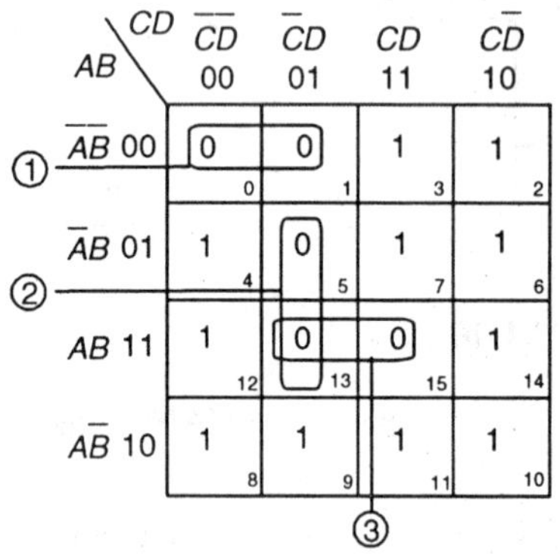

Group (1) generates $\overline{A}\overline{B}\overline{C}$

Group (2) generates $B\overline{C}D$

Group (3) generates ABD

Fig. P3.5(b)

Now from K-map we obtain,

$$\overline{f} = \overline{A}\overline{B}\overline{C} + B\overline{C}D + ABD$$

Taking the complement of this function and applying De Morgan's Theorem, yields:

$$f = (A + B + C)(\overline{B} + C + \overline{D})\ (\overline{A} + \overline{B} + \overline{D}),$$

which is in POS form.

3.6 Find the minimal SOP and POS expressions for

$$f(w, x, y, z) = \Sigma\ (0, 2, 4, 9, 12, 15) + \Sigma_\phi\ (1, 5, 7, 10)$$

SOLUTION:

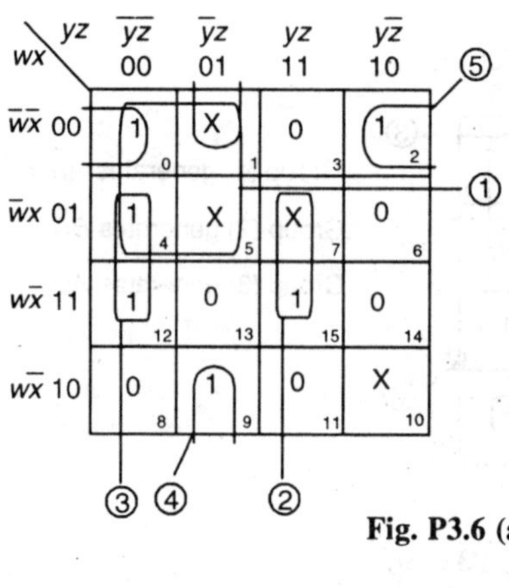

Group (1) generates $\overline{w}\overline{y}$

Group (2) generates xyz

Group (3) generates $x\overline{y}\overline{z}$

Group (4) generates $\overline{x}\overline{y}z$

Group (5) generates $\overline{w}\overline{x}\overline{z}$

Fig. P3.6 (a)

Plotting and grouping of 1s is done as per the procedure explained in theory to get the minimal SOP form of the given function.

From K-map, we get the minimal SOP form as:

$$f = \bar{w}\,\bar{y} + xyz + x\bar{y}\,\bar{z} + \bar{x}\,\bar{y}z + \bar{w}\,\bar{x}\,\bar{z}$$

Grouping of 0s gives the minimal POS form of the given function as follows :

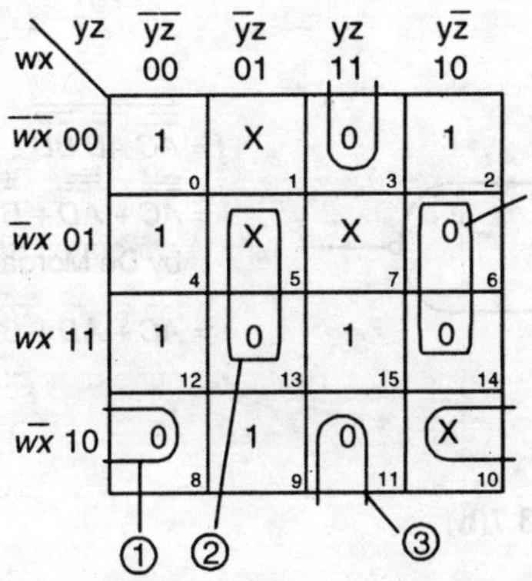

Fig. P3.6 (b)

By K-map simplification we get,

$$\bar{f} = w\bar{x}\,\bar{z} + x\bar{y}z + \bar{x}yz + xy\bar{z}$$

Taking complement on both sides to yield:

$$f = \overline{w\bar{x}\,\bar{z} + x\bar{y}z + \bar{x}yz + xy\bar{z}}$$

Now applying De Morgan's theorem to get the minimal POS form of the given function.

$$f = \overline{(w\bar{x}\bar{z})}\;\overline{(x\bar{y}z)}\,\overline{(\bar{x}yz)}\,\overline{(xy\bar{z})}$$

$$= (\bar{w} + x + z)(\bar{x} + y + \bar{z})(x + \bar{y} + \bar{z})(\bar{x} + \bar{y} + z).$$

3.7 Using K-map, simplify the following Boolean expression and give the implementation of the same using

(i) NAND gates only (SOP form)

(ii) NOR gates only (POS form)

$$f(A, B, C, D) = \Sigma\,(0, 1, 2, 4, 5, 12, 14) + d\,(8, 10)$$

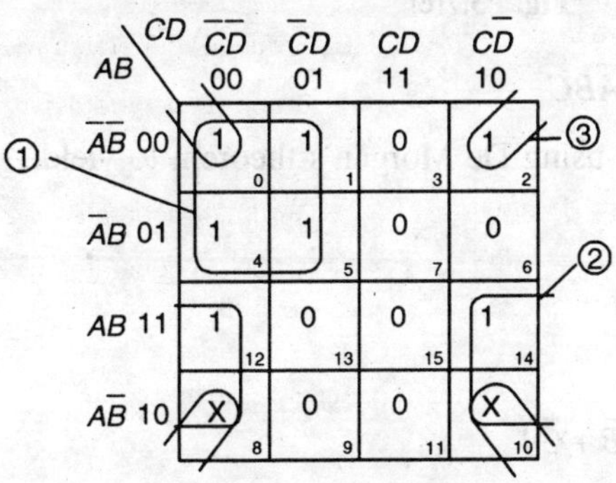

Fig. P3.7(a)

SOLUTION:

Plotting and grouping of 1s is done as per the procedure explained in theory to get the simplified SOP form of the given expression.

From K-map we get, $f = \bar{A}\bar{C} + A\bar{D} + \bar{B}\bar{D}$

NAND Implementation (Refer section 3.4):

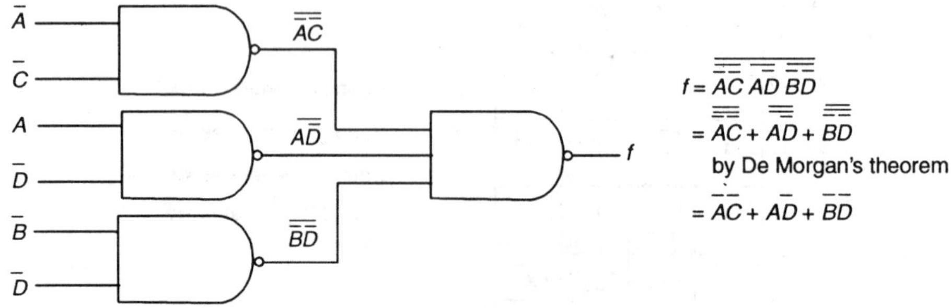

Fig. P3.7(b)

The complementary inputs $\bar{A}$, $\bar{B}$, $\bar{C}$ and $\bar{D}$ can be obtained from NAND gates, for which another 4 NAND gates will be required.

Now grouping of 0s is done instead of 1s as per the procedure explained in theory to get the simplified POS form of the given expression.

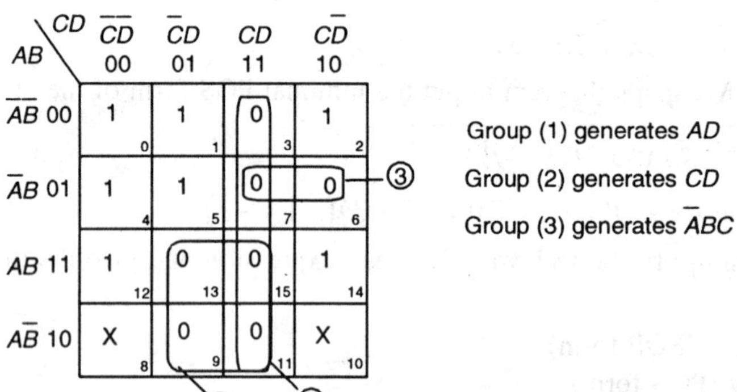

Fig. P3.7(c)

From K-map we get, $\bar{f} = AD + CD + \bar{A}BC$

Taking complement on both sides and using De Morgan's theorem to yield:

$$f = \overline{AD + CD + \bar{A}BC}$$

$$= \overline{AD}\;\overline{CD}\;\overline{\bar{A}BC}$$

$$= (\bar{A} + \bar{D})(\bar{C} + \bar{D})(A + \bar{B} + \bar{C})$$

NOR Implementation (refer section 3.4)

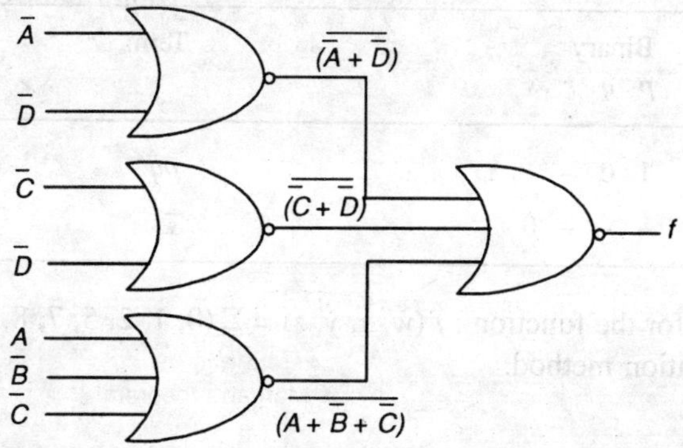

$$f = \overline{\overline{(\bar{A} + \bar{D})} + \overline{(\bar{C} + \bar{D})} + \overline{(A + \bar{B} + \bar{C})}}$$

$$= \overline{\overline{(\bar{A} + \bar{D})}} + \overline{\overline{(\bar{C} + \bar{D})}} + \overline{\overline{(A + \bar{B} + \bar{C})}}$$

by De Morgan's theorem

$$= (\bar{A} + \bar{D}) + (\bar{C} + \bar{D}) + (A + \bar{B} + \bar{C})$$

Fig. P3.7(d)

The complementary inputs $\bar{A}$, $\bar{B}$, $\bar{C}$ and $\bar{D}$ can be obtained from NOR gates, for which another 4 NOR gates will be required.

3.8 Determine the prime-implicants of the function:

F (*p*, *q*, *r*, *s*) = Σ (0, 2, 4, 6, 8, 9, 10, 11, 12, 14) by Quine-McCluskey method using decimal notation.

SOLUTION:

Table P3.8 (a) Determination of prime-implicants of problem 3.8

(a)		(b)	(c)
0 0 0 0	0 ✓	0, 2 (2) ✓	0, 2, 4, 6 (2, 4) ✓
0 0 1 0	2 ✓	0, 4 (4) ✓	0, 2, 8, 10 (2, 8) ✓
0 1 0 0	4 ✓	0, 8 (8) ✓	0, 4, 2, 6 (4, 2) *D*
1 0 0 0	8 ✓	2, 6 (4) ✓	0, 4, 8, 12 (4, 8) ✓
0 1 1 0	6 ✓	2, 10 (8) ✓	0, 8, 2, 10 (8, 2) *D*
1 0 0 1	9 ✓	4, 6 (2) ✓	0, 8, 4, 12 (8, 4) *D*
1 0 1 0	10 ✓	4, 12 (8) ✓	2, 6, 10, 14 (4, 8) ✓
1 1 0 0	12 ✓	8, 9 (1) ✓	2, 10, 6, 14 (8, 4) *D*
1 0 1 1	11 ✓	8, 10 (2) ✓	4, 6, 12, 14 (2, 8) ✓
1 1 1 0	14 ✓	8, 12 (4) ✓	4, 12, 6, 14 (8, 2) *D*
		6, 14 (8) ✓	8, 9, 10, 11 (1, 2) ✓
		9, 11 (2) ✓	8, 10, 9, 11 (2, 1) *D*
		10, 11 (1) ✓	8, 10, 12, 14 (2, 4) ✓
		10, 14 (4) ✓	8, 12, 10, 14 (4, 2) *D*
		12, 14 (2)	*D* ⇒ Discarded term

(d)
0, 2, 4, 6, 8, 10, 12, 14 (2, 4, 8)
0, 2, 8, 10, 4, 6, 12, 14 (2, 8, 4) *D*
0, 4, 8, 12, 2, 6, 10, 14 (4, 8, 2) *D*

Table P3.8 (b) Prime-implicants of problem 3.8

Decimal	Binary p q r s	Term
8, 9, 10, 11 (1, 2)	1 0 – –	$p\bar{q}$
0, 2, 4, 6, 8, 10, 12, 14 (2, 4, 8)	– – – 0	$\bar{s}$

3.9 Determine the set of prime-implicants for the function : $f(w, x, y, z) = \Sigma$ (0, 1, 2, 5, 7, 8, 9, 10, 13, 15) using Quine-McCluskey tabulation method.

SOLUTION:

Table P3.9 (a) Determination of prime-implicants of problem 3.9

(a)		(b)	(c)	
0 0 0 0	0 ✓	0, 1 (1) ✓	0, 1, 8, 9 (1, 8)	
0 0 0 1	1 ✓	0, 2 (2) ✓	0, 2, 8, 10 (2, 8)	
0 0 1 0	2 ✓	0, 8 (8) ✓	0, 8, 1, 9 (8, 1)	$\mathcal{D}$
1 0 0 0	8 ✓	1, 5 (4) ✓	0, 8, 2, 10 (8, 2)	$\mathcal{D}$
0 1 0 1	5 ✓	1, 9 (8) ✓	1, 5, 9, 13 (4, 8)	
1 0 0 1	9 ✓	2, 10 (8) ✓	1, 9, 5, 13 (8, 4)	$\mathcal{D}$
1 0 1 0	10 ✓	8, 9 (1) ✓	5, 7, 13, 15 (2, 8)	
0 1 1 1	7 ✓	8, 10 (2) ✓	5, 13, 7, 15 (8, 2)	$\mathcal{D}$
1 1 0 1	13 ✓	5, 7 (2) ✓		
1 1 1 1	15 ✓	5, 13 (8) ✓		
		9, 13 (4) ✓		
		7,15 (8) ✓	$\mathcal{D} \Rightarrow$ Discarded term.	
		13, 15 (2) ✓		

Table P3.9 (b) Prime-implicants of problem 3.9

Decimal	Binary w x y z	Term
0, 1, 8, 9 (1, 8)	– 0 0 –	$\bar{x}\,\bar{y}$
0, 2, 8, 10 (2, 8)	– 0 – 0	$\bar{x}\,\bar{z}$
1, 5, 9, 13 (4, 8)	– – 0 1	$\bar{y}\,z$
5, 7, 13, 15 (2, 8)	– 1 – 1	$x\,z$

3.10 Reduce the following function to simplest SOP form using tabulation method.

$$F(A, B, C, D, E) = \Sigma(0, 2, 4, 6, 9, 11, 13, 15, 17, 21, 25, 27, 29, 31)$$

SOLUTION:

Table P3.10 (a) Determination of prime-implicants of problem 3.10

(a)			(b)	(c)
00000	0	✓	0, 2 (2) ✓	0, 2, 4, 6 (2, 4)
00010	2	✓	0, 4 (4) ✓	0, 4, 2, 6 (4, 2) $\mathcal{D}$
00100	4	✓	2, 6 (4) ✓	
00110	6	✓	4, 6 (2) ✓	9, 11, 13, 15 (2, 4) ✓
01001	9	✓	9, 11 (2) ✓	9, 11, 25, 27 (2, 16) ✓
10001	17	✓	9, 13 (4) ✓	9, 13, 11, 15 (4, 2) $\mathcal{D}$
01011	11	✓	9, 25 (16) ✓	9, 13, 25, 29 (4, 16) ✓
01101	13	✓	17, 21 (4) ✓	9, 25, 11, 27 (16, 2) $\mathcal{D}$
10101	21	✓	17, 25 (8) ✓	9, 25, 13, 29 (16, 4) $\mathcal{D}$
11001	25	✓	11, 15 (4) ✓	17, 21, 25, 29 (4, 8)
01111	15	✓	11, 27 (16) ✓	17, 25, 21, 29 (8, 4) $\mathcal{D}$
11011	27	✓	13, 15 (2) ✓	11, 15, 27, 31 (4, 16) ✓
11101	29	✓	13, 29 (16) ✓	11, 27, 15, 31 (16, 4) $\mathcal{D}$
11111	31	✓	21, 29 (8) ✓	13, 15, 29, 31(2,16) ✓
			25, 27 (2) ✓	13, 29, 15, 31 (16, 2) $\mathcal{D}$
			25, 29 (4) ✓	25, 27, 29, 31 (2, 4) ✓
			15, 31(16) ✓	25, 29, 27, 31 (4, 2) $\mathcal{D}$
			27, 31 (4) ✓	
			29, 31 (2) ✓	$\mathcal{D} \Rightarrow$ Discarded term

(d)
9, 11, 13, 15, 25, 27, 29, 31 (2, 4, 16)
9, 11, 25, 27, 13, 15, 29, 31 (2, 16, 4) $\mathcal{D}$
9, 13, 25, 29, 11, 15, 27, 31(4, 16, 2) $\mathcal{D}$

Table P3.10 (b) Prime-implicants of problem 3.10

Decimal	Binary A B C D E	Term
0, 2, 4, 6 (2,4)	0 0 – – 0	$\overline{A}\overline{B}\overline{E}$
17, 21, 25, 29 (4, 8)	1 – – 0 1	$A\overline{D}E$
9, 11, 13, 15, 25, 27, 29, 31 (2, 4, 16)	– 1 – – 1	BE

Table P3.10 (c) Prime-implicant selection chart of problem 3.10

		0	2	4	6	9	11	13	15	17	21	25	27	29	31
✓ $\bar{A}\bar{B}\bar{E}$	0, 2, 4, 6	×	×	×	×										
✓ $A\bar{D}E$	17, 21, 25, 29									×	×	×		×	
✓ BE	9, 11, 13, 15, 25, 27, 29, 31					×	×	×	×			×	×	×	×
		✓	✓	✓	✓	✓	✓	✓	✓	✓	✓	✓	✓	✓	✓

Thus the given function is reduced to:

$$F = \bar{A}\bar{B}\bar{E} + A\bar{D}E + BE$$

3.11 Simplify the following function using the tabulation method.

$$f(w, x, y, z) = \Sigma\, m\,(0, 2, 3, 6, 7) + d\,(5, 8, 10, 11, 15)$$

SOLUTION:

Table P3.11(a) Determination of prime-implicants of problem 3.11

(a)		(b)	(c)
0 0 0 0	0 ✓	0, 2 (2) ✓	0, 2, 8, 10 (2, 8)
0 0 1 0	2 ✓	0, 8 (8) ✓	0, 8, 2, 10 (8, 2) $\mathcal{D}$
1 0 0 0	8 ✓	2, 3 (1) ✓	2, 3, 6, 7 (1, 4)
0 0 1 1	3 ✓	2, 6 (4) ✓	2, 3, 10, 11 (1, 8)
0 1 0 1	5 ✓	2, 10 (8) ✓	2, 6, 3, 7 (4, 1) $\mathcal{D}$
0 1 1 0	6 ✓	8, 10 (2) ✓	2, 10, 3, 11 (8, 1) $\mathcal{D}$
1 0 1 0	10 ✓	3, 7 (4) ✓	3, 7, 11, 15 (4, 8)
0 1 1 1	7 ✓	3, 11 (8) ✓	3, 11, 7, 15 (8, 4) $\mathcal{D}$
1 0 1 1	11 ✓	5, 7 (2) ✓	
1 1 1 1	15 ✓	6, 7 (1) ✓	
		10, 11 (1) ✓	
		7, 15 (8) ✓	
		11, 15 (4) ✓	$\mathcal{D} \Rightarrow$ Discarded term

Table P3.11(b) Prime-implicants of problem 3.11

Decimal	Binary $w\ x\ y\ z$	Term
5, 7 (2)	0 1 _ 1	$\bar{w}xz$
0, 2, 8, 10 (2, 8)	_ 0 _ 0	$\bar{x}\bar{z}$
2, 3, 6, 7 (1, 4)	0 _ 1 _	$\bar{w}y$
2, 3, 10, 11 (1, 8)	_ 0 1 _	$\bar{x}y$
3, 7, 11, 15 (4, 8)	_ _ 1 1	yz

Table P3.11(c) Prime-implicant selection chart of problem 3.11

		0	2	3	6	7
$\bar{w}xz$	5, 7					×
✓ $\bar{x}\bar{z}$	0, 2, 8, 10	×	×			
✓ $\bar{w}y$	2, 3, 6, 7		×	×	×	×
✓ $\bar{w}y$	2, 3, 10, 11		×	×		
yz	3, 7, 11, 15			×		×
		✓	✓	✓	✓	✓

Thus we have the simplified function:

$$f(w, x, y, z) = \bar{x}\bar{z} + \bar{w}y$$

Note: The 'don't care' terms are omitted while forming the prime-implicant selection chart.

3.12 Using Quine-McCluskey method, obtain the set of prime-implicants for the function $f(a, b, c, d, e) = \Sigma\,(4, 12, 13, 14, 16, 19, 22, 24, 25, 26, 29, 30) + \Sigma_{\phi}\,(1, 3, 5, 20, 27)$ and hence obtain the minimal form of the given function employing decimal representation.

SOLUTION:

Table P3.12 (a) Determination of prime-implicants of problem 3.12

(a)			(b)		(c)	
0 0 0 0 1	1	✓	1, 3 (2)		4, 5, 12, 13 (1, 8)	
0 0 1 0 0	4	✓	1, 5 (4)		4, 12, 5, 13 (8, 1)	$\mathcal{D}$
1 0 0 0 0	16	✓	4, 5 (1)	✓	24, 25, 26, 27 (1, 2)	
0 0 0 1 1	3	✓	4, 12 (8)	✓	24, 26, 25, 27 (2, 1)	$\mathcal{D}$
0 0 1 0 1	5	✓	4, 20 (16)			
0 1 1 0 0	12	✓	16, 20 (4)			
1 0 1 0 0	20	✓	16, 24 (8)			
1 1 0 0 0	24	✓	3, 19 (16)			
0 1 1 0 1	13	✓	5, 13 (8)	✓		
0 1 1 1 0	14	✓	12, 13 (1)	✓		
1 0 0 1 1	19	✓	12, 14 (2)			
1 0 1 1 0	22	✓	20, 22 (2)			
1 1 0 0 1	25	✓	24, 25 (1)	✓		
1 1 0 1 0	26	✓	24, 26 (2)	✓		
1 1 0 1 1	27	✓	13, 29 (16)			
1 1 1 0 1	29	✓	14, 30 (16)			
1 1 1 1 0	30	✓	19, 27 (8)			
			22, 30 (8)			
			25, 27 (2)	✓		
			25, 29 (4)			
			26, 27 (1)	✓		
			26, 30 (4)			

Table P3.12 (b) Prime-implicants of problem 3.12

Decimal	Binary *A B C D E*	Term
1, 3 (2)	0 0 0 – 1	$\bar{a}\bar{b}\bar{c}e$
1, 5 (4)	0 0 – 0 1	$\bar{a}\bar{b}\bar{d}e$
4, 20 (16)	– 0 1 0 0	$\bar{b}c\bar{d}\bar{e}$
16, 20 (4)	1 0 – 0 0	$a\bar{b}\bar{d}e$
16, 24 (8)	1 – 0 0 0	$a\bar{c}\bar{d}\bar{e}$
3, 19 (16)	– 0 0 1 1	$\bar{b}\bar{c}de$
12, 14 (2)	0 1 1 – 0	$\bar{a}bc\bar{e}$
20, 22 (2)	1 0 1 – 0	$a\bar{b}c\bar{e}$

Table P3.12(b) Prime-implicants of problem 3.12

Decimal	Binary $A\ B\ C\ D\ E$	Term
13, 29 (16)	– 1 1 0 1	$bc\bar{d}e$
14, 30 (16)	– 1 1 1 0	$bcd\bar{e}$
19, 27 (8)	1 – 0 1 1	$a\bar{c}de$
22, 30 (8)	1 – 1 1 0	$acd\bar{e}$
25, 29 (4)	1 1 – 0 1	$ab\bar{d}e$
26, 30 (4)	1 1 – 1 0	$abd\bar{e}$
4, 5, 12, 13 (1, 8)	0 – 1 0 –	$\bar{a}c\bar{d}$
24, 25, 26, 27 (1, 2)	1 1 0 – –	$ab\bar{c}$

Table P3.12(c) Prime-implicant selection chart of problem 3.12

		4	12	13	14	16	19	22	24	25	26	29	30
$\bar{a}\bar{b}\bar{c}e$	1, 3												×
$\bar{a}\bar{b}\bar{d}e$	1, 5												
$\bar{b}c\bar{d}\bar{e}$	4, 20	×											
$a\bar{b}\bar{d}\bar{e}$	16, 20					×							
$a\bar{c}\bar{d}\bar{e}$	16, 24					×			×				
$\bar{b}\bar{c}de$	3, 19						×						
$\bar{a}bc\bar{e}$	12, 14		×		×								
$a\bar{b}c\bar{e}$	20, 22							×					
$bc\bar{d}e$	13, 29			×								×	
$bcd\bar{e}$	14, 30				×								×
$a\bar{c}de$	19, 27						×						
$acd\bar{e}$	22, 30							×					×
$ab\bar{d}e$	25, 29									×		×	
$abd\bar{e}$	26, 30										×		×
$\bar{a}c\bar{d}$	4, 5, 12, 13	×	×	×									
$ab\bar{c}$	24, 25, 26, 27								×	×	×		

There are no essential prime-implicants. Hence we go directly for selection of prime-implicants which cover all the minterms and it is these implicants which are to be included in the minimal set of prime implicants. Since there are many options to choose prime-implicants, one may not get the unique answer.

Thus we obtained the minimal form of the given function as:

$$F = a\bar{c}\bar{d}\bar{e} + \bar{b}\bar{c}de + bcd\bar{e} + acd\bar{e} + ab\bar{d}e + \bar{a}c\bar{d} + ab\bar{c}$$

EXERCISES

3.1 Simplify the following expressions using a K-map

(a) $F = \bar{B}D + \bar{A}B\bar{C} + A(\bar{B}C + B\bar{C})$

(b) $F = A(\bar{B} + C\bar{D}) + \bar{D}(\bar{C} + \bar{A}C) + \bar{A}\bar{B}$

3.2 Using a K-map, reduce the following functions to their minimum sum-of-products form:

(a) $F(A, B, C, D) = \Sigma\ (0, 2, 5, 7, 8, 10, 12, 13)$

(b) $F(P, Q, R, S) = \Sigma\ (0, 2, 3, 5, 6, 7, 8, 9, 11, 13, 15)$

3.3 Using a K-map, reduce the following function to its minimum product-of-sums form:

$f(\text{w, x, y, z}) = \Sigma\ (5, 6, 7, 8, 9, 12, 13, 14, 15)$

3.4 Reduce the expression $Y = \pi\ (2, 8, 9, 10, 11, 12, 14)$ to its simplest POS form and implement in NOR logic.

3.5 Using a K-map, obtain the simplified expression in (i) sum-of-products and (ii) product-of-sums form of the function:

$$F = (\bar{B} + \bar{D})(\bar{A} + \bar{C} + D)(A + \bar{B} + \bar{C} + D)(\bar{A} + B + \bar{C} + \bar{D})$$

and implement the same with

(i) NAND gates only

(ii) NOR gates only

3.6 Using a K-map find minimal SOP and POS expressions for the function: $F(A, B, C, D) = \Sigma\ (2, 5, 7, 11, 14, 15) + d\ (1, 3, 10)$.

3.7 Using a K-map simplify the following Boolean expression and give the implementation of the same using

(i) NAND gates only

(ii) AND, OR and INVERT gates

$f(A, B, C, D) = \Sigma\ (1, 2, 3, 4, 6, 8) + \Sigma_{\phi}\ (0, 7, 9, 12)$

3.8 Determine the set of prime-implicants for the function:

$F(A, B, C, D, E) = \Sigma\ (2, 3, 6, 7, 9, 10, 12, 13, 14, 16, 18, 22, 26, 28, 29, 30)$ using Quine-McCluskey method.

3.9 Find the minimal SOP form of the function $F(A, B, C, D) = \Sigma\ (0, 1, 2, 4, 5, 8, 10, 14, 15)$ using the tabulation method.

3.10 Simplify the following Boolean function by means of the tabulation method in SOP form.

$f(v, w, x, y, z) = \Sigma\ (0, 2, 6, 8, 9, 11, 13, 15, 16, 17, 18, 22)$
$+ d\ (4, 10, 12, 14, 20, 28, 30)$

4

Combinational Logic

When logic gates are connected together to perform any specific function, with no memory elements involved, the resulting network is called *combinational logic*. In combinational logic, the output is at any time dependent on the present combinations of the inputs.

A combinational logic circuit consists of input variables, logic gates and output variables. The logic gates accept signals from the inputs and generate signals to the outputs. The general model of a combinational circuit is shown in Fig. 4.1.

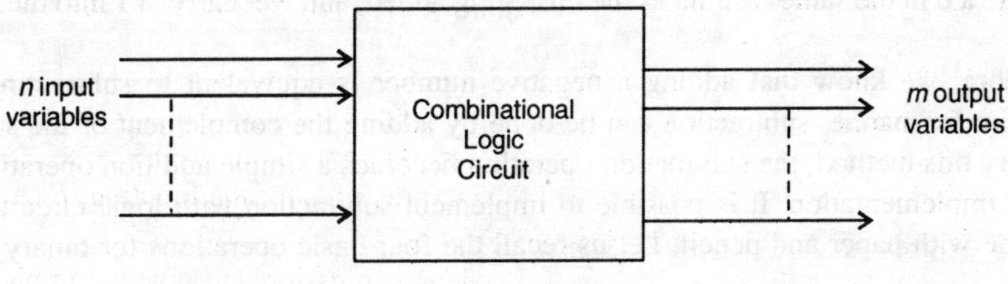

Fig. 4.1 The general model of a combinational circuit

It is worth to note that for *n* input variables, there are 2^n possible combinations of binary input values. For each possible input combination, there is one and only one possible output combination. A combinational circuit can be described by *m* Boolean functions, one for each output variable. Each output function is expressed interms of the *n* input variables.

There are several combinational logic circuits that are employed in the design of digital system and they are available in the form of ICs. In this chapter, we shall study some of the combinational logic circuits such as adders and subtractors, and code converters, including methods of analysis and design of combinational circuits.

4.1 DESIGN PROCEDURE

As a logic designer, one has to start the design of combinational logic circuits from the verbal specifications of the problem. The procedure ends in a set of Boolean functions that can be implemented with logic gates. The design procedure involves the following steps.

Steps:

1. The problem is stated clearly in words.
2. The number of input and output variables is determined.
3. The input and output variables are assigned letter symbols.
4. The truth table that shows the relationship between inputs and outputs is obtained.
5. The simplified Boolean function for each output is obtained by using any of the simplifying techniques.
6. The logic diagram is then drawn.

4.2 ADDERS AND SUBTRACTORS

Adders and subtractors are the two basic building blocks to carry out arithmetic and logic operations on the data.

We know that the addition of two binary digits is the most basic arithmetic operation. It is the key to binary subtraction, multiplication and division. So, let us recall the four basic operations for binary addition:

$$\begin{array}{r} 0 \\ +\,0 \\ \hline 0 \end{array} \qquad \begin{array}{r} 0 \\ +\,1 \\ \hline 1 \end{array} \qquad \begin{array}{r} 1 \\ +\,0 \\ \hline 1 \end{array} \qquad \begin{array}{r} 1 \\ +\,1 \\ \hline 0 \end{array} \quad \text{(Carry 1)}$$

As in normal arithmetic, we can say for the result to the last operation as 'sum 0 with a carry 1'. That is, we write a 0 in the same column as the bits being added, and we 'carry' a 1 into the next column on the left.

From algebra, we know that adding a negative number is equivalent to subtracting a positive number. In a similar manner subtraction can be done by adding the complement of the subtrahend to the minuend. By this method, the subtraction operation becomes a simple addition operation requiring full adders for implementation. It is possible to implement subtraction with logic circuits in a direct manner, as done with paper and pencil. Let us recall the four basic operations for binary subtraction:

$$\begin{array}{r} 0 \\ -\,0 \\ \hline 0 \end{array} \qquad \begin{array}{r} 0 \\ -\,1 \\ \hline 1 \end{array} \text{ (Borrow 1)} \qquad \begin{array}{r} 1 \\ -\,0 \\ \hline 1 \end{array} \qquad \begin{array}{r} 1 \\ -\,1 \\ \hline 0 \end{array}$$

As in normal arithmetic, we can say for the result to the second operation as 'difference 1 with a borrow 1'. That is a 1 is written in the same column, and the fact that a 1 has borrowed is conveyed to the next column on the left.

Half-Adder

A *half-adder* is a combinational circuit that performs the simple addition of two bits producing a sum and a carry.

The truth table for the input-output relationships of a half-adder with input variables x and y and outputs as sum S and carry C is given in Table 4.1.

Table 4.1 Truth table for a half-adder

x	y	C	S
0	0	0	0
0	1	0	1
1	0	0	1
1	1	1	0

From the truth table, we can obtain the simplified expressions as:

$S = x\overline{y} + \overline{x}y$, the same as the Boolean expression for EX-OR gate.

$C = xy$

The block symbol for a half-adder circuit is shown in Fig. 4.2.

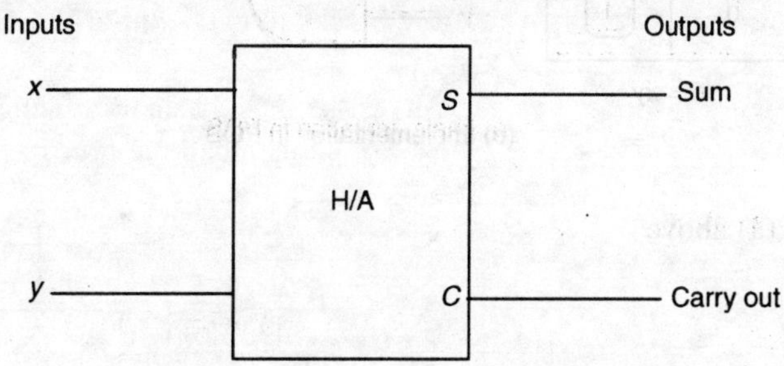

Fig. 4.2 Block symbol for a half-adder

A half-adder can be represented in several ways by using combinations of various logic gates, as shown in Fig. 4.3. Apart from these, other configurations may also be developed.

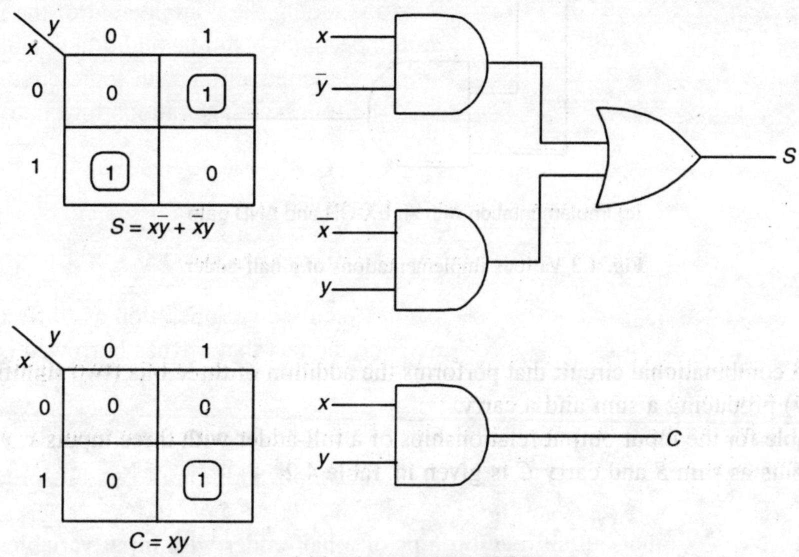

Fig. 4.3 Various implementations of a half-adder

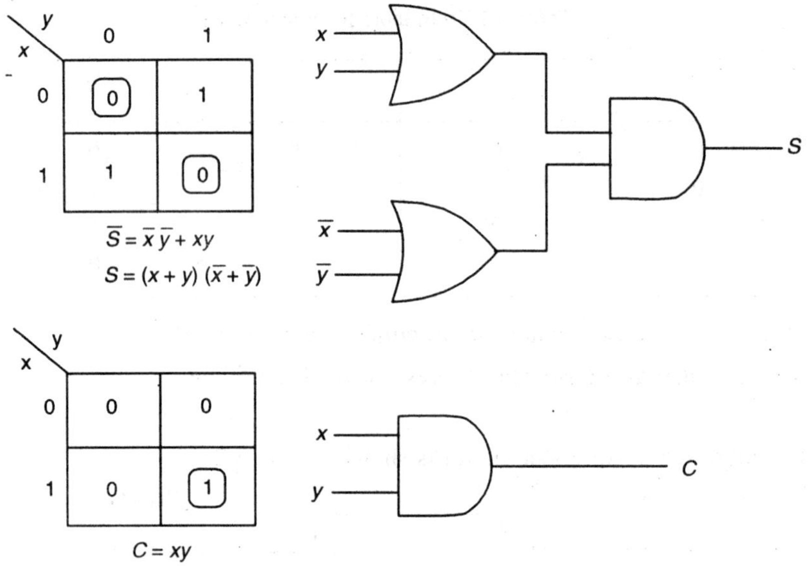

(b) Implementation in POS

$S = x\overline{y} + \overline{x}y$, as in (a) above

$= x \oplus y$

$C = xy$

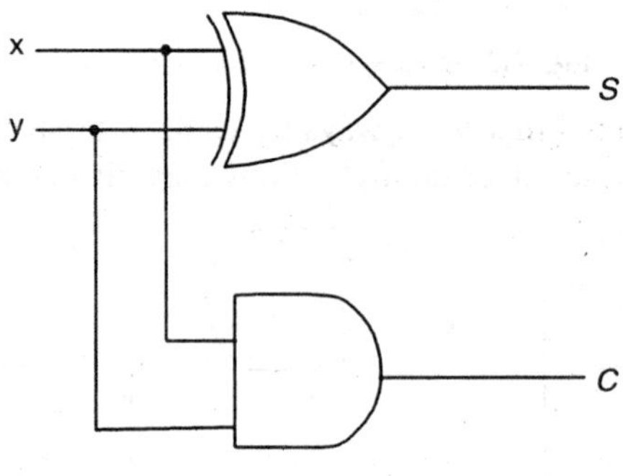

(c) Implementation with an EX-OR and AND gate

Fig. 4.3 Various implementations of a half-adder

Full-Adder

A *full-adder* is a combinational circuit that performs the addition of three bits (two significant bits and a previous carry) producing a sum and a carry.

The truth table for the input-output relationships of a full-adder with three inputs *x*, *y* and an input carry *z* and outputs as sum *S* and carry *C* is given in Table 4.2.

Table 4.2 Truth table for a full-adder

x	y	z (C_{in})	C	S
0	0	0	0	0
0	0	1	0	1
0	1	0	0	1
0	1	1	1	0
1	0	0	0	1
1	0	1	1	0
1	1	0	1	0
1	1	1	1	1

The block symbol for a full-adder circuit is shown in Fig. 4.4.

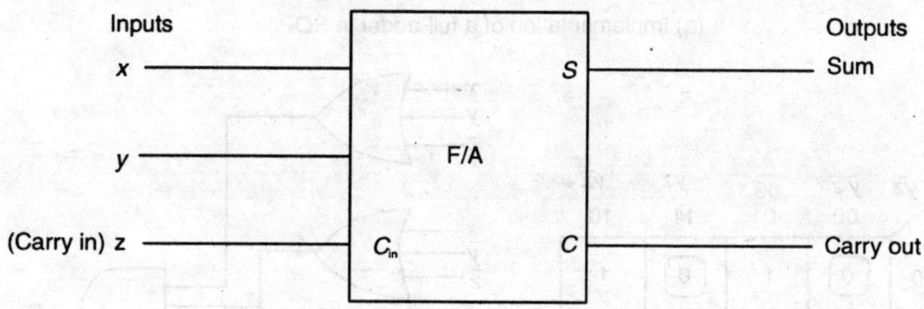

Fig. 4.4 Block symbol for a full-adder

From the truth table, we can plot the K-maps and from that we can have the simplified expressions for sum (S) and carry (C).

The various implementations for a full-adder can be obtained, as shown in Fig. 4.5.

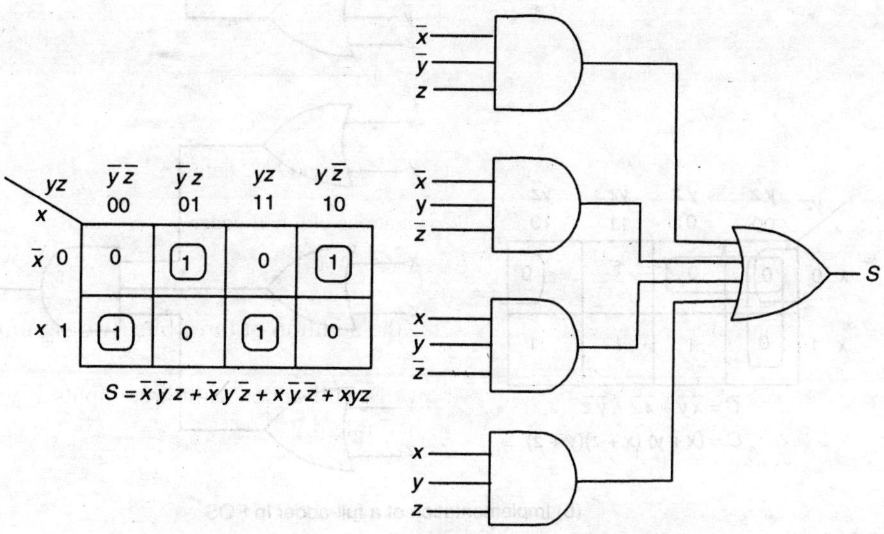

Fig. 4.5 Various implementations of a full-adder

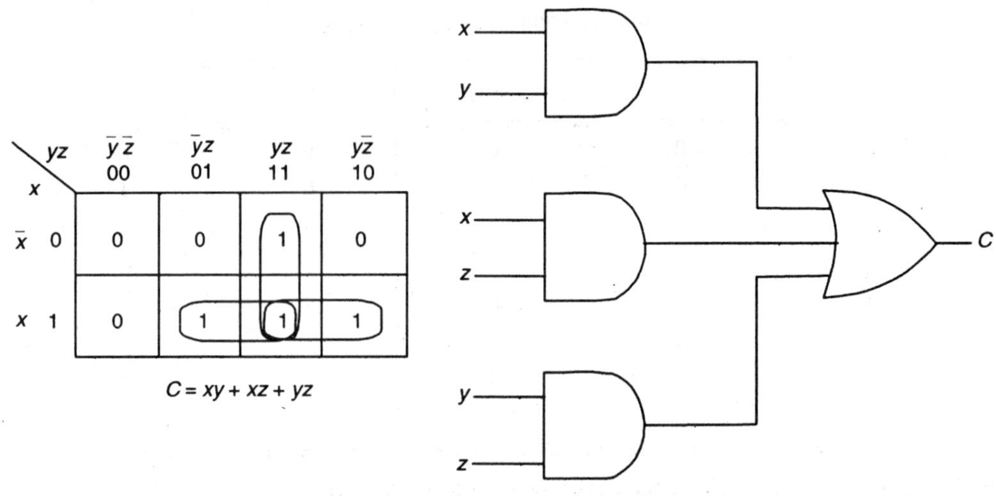

(a) Implementation of a full-adder in SOP

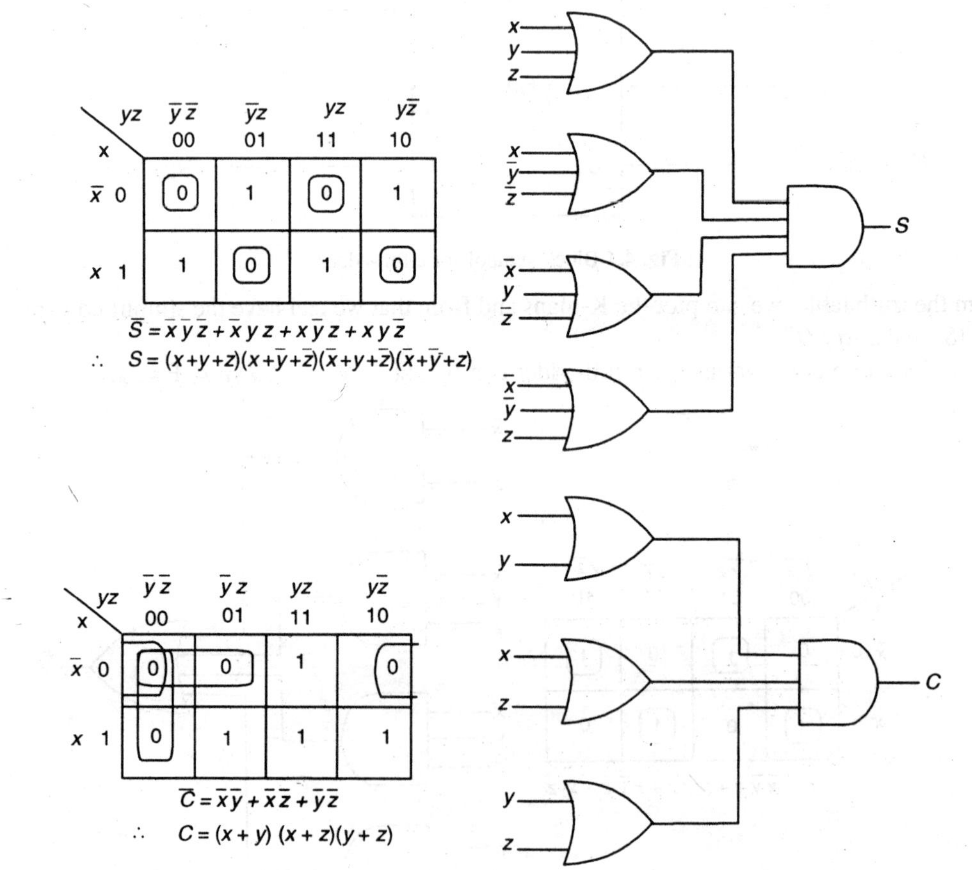

(b) Implementation of a full-adder in POS

Fig. 4.5 Various implementations of a full-adder

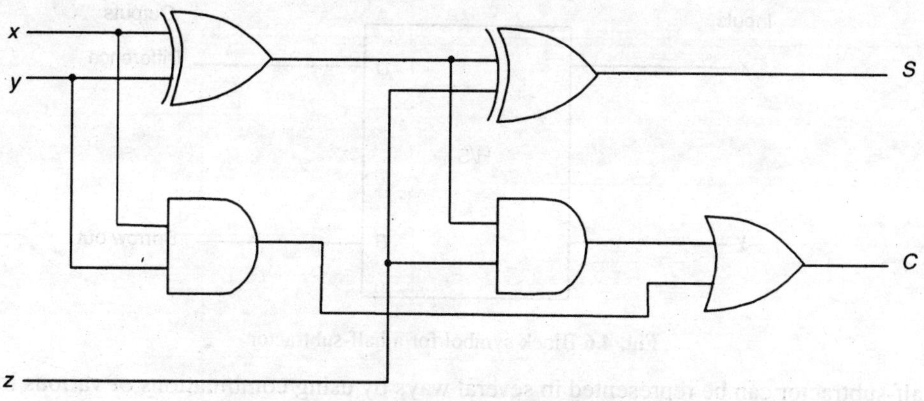

(c) Implementation of a full-adder with two half-adders and an OR gate

Fig. 4.5 Various implementations of a full-adder

$$S = (x \oplus y) \oplus z$$

$$C = (x \oplus y)z + xy$$

These are the same expressions as in (a) above and they can be verified by manipulation (see section 4.7).

Half-Subtractor

A *half-subtractor* is a combinational circuit that performs the simple subtraction of two bits producing a difference and specifying a borrow.

The truth table for the input-output relationships of a half-subtractor with two inputs x and y and outputs as difference D and borrow B is given in Table 4.3.

Table 4.3 Truth table for a half-subtractor

x	y	B	D
0	0	0	0
0	1	1	1
1	0	0	1
1	1	0	0

From the truth table, we can obtain the simplified Boolean expressions as:

$S = x\bar{y} + \bar{x}y$, the same as the Boolean expression for EX-OR gate.

$B = \bar{x}y$

The block symbol for a half-subtractor circuit is shown in Fig. 4.6.

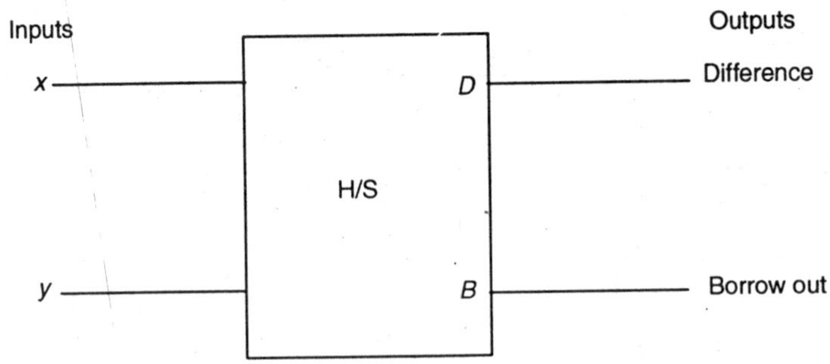

Fig. 4.6 Block symbol for a half-subtractor

A half-subtractor can be represented in several ways by using combinations of various logic gates, as shown in Fig. 4.7. Here we must note that the logic for D is exactly the same as the logic for output S in the half-adder.

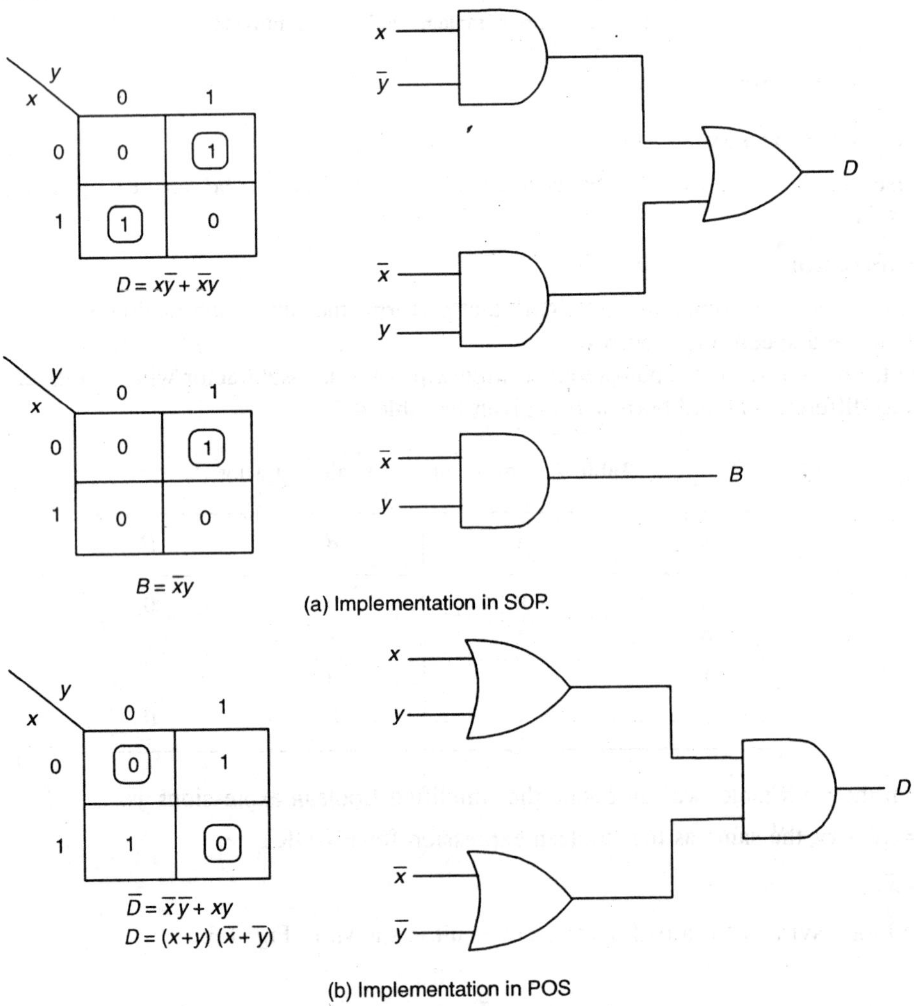

Fig. 4.7 Various implementations of a half-subtractor

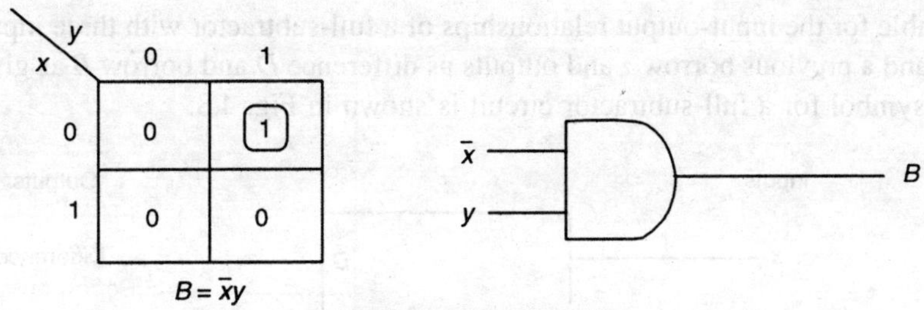

(b) Implementation in POS

$D = x\overline{y} + \overline{x}y$, as in (a) above

$= x \oplus y$

$B = \overline{x}y$

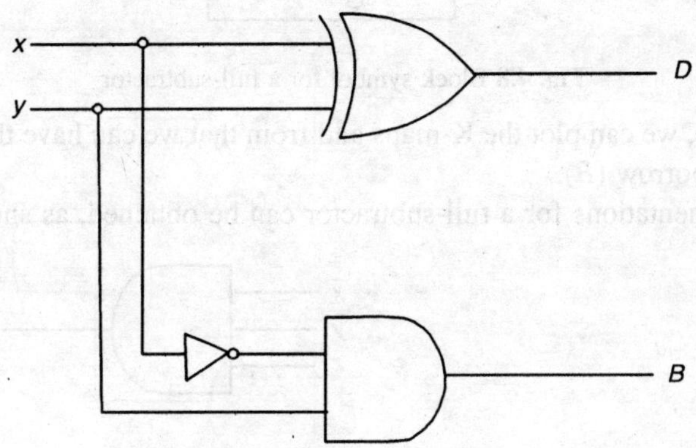

(c) Implementation with an EX-OR and AND gate

Fig. 4.7 Various implementations of a half-subtractor

Full-Subtractor

A *full-subtractor* is a combinational circuit that performs a subtraction between two bits, taking into account that 1 is borrowed by a lower significant stage.

Table 4.4 Truth table for a full-subtractor

x	y	z (B_{in})	B	D
0	0	0	0	0
0	0	1	1	1
0	1	0	1	1
0	1	1	1	0
1	0	0	0	1
1	0	1	0	0
1	1	0	0	0
1	1	1	1	1

The truth table for the input-output relationships of a full-subtractor with three inputs x (minuend), y (subtrahend) and a previous borrow z and outputs as difference D and borrow B as given in Table 4.4.

The block symbol for a full-subtractor circuit is shown in Fig. 4.8.

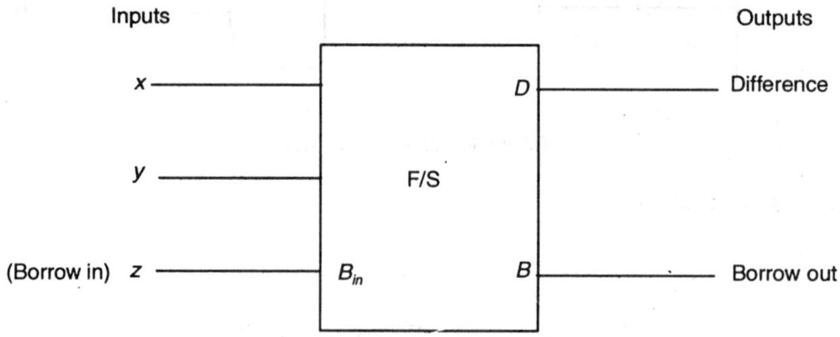

Fig. 4.8 Block symbol for a full-subtractor

From the truth table, we can plot the K-maps and from that we can have the simplified expressions for difference (D) and borrow (B).

The various implementations for a full-subtractor can be obtained, as shown in Fig. 4.9.

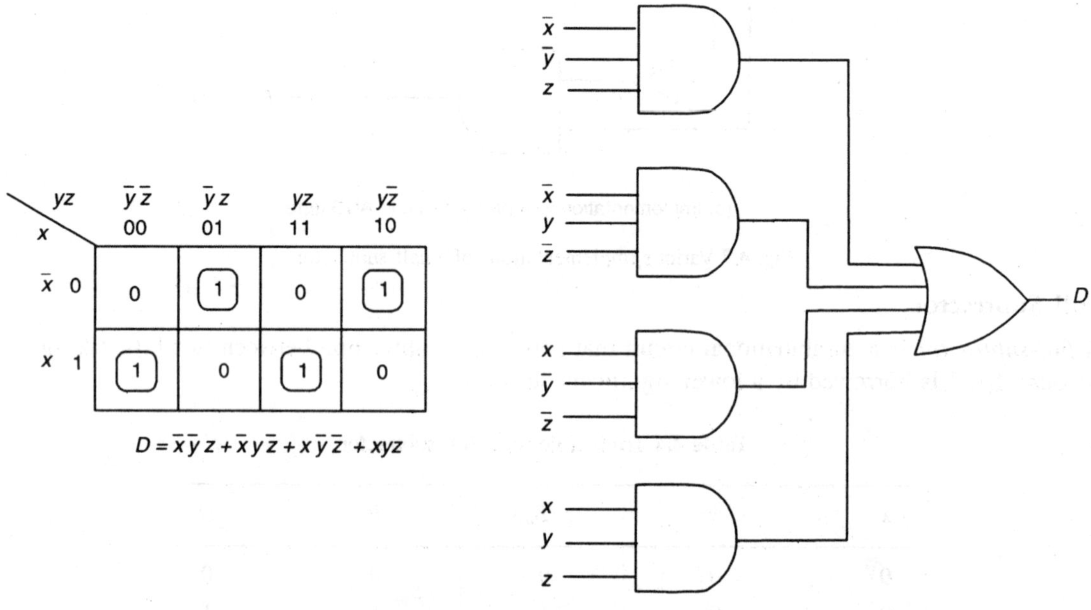

(a) Implementation of a full-subtractor in SOP

Fig. 4.9 Various implementations of a full-subtractor

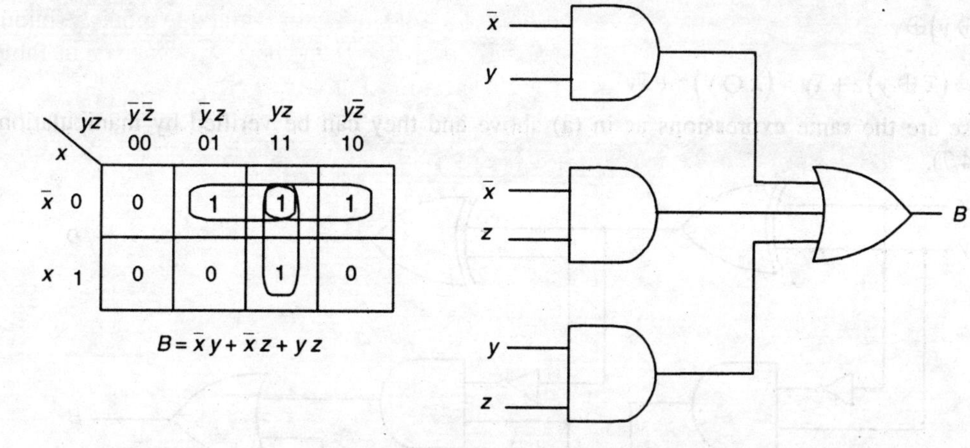

(a) Implementation of a full-subtractor in SOP

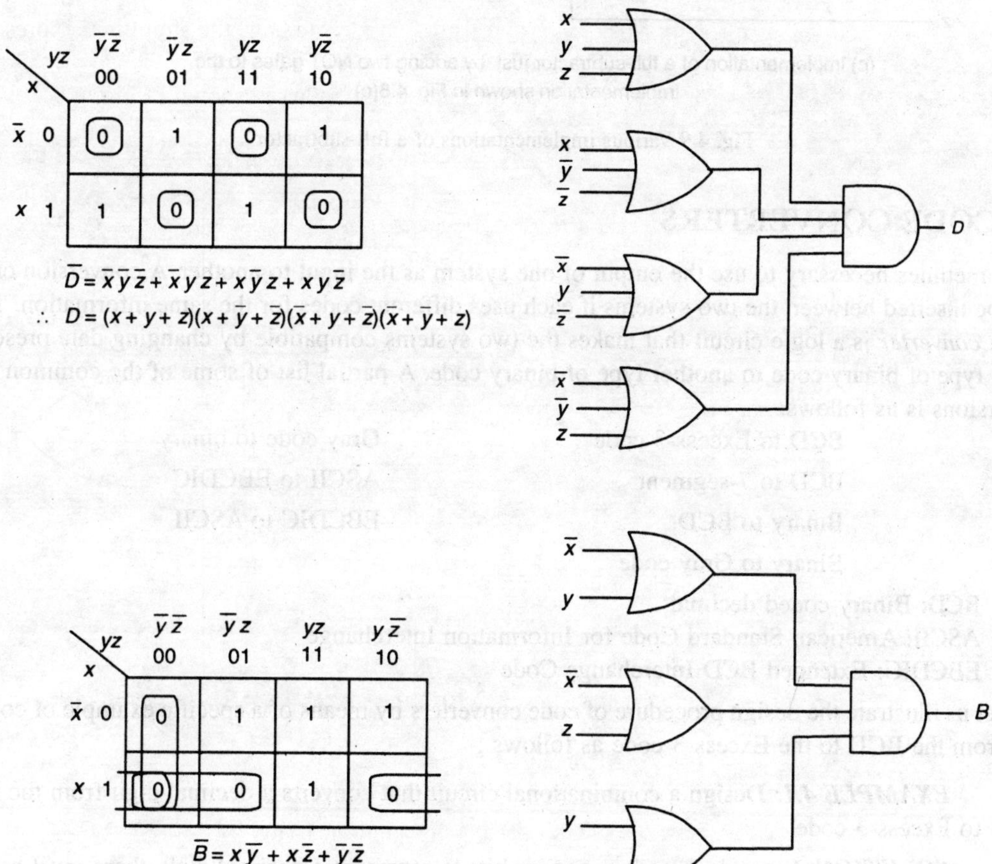

(b) Implementation of a full-subtractor in POS

Fig. 4.9 Various implementations of a full-subtractor

$D = (x \oplus y) \oplus z$

$$B = (\bar{x} \oplus y)z + \bar{x}y = (x \odot y)z + \bar{x}y$$

These are the same expressions as in (a) above and they can be verified by manipulation (see section 4.7).

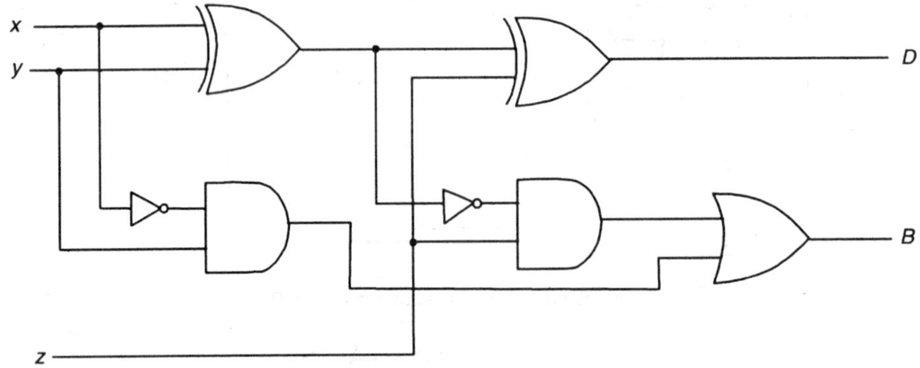

(c) Implementation of a full-subtractor just by adding two NOT gates to the implementation shown in Fig. 4.5(c)

Fig. 4.9 Various implementations of a full-subtractor

4.3 CODE CONVERTERS

It is sometimes necessary to use the output of one system as the input to another. A conversion circuit must be inserted between the two systems if each uses different codes for the same information. Thus, a *code converter* is a logic circuit that makes the two systems compatible by changing data presented in one type of binary code to another type of binary code. A partial list of some of the common code conversions is as follows:

- BCD to Excess-3 code
- BCD to 7-segment
- Binary to BCD
- Binary to Gray code
- Gray code to binary
- ASCII to EBCDIC
- EBCDIC to ASCII

Note: BCD: Binary-coded decimal
ASCII: American Standard Code for Information Interchange
EBCDIC: Extended BCD Interchange Code

Let us illustrate the design procedure of code converters by means of a specific example of conversion from the BCD to the Excess-3 code as follows :

EXAMPLE 4.1: Design a combinational circuit that converts a decimal digit from the BCD to Excess-3 code.

SOLUTION: Since each code uses four bits to represent a decimal digit, there must be four input variables and four output variables. Let us designate the four input binary variables by the symbols A, B, C, and D, and the four output variables by w, x, y and z. The truth table showing the relationships between the input and output variables is given in Table 4.5.

Table 4.5 Truth table for BCD-to-Excess-3 code converter

Input BCD				Output Excess-3 code			
A	*B*	*C*	*D*	*w*	*x*	*y*	*z*
0	0	0	0	0	0	1	1
0	0	0	1	0	1	0	0
0	0	1	0	0	1	0	1
0	0	1	1	0	1	1	0
0	1	0	0	0	1	1	1
0	1	0	1	1	0	0	0
0	1	1	0	1	0	0	1
0	1	1	1	1	0	1	0
1	0	0	0	1	0	1	1
1	0	0	1	1	1	0	0

Note that in BCD 8421 code, the six bit combinations (1010, 1011, 1100, 1101, 1110, and 1111) are not used. These are don't care combinations and the corresponding output variables can be made either a 1 or a 0, whichever gives the best minimization.

The K-maps (Fig. 4.10) are drawn for the truth table (Table 4.5) to obtain a simplified Boolean function for each output. The six don't cares are marked by ×s. One possible way to simplify the functions in SOP form is given under the map of each variable.

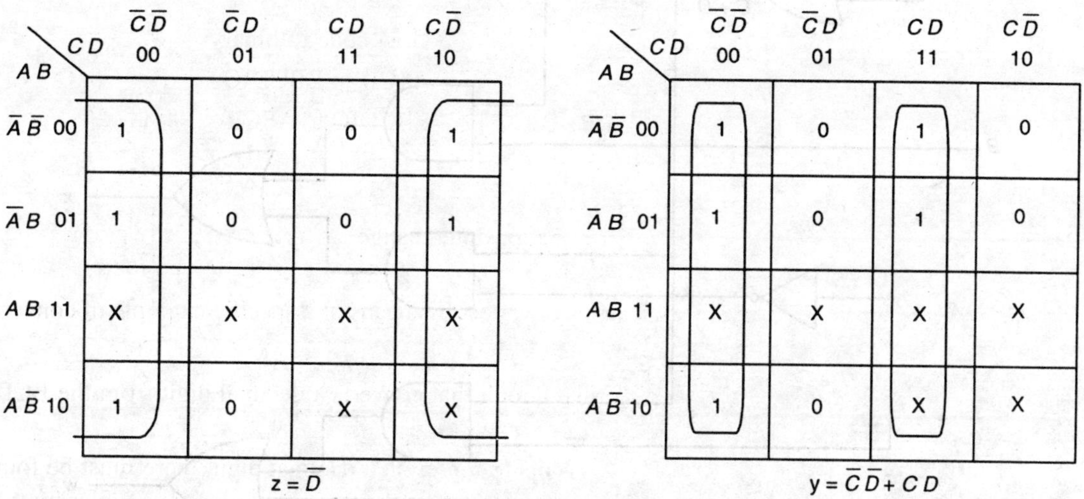

Fig. 4.10 K maps for BCD-to-Excess-3 code converter

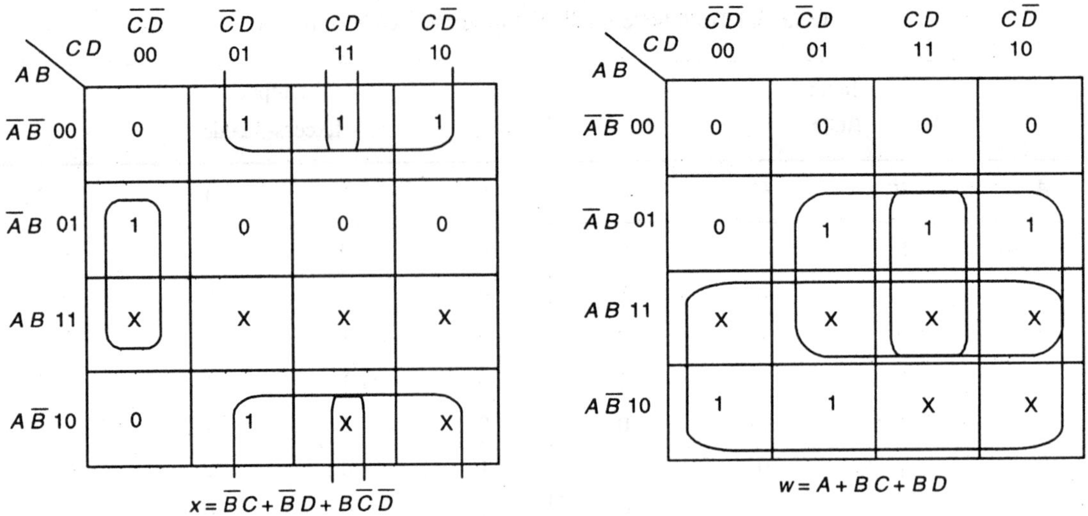

Fig. 4.10 K maps for BCD-to-Excess-3 code converter

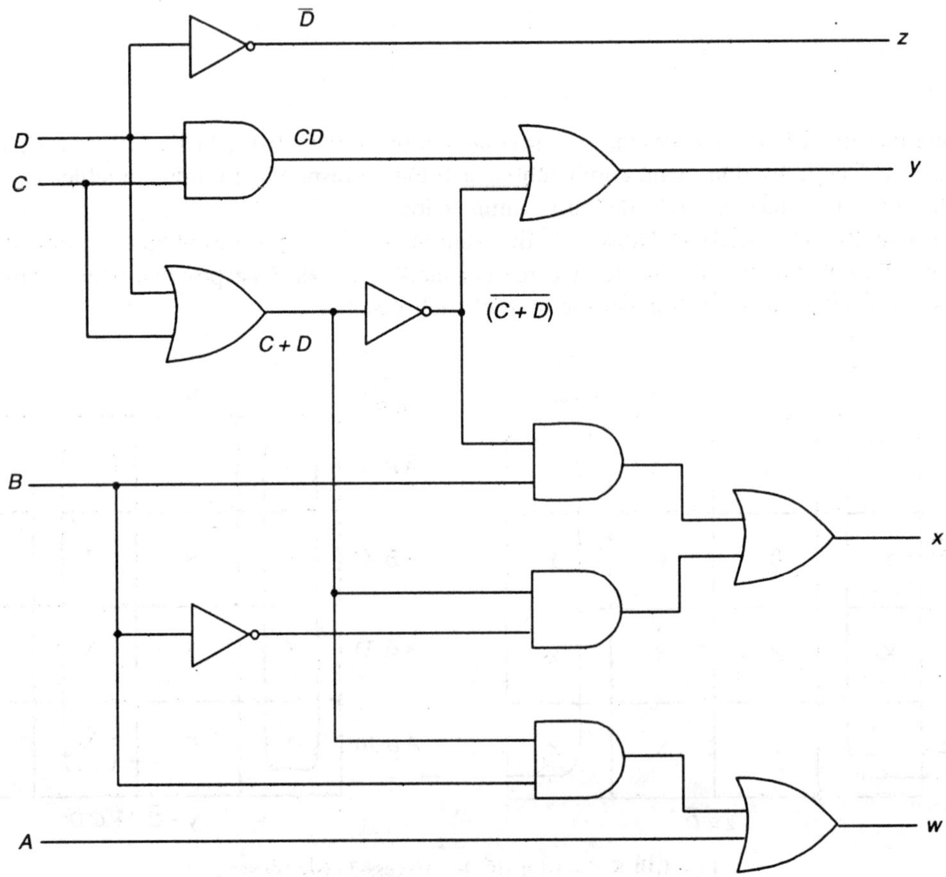

Fig. 4.11 Logic diagram for BCD-to-excess-3 code converter

A logic diagram may be obtained directly from the Boolean expressions derived by the maps. There are other possibilities of implementations which require less number of gates. The expressions which are obtained from maps may be manipulated algebraically so that we can use common gates for two or more outputs. The manipulation can be done as follows:

$$z = \bar{D}$$

$$y = CD + \bar{C}\bar{D}$$

$$= CD + \overline{(C + D)} \qquad \left(\because \bar{C}\bar{D} = \overline{\overline{\bar{C}\bar{D}}} = \overline{(C+D)}\right)$$

$$x = \bar{B}C + \bar{B}D + B\bar{C}\bar{D} = \bar{B}(C + D) + B\overline{(C + D)}$$

$$w = A + BC + BD = A + B(C + D)$$

The logic diagram that implements these expressions is shown in Fig. 4.11. In it we can see that the OR gate whose output is $C + D$ has been used to implement partially each of three outputs.

4.4 ANALYSIS PROCEDURE

The analysis of a combinational circuit is the reverse process of its design procedure. The analysis starts with a given logic diagram and ends with a set of Boolean functions, a truth table, or a verbal explanation of the circuit operation.

The first step in the analysis is to make sure that the given circuit is combinational and not sequential. This requires that a circuit should have logic gates with no feedback paths or memory elements. Once the given logic diagram is ascertained as a combinational circuit, we can proceed to obtain the output Boolean functions and/or the truth table.

The procedure for obtaining the output Boolean functions from a logic diagram involves the following steps.

Steps:

1. Label with arbitrary symbols all gate outputs that are a function of the input variables only. Obtain the Boolean functions for each gate.
2. Label with other arbitrary symbols those gate outputs which are a function of input variables and/or previously labeled gate outputs. Now find the Boolean functions for these gates.
3. Repeat the process of step 2 until the outputs of the circuit are obtained.
4. By repeated substitution of previously defined functions, obtain the output Boolean functions in terms of input variables only.

Derivation of the Truth Table

The procedure for obtaining the truth table directly from a logic diagram is as follows:

1. Determine the number of input variables to the circuit. For n inputs, form the 2^n possible input combinations.
2. Label the outputs of selected gates with arbitrary symbols.
3. Obtain the truth table for the outputs of those gates that are a function of the input variables only.

4. Proceed to obtain the truth table for the outputs of those gates that are a function of previously defined values until the columns for all outputs are determined.

The analysis of the combinational circuit is illustrated by the following example.

EXAMPLE 4.2: Analyze the three-input combinational circuit shown in Fig. 4.12 (a). Obtain the Boolean functions for the two outputs and identify the circuit operation.

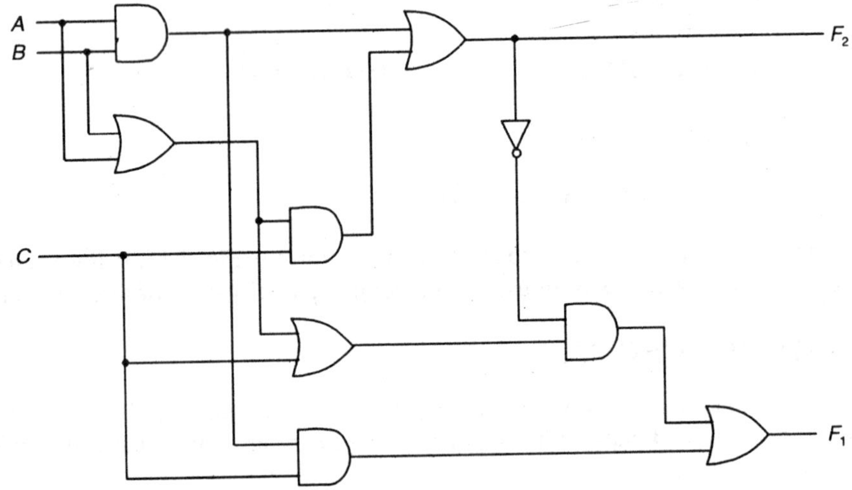

Fig. 4.12 (a)

SOLUTION: The given circuit is combinational. The circuit has three binary inputs, A, B, and C and two binary outputs, F_1 and F_2. The outputs of various gates are labeled with intermediate symbols as shown in Fig. 4.12 (b).

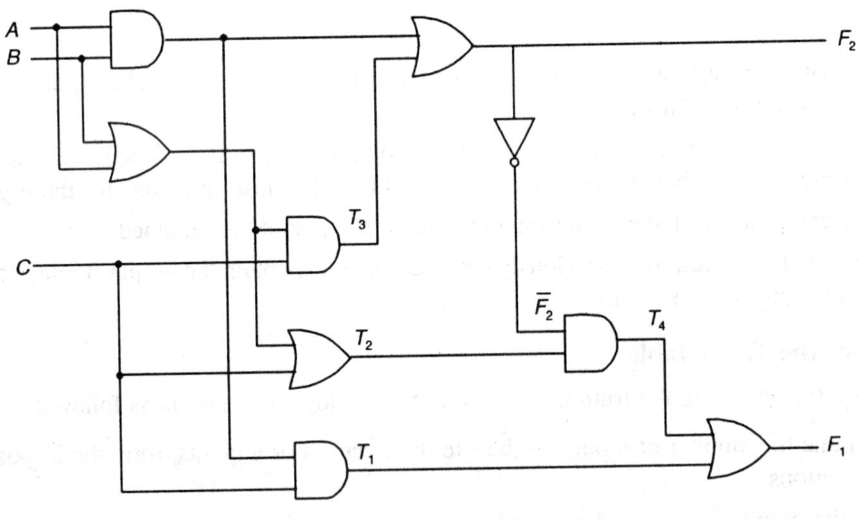

Fig. 4.12 (b)

The Boolean functions for the outputs of gates that are a function of input variables only are:

$$T_1 = ABC$$

$$T_2 = A + B + C$$

$$T_3 = (A + B)\, C$$

The Boolean functions for the outputs of various other gates in terms of intermediate functions are:

$$F_2 = AB + T_3$$

$$T_4 = \overline{F_2}\; T_2$$

$$F_1 = T_4 + T_1$$

A series of substitution yields:

$$\begin{aligned} F_2 &= AB + T_3 \\ &= AB + (A + B)\, C \\ &= AB + AC + BC \\ F_1 &= T_4 + T_1 \\ &= \overline{F_2}\, T_2 + T_1 \\ &= \overline{(AB + AC + BC)}(A + B + C) + ABC \\ &= \overline{AB}\,\overline{AC}\,\overline{BC}(A + B + C) + ABC, \text{ by De Morgan's theorem} \\ &= \underbrace{(\bar{A} + \bar{B})(\bar{A} + \bar{C})}(\bar{B} + \bar{C})(A + B + C) + ABC, \text{ by De Morgan's theorem} \\ &= (\bar{A} + \bar{B}\,\bar{C})(A\bar{B} + \bar{B}C + A\bar{C} + B\bar{C}) + ABC \\ &= \bar{A}\bar{B}C + \bar{A}B\bar{C} + A\bar{B}\bar{C} + ABC \end{aligned}$$

Table 4.6 Truth table for logic diagram of Fig. 4.12

A	B	C	T_1	T_2	T_3	F_2	T_4	F_1
0	0	0	0	0	0	0	0	0
0	0	1	0	1	0	0	1	1
0	1	0	0	1	0	0	1	1
0	1	1	0	1	1	1	0	0
1	0	0	0	1	0	0	1	1
1	0	1	0	1	1	1	0	0
1	1	0	0	1	0	1	0	0
1	1	1	1	1	1	1	0	1

From the truth table (Table 4.6) and output Boolean expressions F_1 and F_2, we conclude that the given logic diagram is a full-adder circuit.

4.5 MULTILEVEL NAND CIRCUITS

We presented the implementation of two-level NAND logic diagram in section 3.4. In this section we are going to present the more general case of multilevel NAND circuits.

We know that the NAND gate is said to be a universal gate, because any Boolean function can be implemented with it as shown in Fig. 4.13.

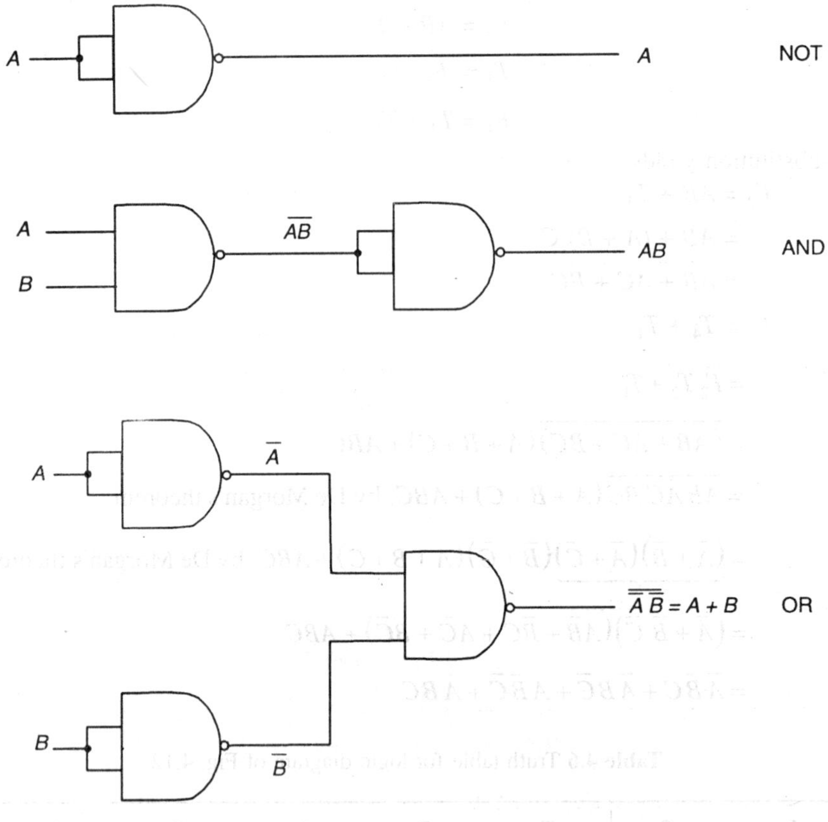

Fig. 4.13 Implementation of NOT, AND, and OR by NAND gates

Boolean Function Implementation-Block Diagram Method

The block diagram procedure for implementing Boolean functions with NAND gates is as follows:

1. Draw the logic diagram with AND, OR, and NOT gates from the given algebraic expression. Assume that both the uncomplemented and complemented inputs are available.
2. Draw an another logic diagram (corresponding to the previous one) with the equivalent NAND logic, as given in Fig. 4.14(b), substituted for each AND, OR, and NOT gate.
3. Remove any two cascaded inverters from the diagram, since double inversion does not perform a logic function. Remove inverters connected to single external inputs and complement the corresponding input variable.

The procedure is illustrated by the following example.

EXAMPLE 4.3: Using the block diagram method, implement the following function with NAND gates only.

$$F = (AB + \bar{C})D + \bar{E}$$

SOLUTION: We proceed according to the procedure given in the block diagram method to obtain NAND implementation (see Fig. 4.14) of the given function $F = (AB + \bar{C})D + \bar{E}$.

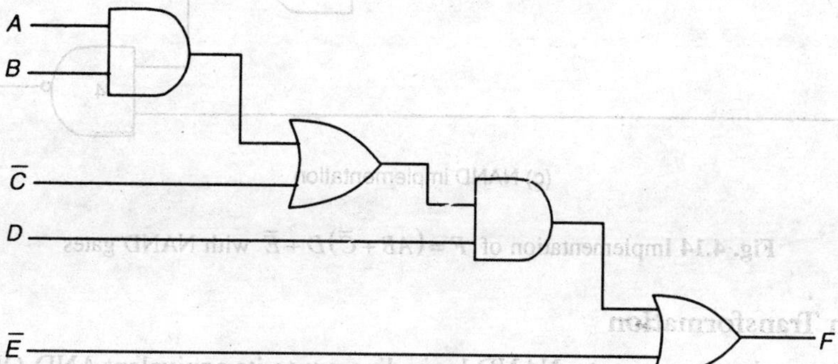

(a) AND/OR implementation

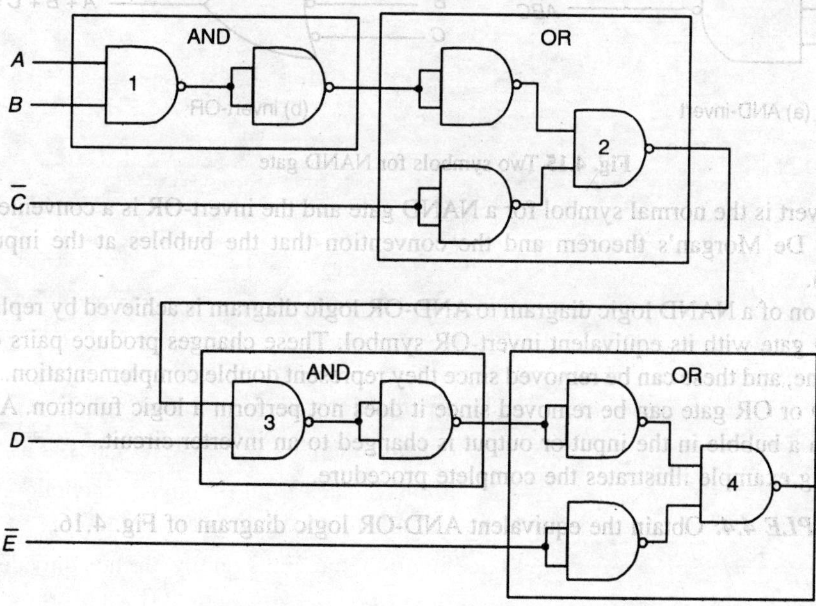

(b) Substituting equivalent NAND functions

Fig. 4.14 Implementation of $F = (AB + \bar{C})D + \bar{E}$ with NAND gates

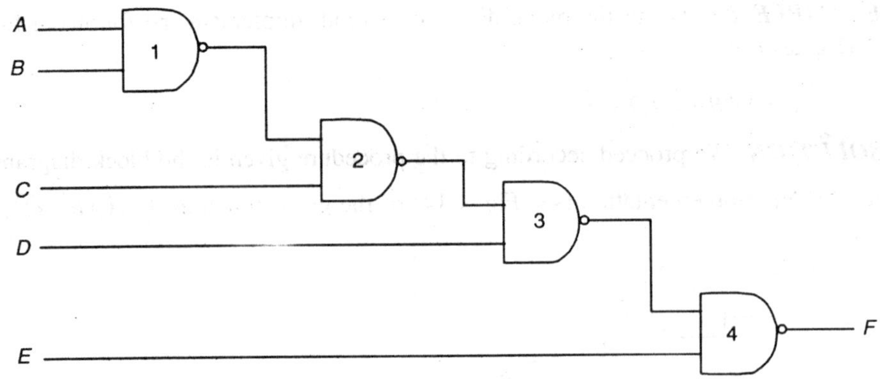

(c) NAND implementation

Fig. 4.14 Implementation of $F = (AB + \bar{C})D + \bar{E}$ with NAND gates

Block Diagram Transformation

It is sometimes convenient to convert a NAND logic diagram to its equivalent AND-OR logic diagram. For this we use the two symbols for NAND gates shown in Fig. 4.15.

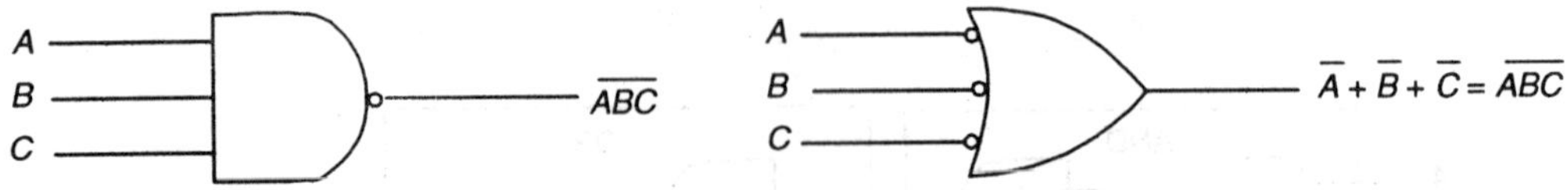

(a) AND-invert (b) invert-OR

Fig. 4.15 Two symbols for NAND gate

The AND-invert is the normal symbol for a NAND gate and the invert-OR is a convenient alternative that utilizes De Morgan's theorem and the convention that the bubbles at the inputs denote complementation.

The conversion of a NAND logic diagram to AND-OR logic diagram is achieved by replacing each odd-level NAND gate with its equivalent invert-OR symbol. These changes produce pairs of bubbles along the same line, and these can be removed since they represent double complementation. Moreover, a one-input AND or OR gate can be removed since it does not perform a logic function. A one-input AND or OR with a bubble in the input or output is changed to an inverter circuit.

The following example illustrates the complete procedure.

EXAMPLE 4.4: Obtain the equivalent AND-OR logic diagram of Fig. 4.16.

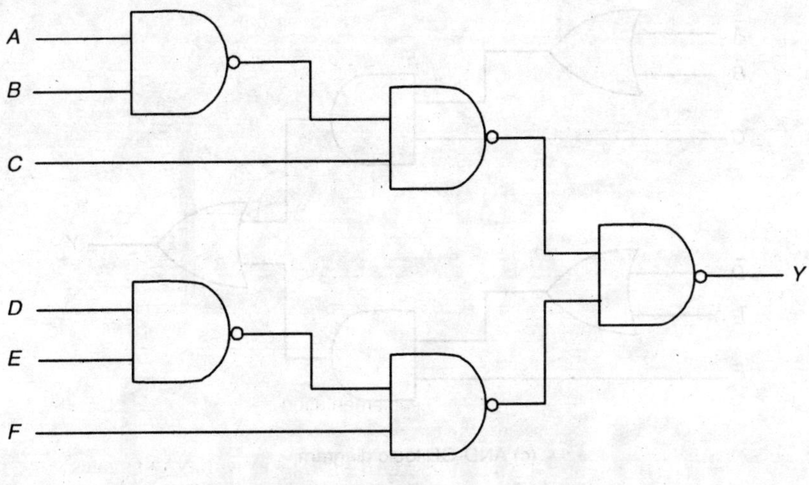

Fig. 4.16

SOLUTION:

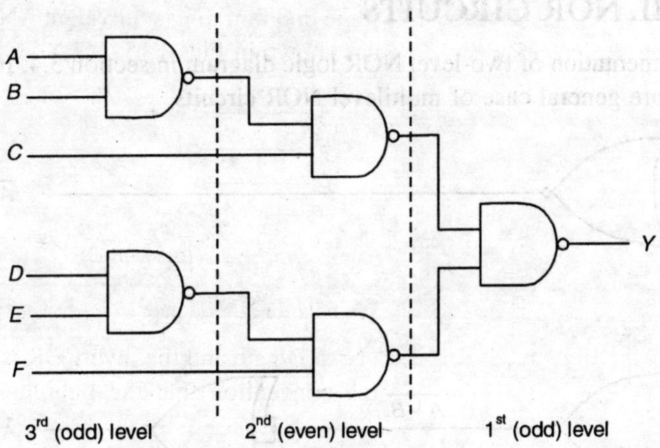

(a) NAND logic diagram

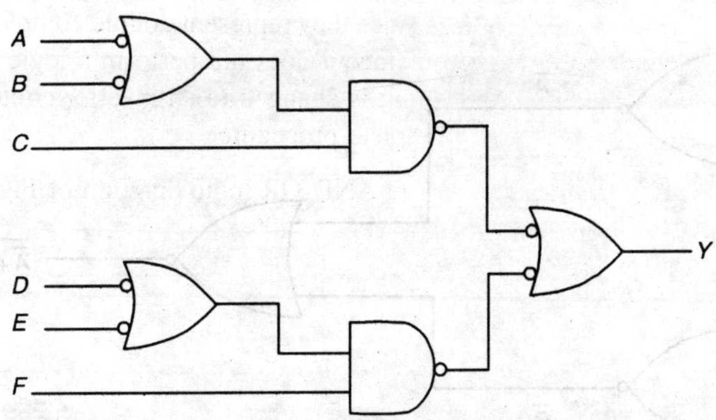

(b) Substitution of invert-OR symbols in odd levels

Fig. 4.17 Conversion of NAND logic diagram to AND-OR

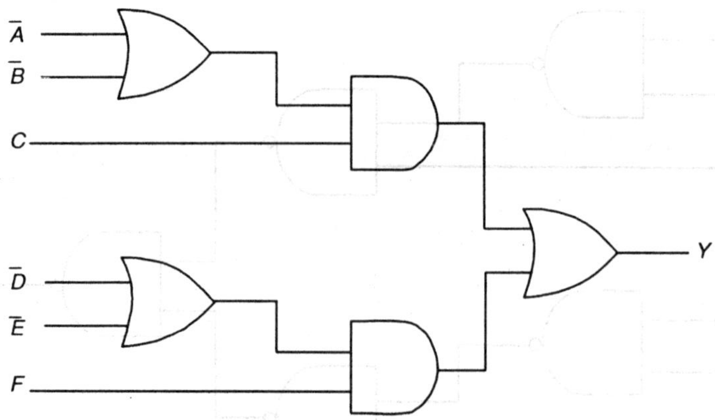

(c) AND-OR logic diagram

Fig. 4.17 Conversion of NAND logic diagram to AND-OR

4.6 MULTILEVEL NOR CIRCUITS

We presented the implementation of two-level NOR logic diagram in section 3.4. In this section we are going to present the more general case of multilevel NOR circuits.

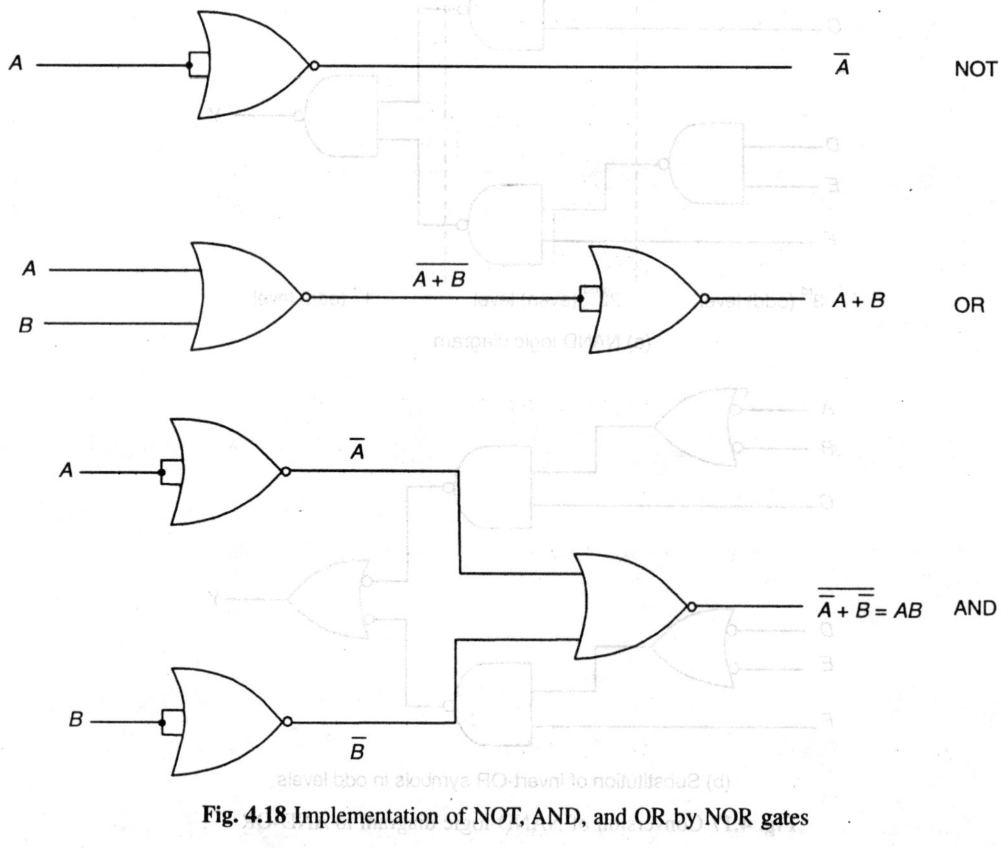

Fig. 4.18 Implementation of NOT, AND, and OR by NOR gates

We know that the NOR gate is said to be a universal gate, because any Boolean function can be implemented with it as shown in Fig. 4.18.

Boolean Function Implementation-Block Diagram Method

The block diagram procedure for implementating Boolean functions with NOR gates is similar to the procedure given in the previous section for NAND gates.

1. Draw the logic diagram with AND, OR, and NOT gates from the given algebraic expression. Assume that both the uncomplemented and complemented inputs are available.
2. Draw an another logic diagram (corresponding to the previous one) with the equivalent NOR logic, substituted for each AND, OR and NOT gate.
3. Remove any two cascaded inverters from the diagram, since double inversion does not perform a logic function. Remove inverters connected to single external inputs and complement the corresponding input variable.

Block Diagram Transformation

It is sometimes convenient to convert a NOR logic diagram to its equivalent AND-OR logic diagram. For this we use the two symbols for NOR gates shown in Fig. 4.19.

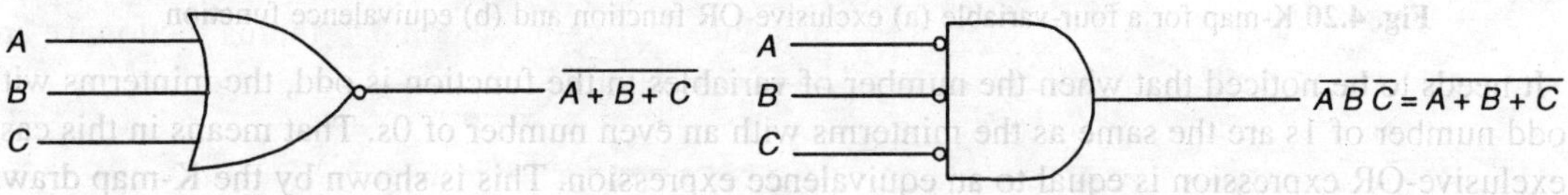

(a) OR-invert (b) Invert-AND

Fig. 4.19 Two symbols for NOR gate

The OR-invert is the normal symbol for a NOR gate and the invert-AND is a convenient alternative that utilizes De Morgan's theorem and the convention that the bubbles at the inputs denote complementation.

The conversion of a NOR logic diagram to AND-OR logic diagram is achieved by replacing each odd-level NOR gate with its equivalent invert-AND symbol. By these changes pairs of bubbles are formed along the same line, and these bubbles can be removed since they represent double complementation. Moreover, a one-input AND or OR gate can be removed since it does not perform a logic function. A one-input AND or OR with a bubble in the input or output is changed to an inverter circuit.

4.7 EXCLUSIVE-OR AND EQUIVALENCE (i.e., EX-NOR) FUNCTIONS

We can write the logic functions to symbolize the action of exclusive-OR and equivalence as:

$$x \oplus y = x\overline{y} + \overline{x}y$$

$$x \odot y = xy + \overline{x}\,\overline{y}$$

The two operations are the complements of each other. Since each operation is commutative and associative, a function of three or more variables can be expressed without parentheses as:

$$F = A \oplus B \oplus C \oplus D$$

$$F = A \odot B \odot C \odot D$$

The two functions are very useful in arithmetic operations and in error detection and correction.

An n-variable exclusive-OR expression is equal to the Boolean function with $2^n/2$ minterms whose equivalent binary numbers have an odd number of 1s whereas an n-variable equivalence expression is equal to the Boolean function with $2^n/2$ minterms whose equivalent binary numbers have even number of 0s. This is shown by the K-maps drawn in Fig. 4.20.

$AB \backslash CD$	$\overline{C}\overline{D}$ 00	$\overline{C}D$ 01	CD 11	$C\overline{D}$ 10
$\overline{A}\overline{B}$ 00	0 (0)	1 (1)	0 (3)	1 (2)
$\overline{A}B$ 01	1 (4)	0 (5)	1 (7)	0 (6)
AB 11	0 (12)	1 (13)	0 (15)	1 (14)
$A\overline{B}$ 10	1 (8)	0 (9)	1 (11)	0 (10)

$F = A \oplus B \oplus C \oplus D$

$= \Sigma\,(1, 2, 4, 7, 8, 11, 13, 14)$

(a)

$AB \backslash CD$	$\overline{C}\overline{D}$ 00	$\overline{C}D$ 01	CD 11	$C\overline{D}$ 10
$\overline{A}\overline{B}$ 00	1 (0)	0 (1)	1 (3)	0 (2)
$\overline{A}B$ 01	0 (4)	1 (5)	0 (7)	1 (6)
AB 11	1 (12)	0 (13)	1 (15)	0 (14)
$A\overline{B}$ 10	0 (8)	1 (9)	0 (11)	1 (10)

$F = A \odot B \odot C \odot D$

$= \Sigma\,(0, 3, 5, 6, 9, 10, 12, 15)$

(b)

Fig. 4.20 K-map for a four-variable (a) exclusive-OR function and (b) equivalence function

It needs to be noticed that when the number of variables in the function is odd, the minterms with an odd number of 1s are the same as the minterms with an even number of 0s. That means in this case an exclusive-OR expression is equal to an equivalence expression. This is shown by the K-map drawn in Fig. 4.21.

$A \backslash BC$	$\overline{B}\overline{C}$ 00	$\overline{B}C$ 01	BC 11	$B\overline{C}$ 10
$\overline{A}$ 0	0 (0)	1 (1)	0 (3)	1 (2)
A 1	1 (4)	0 (5)	1 (7)	0 (6)

$F = A \oplus B \oplus C = A \odot B \odot C = \Sigma\,(1, 2, 4, 7)$

Fig. 4.21 K-map for three-variable function with the minterms having an odd number of 1s

In case if we consider the three-variable function, i.e., a function with an odd number of variables, with the minterms having an even number of 1s (or equivalently, an odd number of 0s), the function can be expressed as the complement of either exclusive-OR function or an equivalence. This is shown by the K-map drawn in Fig. 4.22.

$A \backslash BC$	$\overline{B}\overline{C}$ 00	$\overline{B}C$ 01	BC 11	$B\overline{C}$ 10
$\overline{A}$ 0	1	0	1	0
A 1	0	1	0	1

$F = \overline{A \oplus B \oplus C} = A \oplus B \odot C$

or $F = \overline{A \odot B \odot C} = A \odot B \oplus C$

Fig. 4.22 K-map for three-variable function with the minterms having an even number of 1s

4.8 PARITY GENERATOR AND CHECKER

One-bit errors may occur during transmission of binary information. To catch these errors, an extra bit called a *parity bit* is usually transmitted along with a binary message to make the number of 1s either odd or even. The message, including the parity bit, is transmitted and then checked at the receiving end for errors. An error is detected if the checking parity does not correspond to the one transmitted. The circuit that generates the parity bit in the transmitter is called a *parity generator;* the circuit that checks the parity in the receiver is called a *parity checker.*

The following example illustrates the implementation of parity generator and parity checker for odd-parity system.

EXAMPLE 4.5: Design and implement a parity generator and a parity checker circuits for the system that uses a group of 4 bits as the data to be transmitted, and uses an odd-parity bit. A logic-1 output is required when the four bits received do not constitute an odd parity.

SOLUTION: From the statement it is clear that a 3-bit message is to be transmitted along with an odd-parity bit. For this we need to have the truth tables for the odd-parity generator (Table 4.7) and checker (Table 4.8).

Table 4.7 Truth table for odd-parity generator

3-bit message			Parity bit
x	y	z	P
0	0	0	1
0	0	1	0
0	1	0	0
0	1	1	1
1	0	0	0
1	0	1	1
1	1	0	1
1	1	1	0

We can see that the Table 4.7 corresponds to the K-map of Fig. 4.22; so the function P can be expressed as:

$$P = x \oplus y \odot z$$

or

$$P = x \odot y \oplus z$$

Table 4.8 Truth table for odd-parity checker

Four-bits received				Parity-error check
x	*y*	*z*	*P*	*C*
0	0	0	0	1
0	0	0	1	0
0	0	1	0	0
0	0	1	1	1
0	1	0	0	0
0	1	0	1	1
0	1	1	0	1
0	1	1	1	0
1	0	0	0	0
1	0	0	1	1
1	0	1	0	1
1	0	1	1	0
1	1	0	0	1
1	1	0	1	0
1	1	1	0	0
1	1	1	1	1

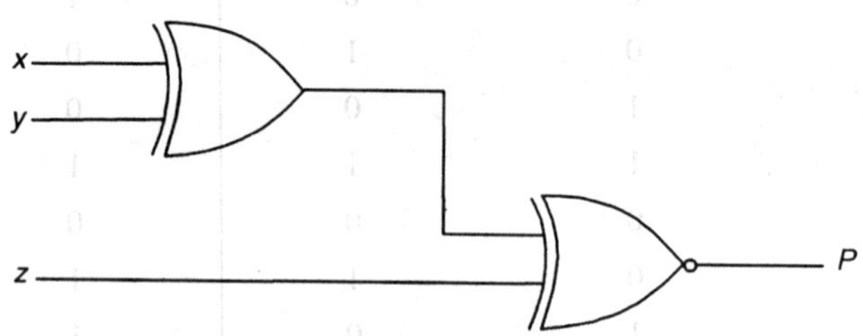

(a) 3-bit odd parity generator

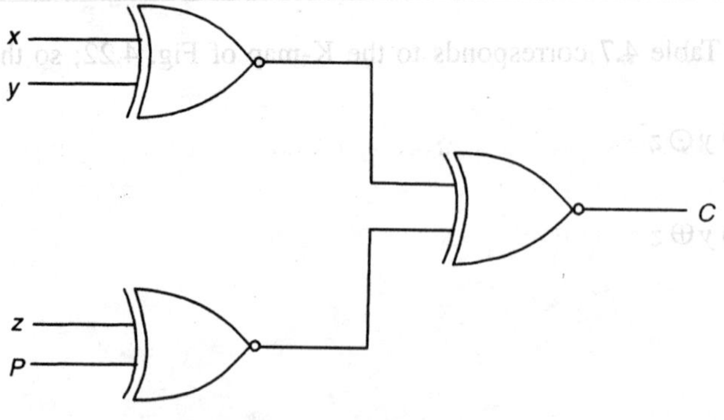

(b) 4-bit odd parity checker

Fig. 4.23 Logic diagrams for parity generator and checker

Also we see that the Table 4.8 corresponds to the K-map of Fig. 4.20(b); so the function C can be expressed as:

$$C = x \odot y \odot z \odot P$$

The logic diagrams for the parity generator and checker can be implemented, as shown in Fig. 4.23.

From the foregoing example we can point out that the parity generator and checker circuits always have an output function that includes half of the minterms whose numerical values have either an even or odd number of 1s. Hence exclusive-OR and/or equivalence gates are ideal for implementation of parity generators and checkers.

SOLVED PROBLEMS

4.1 Design a combinational circuit that detects an error in the representation of a decimal digit in BCD. In other words, obtain a logic diagram whose output is logic-1 when the inputs contain an unused combination in the code.

SOLUTION: Let us first derive the truth table (Table P4.1) for the combinational circuit to be designed.

Table P4.1

	Input BCD				Output
	A	B	C	D	Y
	0	0	0	0	0
	0	0	0	1	0
	0	0	1	0	0
	0	0	1	1	0
	0	1	0	0	0
	0	1	0	1	0
	0	1	1	0	0
	0	1	1	1	0
	1	0	0	0	0
	1	0	0	1	0
Unused combinations	1	0	1	0	1
	1	0	1	1	1
	1	1	0	0	1
	1	1	0	1	1
	1	1	1	0	1
	1	1	1	1	1

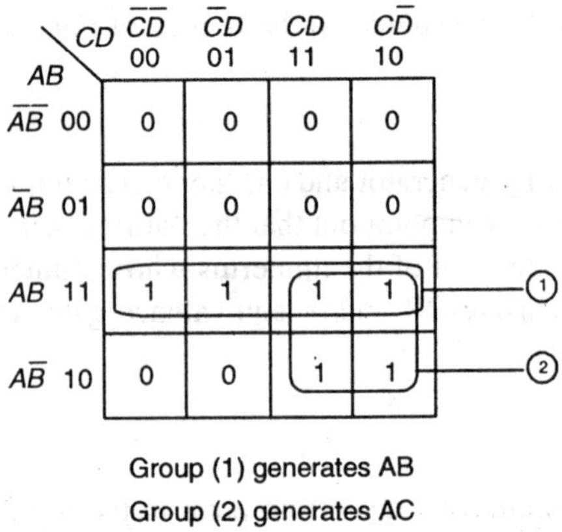

Fig. P4.1(a)

Now the K-map is drawn for the truth table (Table P4.1) to obtain a simplified Boolean function for the output.

From K-map we obtain:

$$Y = AB + AC$$
$$= A\,(B + C)$$

Now the function Y can be implemented, as shown in Fig. P4.1(b).

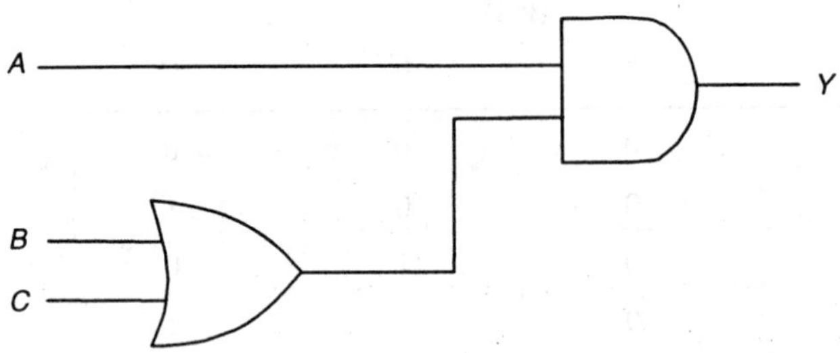

Fig. P4.1(b)

Notice that irrespective of the state of the input variable D, this circuit detects the error when the input contains an unused combination.

4.2 Design a combinational circuit whose input is a four-bit number and whose output is the 2's complement of the input number.

SOLUTION: Let the four input variables be A, B, C, and D and the four output variables be w, x, y, and z.

The truth table showing the relationships between the input and output variables is shown in Table P4.2.

Table P4.2 Truth table for code converter

Input Binary number				Output 2's complement of the input			
A	*B*	*C*	*D*	*w*	*x*	*y*	*z*
0	0	0	0	0	0	0	0
0	0	0	1	1	1	1	1
0	0	1	0	1	1	1	0
0	0	1	1	1	1	0	1
0	1	0	0	1	1	0	0
0	1	0	1	1	0	1	1
0	1	1	0	1	0	1	0
0	1	1	1	1	0	0	1
1	0	0	0	1	0	0	0
1	0	0	1	0	1	1	1
1	0	1	0	0	1	1	0
1	0	1	1	0	1	0	1
1	1	0	0	0	1	0	0
1	1	0	1	0	0	1	1
1	1	1	0	0	0	1	0
1	1	1	1	0	0	0	1

The K-maps (Fig. P4.2 (a)) are drawn for the truth table (Table P4.2) to obtain a simplified Boolean function for each output. The simplified output function in SOP form is given under the map of each variable.

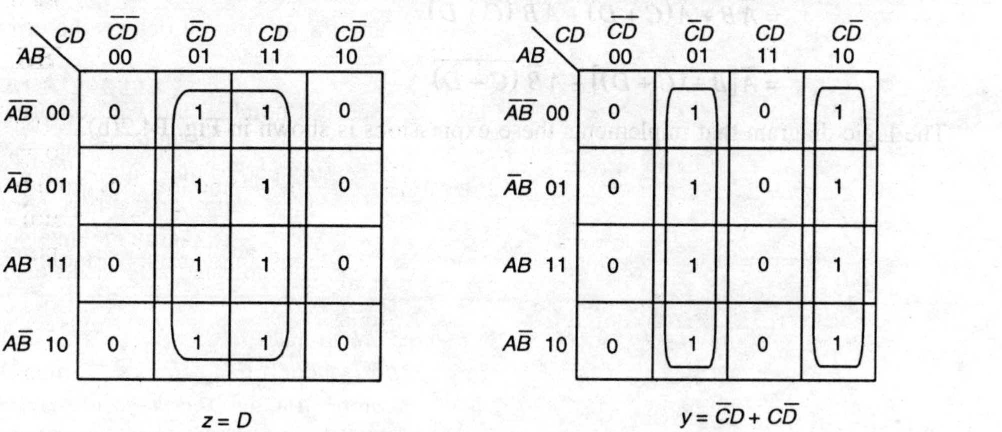

$z = D$ $\qquad$ $y = \overline{C}D + C\overline{D}$

Fig. P4.2(a)

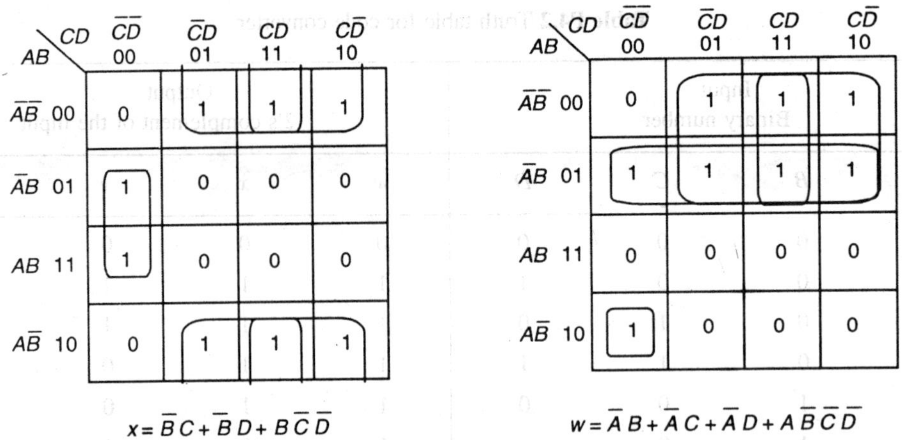

Fig. P4.2(a) (Continued)

The expressions which are obtained from the K-maps may be manipulated algebraically so that we can use common gates for two or more outputs. The manipulation of the expression is as follows:

$$z = D$$

$$y = \bar{C}D + C\bar{D}$$

$$= \overline{CD + \bar{C}\bar{D}} \qquad \because \quad \bar{C}D + C\bar{D} = \overline{CD + \bar{C}\bar{D}}$$

$$= \overline{CD + \overline{(C+D)}}$$

$$x = \bar{B}C + \bar{B}D + B\bar{C}\bar{D}$$

$$= \bar{B}(C+D) + B\overline{(C+D)}$$

$$w = \bar{A}B + \bar{A}C + \bar{A}D + A\bar{B}\bar{C}\bar{D}$$

$$= \bar{A}B + \bar{A}(C+D) + A\bar{B}\,\overline{(C+D)}$$

$$= \bar{A}[B + (C+D)] + A\bar{B}\,\overline{(C+D)}$$

The logic diagram that implements these expressions is shown in Fig. P4.2(b).

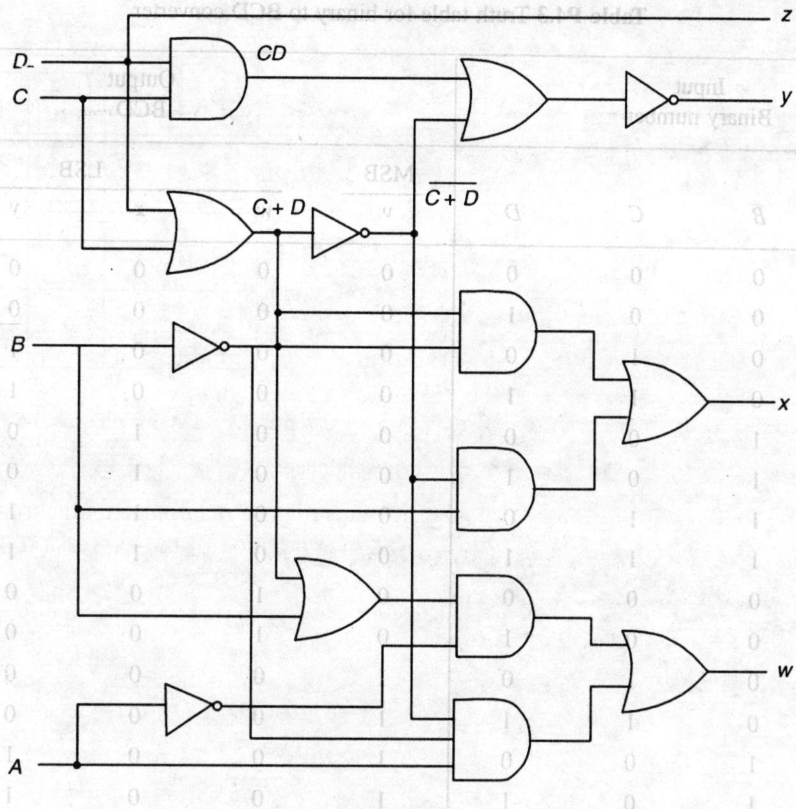

Fig. P4.2(b)

4.3 Design a minimized combinational logic circuit that converts a four-bit binary number to a decimal number in BCD. The output shall also generate a number for inputs corresponding to numerical values in the range of 10 to 15.

SOLUTION: Let the four input variables be *A, B, C,* and *D* and the five output variables (in this case we are getting five) be *v, w, x, y,* and *z.* The truth table relating the input and output variables is shown in Table P4.3.

The K-maps (Fig. P4.3(a)) are drawn for the truth table (Table P4.3) to obtain for each minimized Boolean function for each output. The simplified function, in SOP form is given under the map of each variable.

The simplified expressions which we have got may be manipulated algebraically so that we can use common gates for two or more outputs. The manipulations of the expressions is as follows:

$$z = D$$

$$y = AB\overline{C} + \overline{A}C$$

$$x = \overline{A}B + BC = B(\overline{A} + C)$$

$$w = A\overline{B}\,\overline{C} = A\overline{(B+C)}$$

$$v = AB + AC = A(B + C)$$

Table P4.3 Truth table for binary to BCD converter

Input Binary number				Output BCD				
				MSB	LSB			
A	*B*	*C*	*D*	*v*	*w*	*x*	*y*	*z*
0	0	0	0	0	0	0	0	0
0	0	0	1	0	0	0	0	1
0	0	1	0	0	0	0	1	0
0	0	1	1	0	0	0	1	1
0	1	0	0	0	0	1	0	0
0	1	0	1	0	0	1	0	1
0	1	1	0	0	0	1	1	0
0	1	1	1	0	0	1	1	1
1	0	0	0	0	1	0	0	0
1	0	0	1	0	1	0	0	1
1	0	1	0	1	0	0	0	0
1	0	1	1	1	0	0	0	1
1	1	0	0	1	0	0	1	0
1	1	0	1	1	0	0	1	1
1	1	1	0	1	0	1	0	0
1	1	1	1	1	0	1	0	1

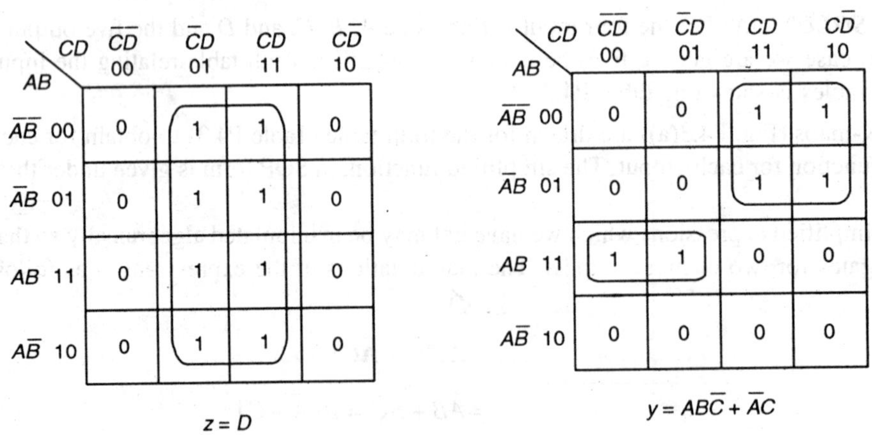

Fig. P4.3(a)

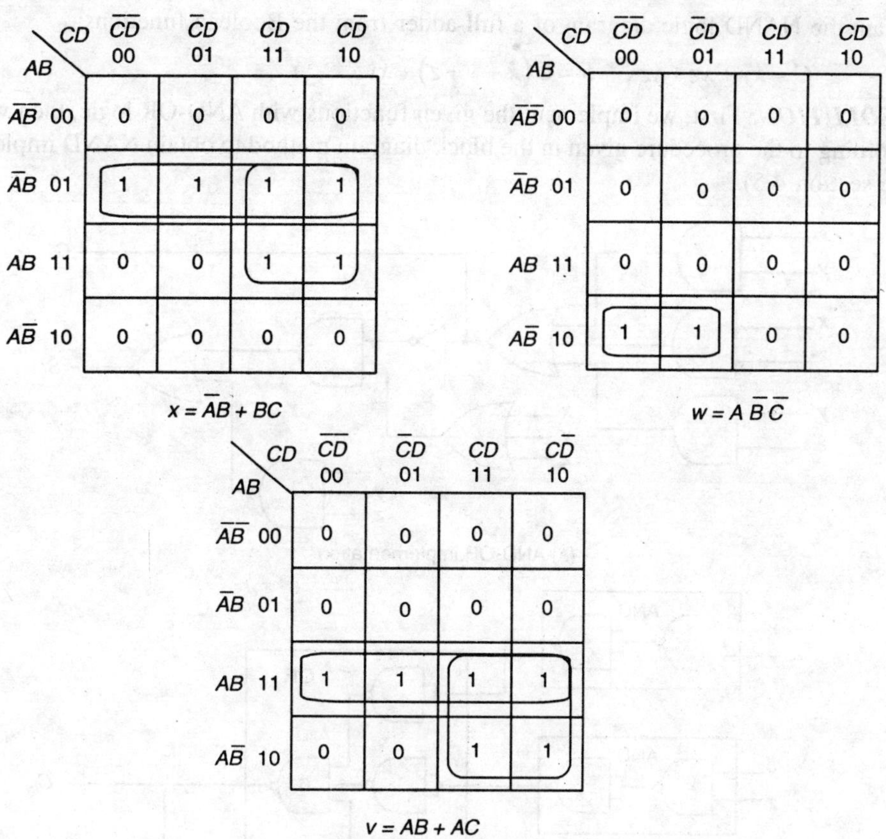

Fig. P4.3(a) (Continued)

The logic diagram that implements these expressions is shown in Fig. P4.3(b).

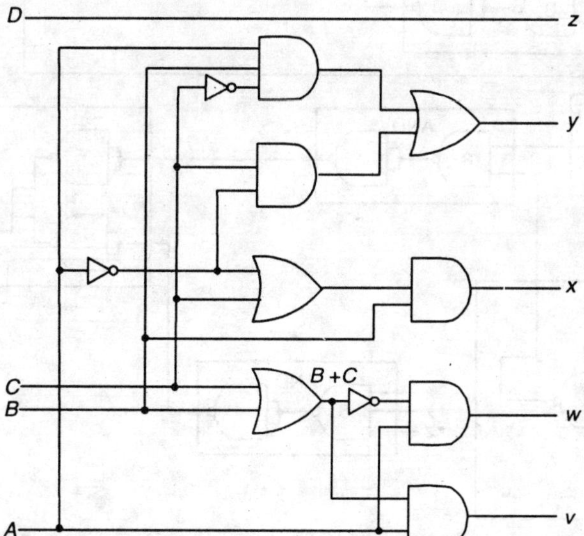

Fig. P4.3(b) Logic diagram for binary to BCD converter of problem 4.3

4.4 Obtain the NAND logic diagram of a full-adder from the Boolean functions:

$$C = xy + xz + yz\,, \quad S = \bar{C}(x + y + z) + xyz$$

SOLUTION: First, we implement the given functions with AND-OR logic, then we proceed according to the procedure given in the block diagram method to obtain NAND implementation (see section 4.5).

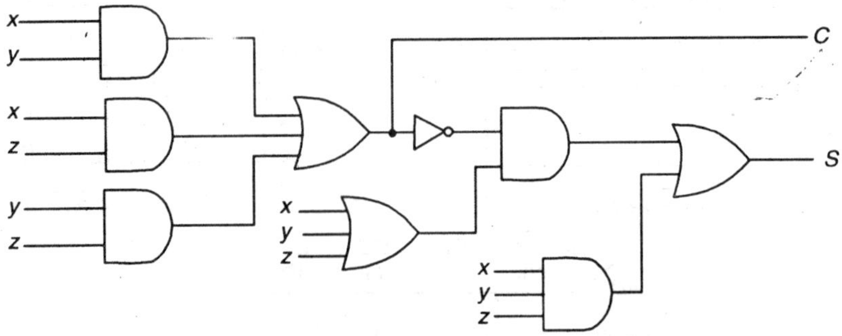

(a) AND-OR implementation

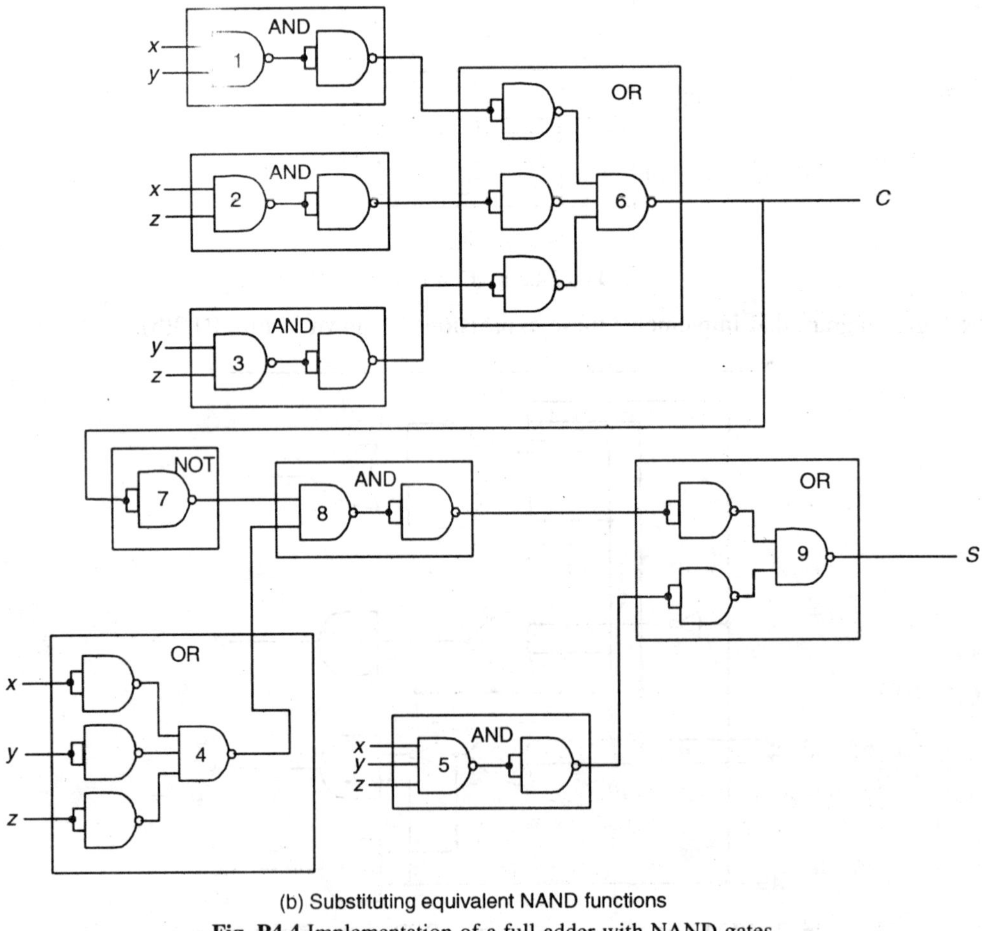

(b) Substituting equivalent NAND functions

Fig. P4.4 Implementation of a full-adder with NAND gates

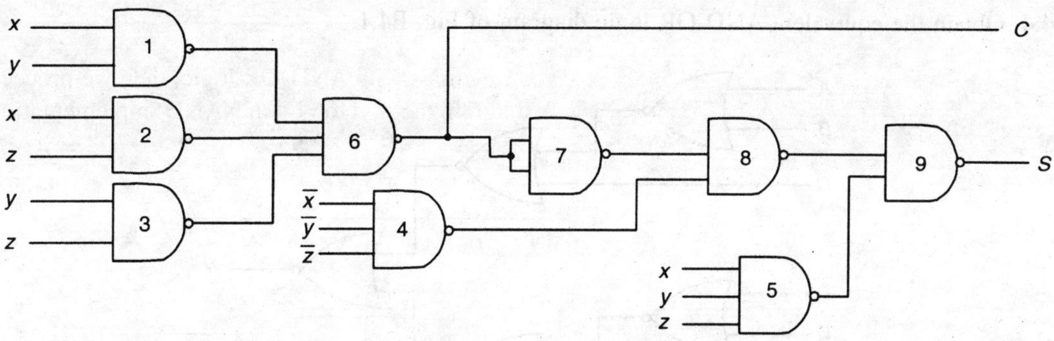

(c) NAND implementation

Fig. P4.4 Implementation of a full-adder with NAND gates

4.5 Show that $A \odot B \odot C \odot D = \Sigma(0, 3, 5, 6, 9, 10, 12, 15)$

SOLUTION:

$$\text{LHS} = A \odot B \odot C \odot D$$

$$= (A \odot B) \odot (C \odot D)$$

$$= \left(AB + \bar{A}\bar{B}\right) \odot \left(CD + \overline{C}\overline{D}\right)$$

$$= \left(AB + \bar{A}\bar{B}\right)\left(CD + \bar{C}\bar{D}\right) + \overline{\left(AB + \bar{A}\bar{B}\right)}\;\overline{\left(CD + \bar{C}\bar{D}\right)}$$

$$= \left(AB + \bar{A}\bar{B}\right)\left(CD + \bar{C}\bar{D}\right) + \left(\bar{A}B + A\bar{B}\right)\left(\bar{C}D + C\bar{D}\right)$$

(By applying De Morgan's theorem)

$$= \underbrace{ABCD}_{1111} + \underbrace{AB\bar{C}\bar{D}}_{1100} + \underbrace{\bar{A}\bar{B}CD}_{0011} + \underbrace{\bar{A}\bar{B}\bar{C}\bar{D}}_{0000} + \underbrace{\bar{A}B\bar{C}D}_{0101} + \underbrace{\bar{A}BC\bar{D}}_{0110} + \underbrace{A\bar{B}\bar{C}D}_{1001} + \underbrace{A\bar{B}C\bar{D}}_{1010}$$

$$= m_{15} + m_{12} + m_3 + m_0 + m_5 + m_6 + m_9 + m_{10}$$

$$= \Sigma(0, 3, 5, 6, 9, 10, 12, 15)$$

$$= \text{RHS}.$$

EXERCISES

4.1 Design a code converter that converts a decimal digit from 8, 4, −2, −1 code to BCD.

4.2 Design a combinational circuit with four input lines that represent a decimal digit in BCD and four output lines that generate the 9's complement of the input digit.

4.3 Using the block diagram method, implement the following function with NOR gates only: $F = \left(AB + \bar{C}\right)D + \bar{E}.$

4.4 Obtain the equivalent AND-OR logic diagram of Fig. E4.1.

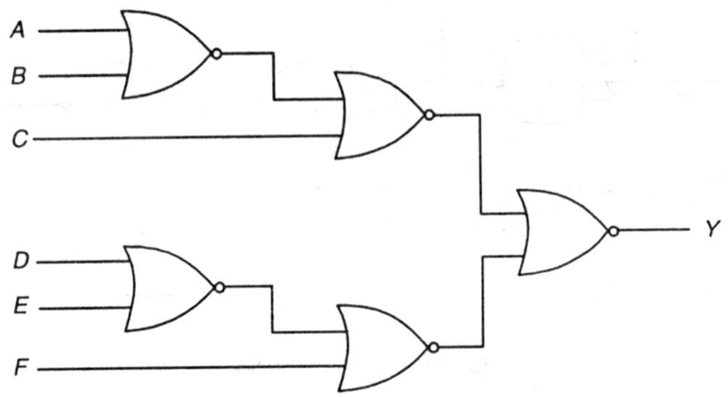

Fig. E4.1

4.5 Obtain the NOR logic diagram of a full-adder from the Boolean functions:

$$C = xy + xz + yz$$

$$S = \bar{C}(x + y + z) + xyz$$

4.6 Design and implement a parity generator and a parity checker circuits for the system that uses a group of 4 bits as the data to be transmitted, and uses an even-parity bit. A logic output is required when the four bits received do not constitute even parity.

4.7 Verify that $A \oplus B \oplus C = A \odot B \odot C$.

4.8 Show that $A \oplus B \oplus C \oplus D = \Sigma\,(1, 2, 4, 7, 8, 11, 13, 14)$.

Combinational Logic with MSI and LSI

5

In the previous chapter, we have learnt the traditional method of combinational circuit design and demonstrated the steps taken to gate-level implementations. Although the basic elements are logic gates (AND, OR and NOT) and flip-flops, the integrated circuit revolution has provided many MSI and LSI ICs that can be used to simplify design and reduce package count, saving both time and money. However, they can be used only if the designer is familiar with the functions that are performed by these ICs and their characteristics.

In this chapter we present standard circuits which are available as MSI and LSI packages. Although each of these circuits can be purchased separately, we shall show how to design each of these circuits. This will enhance our ability to use these circuits, to modify them, or to enlarge them by connecting several packages.

5.1 BINARY PARALLEL ADDER

We have introduced a single full-adder capable of adding two one-bit numbers and an input carry or previous carry in section 4.2. In order to add two binary numbers of n bits each, n numbers of full adders are required. When two binary numbers are added, each column generates a sum and a carry to the next higher-order column. Consider, for example, the addition of two 4-bit binary numbers, $A = A_3 A_2 A_1 A_0 = 1001$ and $B = B_3 B_2 B_1 B_0 = 1011$.

It is possible to add two n-bit numbers serially or in parallel. Here we consider only the parallel method of addition. A parallel method uses n full-adder circuits and are connected in such a manner that all bits of the addend and augend are fed into them simultaneously. The two types of binary parallel adders are described below.

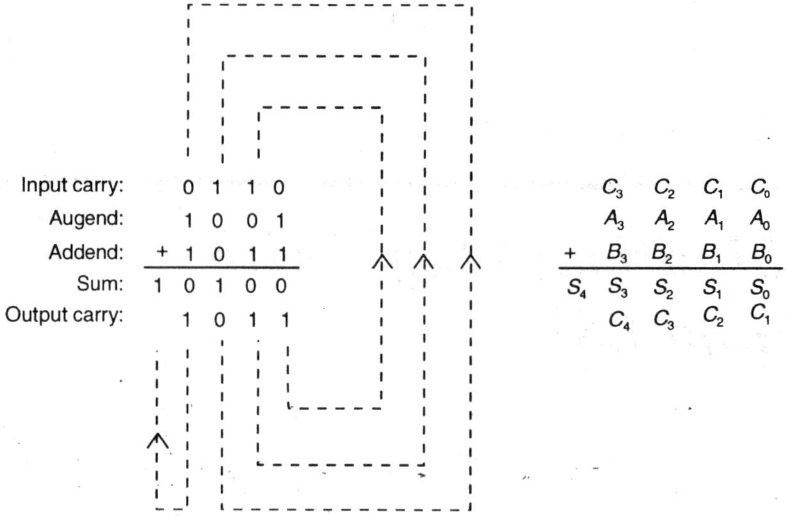

The Ripple-Carry Adder

The ripple-carry adder consists of a number of stages of full-adders, so that the carry-out of each full-adder stage is connected to the carry-in of the next higher-order stage.

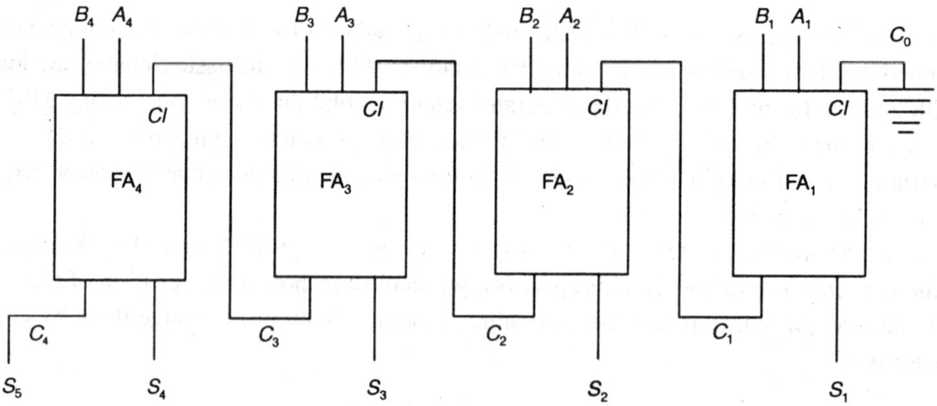

Fig. 5.1 4-bit ripple-carry adder

Figure 5.1 Illustrates a 4-bit ripple-carry adder. Each full adder adds the respective bits in a column of the numbers *A* and *B* and the carry bits are successively connected to the next full-adder. Since FA_1 is the LSB adder, it has no input carry and therefore its input carry $C_0 = 0$. FA_4 is the MSB adder and hence its carry output C_4 gives MSB S_5 of the sum.

An *n*-bit parallel adder requires *n* full-adders. It can also be constructed from available 4-bit, 2-bit, and 1-bit full-adders ICs.

4-bit full-adders is a typical example of an MSI function. It can be used in many applications involving arithmetic operations.

The Look-Ahead-Carry Adder

We have seen that in ripple-carry adder, the sum and carry outputs of any stage cannot be produced until the input carry occurs. This causes a considerable delay in the addition process. The *carry propagation delay* for each full-adder is the time from the application of the input carry until thé output carry occurs. The carry propagation time is a limiting factor on the speed with which two numbers are added in parallel. There are several techniques for speeding up the process, such as look-ahead-carry, asynchronous addition, and conditional sum addition. Among these, only look-ahead-carry technique will be considered here. This method is based on two functions of the full-adder, called the carry generate (G) and the carry propagate (P) functions.

Let us consider the full adder with two binary input bits A_i and B_i at i^{th} stage of a parallel adder as shown in Fig. 5.2.

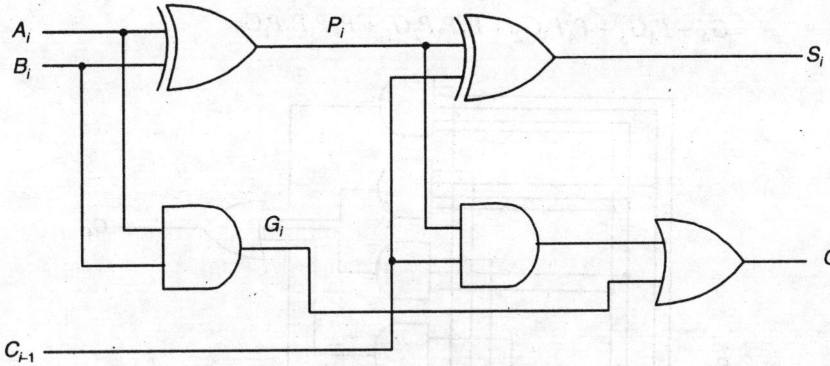

Fig. 5.2 Full-adder

We define the two new binary variables for the ith stage as:

$$\text{Carry propagate, } P_i = A_i \oplus B_i$$

$$\text{Carry generate, } G_i = A_i\, B_i$$

Then, the output sum and carry can be expressed as :

$$\text{Output sum, } S_i = P_i \oplus C_{i-1}$$

$$\text{Output carry, } C_i = G_i + P_i\, C_{i-1}$$

$P_i = 1$ if either A_i or B_i, but not both, is equal to $1 \cdot G_i = 1$ if a carry is generated in the ith stage, that is, if $A_i = B_i = 1$.

Now let us apply this concept to a 4-bit adder. For the full-adder of ith stage, the output carry is dependent on its carry generate (G_i), its carry propagate (P_i), and its carry input (C_{i-1}). The carry generate and carry propagate functions for each stage are immediately available as soon as the input bits and the input carry to the LSB adder are applied, because they are dependent only on these bits. The carry input to each stage is the carry output of the previous stage. Based on this we will now write the Boolean functions for the carry output of each stage.

$$C_1 = G_1 + P_1\, C_0$$

$$C_2 = G_2 + P_2\, C_1$$

$$= G_2 + P_2 (G_1 + P_1 C_0)$$

$$= G_2 + P_2 G_1 + P_2 P_1 C_0$$

$$C_3 = G_3 + P_3 C_2$$

$$= G_3 + P_3 (G_2 + P_2 G_1 + P_2 P_1 C_0)$$

$$= G_3 + P_3 G_2 + P_3 P_2 G_1 + P_3 P_2 P_1 C_0$$

$$C_4 = G_4 + P_4 C_3$$

$$= G_4 + P_4 (G_3 + P_3 G_2 + P_3 P_2 G_1 + P_3 P_2 P_1 C_0)$$

$$= G_4 + P_4 G_3 + P_4 P_3 G_2 + P_4 P_3 P_2 G_1 + P_4 P_3 P_2 P_1 C_0$$

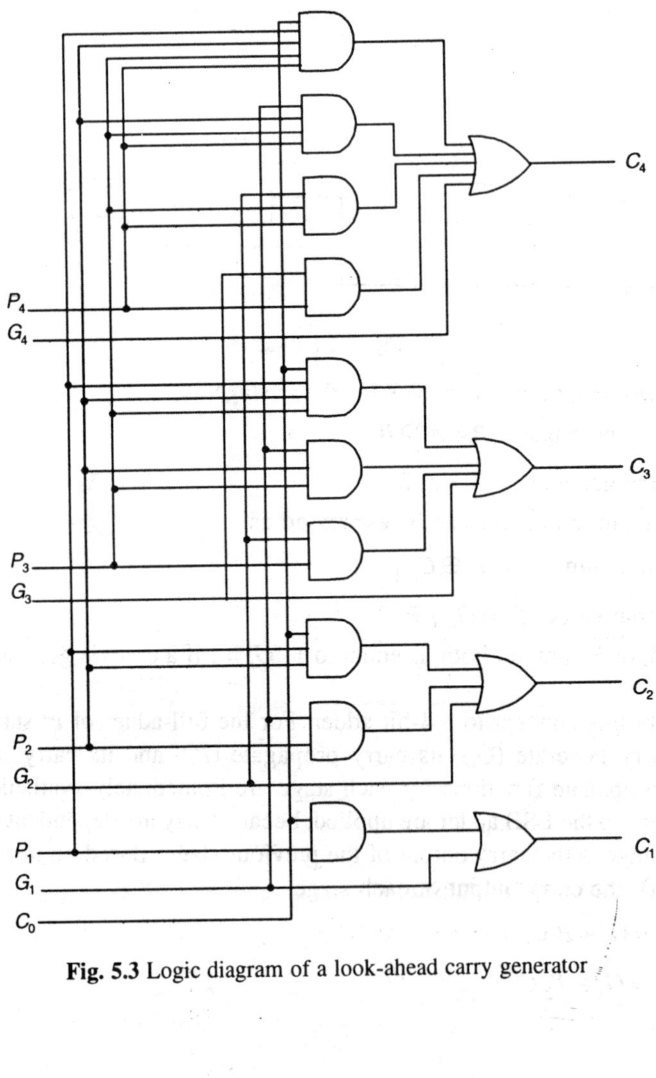

Fig. 5.3 Logic diagram of a look-ahead carry generator

Notice that in each of these expressions the carry output for each full-adder stage is dependent only on the initial carry C_0, its G and P functions, and the G and P functions of the preceding stages. The Boolean functions for C_1, C_2, C_3, and C_4 can be implemented with logic gates to create a look-ahead-carry generator, as shown in Fig. 5.3.

A 4-bit parallel adder with a look-ahead-carry scheme is constructed, as shown in Fig. 5.4.

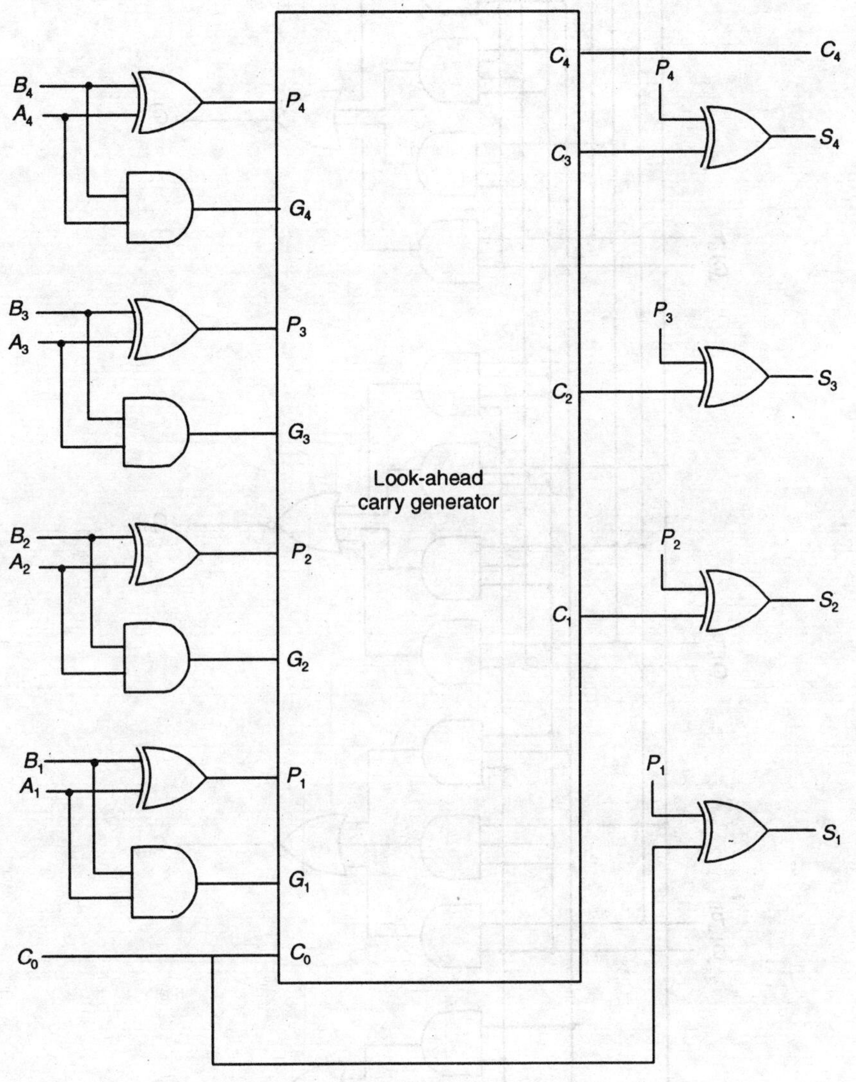

Fig. 5.4 4-bit look-ahead carry adder

The 74S182 Look-Ahead Carry Generator

The 74S182 is a high speed, look-ahead carry generator. It accepts up to four pairs of active LOW carry propagate $(\overline{P}_0, \overline{P}_1, \overline{P}_2, \overline{P}_3)$ and carry generate $(\overline{G}_0, \overline{G}_1, \overline{G}_2, \overline{G}_3)$ signal and an active HIGH carry

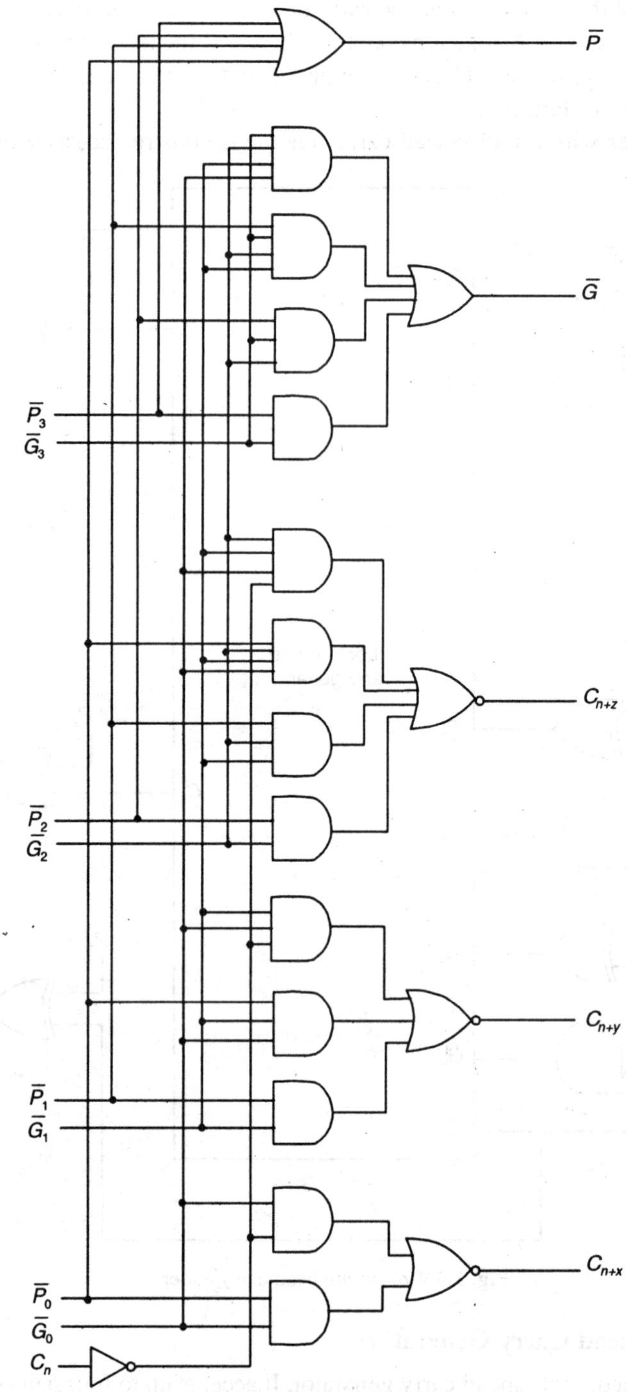

Fig. 5.5 Logic diagram for 74S182

input (C_n) and provides anticipated active HIGH carries (C_{n+x}, C_{n+y}, C_{a+z}) across four groups of binary adders. The 74S182 also has active LOW carry propagate ($\overline{P}$) and carry generate ($\overline{G}$) outputs which may be used for further levels of look-ahead.

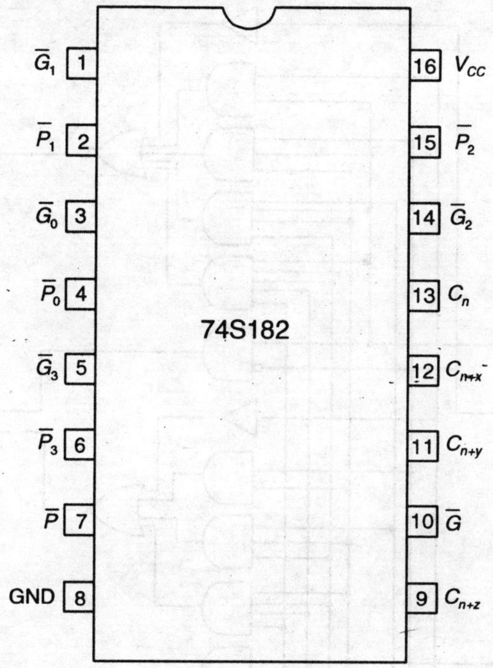

(a) Pinout for 74S182

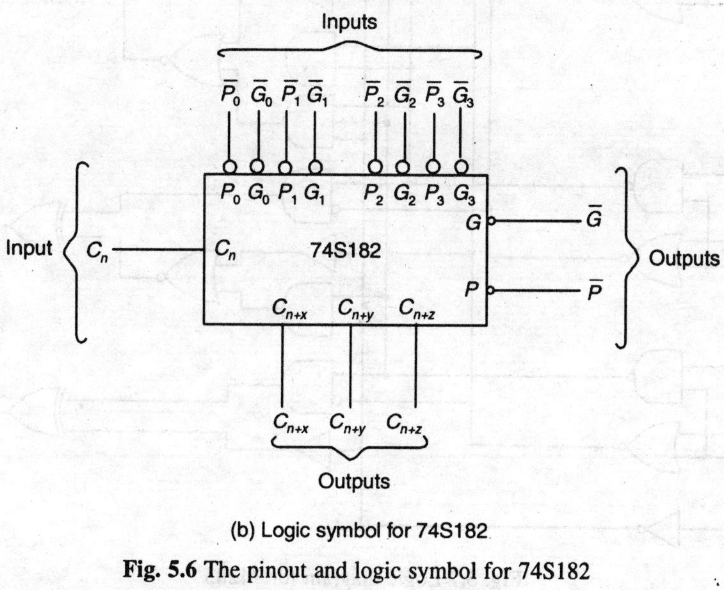

(b) Logic symbol for 74S182

Fig. 5.6 The pinout and logic symbol for 74S182

The logic diagram for the 74S182 is shown in Fig. 5.5. The pinout and logic symbol are given in Fig. 5.6. For the truth table and other details IC data manuals can be referred.

The 74283 4-Bit Binary Parallel Adder

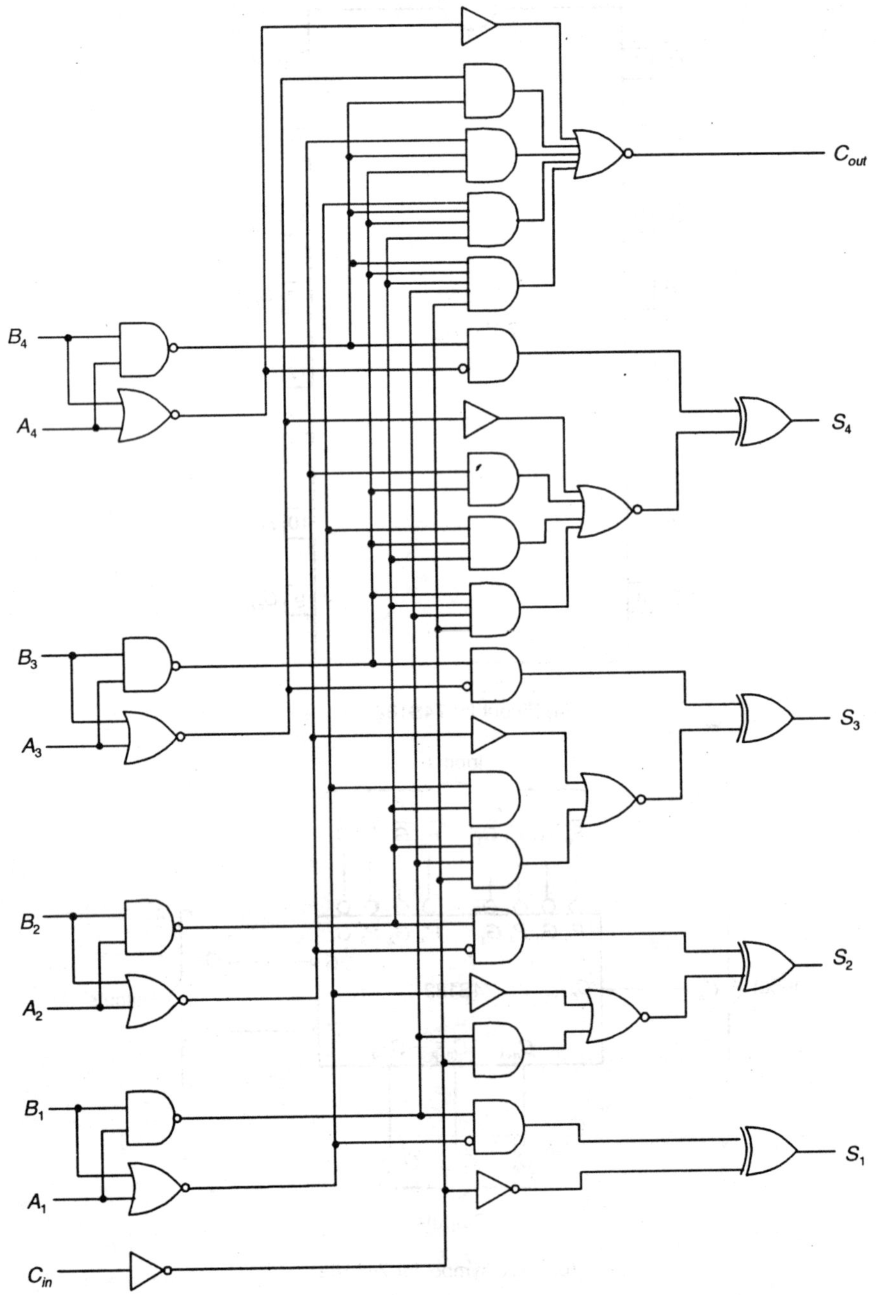

Fig. 5.7 Logic diagram for 74283

The 74283 is one of the most common 4-bit parallel adder IC. It contains four interconnected full adders and the look-ahead carry circuitry needed for high speed operation. These full adders perform the addition of two 4-bit binary words ($A_4\,A_3\,A_2\,A_1$ & $B_4\,B_3\,B_2\,B_1$). The C_{in} is the carry input to the LSB adder. The C_{out} is the carry output of the MSB adder; and $S_4\,S_3\,S_2\,S_1$ is the sum output. Notice that A_1, B_1 and S_1 are the LSBs and A_4, B_4 and S_4 are MSBs.

The logic diagram for 74283 is shown in Fig. 5.7. The pinout and logic symbol are given in Fig. 5.8. For the truth table and other details IC data manuals can be referred.

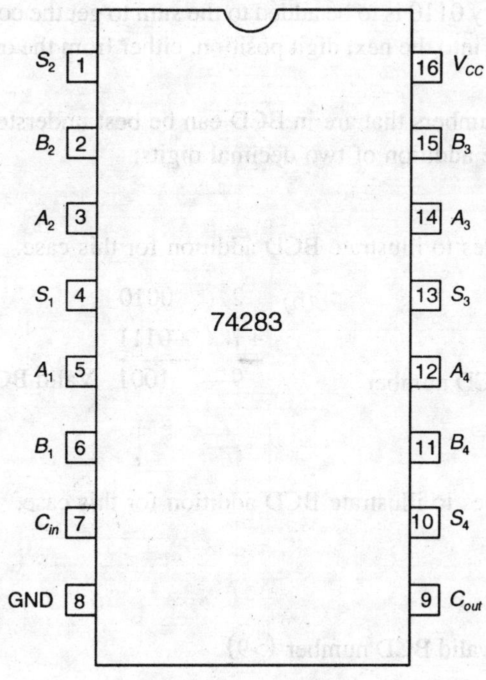

(a) Pinout for 74283

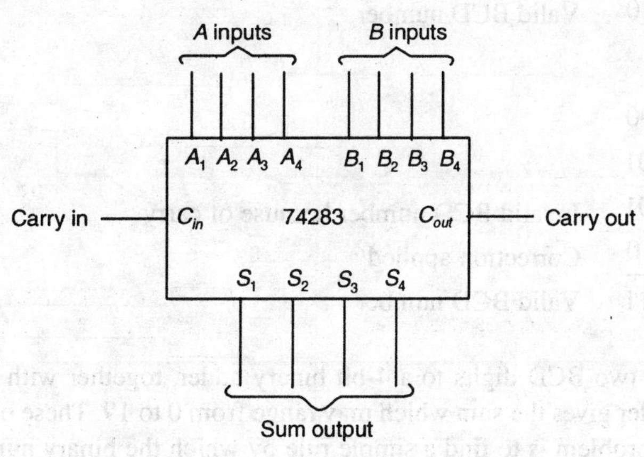

(b) Logic symbol for 74283

Fig. 5.8 The pinout and logic symbol for 74283

5.2 BCD ADDER

BCD (Binary-Coded Decimal)-8421 is a numerical code, and many applications require arithmetic operations with BCD. Two BCD numbers are added as follows:

- The two BCD numbers are added using ordinary binary addition.
- If the 4-bit sum is equal to or less than 9, it is valid and no correction is needed.
- If the 4-bit sum is greater than 9 or if a carry is generated from the 4-bit sum, the sum is invalid and a correction of binary 0110 is to be added to the sum to get the correct BCD result. This case always produces a carry into the next digit position, either from the original addition or from the correction addition.

The addition of decimal numbers that are in BCD can be best understood by considering the two cases that can occur during the addition of two decimal digits:

Case 1: Sum ≤ 9

Consider the following examples to illustrate BCD addition for this case.

(a)	3	0011		(b)	2	0010	
	+5	+0101			+7	+0111	
	8	1000	Valid BCD number		9	1001	Valid BCD number

Case 2: Sum > 9 or a carry

Consider the following examples to illustrate BCD addition for this case.

(a)	3		0011	
	+9		+1001	
	12		1100	Invalid BCD number (>9)
			+0110	Correction applied
			0010	Valid BCD number
		0001		
(b)	8		1000	
	+9		+1001	
	17		1 0001	Invalid BCD number because of carry
			+0110	Correction applied
		0001	0111	Valid BCD number

Suppose we apply two BCD digits to a 4-bit binary adder, together with a possible carry from a previous stage. The adder gives the sum which may range from 0 to 19. These binary numbers are listed in Table 5.1. Now the problem is to find a simple rule by which the binary number in the first column can be converted to the correct BCD-digit representation of the number in the second column.

From the Table 5.1, it is apparent that when the binary sum is equal to or less than 1001, the corresponding BCD number is identical and therefore no correction is needed. When the binary sum is greater than 1001, we get an invalid BCD representation. The addition of binary 0110 to the binary sum converts it to the correct BCD representation and also produces an output carry as required.

The logic circuit that detects the binary sum having invalid BCD representation can be derived from the table entries. From the Table 5.1 we can notice that the binary sum is an invalid BCD number if it has an output carry $K = 1$ or $Z_8 Z_4 = 1$ (i.e., $Z_8 = Z_4 = 1$) or $Z_8 Z_2 = 1$ (i.e., $Z_8 = Z_2 = 1$). Thus, the condition for a correction and an output carry can be expressed by the Boolean function:

$$C = K + Z_8 Z_4 + Z_8 Z_2$$

When $C = 1$, it is necessary to add 0110 to the binary sum and provide an output carry for the next stage.

Table 5.1

Binary sum					BCD sum					Decimal
K	Z_8	Z_4	Z_2	Z_1	C	S_8	S_4	S_2	S_1	
0	0	0	0	0	0	0	0	0	0	0
0	0	0	0	1	0	0	0	0	1	1
0	0	0	1	0	0	0	0	1	0	2
0	0	0	1	1	0	0	0	1	1	3
0	0	1	0	0	0	0	1	0	0	4
0	0	1	0	1	0	0	1	0	1	5
0	0	1	1	0	0	0	1	1	0	6
0	0	1	1	1	0	0	1	1	1	7
0	1	0	0	0	0	1	0	0	0	8
0	1	0	0	1	0	1	0	0	1	9
0	1	0	1	0	1	0	0	0	0	10
0	1	0	1	1	1	0	0	0	1	11
0	1	1	0	0	1	0	0	1	0	12
0	1	1	0	1	1	0	0	1	1	13
0	1	1	1	0	1	0	1	0	0	14
0	1	1	1	1	1	0	1	0	1	15
1	0	0	0	0	1	0	1	1	0	16
1	0	0	0	1	1	0	1	1	1	17
1	0	0	1	0	1	1	0	0	0	18
1	0	0	1	1	1	1	0	0	1	19

Figure 5.9 shows a block diagram of a BCD adder. It includes the correction logic. The function of the BCD adder is as follows: The two 4-bit BCD digits, along with the input carry, are first added in the top 4-bit binary adder to produce the binary sum. When the output carry is equal to zero, nothing is

added to the binary sum. When it is equal to 1, binary 0110 is added to the binary sum through the bottom 4-bit binary adder.

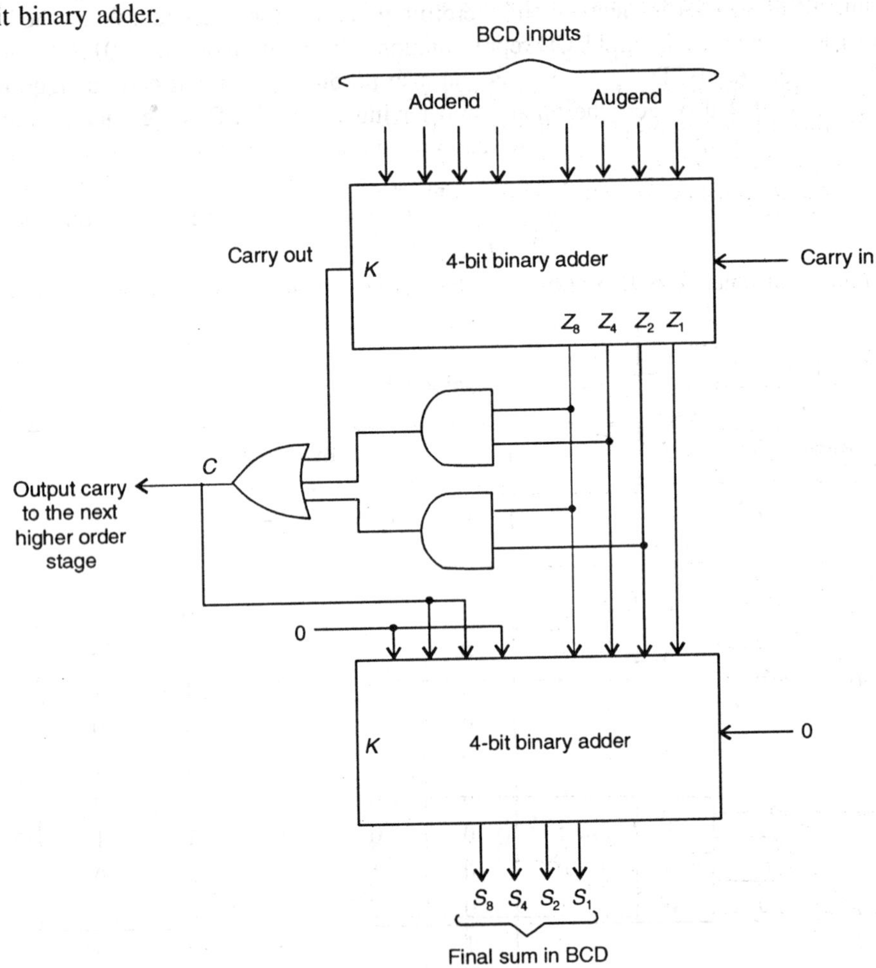

Fig. 5.9 Block diagram of a BCD adder

5.3 MAGNITUDE COMPARATOR

A magnitude comparator is a combinational circuit that compares the magnitude of two numbers, A and B, and determines their relative magnitude. It has three output variables designated as $A > B$, $A = B$, or $A < B$ and they indicate whether $A > B$, $A = B$ or $A < B$.

The circuit for comparing two n-bit numbers has 2^{2n} entries in the truth table and becomes too cumbersome even with $n = 3$. On the other hand, a comparator circuit possesses a certain amount of regularity. We can make use of this well defined regularity for the design of magnitude comparator by deriving an algorithm. We take a 4-bit magnitude comparator for illustration. Let us consider the two binary numbers, A and B, and write as follows:

$$A = A_3A_2A_1A_0$$
$$B = B_3B_2B_1B_0$$

The two numbers are equal if $A_3 = B_3$ and $A_2 = B_2$ and $A_1 = B_1$ and $A_0 = B_0$. The equality relation of each pair of bits can be expressed logically with an equivalence (i.e., EX-NOR) function:

$$x_i = A_i B_i + \bar{A}_i \bar{B}_i \qquad i = 0, 1, 2, 3.$$

where $x_i = 1$ only if the pair of bits in position i are equal (i.e., if $A_i = B_i = 1$ or $A_i = B_i = 0$).

The equality of two numbers, A and B, is indicated by an output variable ($A = B$). This binary variable is equal to 1 if the input numbers are equal, and it is 0 otherwise. For the equality condition to exist, all x_i variables must be equal to 1. This condition is expressed as the AND function of all variables.

$$(A = B) = x_3 x_2 x_1 x_0$$

The binary variable ($A = B$) is equal to 1 only if all pairs of bits of the two numbers are equal.

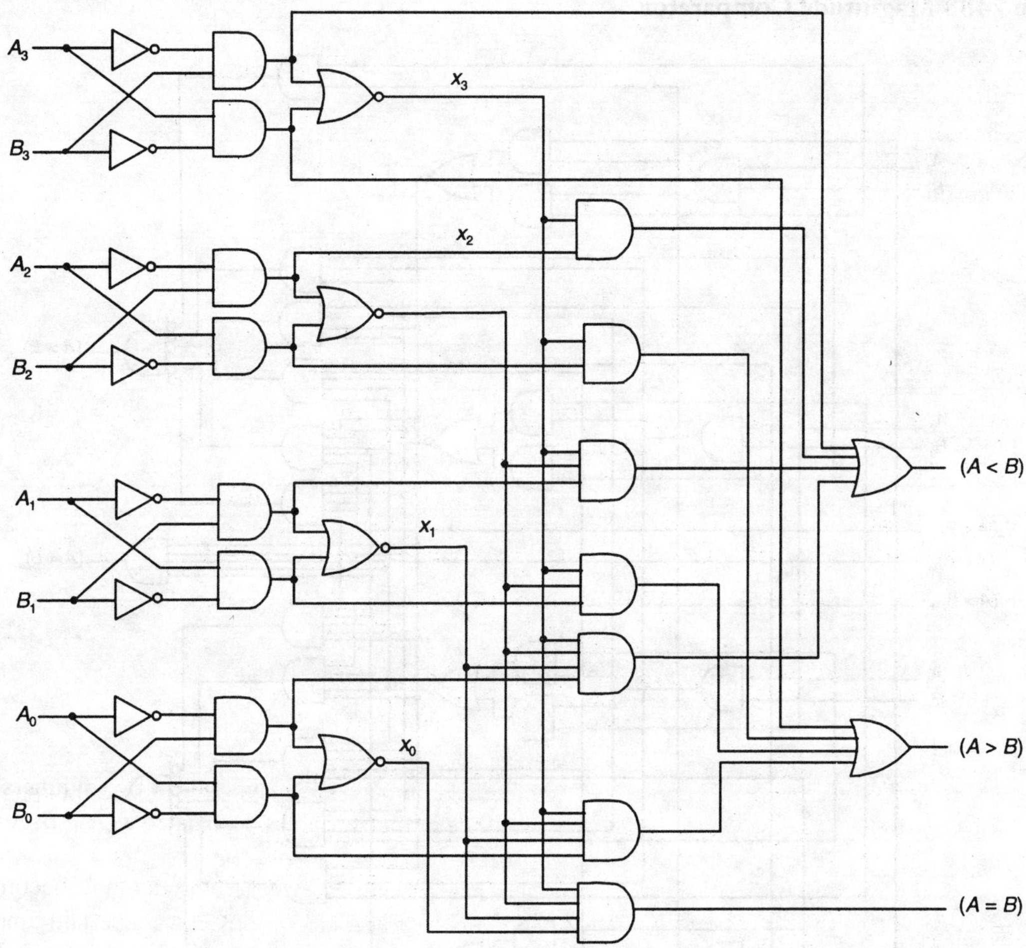

Fig. 5.10 4-bit magnitude comparator

In order to compare two numbers, A and B, to determine which is larger, we start by comparing the MSB of input A to the MSB of input B. If the two bits are equal, then the next most significant bits of A and B are compared. This process continues until a bit of one number differs from the corresponding bit of the other. If the corresponding bit of A is 1 and that of B is 0, we conclude that $A > B$. If the corresponding bit of A is 0 and that of B is 1, we conclude that $A < B$. The sequential comparison can be expressed logically by the following two Boolean functions.

$$(A > B) = A_3\,\bar{B}_3 + x_3\,A_2\,\bar{B}_2 + x_3\,x_2\,A_1\,\bar{B}_1 + x_3\,x_2\,x_1\,A_0\,\bar{B}_0$$

$$(A < B) = \bar{A}_3\,B_3 + x_3\,\bar{A}_2\,B_2 + x_3\,x_2\,\bar{A}_1\,B_1 + x_3\,x_2\,x_1\,\bar{A}_0\,B_0$$

the binary variables $(A > B)$ and $(A < B)$ are equal to 1 when $A > B$ or $A < B$, respectively.

The gate implementation of the three variables just derived is very simple because it involves a certain amount of repetition. The logic diagram of the 4-bit magnitude comparator is shown in Fig. 5.10.

The 7485 Magnitude Comparator

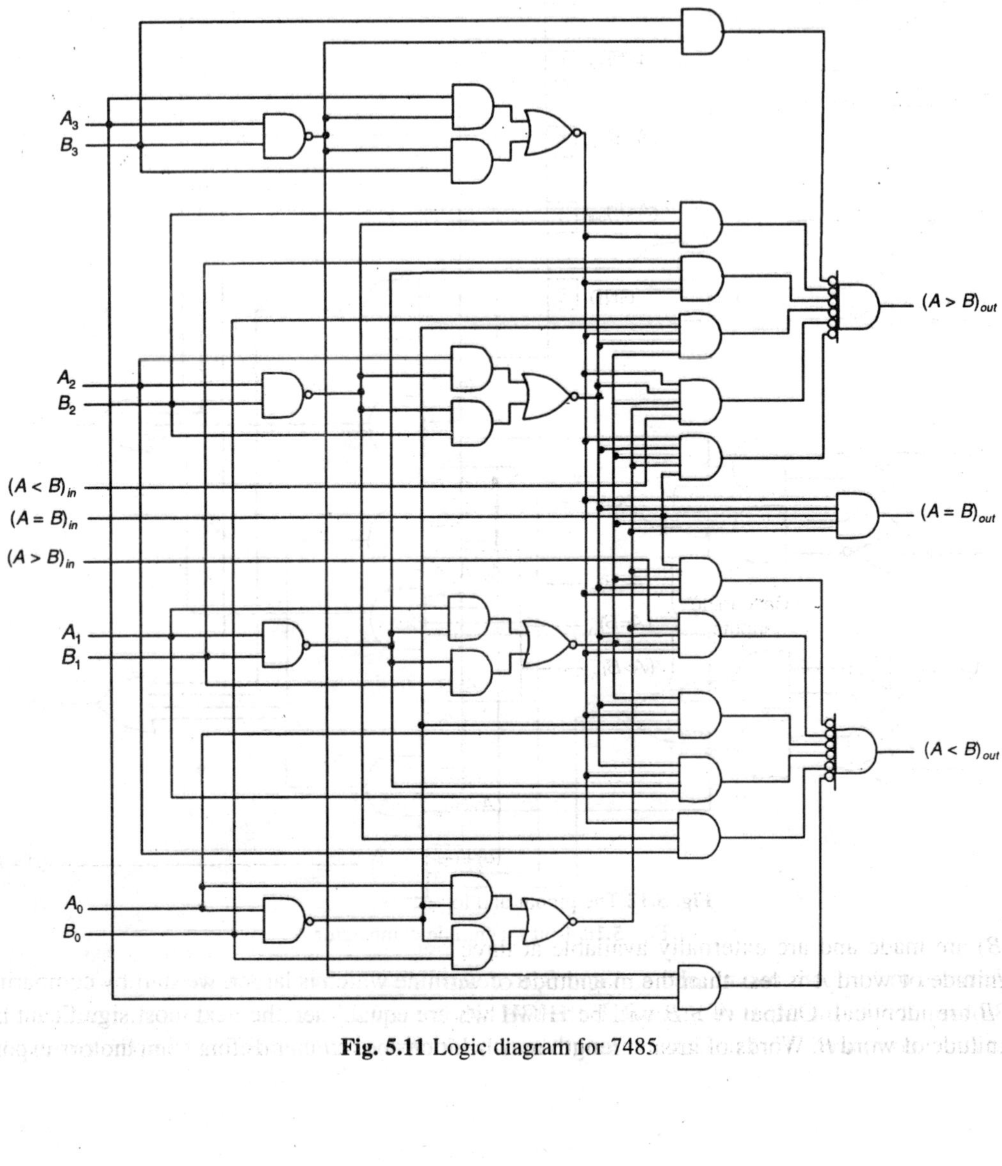

Fig. 5.11 Logic diagram for 7485

The 7485 compares two unsigned 4-bit binary numbers (i.e., words). One of them is $A_3\,A_2\,A_1A_0$ (i.e., word A); the other is $B_3\,B_2\,B_1\,B_0$ (i.e., word B). Three fully decoded decisions about two 4-bit words

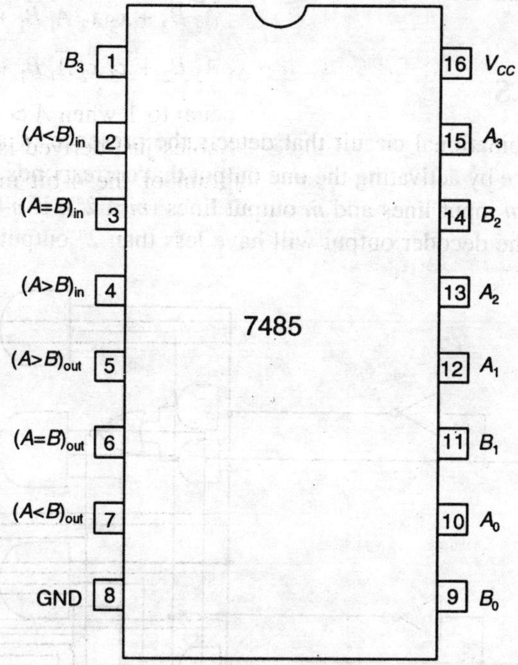

(a) Pinout for 7485

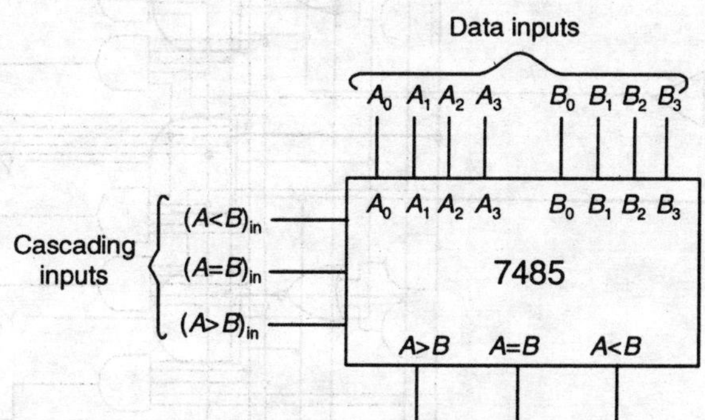

(b) Logic symbol for 7485

Fig. 5.12 The pinout and logic symbol for 7485

(A, B) are made and are externally available at three outputs. Output $A < B$ will be HIGH when the magnitude of word A is less than the magnitude of word B. Output $A = B$ will be HIGH when word A and B are identical. Output $A > B$ will be HIGH when the magnitude of word A is greater than the magnitude of word B. Words of greater length may be compared by connecting comparators in cascade.

The output of the lower-order comparator are connected to the corresponding inputs of the higher-order comparator. The lower-order comparator must have a HIGH on the = input, that is $(A = B)_{in} = 1$.

The logic diagram for 7485 is shown in Fig. 5.11. The pinout and logic symbol are given in Fig. 5.12.

5.4 DECODERS

A *decoder* is a combinational circuit that detects the presence of a specified code on its inputs and indicates that presence by activating the one output that corresponds to the decoded code. In its general form, a decoder has n input lines and m output lines ($m \leq 2^n$). If n-bit decoded information has don't care combinations, the decoder output will have less than 2^n outputs.

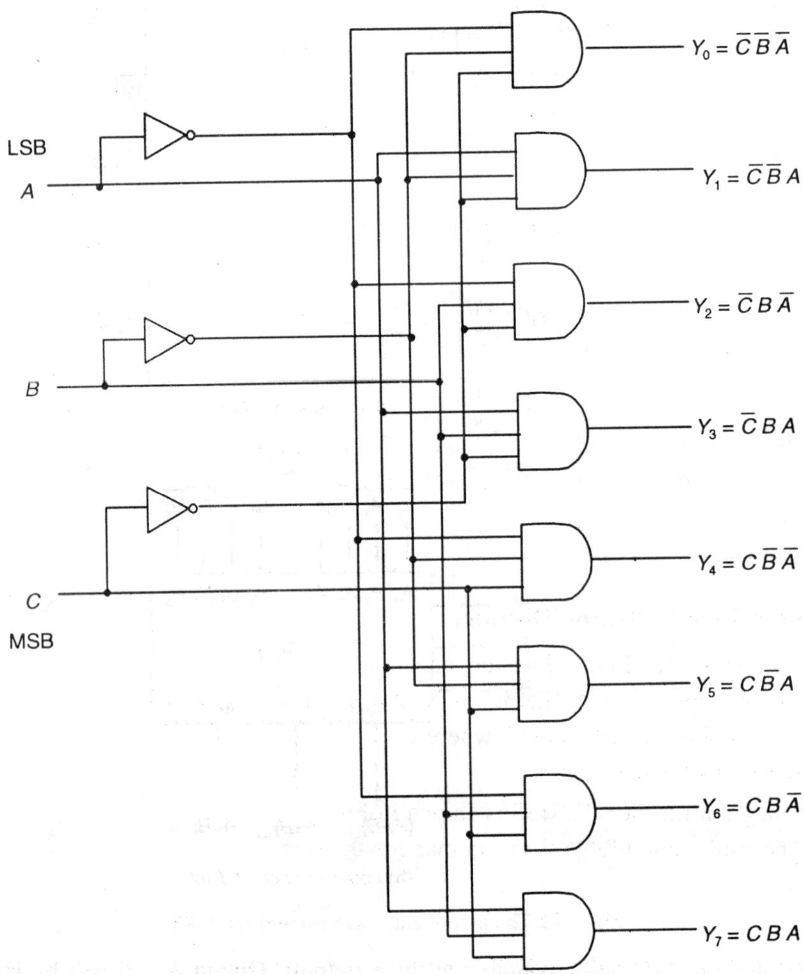

Fig. 5.13 3-to-8 line decoder

The decoders presented here are called n-to m line (or n-line to m-line) decoders. Their purpose is to generate the 2^n (or less) minterms of n input variables.

Decoders have a wide variety of applications. They may be used to route input data to a specified output line. They serve for some code conversions. Or they may be used for data distribution, i.e., demultiplexing.

Figure 5.13 illustrates the 3-to-8 line decoder. The three inputs are decoded into eight outputs, each output representing one of the minterms of the 3-input variables. The truth table for a 3-to-8 line decoder will be as shown in Table 5.2. From the table we can observe that only one of the outputs can be equal to 1 at a time for any combination of the inputs. If the output of the decoder is desired to be active-LOW, it will be set to logic 0 and rest of the states of the output bits are 1.

Table 5.2 Truth table for 3-to-8 line decoder

Inputs			Outputs							
C	B	A	Y_0	Y_1	Y_2	Y_3	Y_4	Y_5	Y_6	Y_7
0	0	0	1	0	0	0	0	0	0	0
0	0	1	0	1	0	0	0	0	0	0
0	1	0	0	0	1	0	0	0	0	0
0	1	1	0	0	0	1	0	0	0	0
1	0	0	0	0	0	0	1	0	0	0
1	0	1	0	0	0	0	0	1	0	0
1	1	0	0	0	0	0	0	0	1	0
1	1	1	0	0	0	0	0	0	0	1

The 74LS138 3-Line to 8-Line Decoder

The 74LS138 decodes one of eight lines dependent on the conditions at the three binary select inputs and the three enable inputs. Notice that it has NAND-gate outputs, so that its outputs are active-LOW. The input code is applied at A, B, and C, where C is the MSB. This decoder can also be referred to as a 3-to-8 decoder or 1-of-8 decoder.

The logic diagram for the 74LS138 is shown in Fig. 5.14. The pinout and logic symbol are given in Fig. 5.15. The truth table (Table 5.3) summarizes the operation.

Table 5.3 Truth table for 74LS138

Inputs					Outputs							
ENABLE		SELECT										
E_3	$\bar{E}_1+\bar{E}_2$	C	B	A	$\bar{Y}_0$	$\bar{Y}_1$	$\bar{Y}_2$	$\bar{Y}_3$	$\bar{Y}_4$	$\bar{Y}_5$	$\bar{Y}_6$	$\bar{Y}_7$
×	1	×	×	×	1	1	1	1	1	1	1	1
0	×	×	×	×	1	1	1	1	1	1	1	1
1	0	0	0	0	0	1	1	1	1	1	1	1
1	0	0	0	1	1	0	1	1	1	1	1	1
1	0	0	1	0	1	1	0	1	1	1	1	1
1	0	0	1	1	1	1	1	0	1	1	1	1
1	0	1	0	0	1	1	1	1	0	1	1	1
1	0	1	0	1	1	1	1	1	1	0	1	1
1	0	1	1	0	1	1	1	1	1	1	0	1
1	0	1	1	1	1	1	1	1	1	1	1	0

Note: '×' represents the 'don't care' condition.

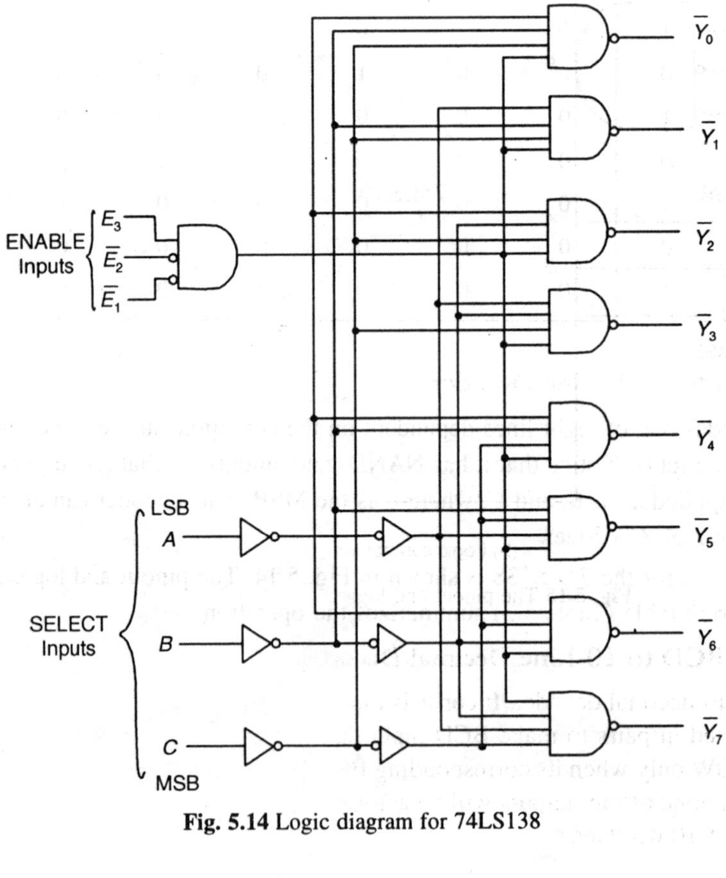

Fig. 5.14 Logic diagram for 74LS138

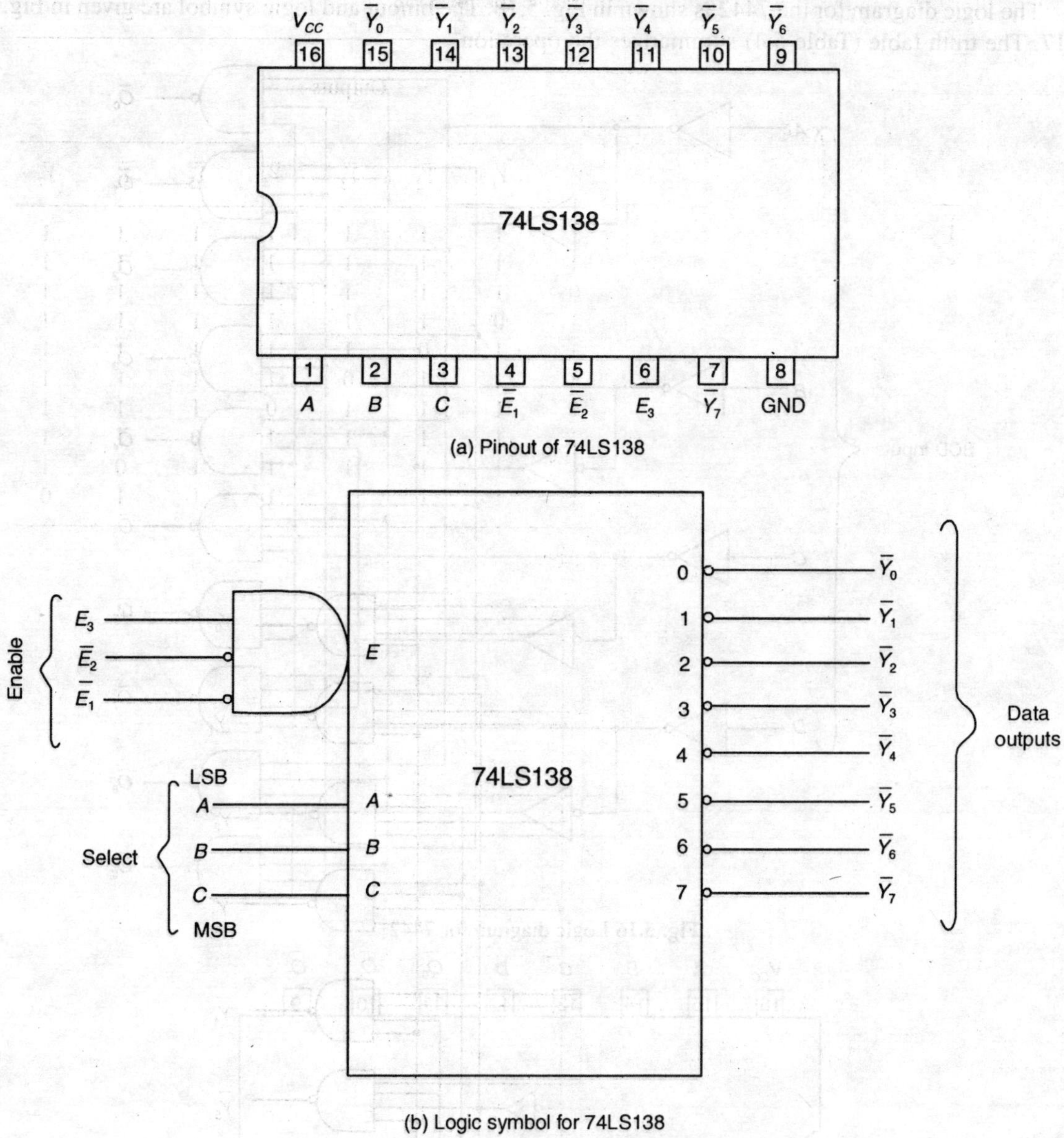

Fig. 5.15 The pinout and logic symbol for 74LS138

The 7442 4-Line BCD to 10-Line Decimal Decoder

The 7442 is a BCD-to-decimal decoder. It consists of eight inverters and ten 4-input NAND gates. The inverters are connected in pairs to make BCD input data available for decoding by the NAND gates. Each output goes LOW only when its corresponding BCD input is applied. For input combinations that are invalid for BCD, none of the outputs will be activated. This decoder can also be referred to as a 4-to-10 decoder or 1-of-10 decoder.

The logic diagram for the 7442 is shown in Fig. 5.16. The pinout and logic symbol are given in Fig. 5.17. The truth table (Table 5.4) summarizes the operation.

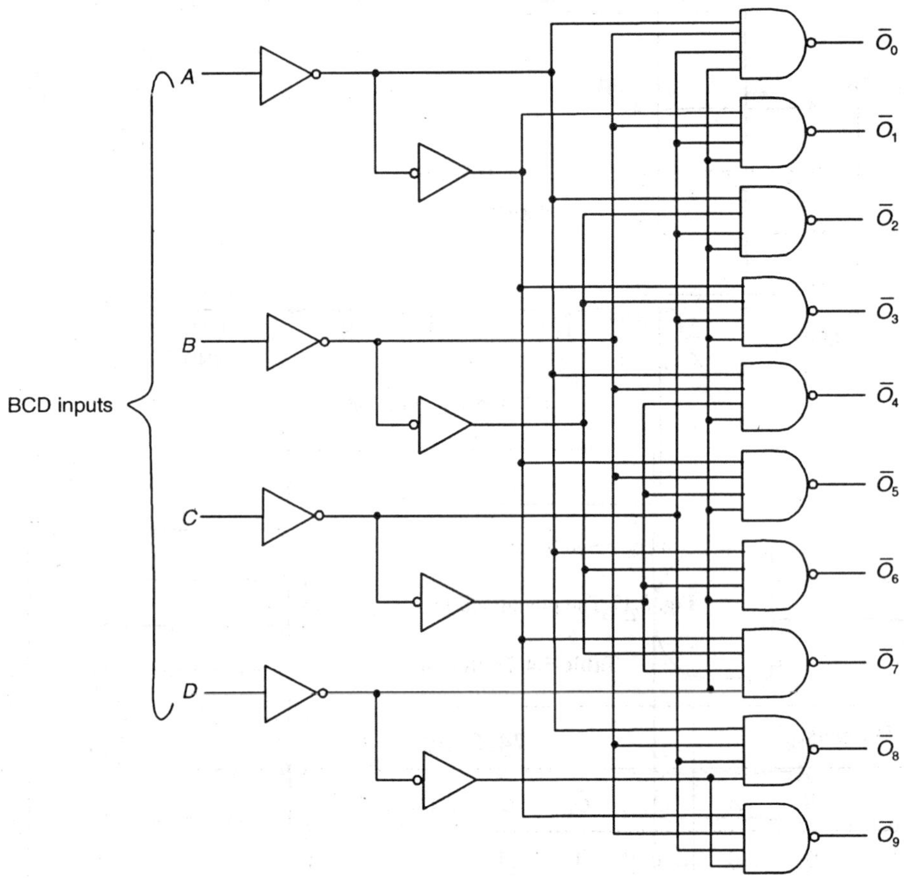

Fig. 5.16 Logic diagram for 7442

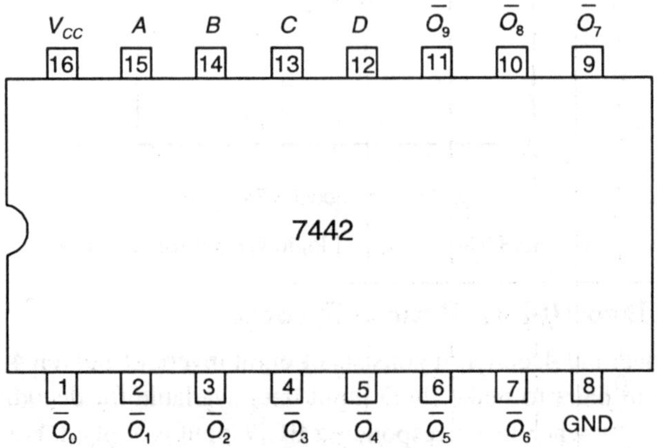

(a) Pinout of 7442

Fig. 5.17 The pinout and logic symbol for 7442

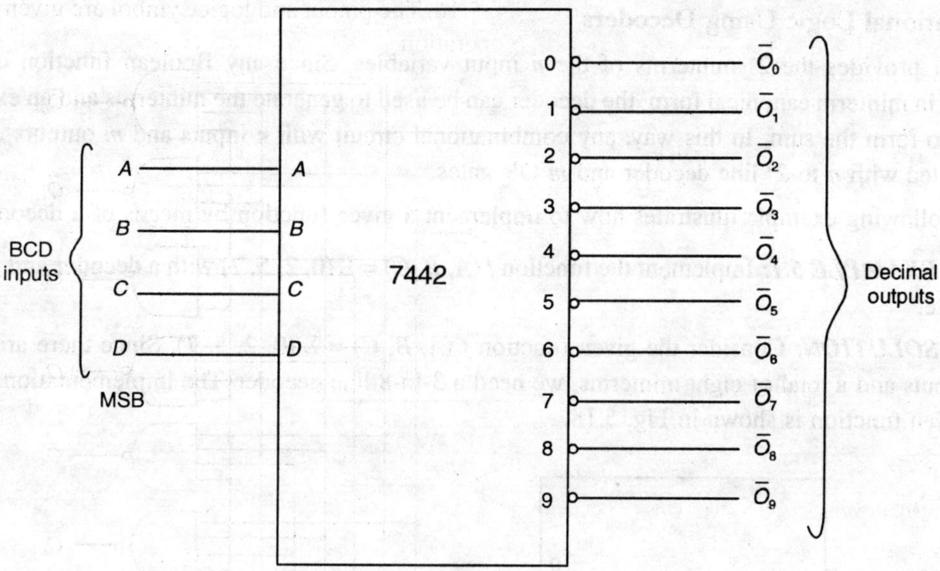

(b) Logic Symbol for 7442

Fig. 5.17 The pinout and logic symbol for 7442

Table 5.4 Truth table for 7442

	BCD inputs				Decimal outputs									
	D	C	B	A	$\overline{O}_0$	$\overline{O}_1$	$\overline{O}_2$	$\overline{O}_3$	$\overline{O}_4$	$\overline{O}_5$	$\overline{O}_6$	$\overline{O}_7$	$\overline{O}_8$	$\overline{O}_9$
	0	0	0	0	0	1	1	1	1	1	1	1	1	1
	0	0	0	1	1	0	1	1	1	1	1	1	1	1
	0	0	1	0	1	1	0	1	1	1	1	1	1	1
	0	0	1	1	1	1	1	0	1	1	1	1	1	1
	0	1	0	0	1	1	1	1	0	1	1	1	1	1
	0	1	0	1	1	1	1	1	1	0	1	1	1	1
	0	1	1	0	1	1	1	1	1	1	0	1	1	1
	0	1	1	1	1	1	1	1	1	1	1	0	1	1
	1	0	0	0	1	1	1	1	1	1	1	1	0	1
	1	0	0	1	1	1	1	1	1	1	1	1	1	0
Invalid	1	0	1	0	1	1	1	1	1	1	1	1	1	1
Invalid	1	0	1	1	1	1	1	1	1	1	1	1	1	1
Invalid	1	1	0	0	1	1	1	1	1	1	1	1	1	1
Invalid	1	1	0	1	1	1	1	1	1	1	1	1	1	1
Invalid	1	1	1	0	1	1	1	1	1	1	1	1	1	1
Invalid	1	1	1	1	1	1	1	1	1	1	1	1	1	1

Combinational Logic Using Decoders

A decoder provides the 2^n minterms of the n input variables. Since any Boolean function can be expressed in minterm canonical form, the decoder can be used to generate the minterms and an external OR gate to form the sum. In this way, any combinational circuit with n inputs and m outputs can be implemented with n-to-2^n line decoder and m OR gates.

The following example illustrates how to implement a given function by means of a decoder.

EXAMPLE 5.1: Implement the function $f(A, B, C) = \Sigma(0, 2, 5, 7)$ with a decoder and an OR gate.

SOLUTION: Consider the given function $f(A, B, C) = \Sigma(0, 2, 5, 7)$. Since there are three inputs and a total of eight minterms, we need a 3-to-8 line decoder. The implementation of the given function is shown in Fig. 5.18.

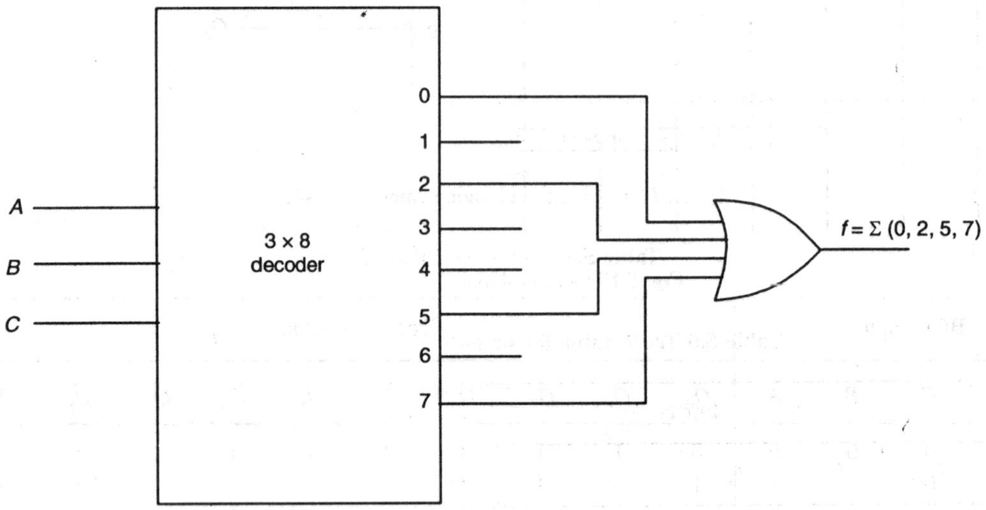

Fig. 5.18 Implementation of a function with decoder

5.5 ENCODERS

An *encoder* is a combinational circuit that performs an operation reverse to that of a decoder. An encoder will have 2^n (or less) input lines and n output lines. The n output lines generate the binary code for upto 2^n input variables.

Figure 5.19 shows the logic circuit for an octal-to-binary encoder. It consists of 8 input lines and produces a 3-bit output code corresponding to the activated input. Notice that I_0 is not connected to any OR gate because the encoder outputs will normally be at 000 when none of the inputs I_1 to I_7, is equal to 1. The truth table (Table 5.5) summarizes the operation. Encoders of this type are not available in IC packages, since they can be easily constructed with OR gates.

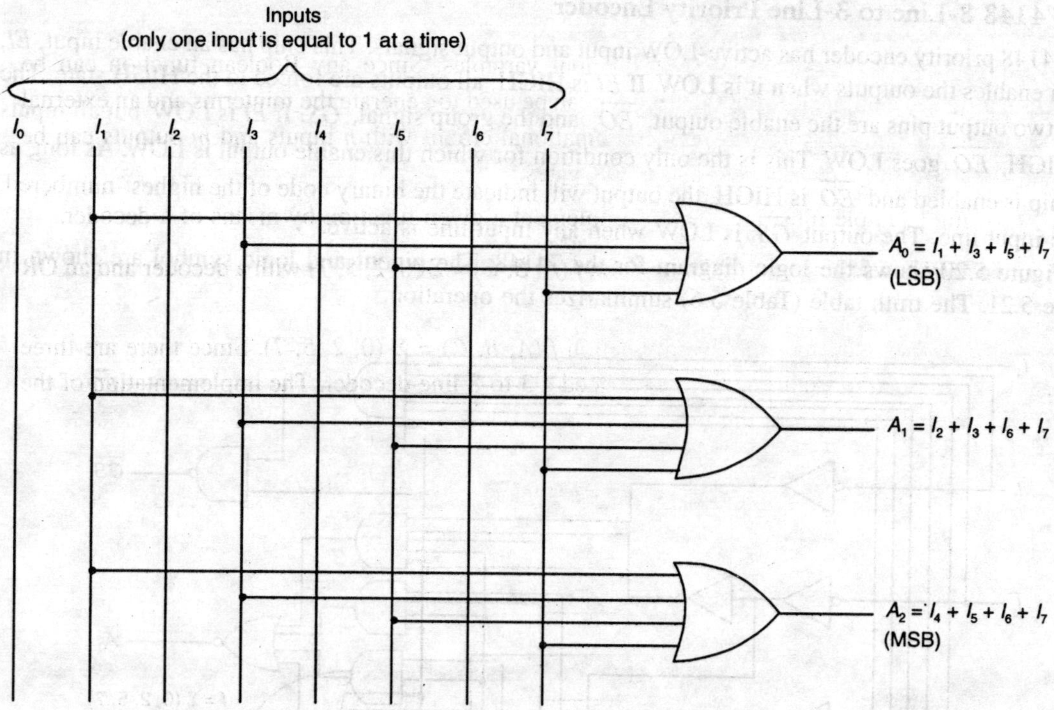

Fig. 5.19 Octal-to-binary encoder

Table 5.5 Truth table for octal-to-binary encoder

Inputs								Outputs		
I_0	I_1	I_2	I_3	I_4	I_5	I_6	I_7	A_2	A_1	A_0
1	0	0	0	0	0	0	0	0	0	0
0	1	0	0	0	0	0	0	0	0	1
0	0	1	0	0	0	0	0	0	1	0
0	0	0	1	0	0	0	0	0	1	1
0	0	0	0	1	0	0	0	1	0	0
0	0	0	0	0	1	0	0	1	0	1
0	0	0	0	0	0	1	0	1	1	0
0	0	0	0	0	0	0	1	1	1	1

The Priority Encoder

It is a modified version of the encoder. This device includes the necessary logic to ensure that when two or more inputs are activated simultaneously, the output code will correspond to the highest numbered input. This type of encoder is available in IC package.

The 74148 8-Line to 3-Line Priority Encoder

The 74148 priority encoder has active-LOW input and output signals. This chip has an enable input, *EI*, which enables the outputs when it is LOW. If *EI* is HIGH, all outputs are forced to the HIGH state. The other two output pins are the enable output, $\overline{EO}$, and the group signal, $\overline{GS}$. If *EI* is LOW, but all inputs are HIGH, $\overline{EO}$ goes LOW. This is the only condition for which this enable output is LOW. As long as the chip is enabled and $\overline{EO}$ is HIGH, the output will indicate the binary code of the highest-numbered, active input line. The output $\overline{GS}$ is LOW when any input line is active.

Figure 5.20 shows the logic diagram for the 74148. The pinout and logic symbol are shown in Figure 5.21. The truth table (Table 5.6) summarizes the operation.

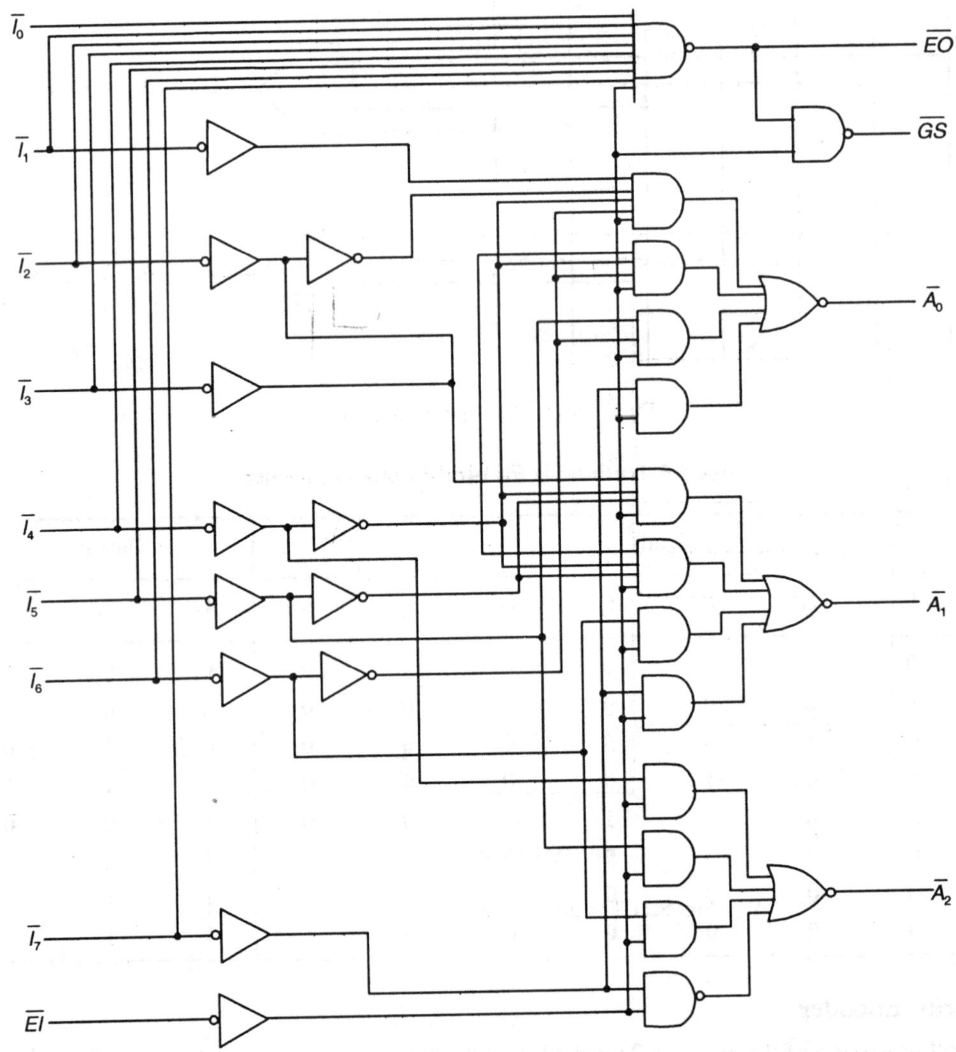

Fig. 5.20 Logic diagram for 74148

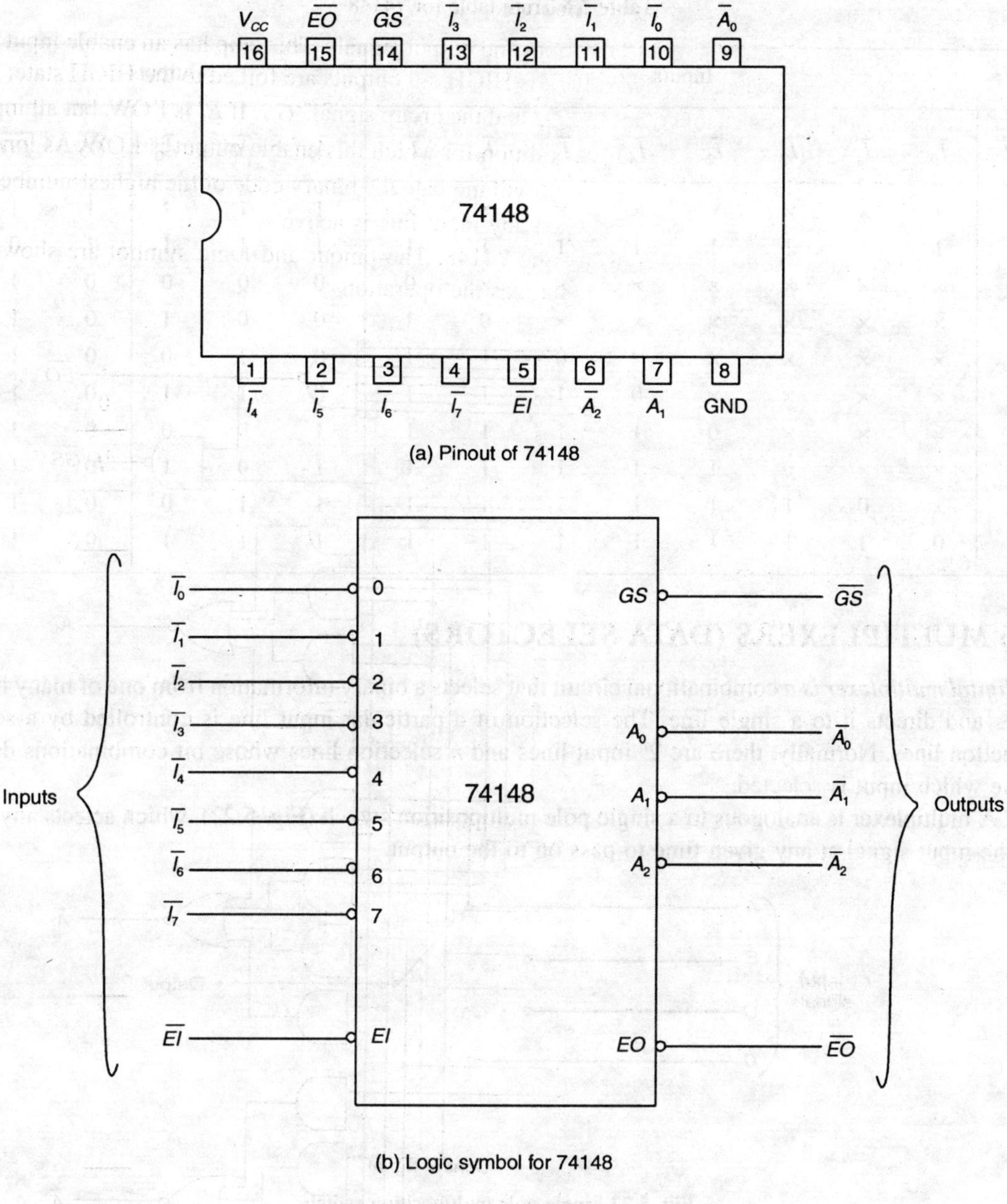

(a) Pinout of 74148

(b) Logic symbol for 74148

Fig. 5.21 The pinout and logic symbol for 74148

Table 5.6 Truth table for 74148

Inputs									Outputs				
$\overline{EI}$	$\overline{I_0}$	$\overline{I_1}$	$\overline{I_2}$	$\overline{I_3}$	$\overline{I_4}$	$\overline{I_5}$	$\overline{I_6}$	$\overline{I_7}$	$\overline{A_2}$	$\overline{A_1}$	$\overline{A_0}$	$\overline{GS}$	$\overline{EO}$
1	×	×	×	×	×	×	×	×	1	1	1	1	1
0	1	1	1	1	1	1	1	1	1	1	1	1	0
0	×	×	×	×	×	×	×	0	0	0	0	0	1
0	×	×	×	×	×	×	0	1	0	0	1	0	1
0	×	×	×	×	×	0	1	1	0	1	0	0	1
0	×	×	×	×	0	1	1	1	0	1	1	0	1
0	×	×	×	0	1	1	1	1	1	0	0	0	1
0	×	×	0	1	1	1	1	1	1	0	1	0	1
0	×	0	1	1	1	1	1	1	1	1	0	0	1
0	0	1	1	1	1	1	1	1	1	1	1	0	1

5.6 MULTIPLEXERS (DATA SELECTORS)

A *digital multiplexer is a* combinational circuit that selects a binary information from one of many input lines and directs it to a single line. The selection of a particular input line is controlled by a set of selection lines. Normally, there are 2^n input lines and n selection lines whose bit combinations determine which input is selected.

A multiplexer is analogous to a single pole multiposition switch (Fig. 5.22), which selects any one of the input signal at any given time to pass on to the output.

Fig. 5.22 Single pole multiposition switch

Figure 5.23(a) shows a logic diagram of a 4-line to 1-line multiplexer. Each of the four lines, I_0 through I_3, is applied to one input of an AND gate. Selection lines S_1 and S_0 are decoded to select a particular AND gate. For instance, consider the case when $S_1 = 0$ and $S_0 = 0$. Here I_0 is gated with $\overline{S_1}\,\overline{S_0}$ so that I_0 will pass through its AND gate to output only when $S_1 = 0$ and $S_0 = 0$. The truth table shown in Fig. 5.23(c) lists the outputs for each possible bit combination of the selection lines. The block diagram representation of the multiplexer is shown in Fig. 5.23(b).

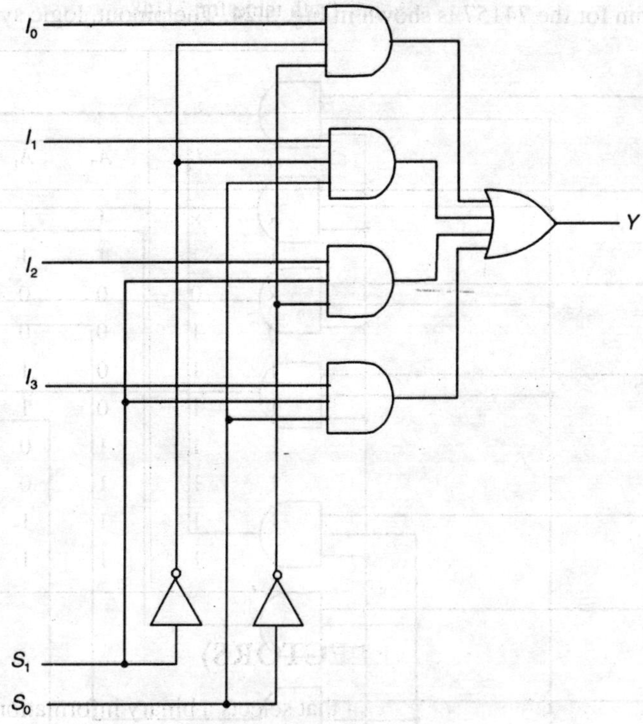

(a) Logic diagram

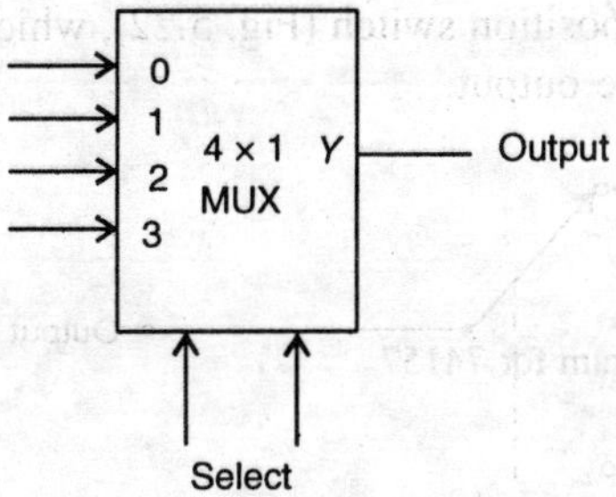

(b) Block diagram

S_1	S_0	Y
0	0	I_0
0	1	I_1
1	0	I_2
1	1	I_3

(c) Truth table

Fig. 5.23 4-to-1 line multiplexer

The 74157 Quadruple 2-Line to 1-Line Multiplexer

The 74157 is a very useful multiplexer IC. It contains four two-input multiplexers. A 4-bit word is selected from one of two sources and is routed to the four outputs. The control signal labeled SELECT determines which 4-bit input word is transmitted to the output. It also includes a separate ENABLE (STROBE) input. The ENABLE must be LOW for the multiplexer to work properly. When the ENABLE is HIGH, the multiplexer is inoperative.

The logic diagram for the 74157 is shown in Fig. 5.24. The pinout, logic symbol and truth table are given in Fig. 5.25.

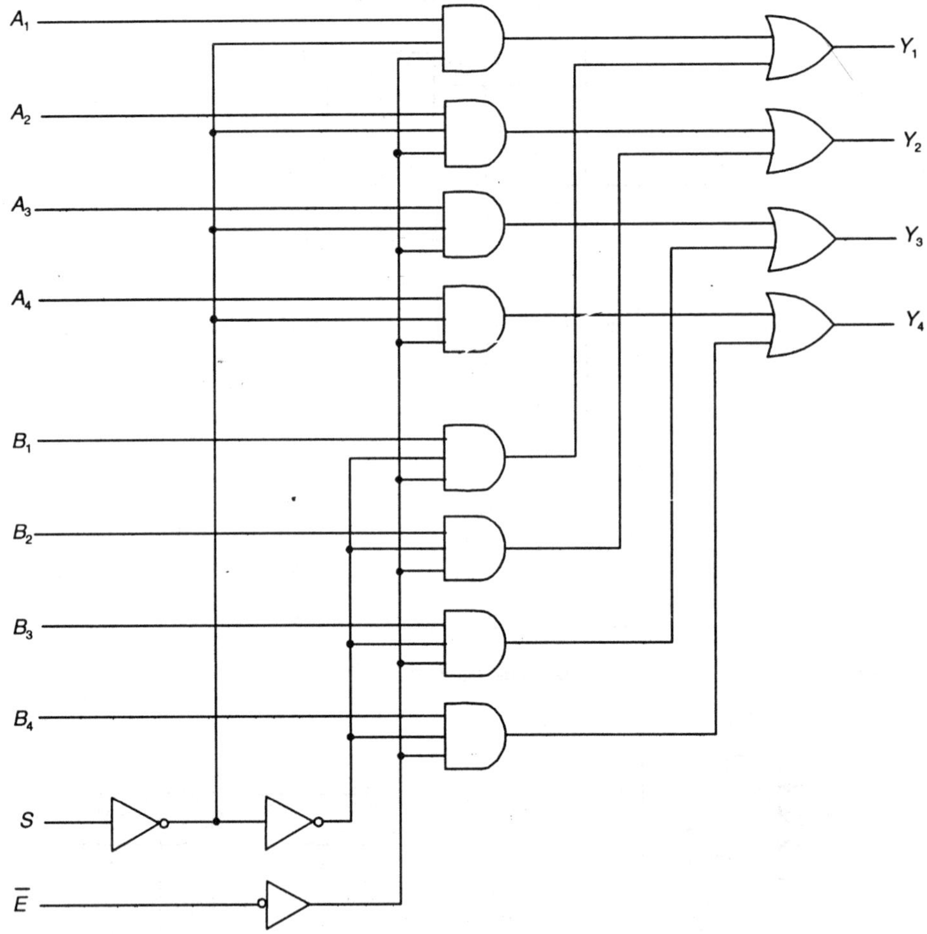

Fig. 5.24 Logic diagram for 74157

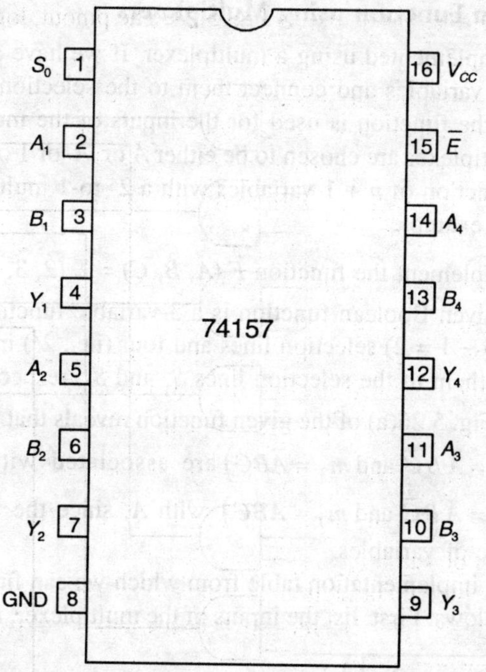

(a) Pinout for 74157

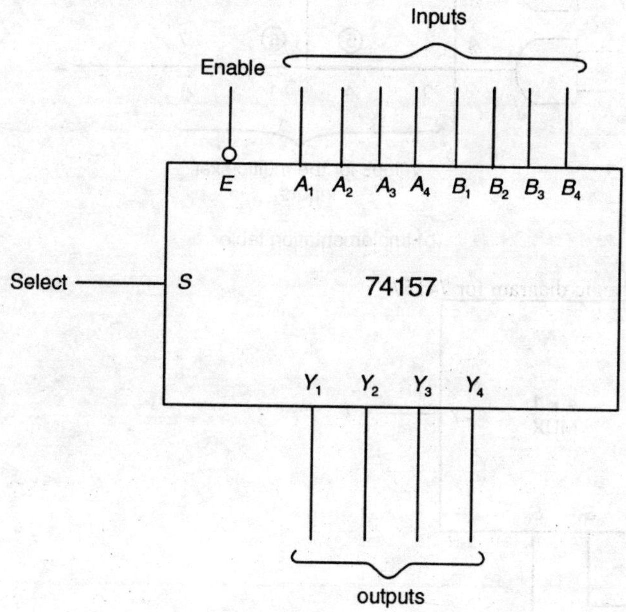

(b) Logic symbol for 74157

$\bar{E}$	S	Y_1	Y_2	Y_3	Y_4
1	X	0	0	0	0
0	0	A_1	A_2	A_3	A_4
0	1	B_1	B_2	B_3	B_4

(c) Truth table

Fig. 5.25 The pinout, logic symbol and truth table for 74157

Implementation of Boolean Function using Multiplexers

A Boolean function can be implemented using a multiplexer. If we have a Boolean function of $n + 1$ variables, we take n of these variables and connect them to the selection lines of a multiplexer. The remaining single variable of the function is used for the inputs of the multiplexer. If A is this single variable, the inputs of the multiplexer are chosen to be either A or $\bar{A}$ or 1 or 0. In this way it is possible to implement any Boolean function of $n + 1$ variables with a 2^n-to-1 multiplexer. We demonstrate the procedure with the following example.

***EXAMPLE 5.2*:** Implement the function $F(A, B, C) = \Sigma\,(2, 3, 5, 6)$ using multiplexer.

***SOLUTION*:** The given Boolean function is a 3-variable function. Hence we need a multiplexer with two (i.e., $3 - 1 = 2$) selection lines and four (i.e., 2^2) inputs. We take two variables B and C, and connect them to the selection lines S_1 and S_0, respectively.

The truth table shown in Fig. 5.26(a) of the given function reveals that the first half of the minterms $\left(m_0 = \bar{A}\bar{B}\bar{C},\ m_1 = \bar{A}\bar{B}C,\ m_2 = \bar{A}B\bar{C} \text{ and } m_3 = \bar{A}BC\right)$ are associated with $\bar{A}$ and the second half $\left(m_4 = A\bar{B}\bar{C},\ m_5 = A\bar{B}C,\ m_6 = AB\bar{C} \text{ and } m_7 = ABC\right)$ with A, since the variable A is in the highest order position in the sequence of variables.

Now we go for preparing implementation table from which we can find values for the multiplexer inputs. The procedure is as follows. First, list the inputs of the multiplexer, I_0 through I_3, and under them

Minterm	A	B	C	F
0	0	0	0	0
1	0	0	1	0
2	0	1	0	1
3	0	1	1	1
4	1	0	0	0
5	1	0	1	1
6	1	1	0	1
7	1	1	1	0

(a) Truth table

	I_0	I_1	I_2	I_3
$\bar{A}$	0	1	②	③
A	4	⑤	⑥	7
	0	A	1	$\bar{A}$

Values for the multiplexer inputs

(b) Implementation table

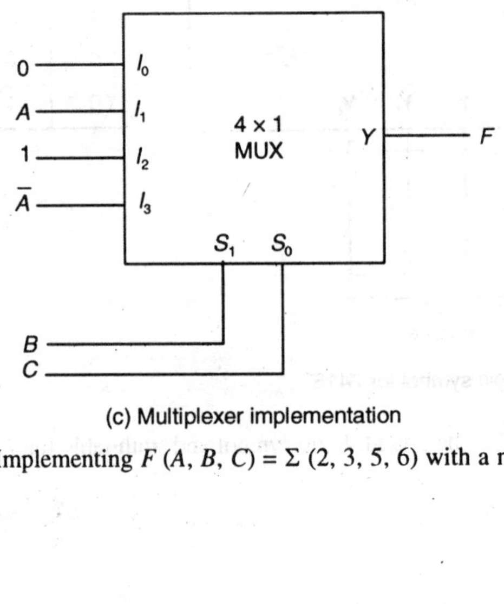

(c) Multiplexer implementation

Fig. 5.26 Implementing $F(A, B, C) = \Sigma\,(2, 3, 5, 6)$ with a multiplexer

list all the minterms in two rows. The first row contains all those minterms that are associated with $\bar{A}$, and the second row minterms associated with A, as shown in Fig. 5.26(b). Encircle all the minterms of the given function and inspect each column separately.
Values for the multiplexer inputs can be obtained from the following rules:

- If the two minterms in a column are not encircled, 0 is applied to the corresponding multiplexer input.
- If the two minterms in a column are encircled, 1 is applied to the corresponding multiplexer input.
- If only the bottom minterm in a column is encircled, A is applied to the corresponding multiplexer input.
- If only the top minterm in a column is encircled, $\bar{A}$ is applied to the corresponding multiplexer input.

After finding values for the multiplexer inputs, the given function is easily implemented, as shown in Fig. 5.26(c).

5.7 DEMULTIPLEXERS (DATA DISTRIBUTORS)

A *demultiplexer* performs the reverse operation of a multiplexer. It takes information on a single line and transmits this information on one of several output lines. Normally there are 2^n output lines and n selection lines whose bit combinations determine which output is selected.

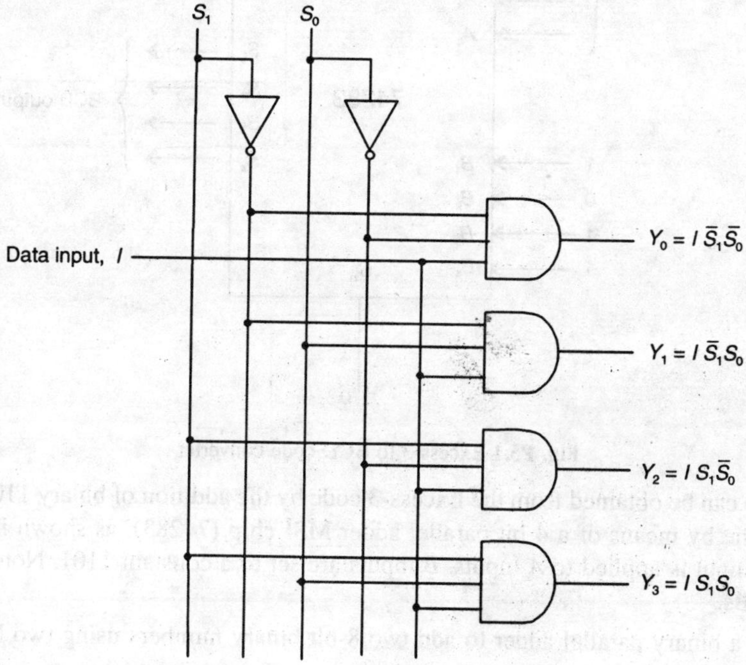

Fig. 5.27 1-to-4 line demultiplexer

Figure 5.27 shows the logic diagram of 1-to-4 line demultiplexer. The input data line is connected to all four AND gates, but only one of these gates will be enabled by the selection lines. For example with the selection lines $S_1 S_0 = 00$, only the top AND gate will be enabled, and data input I will appear at output Y_0. Similarly the other bit combinations of n selection lines cause input I to reach the other outputs.

A decoder with an enable input is referred to as a *decoder/demultiplexer*. Enable input is an extra input added to the decoder gates. This type of decoder can therefore be used as a demultiplexer, with the binary code inputs serving as the SELECT inputs and the ENABLE input serving as the data input I.

SOLVED PROBLEMS

5.1 Implement an Excess-3 to BCD code converter by using 4-bit parallel binary adder MSI chip (74283).

SOLUTION:

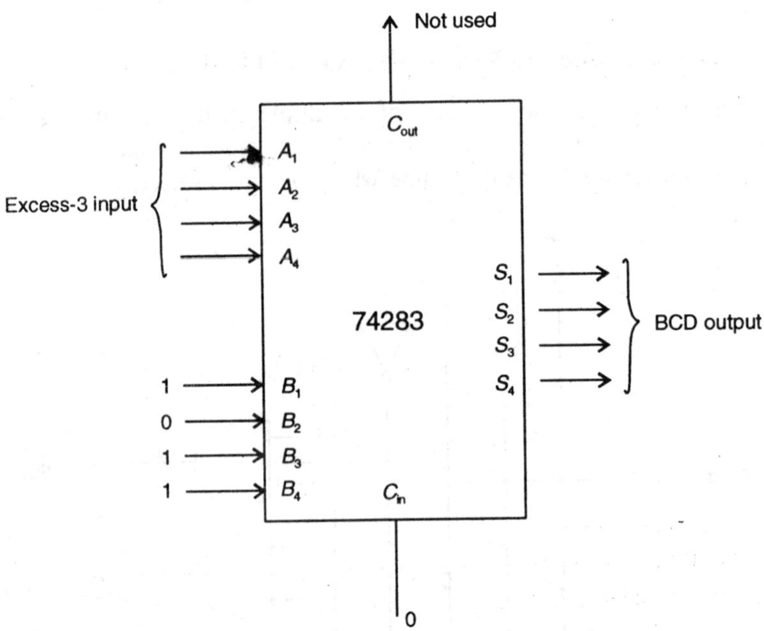

Fig. P5.1 Excess-3 to BCD code converter

BCD code can be obtained from the Excess-3 code by the addition of binary 1101. This addition can be done by means of a 4-bit parallel adder MSI chip (74283), as shown in Fig. P5.1. The Excess-3 input is applied to A inputs. B inputs are set to a constant 1101. Note that A_1, B_1 and S_1 are LSBs.

5.2 Construct a binary parallel adder to add two 8-bit binary numbers using two MSI chips.

SOLUTION:

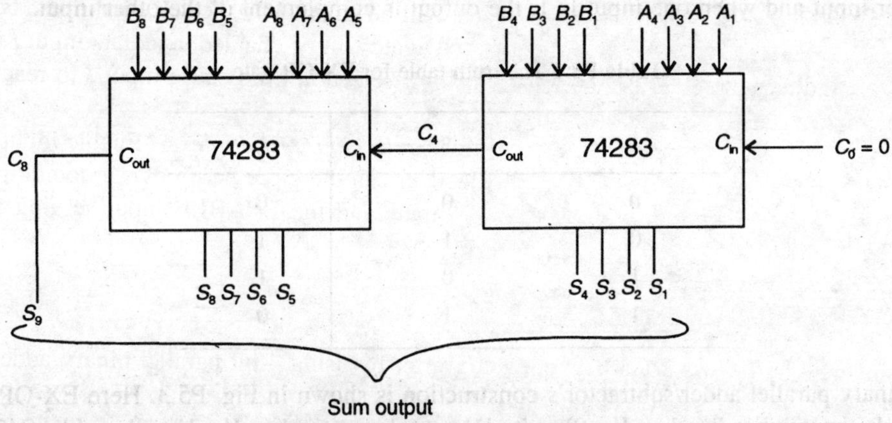

Fig. P5.2 8-bit binary parallel adder

Fig. P5.2 shows an 8-bit binary parallel adder using two 4-bit binary parallel adders. Here A and B are two 8-bit binary inputs to be added and $S_9\ S_8\ ......\ S_1$ is their sum. Note that A_1, B_1 and S_1 are the LSBs. Also notice that the carry input of the right adder is zero and its carry output is connected to the carry input of the left adder.

5.3 Using 4 EX-OR gates and a 4-bit binary parallel adder MSI circuit, construct a 4-bit parallel adder/subtractor. Use an input select variable V so that when $V = 0$, the circuit adds and when $V = 1$, the circuit subtracts. Use 2's complement subtraction.

SOLUTION:

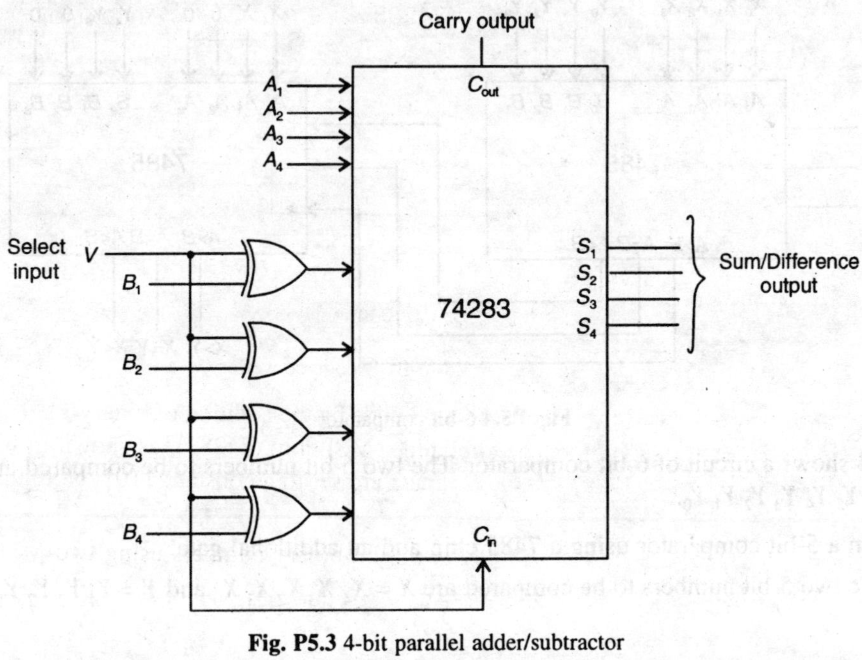

Fig. P5.3 4-bit parallel adder/subtractor

The truth table (Table P5.1) of the EX-OR gate reveals that when one input is 0, the output is same as the other input and when one input is 1, the output is complement of the other input.

Table P5.1 The truth table for EX-OR gate

x	y	F
0	0	0
0	1	1
1	0	1
1	1	0

The binary parallel adder/subtractor's construction is shown in Fig. P5.3. Here EX-OR gates are used to apply the number B (when $V = 0$) or its 1's complement (when $V = 1$) to the adder 74283. When $V = 0$, the circuit adds the two binary inputs (A and B) with carry input equal to 0. The output will be the sum of the inputs. When $V=1$, the circuit adds the number A and 1's complement of the number B along with the carry input equal to 1. (The reason for taking carry input equal to 1 is to add 1 to the 1's complement of the number B to obtain its 2's complement). When $A > B$, there is always a carry (i.e., carry output equal to 1), the difference output is considered as answer by discarding carry. When $A<B$, there is no carry, the difference output will be in the 2's complement form.

5.4 Construct a 6-bit comparator using two 7485 chips.

SOLUTION:

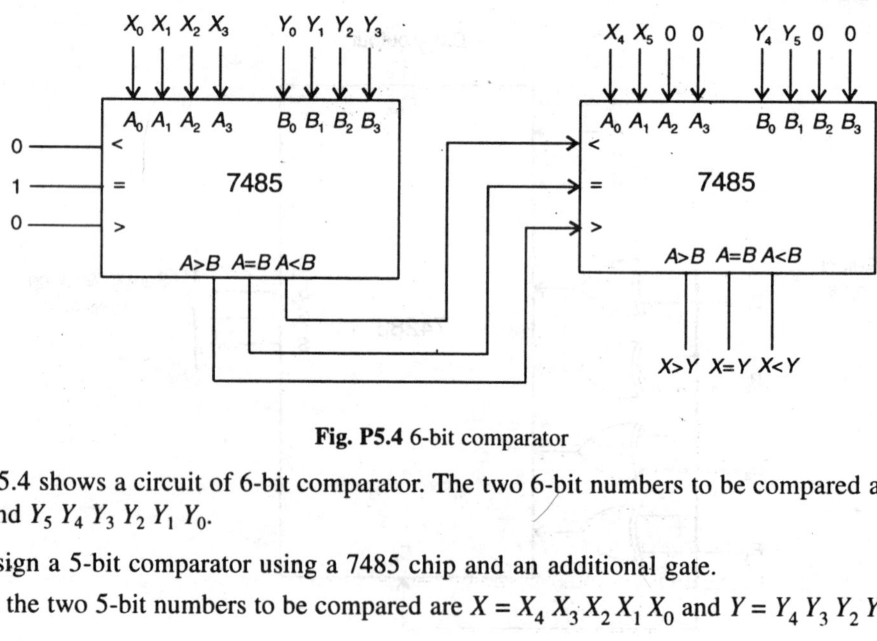

Fig. P5.4 6-bit comparator

Fig. P5.4 shows a circuit of 6-bit comparator. The two 6-bit numbers to be compared are $X_5\ X_4\ X_3\ X_2\ X_1\ X_0$ and $Y_5\ Y_4\ Y_3\ Y_2\ Y_1\ Y_0$.

5.5 Design a 5-bit comparator using a 7485 chip and an additional gate.

Let the two 5-bit numbers to be compared are $X = X_4\,X_3\,X_2\,X_1\,X_0$ and $Y = Y_4\,Y_3\,Y_2\,Y_1\,Y_0$.

SOLUTION:

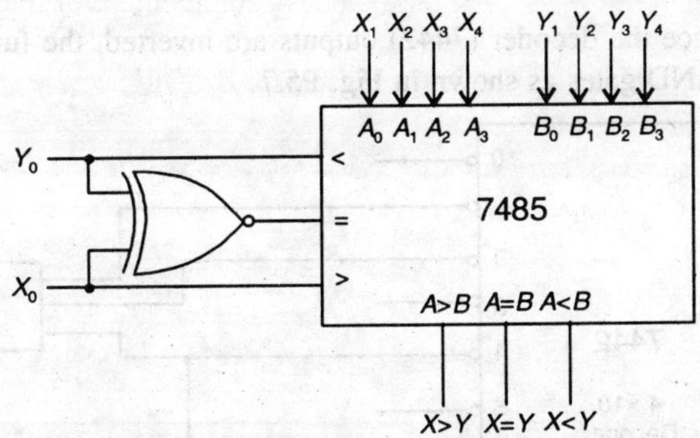

Fig. P5.5 5-bit comparator

5.6 Given a 3 × 8 decoder. Construct a 4 × 16 decoder.

SOLUTION:

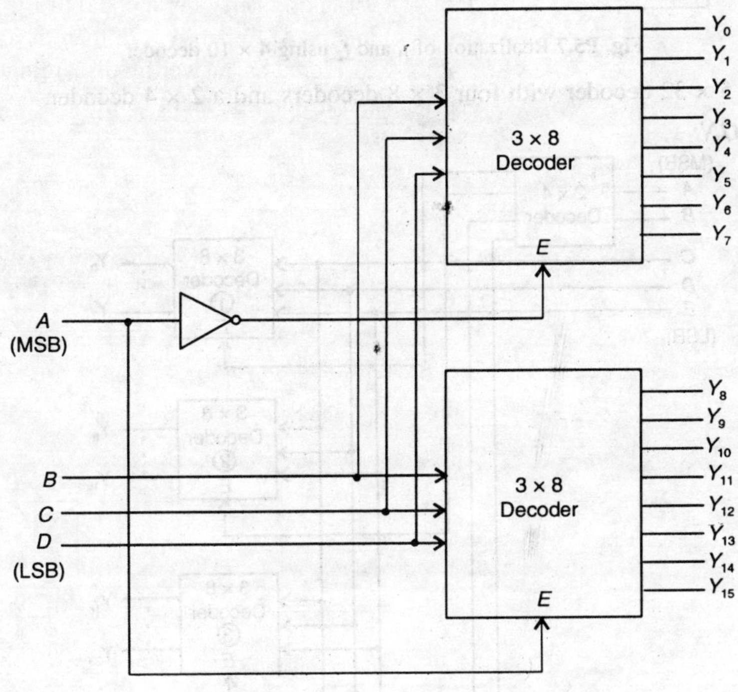

Fig. P5.6 4 × 16 decoder constructed with two 3 × 8 decoders

In order to construct a 4 × 16 decoder (Fig. P5.6) the most significant bit A and its complement, that is $\bar{A}$, are connected to the enable inputs of the bottom and top decoders, respectively. When $A = 0$, the top decoder is enabled and the bottom decoder is disabled to generate minterms 0000 to 0111. When $A = 1$, the bottom decoder is enabled and the top decoder is disabled to generate minterms 1000 to 1111.

5.7 Realize the functions $f_1\ (A, B, C, D) = \Sigma\ (1, 2, 4)$ and $f_2\ (A, B, C, D) = \Sigma\ (4, 7, 9)$ using the decoder 7442.

SOLUTION: Since the decoder (7442) outputs are inverted, the functions f_1 and f_2 can be generated using NAND gates as shown in Fig. P5.7.

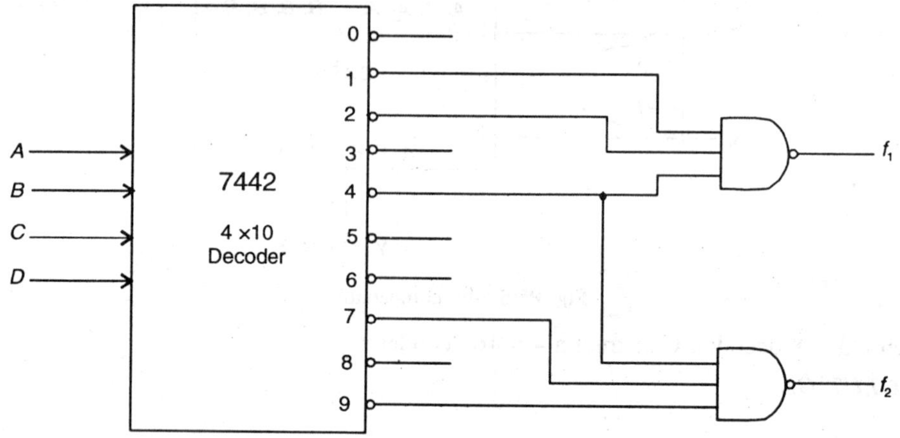

Fig. P5.7 Realization of f_1 and f_2 using 4 × 10 decoder

5.8 Construct a 5 × 32 decoder with four 3 × 8 decoders and a 2 × 4 decoder.

SOLUTION:

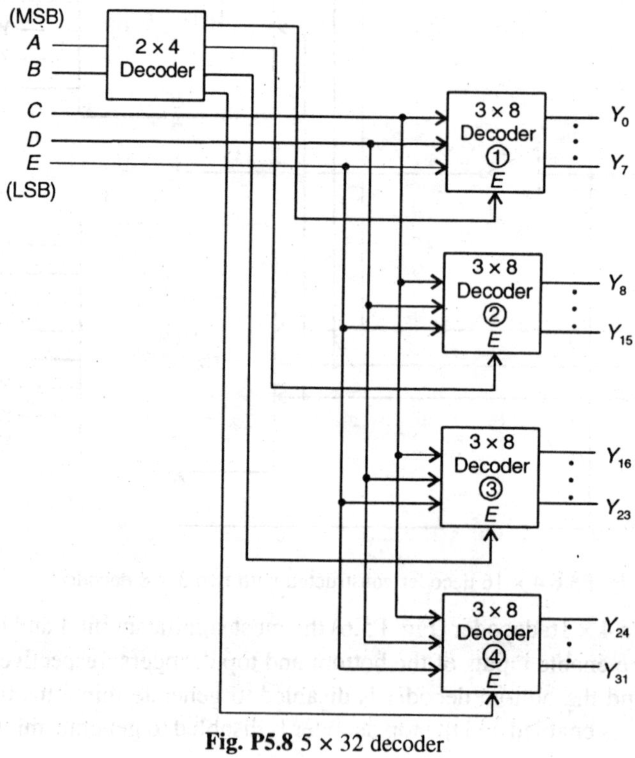

Fig. P5.8 5 × 32 decoder

In order to construct 5 × 32 decoder (Fig. P5.8) the higher order bits A and B are applied to 2 × 4 decoder. Depending on the values of AB, the decoders (1) to (4) are enabled one at a time, and the remaining decoders are disabled. For instance, when $AB = 00$, the decoder (1) is enabled and the other decoders are disabled.

5.9 Design a BCD-to-decimal decoder such that it gives an output of all 0s when any invalid combination occurs.

SOLUTION: The BCD code has four bits. Therefore, the decoder should have four inputs to accept the coded digit and ten outputs, one for each decimal digit. This gives a 4 × 10 decoder. The truth table for this decoder is shown in Table P5.2.

Table P5.2 Truth table for the decimal decoder

	BCD Inputs				Decimal Outputs									
	A	B	C	D	D_0	D_1	D_2	D_3	D_4	D_5	D_6	D_7	D_8	D_9
	0	0	0	0	1	0	0	0	0	0	0	0	0	0
	0	0	0	1	0	1	0	0	0	0	0	0	0	0
	0	0	1	0	0	0	1	0	0	0	0	0	0	0
	0	0	1	1	0	0	0	1	0	0	0	0	0	0
	0	1	0	0	0	0	0	0	1	0	0	0	0	0
	0	1	0	1	0	0	0	0	0	1	0	0	0	0
	0	1	1	0	0	0	0	0	0	0	1	0	0	0
	0	1	1	1	0	0	0	0	0	0	0	1	0	0
	1	0	0	0	0	0	0	0	0	0	0	0	1	0
	1	0	0	1	0	0	0	0	0	0	0	0	0	1
Invalid	1	0	1	0	0	0	0	0	0	0	0	0	0	0
	1	0	1	1	0	0	0	0	0	0	0	0	0	0
	1	1	0	0	0	0	0	0	0	0	0	0	0	0
	1	1	0	1	0	0	0	0	0	0	0	0	0	0
	1	1	1	0	0	0	0	0	0	0	0	0	0	0
	1	1	1	1	0	0	0	0	0	0	0	0	0	0

From the truth table, we can obtain the expressions for D_0 through D_9 as follows:

$$D_0 = \overline{A}\overline{B}\overline{C}\overline{D}$$

$$D_1 = \overline{A}\overline{B}\overline{C}D$$

$$D_2 = \overline{A}\overline{B}C\overline{D}$$

$$D_3 = \bar{A}\bar{B}CD$$

$$D_4 = \bar{A}B\bar{C}\bar{D}$$

$$D_5 = \bar{A}B\bar{C}D$$

$$D_6 = \bar{A}BC\bar{D}$$

$$D_7 = \bar{A}BCD$$

$$D_8 = A\bar{B}\bar{C}\bar{D}$$

$$D_9 = A\bar{B}\bar{C}D$$

With these expressions a BCD-to-decimal decoder circuit can be constructed as shown in Fig. P5.9. An analysis of the circuit shows that the six invalid input combinations will produce an output of all 0s.

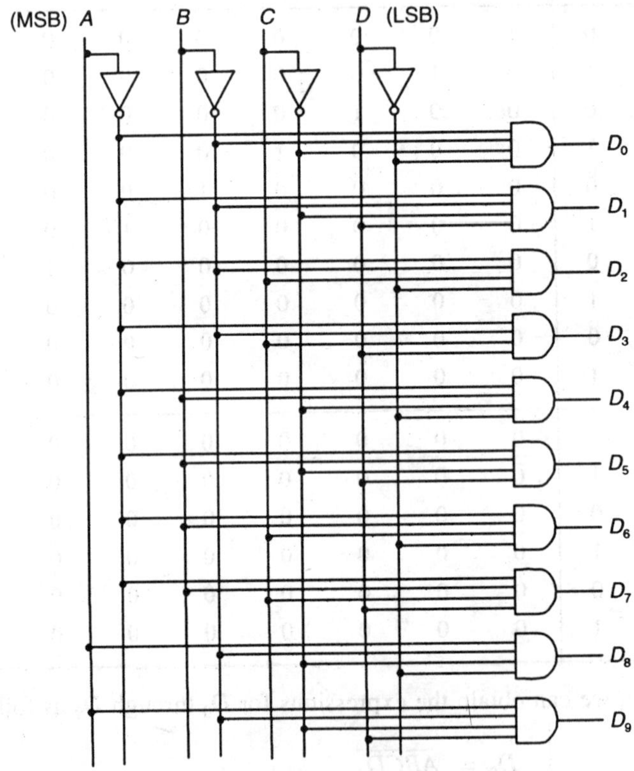

Fig. P5.9 BCD-to-decimal decoder

5.10. Design a 4-line to 2-line priority encoder. Include an output E to indicate that at least one input is a 1.

SOLUTION: The truth table of a 4-line to 2-line priority encoder is shown in Table P5.3.

Table P5.3 Truth table for 4-line to 2-line priority encoder

Inputs				Outputs	
D_0	D_1	D_2	D_3	x	y
×	×	×	1	1	1
×	×	1	0	1	0
×	1	0	0	0	1
1	0	0	0	0	0

Considering the four input combinations which produce output 1, we can obtain the minterms. By K-map simplification, we get the Boolean expressions for the outputs x and y as follows:

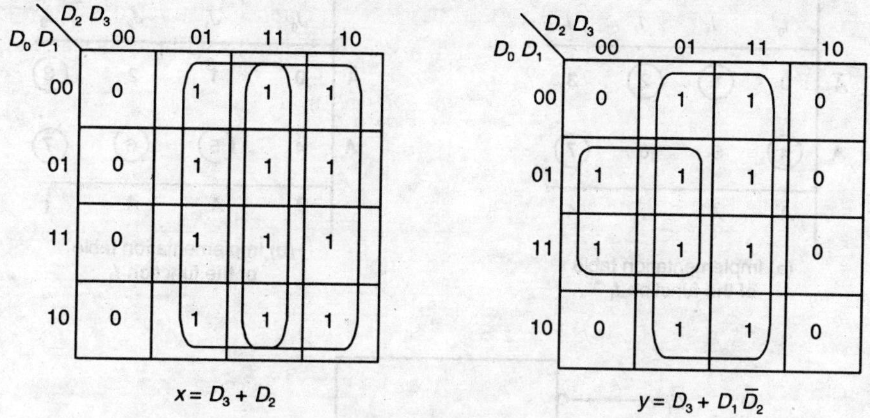

(a) K-map simplification

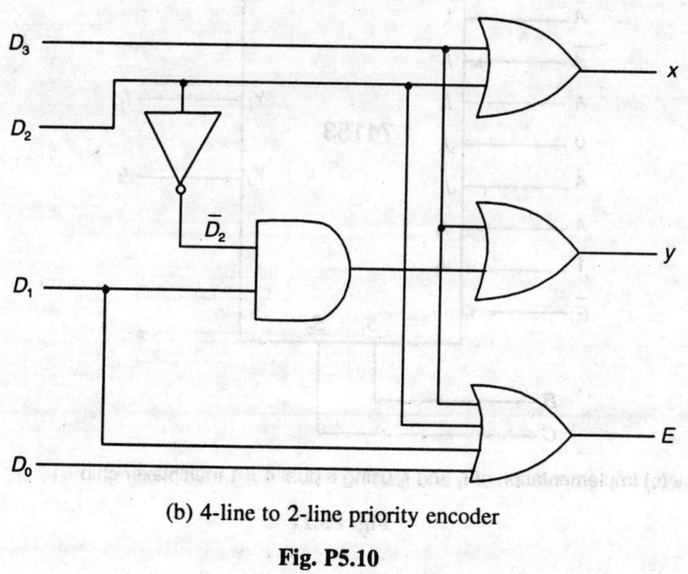

(b) 4-line to 2-line priority encoder

Fig. P5.10

Boolean expression for E can be obtained by ORing D_0, D_1, D_2 AND D_3. That is,

$$E = D_0 + D_1 + D_2 + D_3$$

Knowing the Boolean expressions for x, y and E a 4-line to 2-line priority encoder is constructed as shown in Fig. P5.10(b).

5.11 Implement the following two functions using a dual 4 : 1 multiplexer chip.

$$f_1(A, B, C) = \Sigma(1, 2, 4, 7)$$

$$f_2(A, B, C) = \Sigma(3, 5, 6, 7)$$

SOLUTION: A dual 4 : 1 multiplexer chip (74153) which has common selection lines is used here to implement the given functions.

The given functions are of 3-variables. Hence a 4 : 1 multiplexer with two selection lines is used to implement each function.

	I_0	I_1	I_2	I_3
$\bar{A}$	0	(1)	(2)	3
A	(4)	5	6	(7)
	A	$\bar{A}$	$\bar{A}$	A

(a) Implementation table of the function f_1

	J_0	J_1	J_2	J_3
$\bar{A}$	0	1	2	(3)
A	4	(5)	(6)	(7)
	0	A	A	1

(b) Implementation table of the function f_2

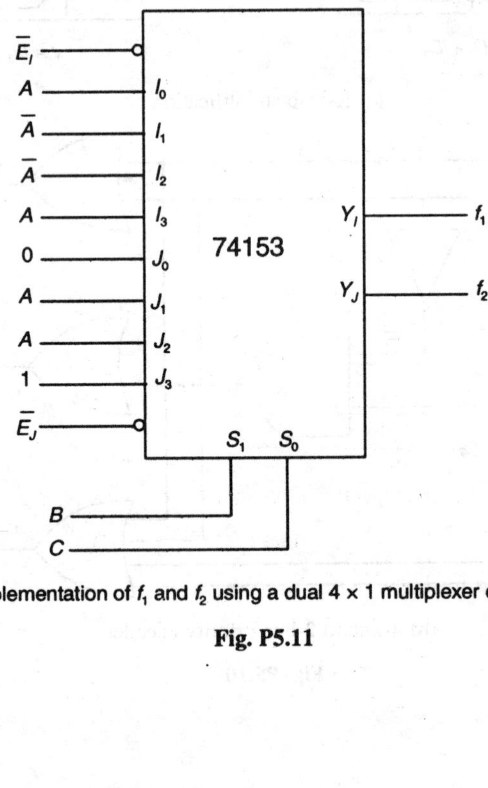

(c) Implementation of f_1 and f_2 using a dual 4 × 1 multiplexer chip

Fig. P5.11

Let the variables B and C be connected to the two selection lines S_1 and S_0, respectively. Now, let us prepare the implementation tables to find values for the multiplexer inputs.

5.12 Implement the following two functions using a dual 4 : 1 multiplexer chip.

$$f_1(A, B, C) = \Sigma\,(2, 5, 6, 7) + \Sigma d(1, 4)$$

$$f_2(A, B, C) = \Sigma\,(3, 4, 6, 7) + \Sigma d(1, 5)$$

SOLUTION: The given function includes don't care conditions. They may be considered as either 0 or 1. If considered as 1 these terms are encircled in implementation table to eliminate either A or $\bar{A}$. Rest of the procedure is similar to the previous problem.

	I_0	I_1	I_2	I_3
$\bar{A}$	0	(1)	(2)	3
A	4	(5)	(6)	(7)
	0	1	1	A

(a) Implementation table of the function f_1

	J_0	J_1	J_2	J_3
$\bar{A}$	0	1	2	(3)
A	(4)	5	(6)	(7)
	A	0	A	1

(b) Implementation table of the function f_2

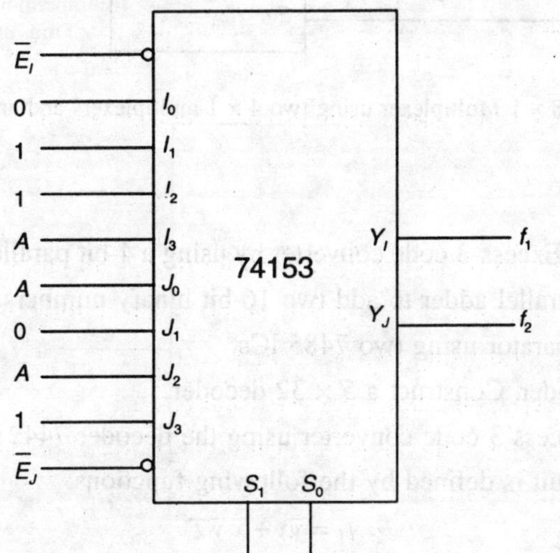

(c) Implementation of f_1 and f_2 using a dual 4 × 1 multiplexer chip

Fig. P5.12

5.13 Implement an 8 × 1 multiplexer using two 4 × 1 multiplexers and an OR gate.

SOLUTION: An implementation of an 8 × 1 multiplexer is shown in Fig. P5.13. The circuit has a total of 8 inputs. Here the enable input E is used as the most significant data-select bit (S_2).

Thus the circuit will have three selection lines S_2, S_1, and S_0. When $S_2 = 0$, the upper MUX is enabled, and one of the data inputs (A_0 through A_3) is selected by the S_1 S_0 inputs. When $S_2 = 1$, the lower MUX is enabled, and one of the data inputs (A_4 through A_7) is selected by the same S_1 S_0 inputs. The two multiplexer outputs (Y_1 and Y_2) are then combined in the OR gate to produce a single output Y.

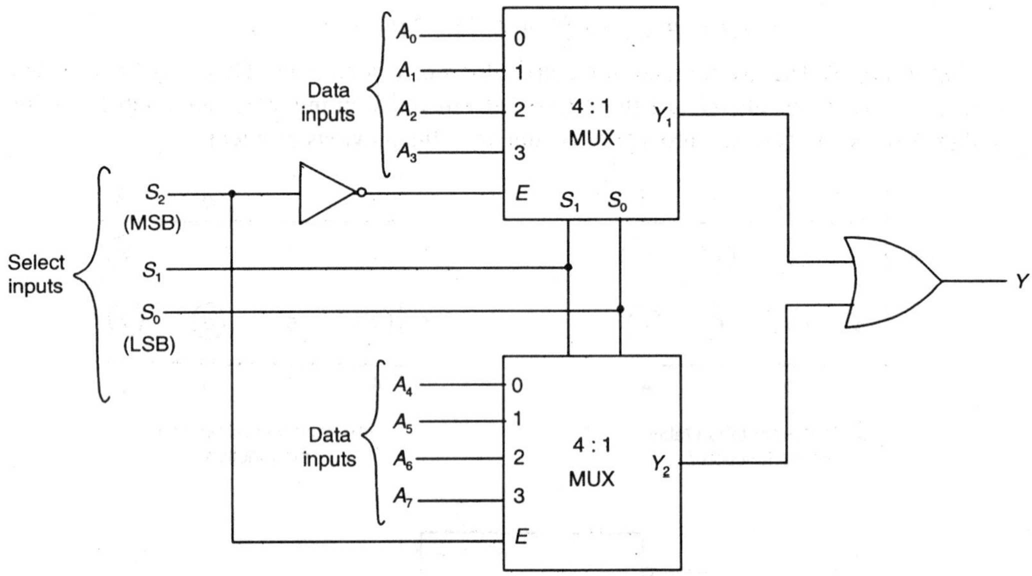

Fig. P5.13 8 × 1 Multiplexer using two 4 × 1 multiplexers and an OR gate

EXERCISES

5.1 Implement a BCD to Excess-3 code converter by using a 4-bit parallel adder MSI chip (74283).

5.2 Construct a binary parallel adder to add two 16-bit binary numbers using four 74283 ICs.

5.3 Design an 8-bit comparator using two 7485 ICs.

5.4 Given a 14 × 16 decoder. Construct a 5 × 32 decoder.

5.5 Realize a BCD to Excess-3 code converter using the decoder 7442 and four NAND gates.

5.6 A combinational circuit is defined by the following functions:

$$f_1 = \bar{y}x + \bar{x}\,\bar{y}\,\bar{z}$$

$$f_2 = x\bar{y} + \bar{x}y$$

Design the circuit with a decoder and external gates.

5.7 A combinational circuit is defined by the following functions:

$$f_1\,(x, y, z) = \Sigma\,(0, 1, 6)$$
$$f_2\,(x\ y, z) = \Sigma\,(0, 1, 6, 7)$$

Implement the combinational circuit using the decoder 74LS318 and external NAND gates.

5.8 Implement a 4 × 64 decoder using one 2 × 4 decoder and four 4 × 16 decoders.

5.9 Implement the following two functions using a dual 4 × 1 multiplexer chip (74153).

$$f_1(A, B, C) = ABC + \overline{A}\overline{B}C + \overline{A}B\overline{C} + A\overline{B}C$$

$$f_2(A, B, C) = \overline{A}\overline{B}C + \overline{A}\overline{B}\overline{C} + A\overline{B}C$$

5.10 Implement a 16 × 1 multiplexer using two 8 × 1 multiplexers and an OR gate.

Sequential Logic

6

So far we have discussed combinational logic circuits whose outputs at any instant are entirely dependent upon the inputs present at that time. Most digital systems in practice are sequential circuits which employ memory elements in addition to logic gates. Their outputs are a function of the inputs and the state of the memory elements.

Figure 6.1 shows a block diagram of a sequential circuit that combines combinational logic circuit with memory elements. The combinational circuit receives binary information from external inputs. These inputs, together with the present state of the memory elements, determine the binary value of the output terminals. From the process it is clear that the external outputs in a sequential circuit are a function of both its external inputs and the present state of the memory elements.

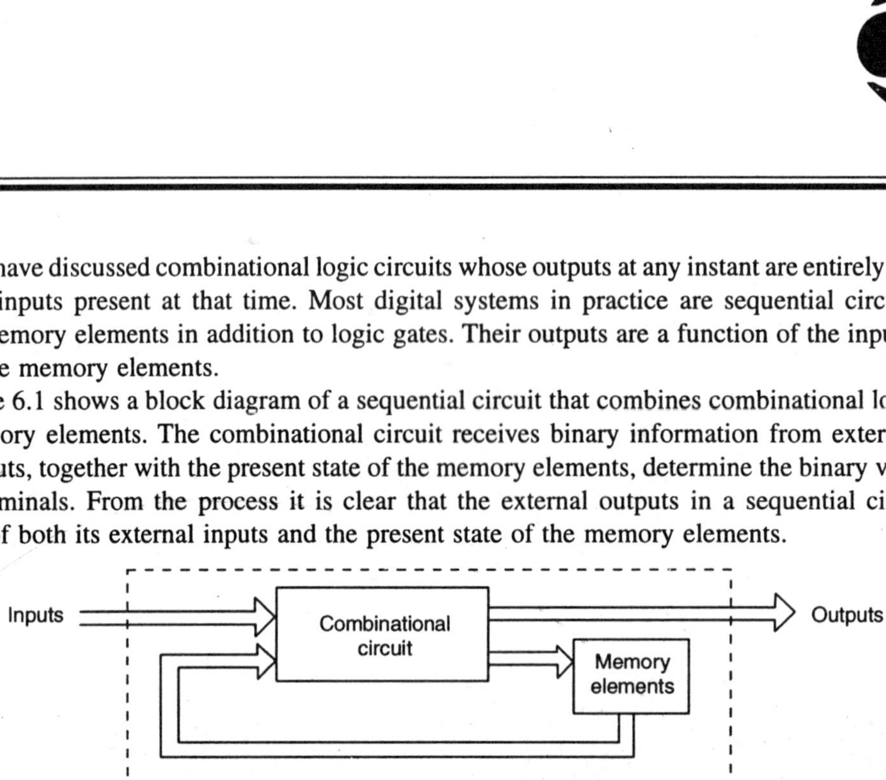

Fig. 6.1 Block diagram of a sequential circuit

There are two main types of sequential circuits:

(1) Synchronous sequential circuit, and (2) Asynchronous sequential circuit.

A synchronous sequential circuit is a system whose behaviour can be defined from the knowledge of its signals at discrete instants of time. On the other hand, an *asynchronous* sequential circuit is a system whose behaviour depends upon the order in which its input signals change and can be affected at any instant of time. Synchronous sequential circuits whose memory elements use clock as one of the inputs are called *clocked sequential circuits.* These are the circuits which are encountered most frequently.

The most important memory elements used in clocked sequential circuits are called flip-flops. In this chapter we will study the various types of flip-flops and their applications.

6.1 FLIP-FLOPS

A device that exhibits two different stable states is useful as a memory element. Any electrical circuit that has this characteristic falls into the category of devices commonly known as *flip-flops*. In general we can say that *flip-flop* is a bistable element or device that can flip into one stable state or flop back again to the other on command. It is like a toggle switch, which has two stable states: ON and OFF. It is either ON or OFF depending on the position of the switch. Thus it can be said that the switch has a memory. Similarly flip-flop is said to have memory which can store 1 bit of data. The flip-flop is also known by the names bistable multivibrator, binary and toggle.

Flip-flops operate in one of two modes: direct or clocked. Direct-mode flip-flops respond directly to applied inputs. On the other hand clocked-mode flip-flops respond to applied inputs only in presence of clock signal. We can make four basic categories of flip-flops as follows :

1. The latches } Direct-mode
2. The edge-triggered flip-flops
3. The pulse-triggered (master-slave) flip-flops } Clocked-mode
4. The data lock-out flip-flops.

A general logic symbol used for a flip-flop is drawn in Fig. 6.2. There are two possible output states:

1. $Q = 1$, $\overline{Q} = 0$; that is, HIGH or 1 or SET state.
2. $Q = 0$, $\overline{Q} = 1$; that is, LOW or 0 or RESET or CLEAR state.

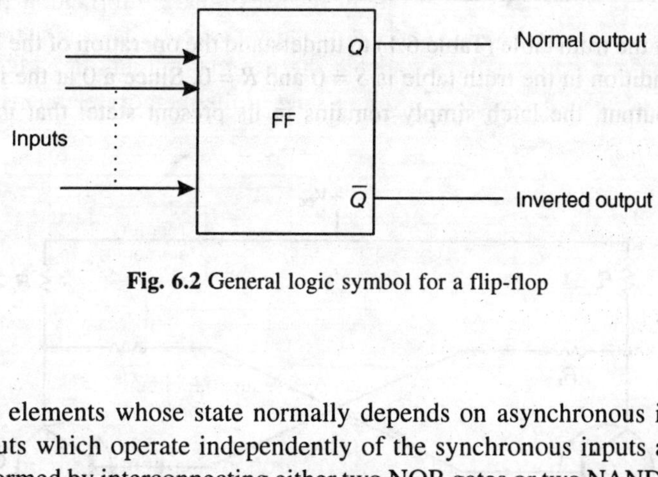

Fig. 6.2 General logic symbol for a flip-flop

6.2 LATCHES

Latches are bistable elements whose state normally depends on asynchronous inputs. Asynchronous inputs are those inputs which operate independently of the synchronous inputs and clock input.

A latch can be formed by interconnecting either two NOR gates or two NAND gates. The NOR gate version is called as NOR gate *S-R* latch and the NAND gate version is called as NAND gate *S-R* latch. Both the circuits are classified as asynchronous sequential circuits.

The NOR Gate *S-R* Latch

The construction of NOR gate latch is shown in Fig. 6.3. The two NOR gates are cross coupled so that the output of one gate is connected to one of the inputs of the other gate. The latch has two outputs, Q and $\overline{Q}$. Under Normal operation, these outputs will always be the inverse of each other. There are two latch inputs: the RESET (CLEAR) input is the input that resets Q to the 0 state; the SET input is the input that sets Q to the 1 state.

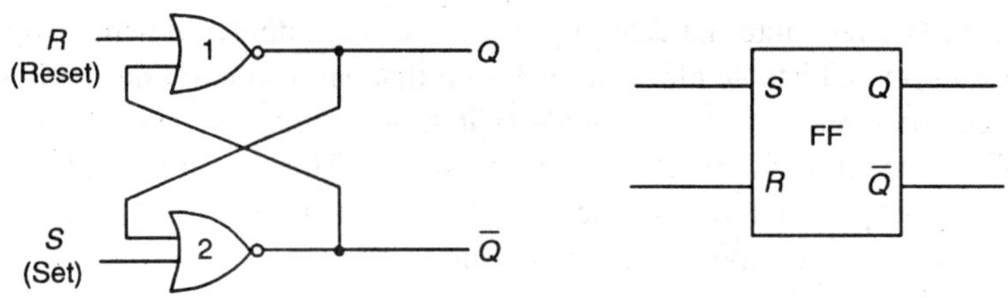

(a) Construction (b) Block symbol

Fig. 6.3 NOR gate *S-R* latch

Table 6.1 Truth table for NOR gate *S-R* latch

Inputs		Outputs		Comments
S	R	Q	$\bar{Q}$	
0	0	Previous state		No change
0	1	0	1	Latch resets
1	0	1	0	Latch sets
1	1	0	0	Invalid

Let us make use of the truth table (Table 6.1) to understand the operation of the NOR gate *S-R* latch.

The first input condition in the truth table is $S = 0$ and $R = 0$. Since a 0 at the input of a NOR gate has no effect on its output, the latch simply remains in its present state; that is, Q and $\bar{Q}$ remain unchanged.

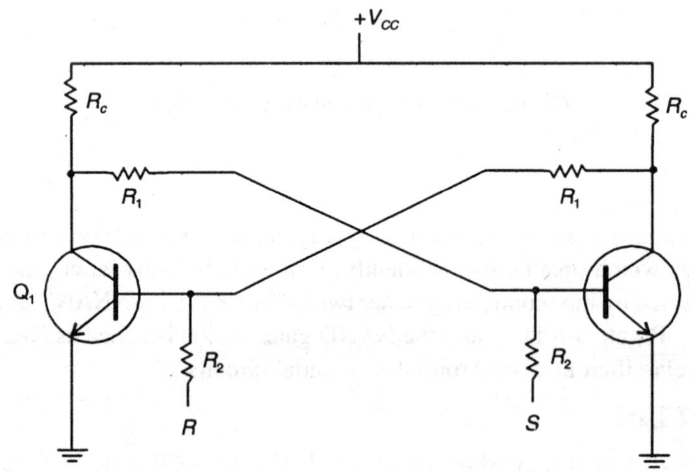

Fig. 6.4 The basic *S-R* flip-flop(latch)

The second input condition is $S = 0$ and $R = 1$ (which takes control of the NOR gate 1). This condition forces the output Q to go to 0 and $\bar{Q}$ to go to 1. Thus 1 at the R input is said to RESET the latch.

The third input condition is $S = 1$ (which takes control of the NOR gate 2) and $R = 0$. This condition forces the output Q to go to 1 and $\bar{Q}$ to go to 0. Thus 1 at the S input is said to SET the latch.

The last input condition in the truth table is $S = 1$ and $R = 1$. This condition is called as *race condition.* This is an invalid condition, which is never used as it leads to unpredictable operation. We can understand this clearly from the flip-flop (i.e., latch) circuit which consists of two interconnected transistors, as shown in Fig. 6.4.

In Fig. 6.4, if both the inputs R and S are at 1, then both the transistors (Q_1 and Q_2) saturate. Subsequently when both the inputs are at 0, the transistors are in race to come out of saturation. It is a *race* between the two transistors as to which one reaches the 'cut off' state first. The faster transistor with shorter saturation delay time wins the race and latches the circuit.

The NAND Gate *S-R* Latch

The construction of the NAND gate *S-R* latch is shown in Fig. 6.5. It is similar to the NOR gate *S-R* latch except that Q and $\bar{Q}$ outputs have reversed positions.

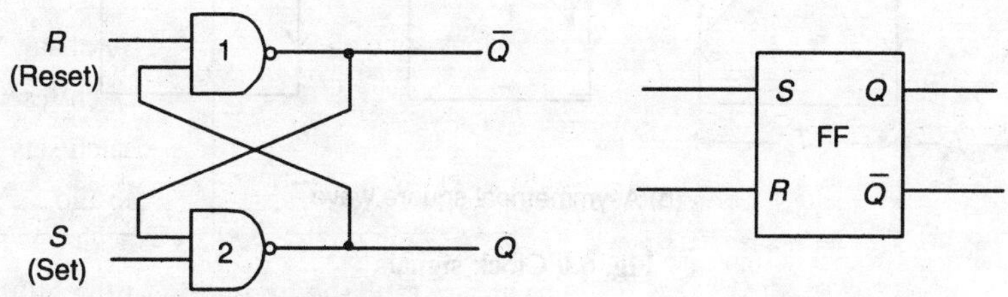

(a) Construction (b) Block symbol

Fig. 6.5 NAND gate *S-R* latch

As in the NOR gate *S-R* latch, in this latch two NAND gates are cross coupled. Notice that the truth table (Table 6.2) for the NAND gate *S-R* latch is different from that for the NOR gate *S-R* latch. To understand how this circuit functions, it has to be remembered that a '0' on any input to a NAND gate takes control of the gate to force its output to a '1'. Thus $S = 1$ and $R = 0$ (which takes control of the NAND gate 1) will reset the latch ($Q = 0$ and $\bar{Q} = 1$). And $S = 0$ (which takes control of the NAND gate 2 and $R = 1$) will set the latch ($Q = 1$ and $Q = 0$). When $S = 1$ and $R = 1$, the latch will remain in its previous state and the condition of race will occur when $S = 0$ and $R = 0$.

Table 6.2 Truth table for NAND gate *S-R* latch

Inputs		Outputs		Comments
S	R	Q	$\bar{Q}$	
1	1	Previous state		No change
1	0	0	1	Latch resets
0	1	1	0	Latch sets
0	0	1	1	Invalid

6.3 CLOCK SIGNALS AND CLOCKED-MODE FLIP-FLOPS

Clock Signals

In synchronous systems, it is generally necessary to have a time reference for various operations to take place within the system. A periodic waveform called a clock signal is generated to establish this time reference. The clock signal could be a symmetrical or an asymmetrical square wave as shown in Fig. 6.6.

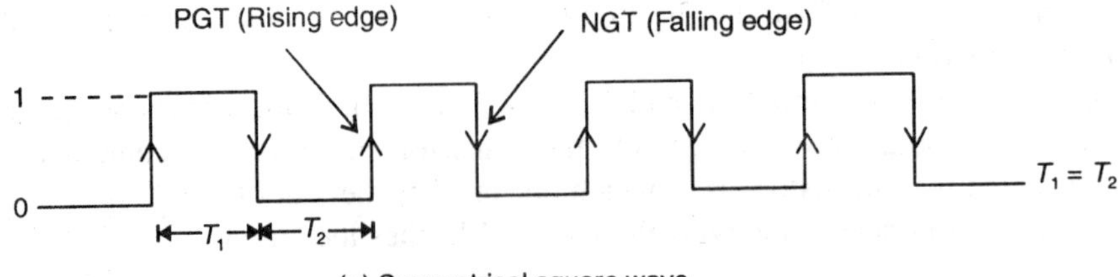

(a) Symmetrical square wave

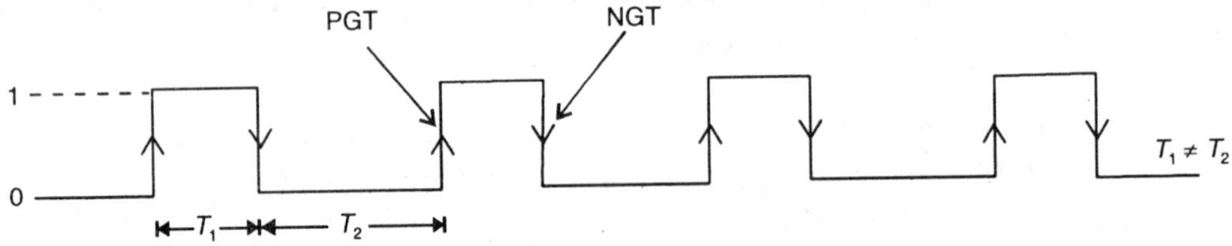

(b) Asymmetrical square wave

Fig. 6.6 Clock signals

In most of the clock driven components, the actions are initiated only when the clock makes a transition. As indicated in Fig. 6.6, there are two transitions: the positive-going transition (PGT), when the clock changes from 0 to 1 and the negative-going transition (NGT), when the clock changes from 1 to 0. A PGT is sometimes referred to as a *rising edge* and the NGT as *a falling edge.*

Clocked-Mode Flip-Flops

A *clocked-mode flip-flop* is one whose output can change states only in synchronization with the clock signal. To initiate the study of different clocked flip-flops, let us describe some of the features that are common to all of them.

Clocked-mode flip-flops have a clock input that is typically labeled *CLK, CK*, or *CP*. In most clocked flip-flops the *CLK* input is edge-triggered. It means that the flip-flop changes state only either

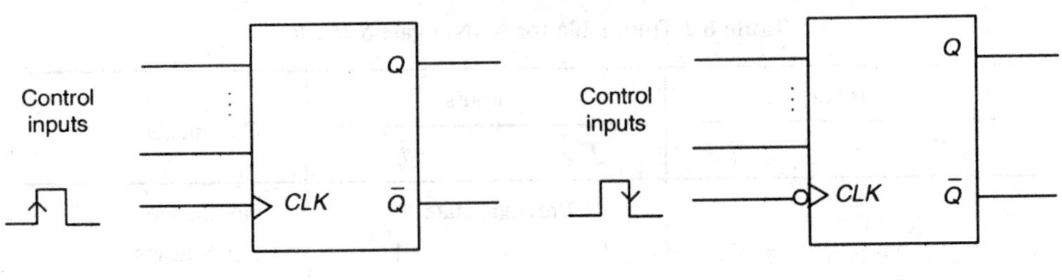

(a) Positive edge-triggered (b) Negative edge-triggered

Fig. 6.7 Clocked-mode flip-flops

at the PGT or at the NGT of the clock signal. A small triangle (▷) present at the clock input indicates a positive edge-triggering while the bubble with triangle (○▷) indicates a negative edge-triggering as shown in Fig. 6.7.

Clocked-mode flip-flops have one or more control inputs. A change in control inputs have no effect on the output until a clock transition accurs; that is changes in the output occur in synchronization with the clock. Hence they are called synchronous control inputs.

Finally, we can simply conclude that the control inputs control the WHAT (i.e., what state the output will go to); the *CLK* input determines the WHEN (i.e., at what instant the output has to change).

Setup Time and Hold Time

'Setup time' and 'hold time' are the two prerequisites that must be met if a clocked flip-flop is to operate satisfactorily. These are illustrated in Fig. 6.8 and 6.9 for a flip-flop that triggers on a PGT.

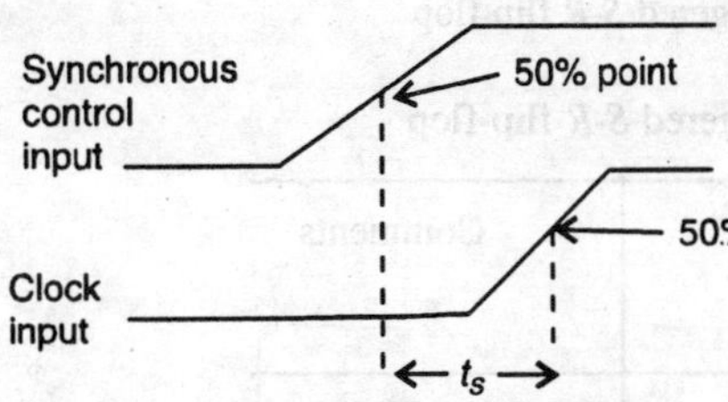

Fig. 6.8 Setup time (t_s)

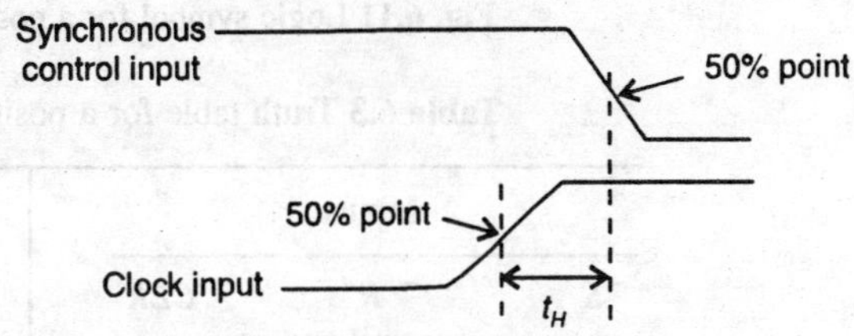

Fig. 6.9 Hold time (t_H)

Setup time (t_s): The synchronous input must be present for a certain minimum time before the transition is applied. This time is referred to as the *setup time.*

Hold time (t_H): The synchronous input must be present for a certain minimum time after the transition is applied. This time is referred to as the *hold time.*

IC manufacturers usually specify the minimum acceptable t_S and t_H values in the nanosecond range.

Edge-Triggered *S-R* Flip-flop

The Basic flip-flop, i.e., the *S-R* latch, is an asynchronous sequential circuit. By adding two AND gates to the basic circuit, it can be made to respond to inputs only during the occurance of a clock pulse. Figure 6.10 shows a logic diagram for an edge triggered *S-R* flip-flop.

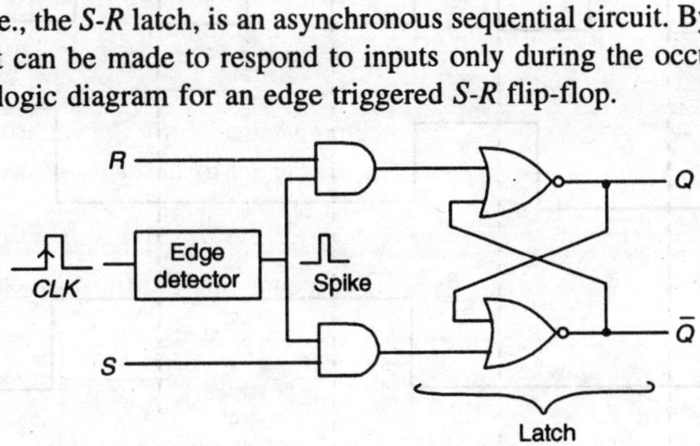

Fig. 6.10 Logic diagram for an edge-triggered *S-R* flip-flop

The two AND gates at the *S* and *R* inputs as shown in Fig. 6.10 will result in a flip flop that can trigger on a PGT. Thus $S = 1$, $R = 0$ and $CLK = 1$ will set the flip-flop. And $S = 0$, $R = 1$ and $CLK = 1$ will reset the flip-flop. An invalid condition occurs when both *S* and *R* equal to 1.

Figure 6.11 shows the logic symbol for an edge-triggered *S-R* flip-flop that is triggered by the PGT of the clock signal. The truth table for the flip-flop is given in Table 6.3. This table shows how the flip-flop output will respond to the PGT at the *CLK* input for various values of the inputs.

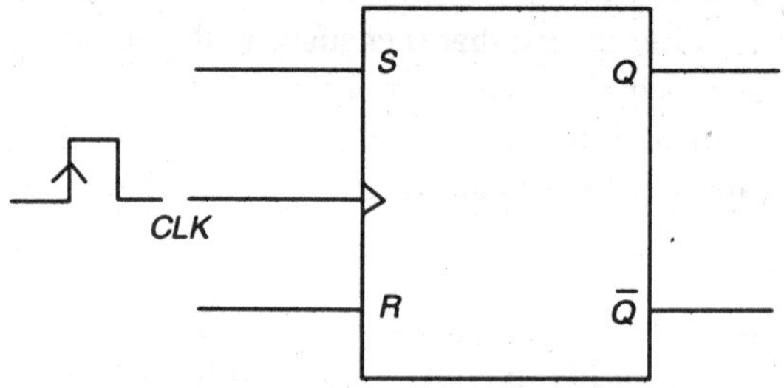

Fig. 6.11 Logic symbol for a positive edge-triggered *S-R* flip flop

Table 6.3 Truth table for a positive edge-triggered *S-R* flip-flop

Inputs			Output	Comments
S	*R*	*CLK*	*Q*	
0	0	↑	Q_P	No change
0	1	↑	0	RESET
1	0	↑	1	SET
1	1	↑	?	Invalid

Note: ↑ = PGT, Q_P = Prior output state

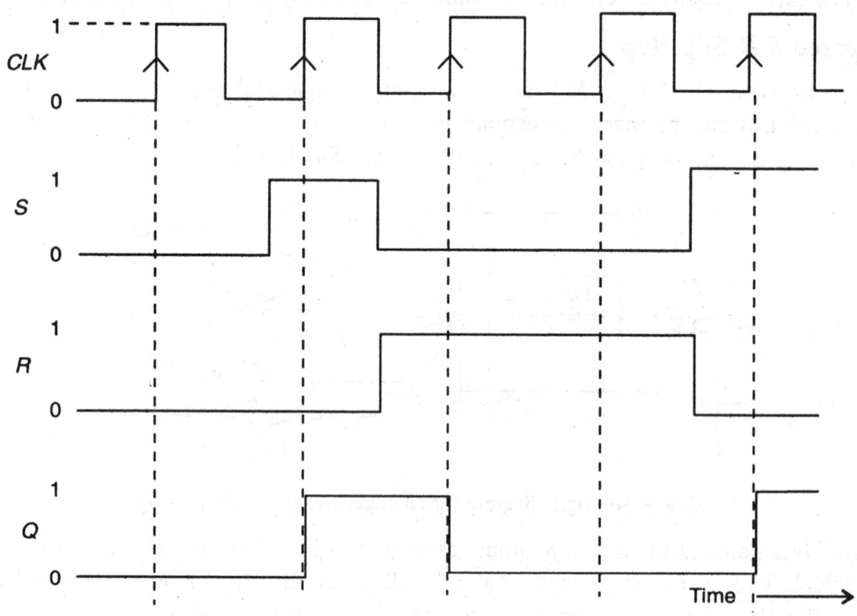

Fig. 6.12 Waveforms

The output Q of an edge-triggered S-R flip-flop for the inputs S and R and the clock is shown in Fig. 6.12. It is assumed that the flip-flop is initially RESET.

The Edge-Triggered *D* Flip-Flop

The S-R Flip-flop can be modified to prevent the invalid condition by simply introducing an inverter in one of the inputs as shown in Fig. 6.13. Such a circuit with only one input in addition to the clock is known as D flip-flop. It receives designation D from its ability to transfer 'data' into a flip-flop.

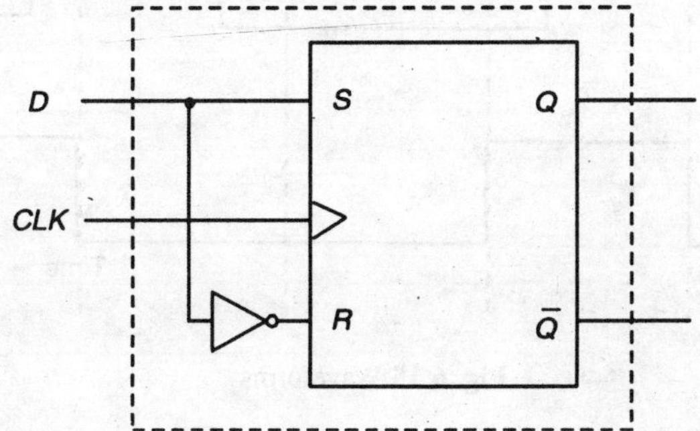

Fig. 6.13 A positive edge-triggered D flip-flop formed with an S-R flip-flop and inverter

The operation of the D flip-flop is very simple; Q will go to the same state that is present at the D input when a PGT occurs at CLK. It means if $D = 1$, a PGT will result in $Q = 1$ and if $D = 0$, a PGT will result in $Q = 0$. The operation of the positive edge-triggered D flip-flop is summarized in Table 6.4. Notice that the truth table is restricted to the middle two entries of the Table 6.3. The logic symbols for edge-triggered D flip-flops are shown in Fig. 6.14.

Table 6.4. Truth table for a positive edge-triggered D flip-flop

Inputs		Output	Comments
D	CLK	Q	
1	↑	1	SET
0	↑	0	RESET

Note: ↑ = PGT

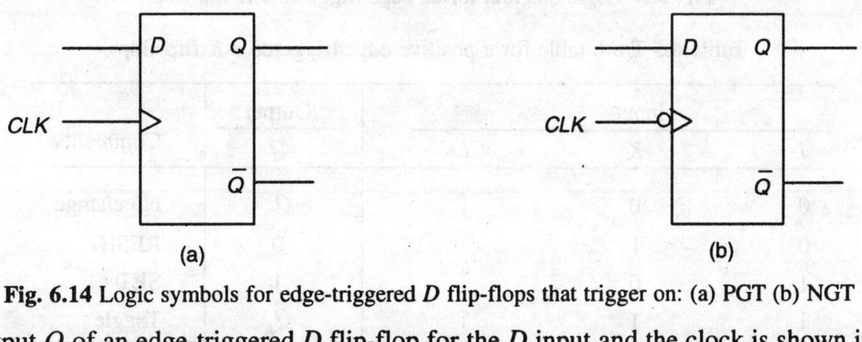

Fig. 6.14 Logic symbols for edge-triggered D flip-flops that trigger on: (a) PGT (b) NGT

The output Q of an edge-triggered D flip-flop for the D input and the clock is shown in Fig. 6.15. It is assumed that the flip-flop is initially RESET.

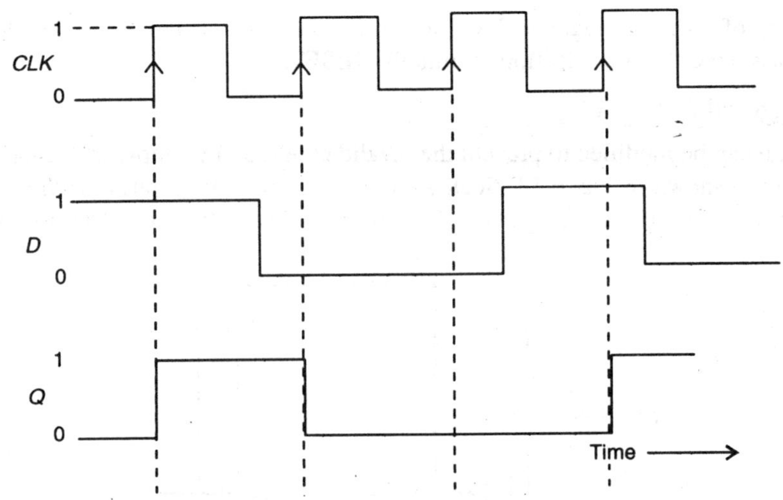

Fig. 6.15 Waveforms

Edge-Triggered *J-K* Flip-Flop

The *J-K* flip-flop is a versatile and the most widely used flip-flop. It has two data inputs, *J* and *K*, in addition to the clock. Inputs *J* and *K* behave like inputs *S* and *R* to set and reset the flip-flop. Note that *J* corresponds to *S* and *K* corresponds to *R*.

The *S-R* flip-flop can be modified to form a *J-K* flip-flop. Figure 6.16 shows a logic diagram for an edge-triggered *J-K* flip-flop.

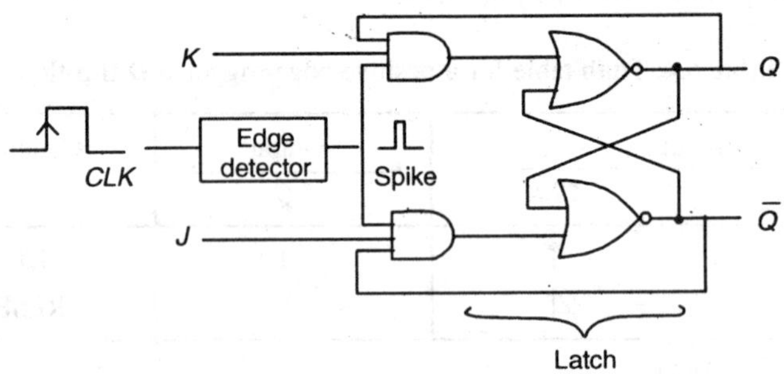

Fig. 6.16 Logic diagram for an edge-triggered *J-K* flip-flop

Table 6.5 Truth table for a positive edge-triggered *J-K* flip-flop

Inputs			Output	Comments
J	*K*	*CLK*	*Q*	
0	0	↑	Q_p	No change
0	1	↑	0	RESET
1	0	↑	1	SET
1	1	↑	$\bar{Q}_p$	Toggle

Note: ↑ = PGT, Q_p = Prior output state

The truth table for the *J-K* flip-flop is given in Table 6.5. As shown in the truth table, the logical operation of the *J-K* flip-flop is identical to that of the *S-R* flip-flop in SET, RESET and No change conditions. The difference in operation occurs when both *J* and *K* are equal to 1. When both *J* and *K* are '1', the clock spike is transmitted through one AND gate only—the one whose input is connected to the flip-flop output which is presently equal to 1. Thus, if $Q = 1$, the output of the upper AND gate becomes 1 upon application of a clock spike, and the flip-flop is cleared (i.e., $Q = 0$ and $\bar{Q} = 1$). Now, as $\bar{Q} = 1$, the output of the lower AND gate becomes 1 upon the application of next clock spike, and the flip-flop is set (i.e, $Q = 1$ and $\bar{Q} = 0$). Thus the flip-flop changes to the opposite state, on each successive clock. This is called *toggle* operation.

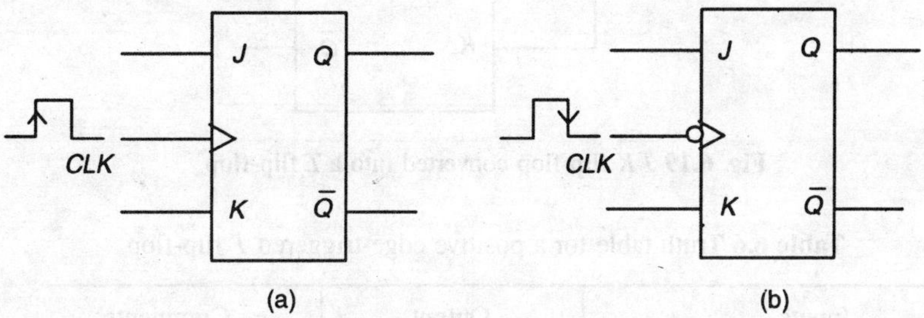

Fig. 6.17 Logic symbols for edge-triggered *J-K* flip-flops that change on: (a) PGT (b) NGT

Fig. 6.17 shows logic symbols for edge-triggered *J-K* flip-flops.

The output *Q* of an edge-triggered *J-K* flip-flop for the inputs *J* and *K* and the clock is shown in Fig. 6.18. It is assumed that the flip-flop is initially RESET.

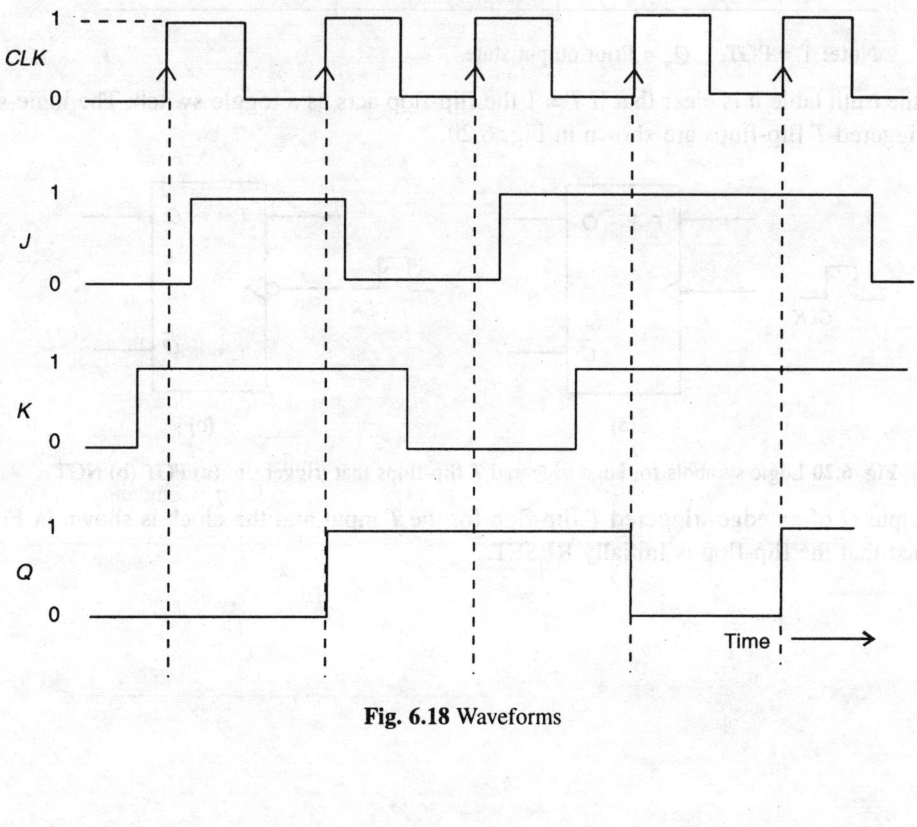

Fig. 6.18 Waveforms

Edge-Triggered T Flip-Flop

The T flip-flop is a single-input version of the J-K flip-flop. As shown in Fig. 6.19, the T flip-flop is obtained from a J-K flip-flop if both the inputs J and K are tied together. It receives designation T from its ability to 'toggle'. Its truth table is given in Table 6.6.

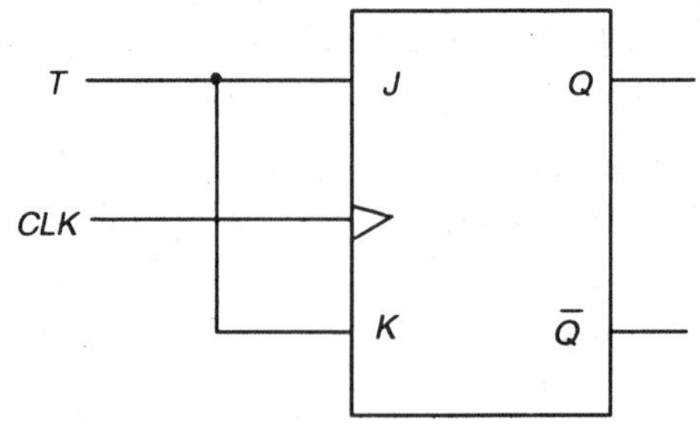

Fig. 6.19 J-K flip-flop converted into a T flip-flop

Table 6.6 Truth table for a positive edge-triggered T flip-flop

Inputs		Output	Comments
T	CLK	Q	
0	↑	Q_p	No change
1	↑	$\bar{Q}_p$	Toggle

Note: ↑ = PGT, Q_p = Prior output state

From the truth table it is clear that if $T = 1$ the flip-flop acts as a toggle switch. The logic symbols for edge triggered T flip-flops are shown in Fig. 6.20.

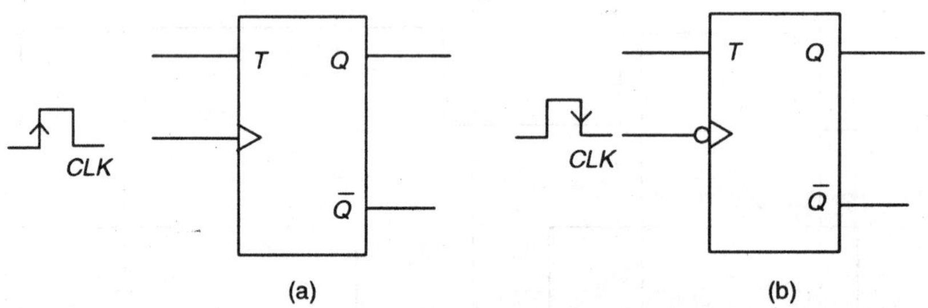

Fig. 6.20 Logic symbols for edge triggered T flip-flops that trigger on: (a) PGT (b) NGT

The output Q of an edge-triggered T flip-flop for the T input and the clock is shown in Fig. 6.21. It is assumed that the flip-flop is initially RESET.

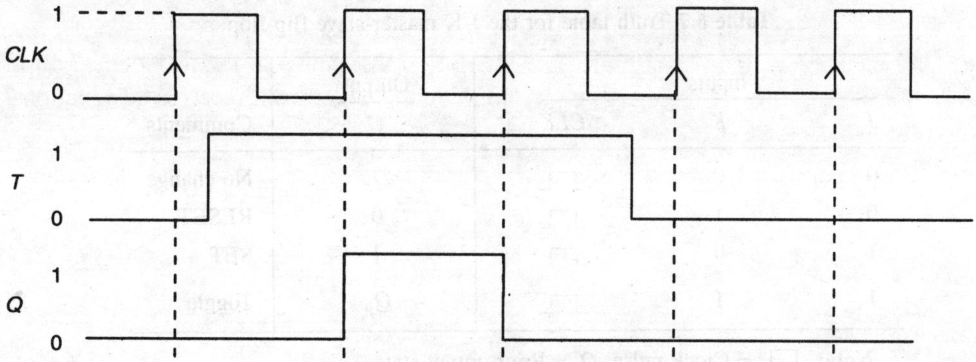

Fig. 6.21 Waveforms

J-K Master-Slave Flip-Flop

A master-slave or pulse-triggered flip-flop is constructed from two separate flip-flops. One serves as a master and the other as a slave. The master-slave flip-flop operates from a complete clock-pulse. It means that the data present at the inputs is transmitted to the master flip-flop on the leading edge of a pulse and is held there until the trailing edge of the clock pulse occurs, after which it is allowed to pass through to the slave flip-flop. As with the edge-triggered flip-flops, there are four basic types of master-slave flip-flops: *S-R*, *D*, *J-K* and *T*. Let us consider the *J-K* master-slave flip-flop which is the most popular and useful.

The logic diagram of a *J-K* master-slave flip-flop is shown in Fig. 6.22.

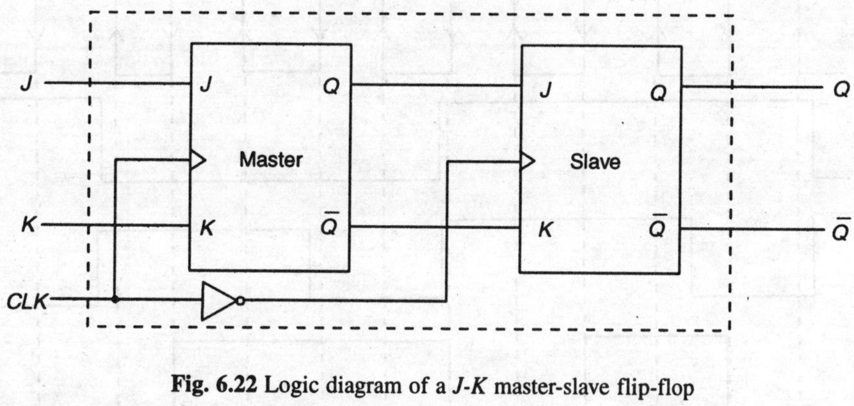

Fig. 6.22 Logic diagram of a *J-K* master-slave flip-flop

The truth table for the *J-K* master-slave flip-flop is given in Table 6.7.

The function of the flip-flop is as follows. The master responds to its *J* and *K* inputs before the slave. If $J = 1$ and $K = 0$ during PGT of the clock pulse, the output *Q* of the master switches to 1. This $Q = 1$ derives the *J* input of the slave. When the NGT of the clock pulse occurs, the slave now switches its output *Q* to 1. It means slave copies the master on the NGT. Similarly it functions when $J = 0$ and $K = 1$ and the slave switches its output *Q* to 0. If both *J* and *K* inputs are equal to 1, the master toggles on the PGT and the slave then toggles on the NGT.

Table 6.7 Truth table for the J-K master-slave flip-flop

Inputs			Output	
J	*K*	*CLK*	*Q*	Comments
0	0	⎍	Q_p	No change
0	1	⎍	0	RESET
1	0	⎍	1	SET
1	1	⎍	$\bar{Q}_p$	Toggle

Note: ⎍ = Clock pulse, Q_p = Prior output state

Logic symbols for a *J-K* master-slave flip-flop are given in Fig. 6.23.

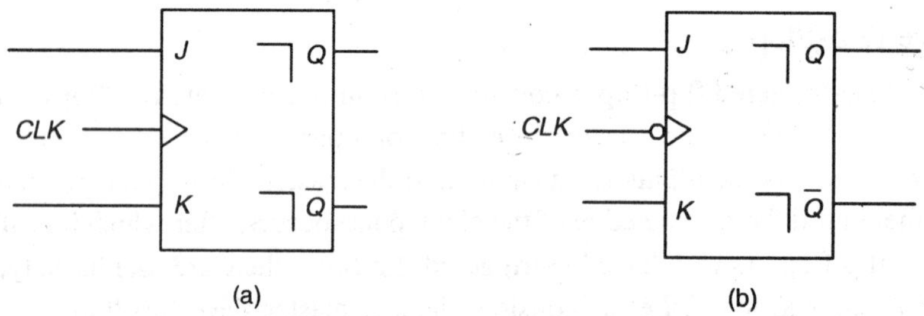

Fig. 6.23 Logic symbols for a *J-K* master-slave flip-flops that trigger on: (a) Positive pulse (b) Negative pulse

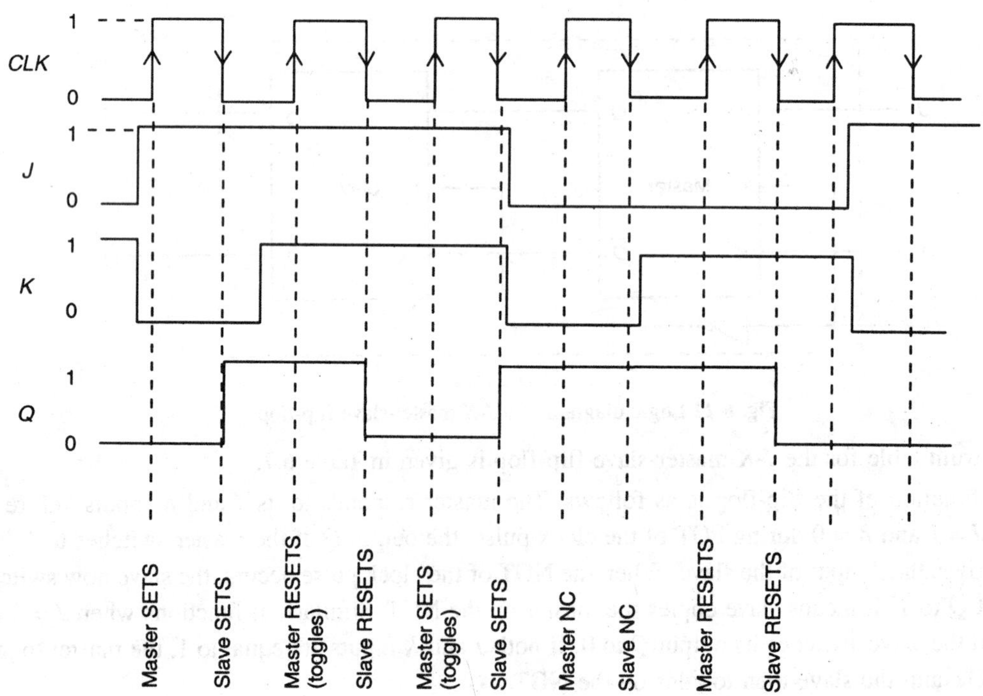

Fig. 6.24 Waveforms

The output Q of a J-K master-slave flip-flop for the inputs J and K and the clock is shown in Fig. 6.24. It is assumed that the flip-flop is initially RESET.

Asynchronous Inputs

The inputs S, R, J, K, D and T of the clocked flip-flop are called *synchronous inputs*, because their effect on the flip-flop output is synchronized with the clock input. Most clocked flip-flops also have *asynchronous inputs* that affect the state of the flip-flop independent of the clock. These inputs are normally labeled as preset (*PRE*) and clear (*CLR*), or direct set (S_D) and direct reset (R_D) by some manufacturers. An active level on the preset input will SET the flip-flop, and an active level on the clear input will RESET the flip-flop, overriding all the synchronous inputs. When these inputs are active-LOW an overbar is used to indicate their status (i.e., $\overline{PRE}$ and $\overline{CLR}$) and a bubble is used in the flip-flop symbol.

The truth table (Table 6.8) shows how these inputs affect the flip-flop response.

Table 6.8. Truth table showing the affect of asynchronous inputs on the flip-flop response

$\overline{PRE}$	$\overline{CLR}$	Flip-flop response
1	1	Clocked operation
0	1	$Q = 1$
1	0	$Q = 0$
0	0	Not used

Note: For clocked operation, preset and clear inputs should be kept at 1 (i.e. HIGH).

Figure 6.25 shows the logic diagram for an edge-triggered J-K flip-flop with $\overline{PRE}$ and $\overline{CLR}$ inputs.

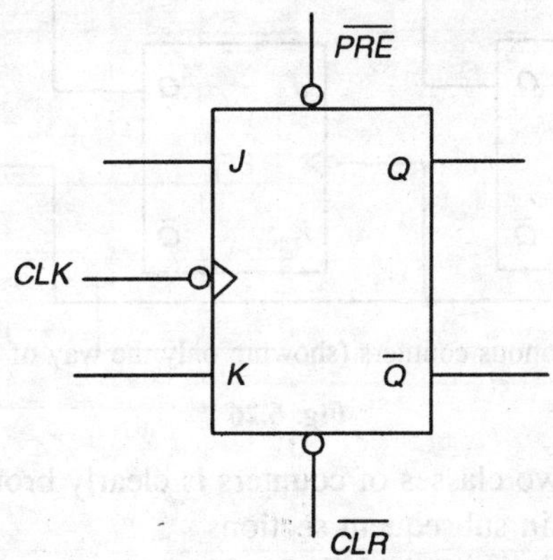

Fig. 6.25 Logic symbol for a J-K flip-flop with active-LOW asynchronous inputs

6.4 COUNTERS

A *counter* is a sequential logic circuit that can be used to count the number of electronic events, such as pulses, by progressing through a sequence of binary states. Flip-flops can be connected together to form a counter. The number of flip-flops used and the way in which they are connected determine the number of states and the sequence of states that the counter goes through in each complete cycle. If, starting from some initial state, the counter returns to that initial state after N cycles of the input clock, the counter is called *MODULO-N* or simply *MOD-N* counter. If a counter has n flip-flops and if the counter advances through every possible state, the counter will have maximum number of states and its MOD number is equal to 2^n. Counters can also be designed to have a number of states in their sequence that is less than 2^n. The resulting sequence is called a *truncated* sequence. Note that the maximum count of a binary counter is $2^n–1$; the number of stable states is 2^n, where n represents the number of flip-flops. For instance, the 3 flip-flop binary counter will have a maximum count of $2^3–1$, which equals 7; the number of stable states equals to $2^3 = 8$ (000 through 111) and hence it can be referred to as a MOD-8 counter.

Counters are classified into two broad categories in accordance with the way they are clocked. (1) Asynchronous (Ripple) counters, (2) Synchronous counters.

In asynchronous counters, all the flip-flops are not clocked simultaneously. Only the first flip-flop is clocked by the external clock pulse, and then each successive flip-flop is clocked by the output of the previous flip-flop.

In synchronous counters, all the flip-flops are clocked simultaneously by the external clock pulse.

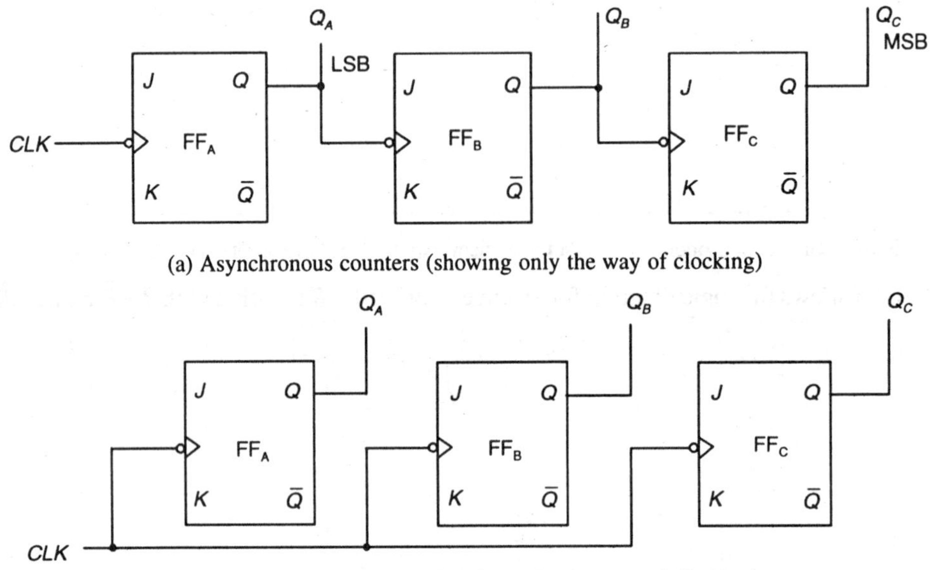

(a) Asynchronous counters (showing only the way of clocking)

(b) Synchronous counters (showing only the way of clocking)

Fig. 6.26

The difference between the two classes of counters is clearly brought out in Fig. 6.26. These two classes of counters are discussed in subsequent sections.

In a counter, the sequence of states may follow a binary count or any other sequence of states. A counter that follows the binary sequence is called a *binary counter*. A counter, whether it is asynchronous or synchronous, can be an up-counter, a down counter or an up-down counter. In an *up-counter*, the binary count is incremented by 1 with every input count pulse. In a *down-counter*, the binary count is decremented by 1 with every input count pulse. In an up-down counter the binary count is either incremented or decremented by 1 according to the state of a direction control input. For instance, the MOD-16 up-counter will count from 0000 up to 1111, whereas the down-counter will count from 1111 down to 0000.

6.5 ASYNCHRONOUS (RIPPLE) COUNTERS*

The binary ripple counter is simple and straight-forward in operation and construction. It consists of a series connection of *T* or *J-K* flip-flops, with the output of each flip-flop connected to the *CLK* input of the next higher-order flip-flop. The flip-flop holding the LSB receives the incoming count pulses.

3-bit Asynchronous Binary Up-Counter

Figure 6.27(a) shows a 3-bit asynchronous binary up-counter. Notice that all flip-flops are connected for toggle operation. Initially all flip-flops are in the logic-0 state, that is, $Q_A = Q_B = Q_c = 0$. The clock pulses are applied only to the *CLK* input of FF_A. Thus, FF_A will toggle (changes to its opposite state) at the NGT of the input clock pulse. The normal output of FF_A, that is, Q_A acts as the *CLK* input for FF_B, and so FF_B will toggle at the NGT of Q_A. Similarly Q_B acts as the *CLK* input for FF_C, and so FF_C will toggle at the NGT of Q_B. (Flip-flop outputs Q_C, Q_B, Q_A) represent a 3-bit binary number with Q_C as the MSB). Before arrival of the eighth clock pulse all flip-flops are in the 1 state. Clock pulse 8 causes Q_A, Q_B and Q_C to go to 0 state in turn. It means that the counter has gone through one complete cycle (000 through 111) and has recycled back to 000.

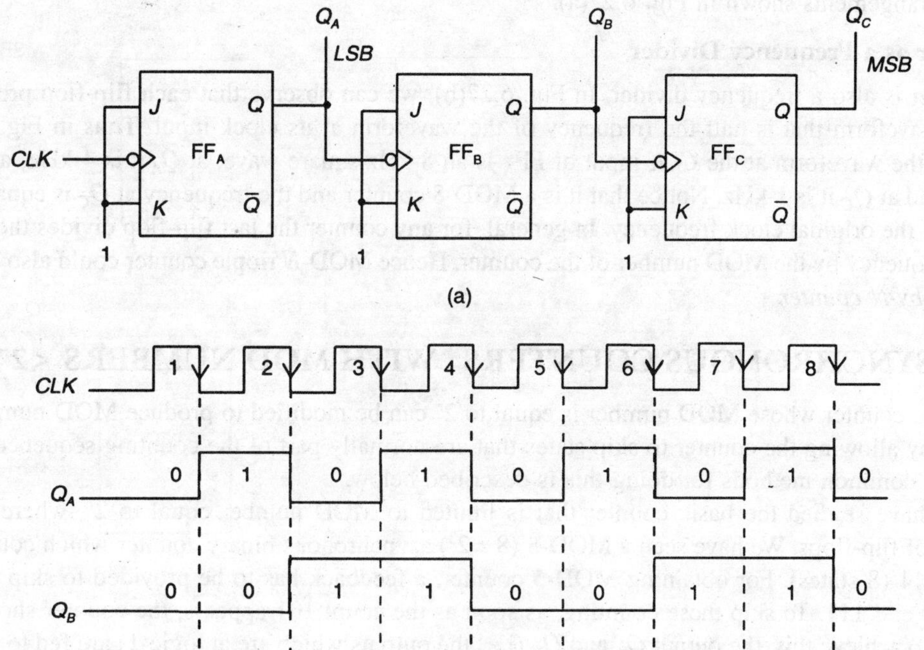

Fig. 6.27 3-bit asynchronous binary up-counter with its timing diagram for one complete cycle

Table 6.9 shows the sequence of counter states.

---

*Also called serial counters.

Table 6.9 Count sequence for 3-bit asynchronous binary up-counter

Count	Output		
	Q_C	Q_B	Q_A
0	0	0	0
1	0	0	1
2	0	1	0
3	0	1	1
4	1	0	0
5	1	0	1
6	1	1	0
7	1	1	1

The counter with MOD number = 2^n can be easily obtained by connecting 'n' number of flip-flops in the arrangements shown in Fig. 6.27(a).

Counter as a Frequency Divider

A counter is also a frequency divider. In Fig. 6.27(b), we can observe that each flip-flop provides an output waveform that is half the frequency of the waveform at its clock input. Thus in Fig. 6.27(b), suppose the waveform at the *CLK* input of FF_A is an 8-kHz square wave, at Q_A it is 4-kHz, at Q_B it is 2-kHz and at Q_C it is 1-kHz. Notice that it is a MOD-8 counter and the frequency at Q_C is equal to one-eighth of the original clock frequency. In general, for any counter the last flip-flop divides the original clock frequency by the MOD number of the counter. Hence MOD-*N* ripple counter could also be called a *divide-by-N counter.*

6.6 ASYNCHRONOUS COUNTERS* WITH MOD NUMBERS $<2^n$

The basic counter whose MOD number is equal to 2^n can be modified to produce MOD numbers less than 2^n by allowing the counter to skip states that are normally part of the counting sequence. One of the most common methods for doing this is described below.

We have studied the basic counter that is limited to MOD number equal to 2^n, where n is the number of flip-flops. We have seen a MOD-8 ($8 = 2^3$) asynchronous binary counter which counts from 000 to 111 (8 states). For obtaining MOD-5 counter, a feedback has to be provided to skip counting 101, 110 and 111. To skip these counting, as soon as the count 101 appears, the counter should reset to 000. To achieve this, the output Q_A and Q_C (i.e., the outputs which are at logic-1) are fed to a NAND gate; the NAND gate output is fed to all flip-flops through clear (CLR) input, as shown in Fig. 6.28(a), so that the counter is reset to 000.

Table 6.10 helps to understand the operation of the counter.

Note that there is a *glitch* on the Q_A waveform. The cause for this glitch is the momentary occurance of the 101 state before clearing. This glitch is very narrow and so would not produce any visible indication. Also note that the Q_C output has a frequency equal to one-fifth of the input clock frequency.

*Also called truncated counters.

Table 6.10 Count sequence for MOD-5 asynchronous binary counter

Count	Output Q_C	Q_B	Q_A	
0	0	0	0	
1	0	0	1	
2	0	1	0	
3	0	1	1	
4	1	0	0	
5	1	0	1	(temporary state)*
0	0	0	0	

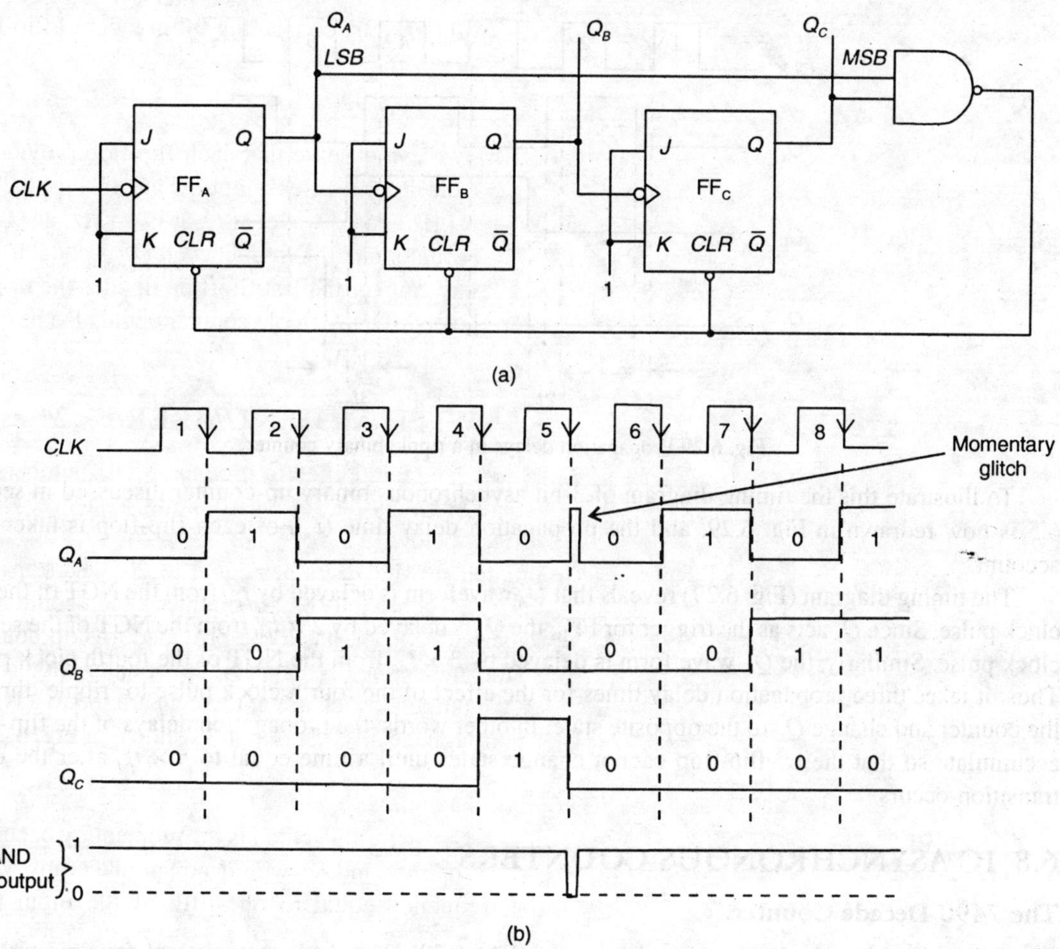

Fig. 6.28 MOD-5 asynchronous binary counter and its timing diagram

*It remains only for few nanoseconds and then clears the counter.

The counter with any desired MOD number (< 2^n) can be obtained in a similar way as described above. However, in general, the asynchronous counter can be designed using the following procedure.

Design Procedure to Construct Asynchronous (Ripple) Counters

1. Find the smallest number of flip-flops such that $2^n \geq$ MOD number and connect them as a ripple counter. If 2^n = MOD number, then do not go for the following steps (Note n = Number of flip-flops).
2. Connect all flip-flop outputs for which $Q = 1$ at the count equal to MOD number, as inputs to a NAND gate if *CLR* input is active low (or to an AND gate if *CLR* input is active high).
3. Connect the NAND/AND gate output to the clear (*CLR*) inputs of all the flip-flops.

6.7 PROPAGATION DELAY IN RIPPLE COUNTERS

The major disadvantage of the ripple counters is that the propagation delays of the flip-flops add up as the transition 'ripples' through the chain of flip-flops.

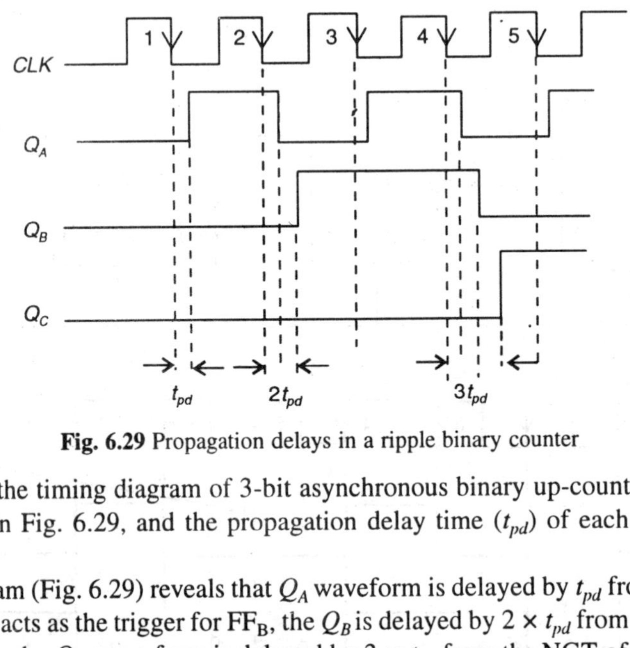

Fig. 6.29 Propagation delays in a ripple binary counter

To illustrate this the timing diagram of 3-bit asynchronous binary up-counter discussed in section 6.5 is now redrawn in Fig. 6.29, and the propagation delay time (t_{pd}) of each flip-flop is taken into account.

The timing diagram (Fig. 6.29) reveals that Q_A waveform is delayed by t_{pd} from the NGT of the first clock pulse. Since Q_A acts as the trigger for FF_B, the Q_B is delayed by $2 \times t_{pd}$ from the NGT of the second clock pulse. Similarly, the Q_C wave form is delayed by $3 \times t_{pd}$ from the NGT of the fourth clock pulse. Thus, it takes three propagation delay times for the effect of the fourth clock pulse to 'ripple' through the counter and change Q_C to the opposite state. In other words, the propagation delays of the flip-flops accumulate so that the nth flip-flop cannot change states until a time equal to $n \times t_{pd}$ after the clock transition occurs.

6.8 IC ASYNCHRONOUS COUNTERS

The 7490 Decade Counter

The 7490 is a 4-bit, ripple-type decade counter (Fig. 6.30). The device consists of four master-slave flip-flops internally connected to provide a divide-by-2 counter and a divide-by-5 counter. Each counter has a separate clock input.

A gated AND asynchronous Master Reset ($MR_1 \cdot MR_2$) is provided which overrides both clocks and resets (clears) all the flip-flops. Similarly a gate AND asynchronous Master Set ($MS_1 \cdot MS_2$) is provided which overrides the clocks and the MR inputs, setting the outputs to BCD count of 9 (i.e., 1001).

Since the output from the divide-by-2 counter is not internally connected to the succeeding stages, the device may be operated in various counting modes.

1. When used as a BCD (8421) counter, the output Q_0 must be externally connected to the input $\overline{CP_1}$. The input count pulses are applied at the input $\overline{CP_0}$.
2. If a symmetrical bi-quinary divide-by-10 counter is desired, the output Q_3 must be externally connected to the input $\overline{CP_0}$. The input count pulses are then applied to the $\overline{CP_1}$ input and a divide-by-10 square wave is obtained at output Q_0.
3. When used as a divide-by-2 counter and divide-by-5 counter, no external interconnections are required. The first flip-flop is used as a binary element for the divide-by-2 function ($\overline{CP_0}$ as the input and Q_0 as the output). The $\overline{CP_1}$ input is used to obtain divide-by-5 operation at the output Q_3.

The logic diagram for the 7490 is given in Fig. 6.30. The pinout and logic symbol are shown in Fig. 6.31. The truth table for different modes are given in Table 6.11.

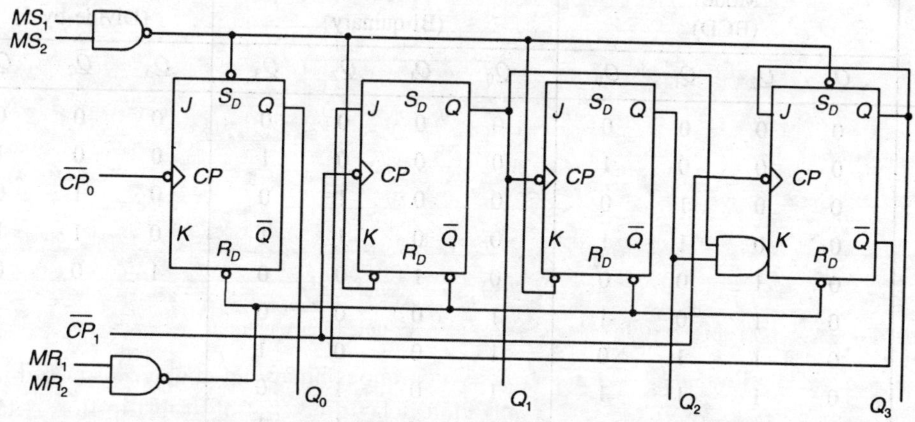

Fig. 6.30 Logic diagram for 7490

Note: • $\overline{CP_0}, \overline{CP_1} \rightarrow$ Clock inputs. • $\overline{R_D}, \overline{S_D} \rightarrow$ Reset and Set inputs.

• The J and K inputs shown without connection are for reference only and are functionally at logic-1.

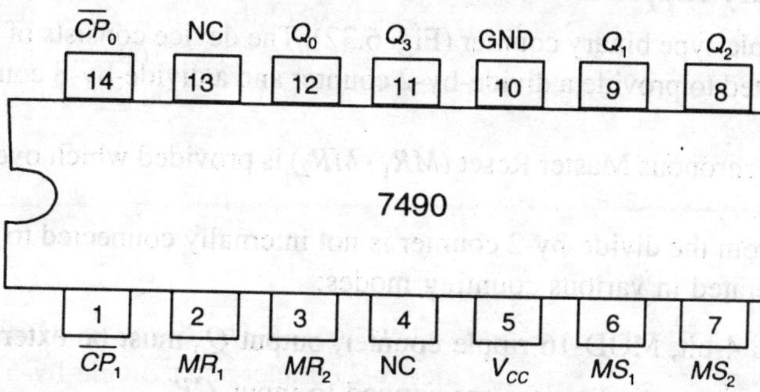

Fig. 6.31 (a) The pinout of 7490

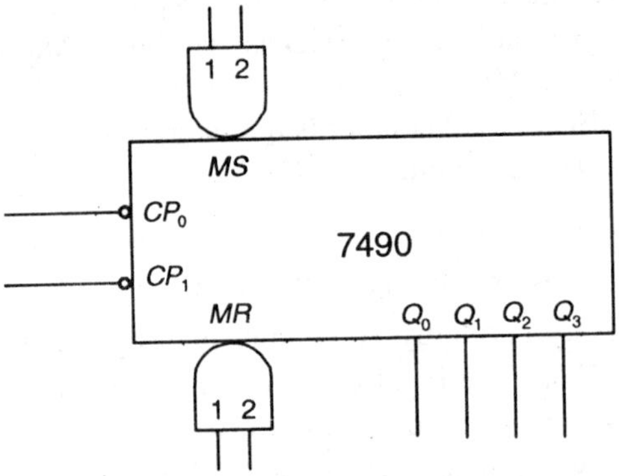

Fig. 6.31 (b) Logic symbol for 7490

Table 6.11 Truth table for 7490

	Mode1 (BCD)				Mode 2 (Bi-quinary)				Mode 3 (Divide-by-5)		
Count	Q_3	Q_2	Q_1	Q_0	Q_0	Q_1	Q_2	Q_3	Q_3	Q_2	Q_1
0	0	0	0	0	0	0	0	0	0	0	0
1	0	0	0	1	0	0	0	1	0	0	1
2	0	0	1	0	0	0	1	0	0	1	0
3	0	0	1	1	0	0	1	1	0	1	1
4	0	1	0	0	0	1	0	0	1	0	0
5	0	1	0	1	1	0	0	0			
6	0	1	1	0	1	0	0	1			
7	0	1	1	1	1	0	1	0			
8	1	0	0	0	1	0	1	1			
9	1	0	0	1	1	1	0	0			

The 7493 4-Bit Binary Ripple Counter

The 7493 is a 4-bit, ripple-type binary counter (Fig. 6.32). The device consists of four master-slave flip-flops internally connected to provide a divide-by-2 counter and a divide-by-8 counter. Each counter has a separate clock input.

A gated AND asynchronous Master Reset $(MR_1 \cdot MR_2)$ is provided which overrides both clocks and resets all the flip-flops.

Since the output from the divide-by-2 counter is not internally connected to the succeeding stages, the device may be operated in various counting modes:

1. When used as a 4-bit, MOD-16 ripple counter, output Q_0 must be externally connected to the input $\overline{CP_1}$. The input count pulses are applied to input $\overline{CP_0}$.

2. When used as a 3-bit, MOD-8 ripple counter, the input count pulses are applied to input $\overline{CP_1}$.

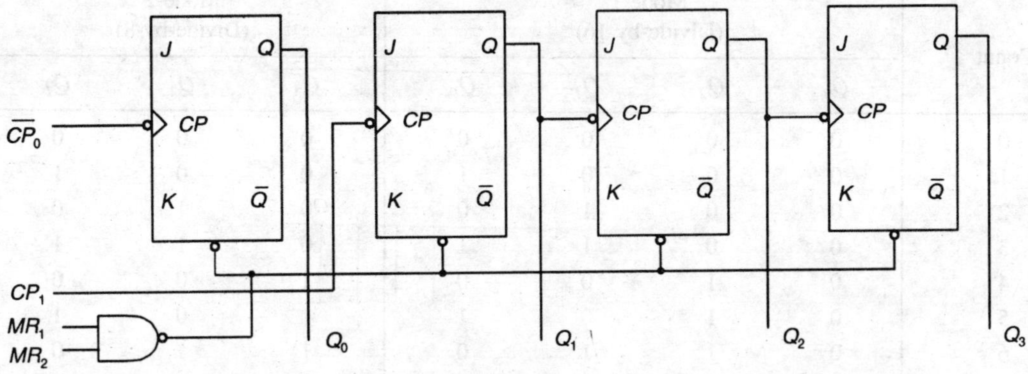

Fig. 6.32 Logic diagram for 7493

Note: • $\overline{CP_0}, \overline{CP_1} \rightarrow$ Clock inputs.

• The *J* and *K* inputs shown without connection are for reference only and are functionally at logic-1.

The logic diagram for the 7493 is given in Fig. 6.32. The pinout and logic symbol are shown in Fig. 6.33. The truth table for different modes are given in Table 6.12.

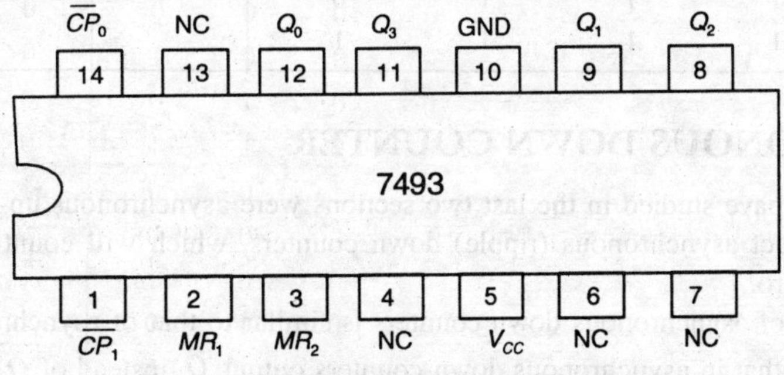

(a) Pinout of 7493

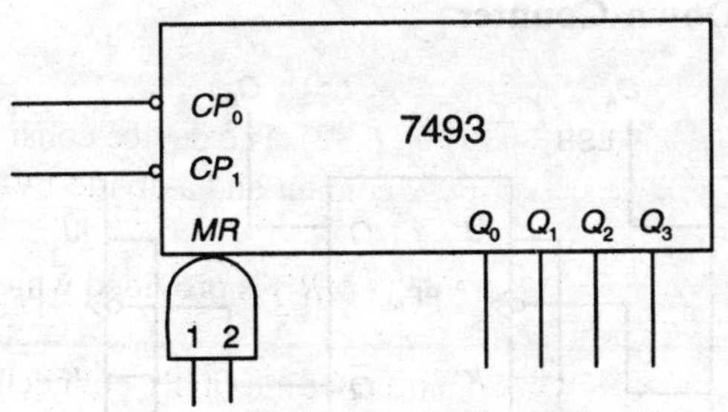

(b) Logic symbol for 7493

Fig. 6.33 The pinout and logic symbol for 7493

Table 6.12 Truth table for 7493

Count	Mode 1 (Divide-by-16)				Mode 2 (Divide-by-8)		
	Q_3	Q_2	Q_1	Q_0	Q_3	Q_2	Q_1
0	0	0	0	0	0	0	0
1	0	0	0	1	0	0	1
2	0	0	1	0	0	1	0
3	0	0	1	1	0	1	1
4	0	1	0	0	1	0	0
5	0	1	0	1	1	0	1
6	0	1	1	0	1	1	0
7	0	1	1	1	1	1	1
8	1	0	0	0			
9	1	0	0	1			
10	1	0	1	0			
11	1	0	1	1			
12	1	1	0	0			
13	1	1	0	1			
14	1	1	1	0			
15	1	1	1	1			

6.9 ASYNCHRONOUS DOWN COUNTER

The counters that we have studied in the last two sections were asynchronous up-counters. It is very simple task to construct asynchronous (ripple) down counters, which will count downward from a maximum count to zero.

The construction of asynchronous down counters is similar to that of asynchronous up-counters; the only difference is that in asynchronous down-counters output $\overline{Q}$ instead of Q of each flip-flop is connected to the *CLK* input of the next higher order flip-flop.

3-Bit Asynchronous Binary Down-Counter

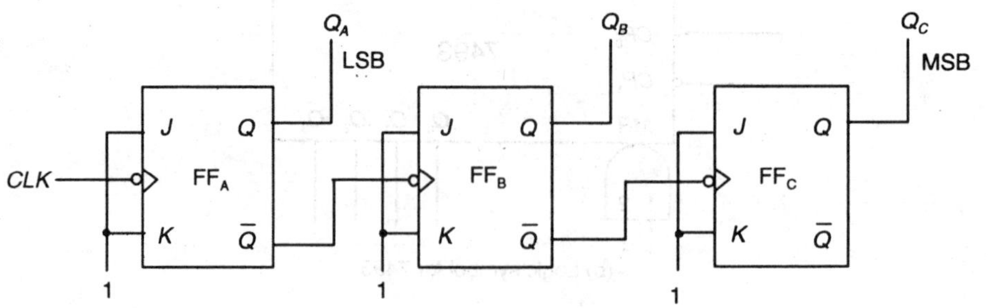

(a)

Fig. 6.34 3-bit asynchronous binary down-counter with its timing diagram for one complete cycle

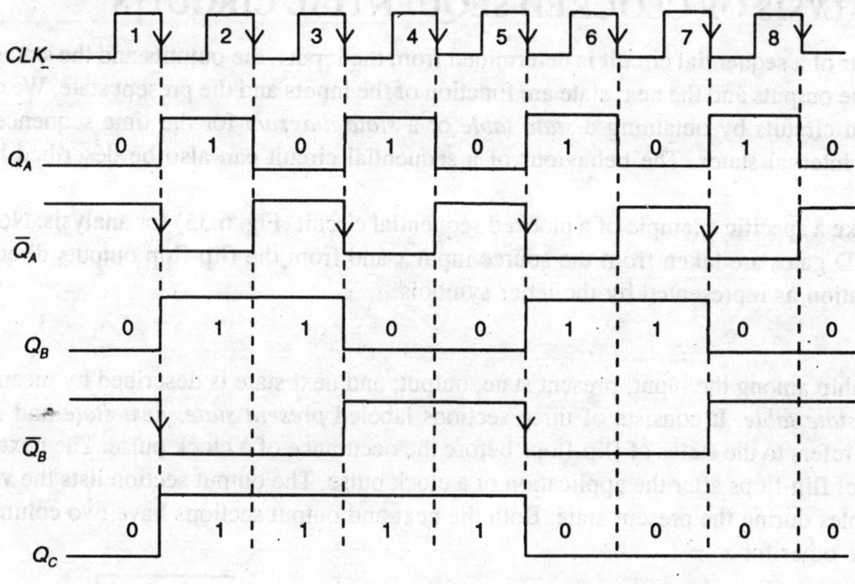

(b)

Fig. 6.34 3-bit asynchronous binary down-counter with its timing diagram for one complete cycle

Figure 6.34(a) shows a 3-bit asynchronous binary down counter. Notice that all flip-flops are connected for toggle operation. Initially $Q_A = Q_B = Q_C = 0$. The clock pulses are applied only to the *CLK* input of flip-flop FF_A. Thus, FF_A will toggle at the NGT of each clock pulse. The output $\overline{Q}_A$ acts as the clock for FF_B, and so FF_B will toggle at the NGT of $\overline{Q}_A$. Similarly the output $\overline{Q}_B$ acts as the clock for FF_C, and so will toggle at the NGT of $\overline{Q}_B$. (Flip-flop outputs Q_C, Q_B, Q_A represent a 3-bit binary number with Q_C as the MSB). Before arrival of the eighth clock pulse the counter is in the state 001. Clock pulse 8 causes the counter to go to the state 000 in turn. It means that the counter has gone through one complete cycle (111 through 000) and has recycled back to 000.

Table 6.13 shows the sequence of counter states.

Table 6.13 Count sequence for 3-bit asynchronous binary down-counter

Output		
Q_C	Q_B	Q_A
1	1	1
1	1	0
1	0	1
1	0	0
0	1	1
0	1	0
0	0	1
0	0	0

6.10 ANALYSIS OF CLOCKED SEQUENTIAL CIRCUITS

The behaviour of a sequential circuit is determined from the inputs, the outputs and the states of its flip-flops. Both the outputs and the next state are function of the inputs and the present state. We can analyze the sequential circuits by obtaining a *state table* or a *state diagram* for the time sequence of inputs, outputs, and internal states. The behaviour of a sequential circuit can also be described by Boolean expressions.

Let us take a specific example of a clocked sequential circuit (Fig. 6.35) for analysis. Note that here inputs to AND gates are taken from the source input x and from the flip-flop outputs directly or after complementation as represented by the letter symbols.

State Table

The relationship among the input, present state, output, and next state is described by means of a table known as a *state table.* It consists of three sections labeled *present state, next state* and *output.* The present state refers to the states of flip-flops before the occurance of a clock pulse. The next state refers to the states of flip-flops after the application of a clock pulse. The output section lists the values of the output variables during the present state. Both the next and output sections have two columns, one for $x = 0$ and the other for $x = 1$.

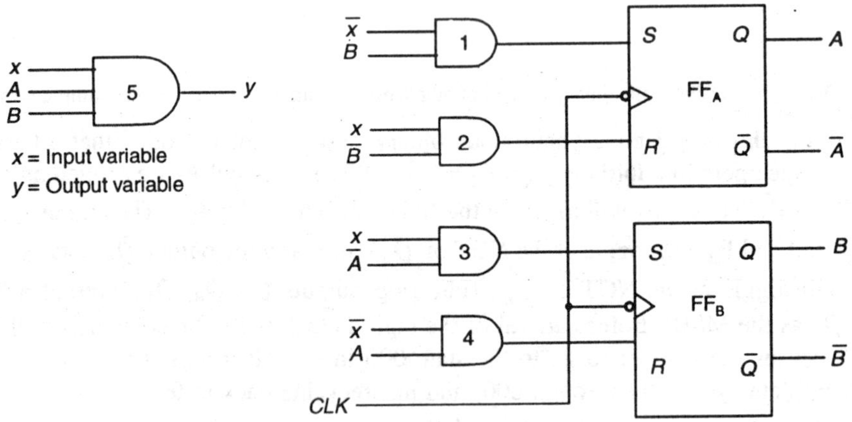

Fig. 6.35 Example of clocked sequential circuit

Derivation of the state table

The state table (Table 6.14) for the circuit of Fig. 6.35 can be derived as follows: Referring the sequential circuit given in Fig. 6.35, let us start the derivation from an assumed initial state 00 (i.e., state of FF_A and FF_B are equal to 0).

Step 1: With the present state $AB = 00$ and input $x = 0$; none of the AND gates produce a logic-1 signal. Therefore, the next state remains unchanged, that is, again next state $AB = 00$.

With the present state $AB = 00$ and input $x = 1$, gate (2) produces a logic-1 at the R input of FF_A and gate (3) produces a Logic-1 at the S input of FF_B. When a clock pulse occurs, FF_A is cleared and FF_B is set, making the next state $AB = 01$. This information is now entered in the first row of the state table.

Step 2: With the present state $AB = 01$ and input $x = 0$, gate (1) produces a logic-1 at the S input of FF_A. When a clock pulse occurs, FF_A is set and FF_B remains unchanged, making the next state $AB = 11$.

Table 6.14 State table for the circuit of Fig. 6.35

Present state	Next state		Output	
	$x = 0$	$x = 1$	$x = 0$	$x = 1$
AB	*AB*	*AB*	*y*	*y*
00	00	01	0	0
01	11	01	0	0
10	10	00	0	1
11	10	11	0	0

With the present state $AB = 01$ and input $x = 1$, gate (3) produces a logic-1 at the S input of FF_B. When a clock pulse occurs, FF_A remains unchanged, and FF_B is set again. Therefore, the next state remains unchanged, that is, next state $AB = 01$.

In this way, in another two steps, we can derive the next state starting from the other two possible present states (10 and 11).

We can easily determine the entries for the output section by examining the AND gate (5) for all possible input and present states. We get $y = 1$ only when input $x = 1$, and the present state $AB = 10$. Therefore, the output columns are entered with 0s except this possibility.

The same procedure is used to obtain the state table of any sequential circuit. Note that a sequential circuit with m flip-flops and n input variables will have 2^m rows, one for each state. The next state and output sections each will have 2^n columns, one for each input combination.

State Diagram

A *state diagram* is a graphical representation of a state table. Both the state diagram and the state table provide the same information. One can be obtained directly from the other. In the state diagram, a state

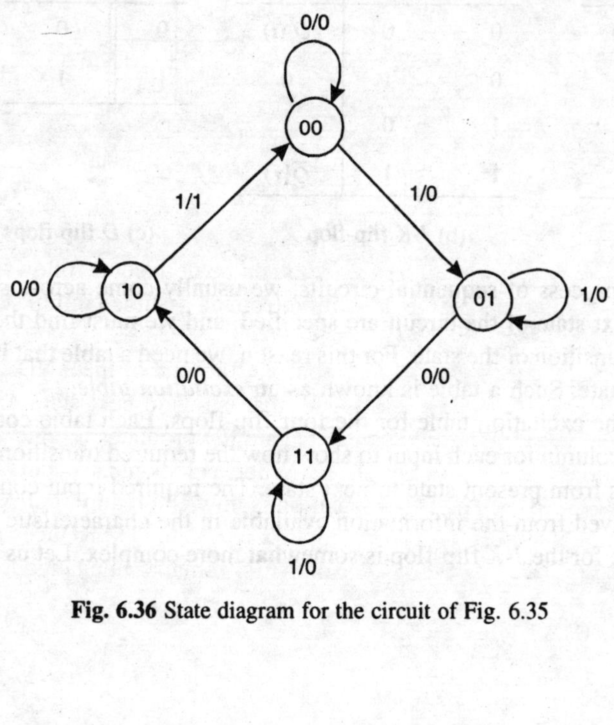

Fig. 6.36 State diagram for the circuit of Fig. 6.35

is represented by a circle, and the transition between the two states is indicated by directed lines connecting the circles. The state diagram of the sequential circuit of Fig. 6.35 is drawn as shown in Fig. 6.36.

In the state diagram (Fig. 6.36), each circle represents one possible state as indicated by the binary number inside the circle. Each directed line represents the occurance of a clock pulse and is labeled with two binary numbers separated by a slash(/). The labels of the directed lines specify the inputs and the corresponding outputs. For example, the directed line from state 00 to 01 is labeled 1/0, meaning that the sequential circuit is in a present state 00 while input $x = 1$ and output $y = 0$, and that on the termination of the next clock pulse, the circuit goes to next state 01. A directed line connecting a circle with itself indicates that no change of state occurs.

6.11 FLIP-FLOP EXCITATION TABLES

The truth tables for various flip-flops have already been presented in section 6.3. Since the truth table of a flip-flop defines the logical property of the flip-flop and completely characterizes its operation, it is also referred to as the *characteristic table.*

The characteristic table for *S-R*, *J-K*, *D* and *T* flip-flops is shown in Table 6.15, in a somewhat different way. Table 6.15 defines the state of each flip-flop as a function of its inputs and previous state. $Q(t)$ refers to the present state (before a pulse is received) and $Q(t+1)$ to the next state (after the pulse is received). The characteristic table for *S-R* flip-flop shows that the next stage is equal to the present state when $S = R = 0$. When $S = 0$ and $R = 1$, the next clock pulse clears the flip-flop. When $S = 1$ and $R = 0$, the next clock pulse sets the flip-flop. The question mark (?) for the next state when $S = R = 1$ designates an indeterminate next state. Similarly we can interpret the other characteristic tables.

Table 6.15 Flip-flop characteristic tables

S	R	$Q(t+1)$
0	0	$Q(t)$
0	1	0
1	0	1
1	1	?

(a) *S-R* flip-flop

J	K	$Q(t+1)$
0	0	$Q(t)$
0	1	0
1	0	1
1	1	$\bar{Q}(t)$

(b) *J-K* flip-flop

D	$Q(t+1)$
0	0
1	1

(c) *D* flip-flop

T	$Q(t+1)$
0	$Q(t)$
1	$\bar{Q}(t)$

(d) *T* flip-flop

During the design process of sequential circuits, we usually come across situations in which the present state and the next state of the circuit are specified, and we must find the input conditions that will cause the desired transition of the state. For this reason, we need a table that lists the required inputs for a given change of state. Such a table is known as an *excitation table.*

Table 6.16 shows the excitation table for the four flip-flops. Each table consists of two columns, $Q(t)$ and $Q(t+1)$, and a column for each input to show how the required transition is achieved. There are four possible transitions from present state to next state. The required input conditions for each of the four transitions are derived from the information available in the characteristic table.

The excitation table for the *J-K* flip-flop is somewhat more complex. Let us examine the each case of this table.

Table 6.16 Flip-flop excitation tables

Present state $Q(t)$	Next state $Q(t+1)$	S	R
0	0	0	×
0	1	0	0
1	0	1	1
1	1	×	0

(a) *S-R* flip-flop

Present State $Q(t)$	Next State $Q(t+1)$	J	K
0	0	0	×
0	1	1	×
1	0	×	1
1	1	×	0

(b) *J-K* flip-flop

Present State $Q(t)$	Next State $Q(t+1)$	D
0	0	0
0	1	1
1	0	0
1	1	1

(c) *D* flip-flop

Present State $Q(t)$	Next State $Q(t+1)$	T
0	0	0
0	1	1
1	0	1
1	1	0

(d) *T* flip-flop

0 → 0 Transition: The flip-flop present state is at 0 and is required to remain at 0 when a clock pulse is applied. This can be obtained with two different sets of input conditions. If $J = 0$ and $K = 0$ (no-change condition), the flip-flop will not change states and the zero value for Q remain after the clock transition. A second set of inputs that results in this output condition is $J = 0$ and $K = 1$ (clear conditon). This always forces the flip-flop to the 0-state after the occurance of the pulse. The first row of the excitation table combines these input conditions to yield $J = 0$ and $K = \times$ for the 0 to 0 output transition.

0 → 1 Transition: The flip-flop present state is at 0 and is required to change to a 1 when a clock pulse is applied. This can happen when either $J = 1$ and $K = 0$ (set condition) or $J = 1$ and $K = 1$ (toggle condition). These conditions can be combined to yield $J = 1$ and $K = \times$ for the 0 to 1 output transition.

1 → 0 Transition: The flip-flop present state is at 1 and is required to change to a 0 when a clock pulse is applied. This can happen when either $J = 0$ and $K = 1$ (clear condition) or $J = 1$ and $K = 1$ (toggle condition). These conditions can be combined to yield $J = \times$ and $K = 1$ for the 1 to 0 output transition.

1 → 1 Transition: The flip-flop present state is at 1 and is required to remain at 1 when a clock pulse is applied. This can happen when either $J = 0$ and $K = 0$ (no-change condition) or $J = 1$ and $K = 0$ (set condition). These conditions can be combined to yield $J = \times$ and $K = 0$ for the 1 to 1 output transition.

The same type of explanation leads to find the required input conditions in the remaining flip-flop excitation table.

6.12 SYNCHRONOUS (PARALLEL) COUNTERS

We have noticed that in asynchronous counters, the input clock pulse ripples through from flip-flop to flip-flop. Because of this ripple action, their speed is low. The speed of operation can be improved by keeping all the flip-flops of a counter under the control of the same clock pulse. Such a counter is known as a *synchronous counter.* Synchronous counters can be designed for any count sequence (need not be straight binary). These counters can be designed following a systematic approach.

The design of synchronous binary counters is so simple that there is no need to go through a rigorous sequential logic design process. That is why we design the binary counter by inspection of counting sequence and study its operation in this section. We will discuss a systematic design procedure, which can be generalized to other types of counters, in the later section.

Since in synchronous counter, the clock pulses are applied to all the flip-flops, some means must be used to control when a flip-flop is to toggle and when it is to remain unaffected by a clock pulse. This can be achieved by using the J and K inputs of the *J-K* flip-flop.

Synchronous Counter Design by Inspection

Let us design a MOD-16 counter by this procedure. The count sequence for this counter is given in Table 6.17.

Table 6.17 Count sequence for MOD-16 counter

Count	Flip-flop states			
	Q_D	Q_C	Q_B	Q_A
0	0	0	0	0
1	0	0	0	1
2	0	0	1	0
3	0	0	1	1
4	0	1	0	0
5	0	1	0	1
6	0	1	1	0
7	0	1	1	1
8	1	0	0	0
9	1	0	0	1
10	1	0	1	0
11	1	0	1	1
12	1	1	0	0
13	1	1	0	1
14	1	1	1	0
15	1	1	1	1

Table 6.17 reveals that:

- Q_A has to change state at each NGT (for the negative edge triggered flip-flop). For this reason the J and K inputs of the flip-flop FF_A are permanently connected to logic 1 so that it will toggle on each NGT of the clock input.
- Q_B has to change state on each NGT that occurs while $Q_A = 1$. This is achieved by connecting output Q_A to the J and K inputs of flip-flop FF_B so that these J and K inputs equal to 1 only when $Q_A = 1$.
- Q_C has to change state on each NGT that occurs while $Q_A = 1$ and $Q_B = 1$. This is achieved by connecting an AND gate to the J and K inputs of flip-flop FF_C so that these J and K inputs equal to 1 only when $Q_A = 1$ and $Q_B = 1$.
- Q_D has to change state on each NGT that occurs while $Q_A = 1$, $Q_B = 1$ and $Q_C = 1$. This is achieved by connecting an AND gate to the J and K inputs of flip-flop FF_D so that these J and K inputs equal to 1 only when $Q_A = 1$, $Q_B = 1$ and $Q_C = 1$.

Thus we can determine the logic circuitry consisting of AND gate that feeds the J and K inputs of each flip-flop and construct a 4-bit, MOD-16 synchronous binary counter as shown in Fig. 6.37. One can easily verify the circuit operation by tracing signals through the circuit.

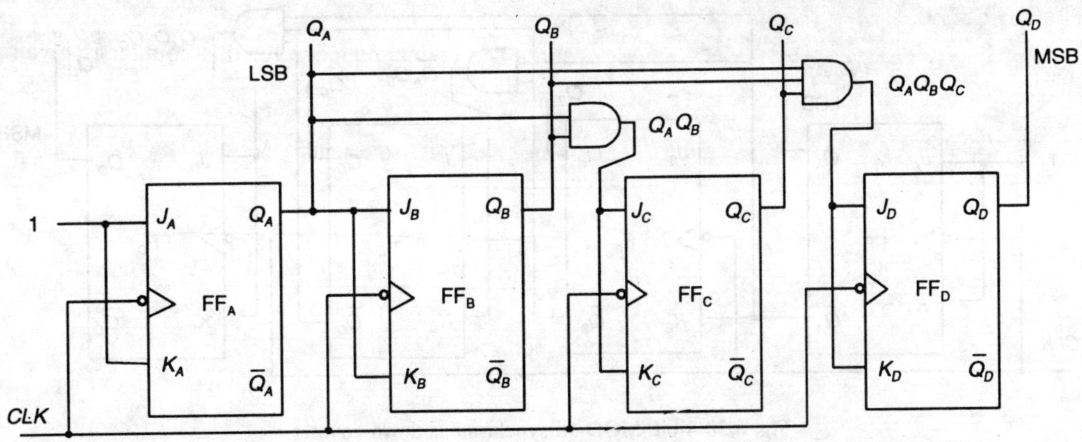

Fig. 6.37 4-bit, MOD-16 synchronous counter

6.13 SYNCHRONOUS DOWN AND UP/DOWN COUNTERS

We saw that a ripple counter could be made to count down by using $\overline{Q}$ output of each flip-flop to drive the next flip-flop in the counter. A synchronous down counter can be constructed in a similar way, that is, by using $\overline{Q}$ outputs to drive the J and K inputs of the following flip-flops.

Fig. 6.38 shows a 4-bit, MOD-16 synchronous down counter. This counter is obtained by converting the synchronous up-counter of Fig. 6.37 by connecting $\overline{Q}_A$, $\overline{Q}_B$ and $\overline{Q}_C$ in place of Q_A, Q_B and Q_C. Table 6.18 shows the sequence of counter states.

Table 6.18 Count sequence for MOD-16 down counter

Flip-flop states			
Q_D	Q_C	Q_B	Q_A
1	1	1	1
1	1	1	0
1	1	0	1
1	1	0	0
1	0	1	1
1	0	1	0
1	0	0	1
1	0	0	0
0	1	1	1
0	1	1	0
0	1	0	1
0	1	0	0
0	0	1	1
0	0	1	0
0	0	0	1
0	0	0	0

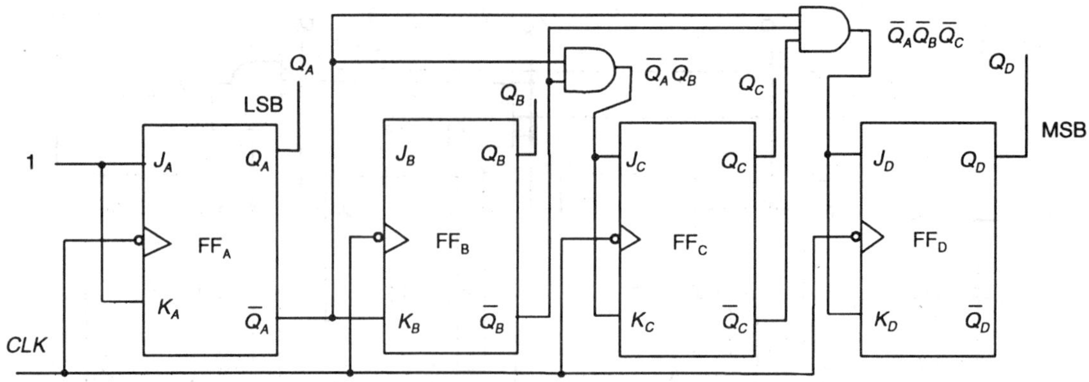

Fig. 6.38 4-bit, MOD-16 synchronous down-counter

In a synchronous up/down counter, the control inputs (count-up and count-down) are used to control whether the Q outputs or the $\bar{Q}$ outputs are fed to the J and K inputs of the following flip-flops. The counter in Fig. 6.39 is a 3-bit, MOD-8 up/down counter that will count from 000 up to 111 when the count-up control input is 1 and from 111 down to 000 when the count-down input is 1.

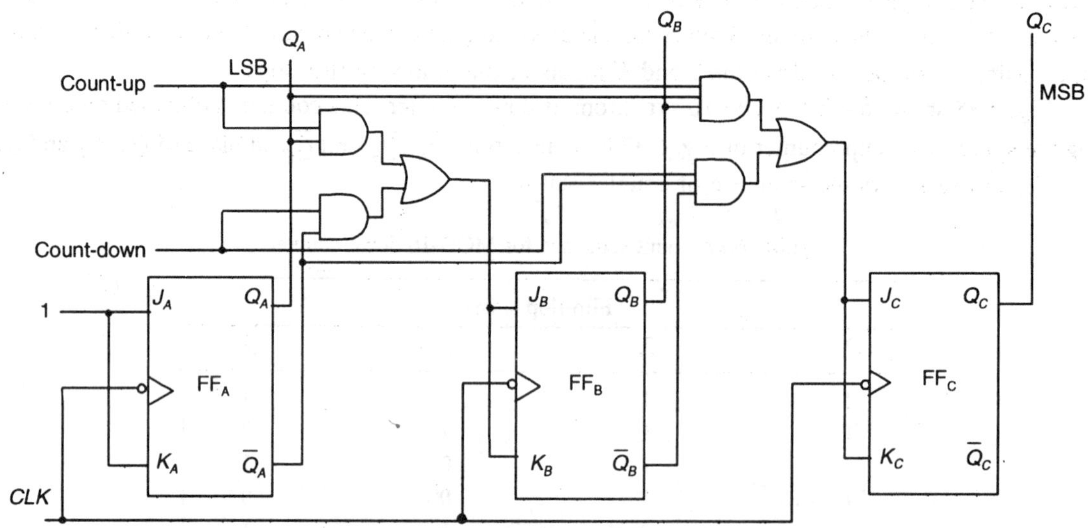

Fig. 6.39 3-bit, MOD-8 synchronous up/down counter

6.14 PRESETTABLE COUNTERS

A counter is designated as a presettable counter if it incorporates logic such that it can be preset to any desired state. The presetting operation is also referred to as loading the counter. A presettable counter is a basic building block that can be used to implement a counter that has any modulus. Nearly all the presettable counters available as TTL MSI are constructed by using four flip-flops (usually master-slave J-K types), and they are generally referred to as 4-bit counters. They may use either asynchronous or synchronous presetting. For instance, the 74193 is a synchronous binary counter that can operate in either a count-down or count-up mode.

The 74193 Presettable 4-Bit Binary Up/Down Counter

The 74193 is a 4-bit synchronous up-down (reversible) binary counter. It has a master reset (*MR*) input and can be reset to any desired count with the parallel load inputs. The logic diagram for 74193 is

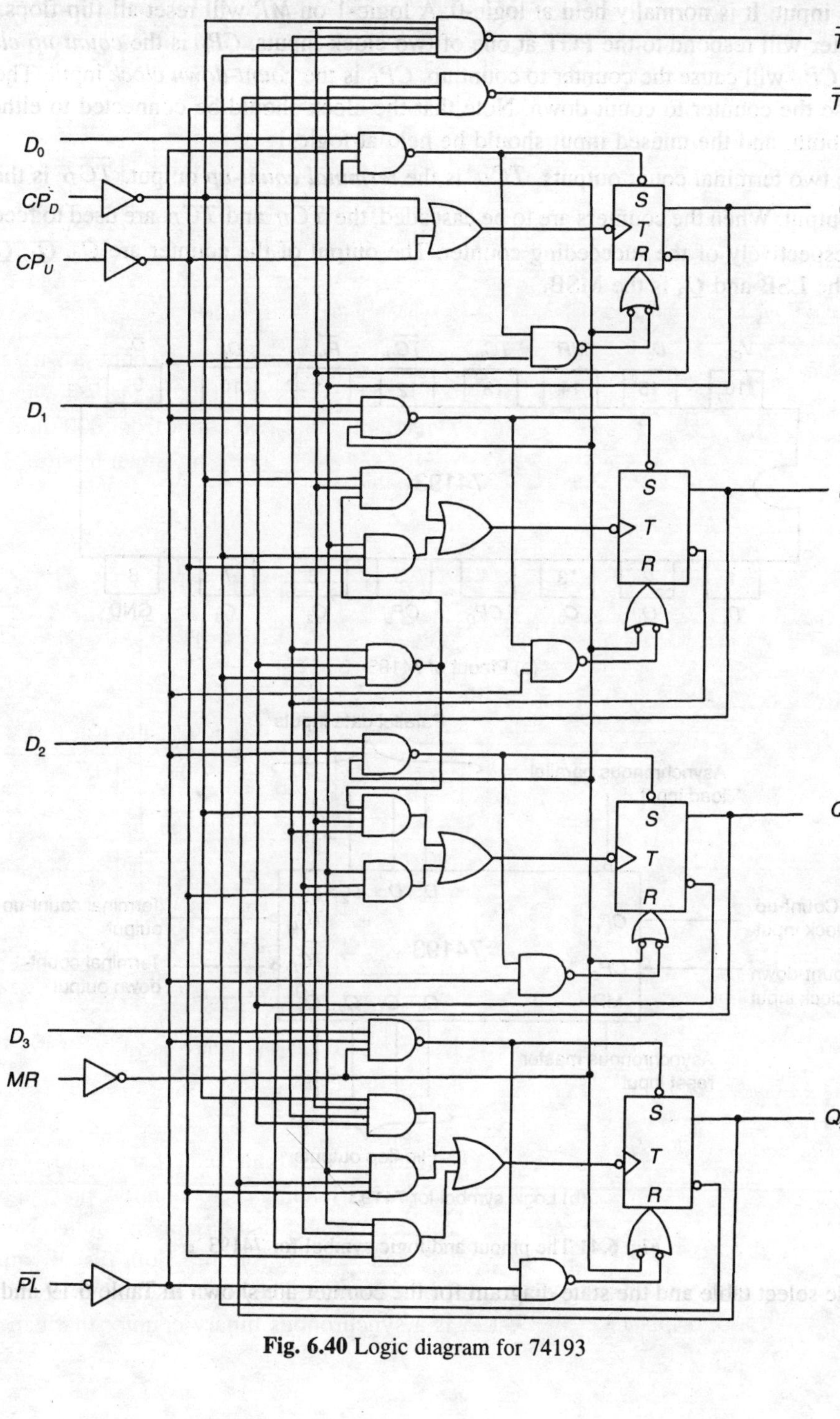

Fig. 6.40 Logic diagram for 74193

shown in Fig. 6.40. The pinout and logic symbol for this IC are shown in Fig. 6.41. Pin $\overline{PL}$ is a control input for loading data into pins D_0, D_1, D_2 and D_3. When the device is used as a counter, these four pins are left open and $\overline{PL}$ must be held at a logic-1. Pin *MR* is the master reset. It is an active-HIGH master asynchronous input. It is normally held at logic-0. A logic-1 on *MR* will reset all flip-flops.

The counter will respond to the PGT at one of two clock inputs. CP_U is the *count-up clock* input. The clock on CP_U will cause the counter to count up. CP_D is the *count-down clock* input. The clock on CP_D will cause the counter to count down. Note that the clock should be connected to either CP_U or CP_D, but not both, and the unused input should be held at logic-1.

There are two terminal count outputs. $\overline{TC_U}$ is the *terminal count-up* output. $\overline{TC_D}$ is the *terminal count-down* output. When the counters are to be cascaded, the $\overline{TC_U}$ and $\overline{TC_D}$ are used to feed CP_U and CP_D inputs respectively of the succeeding counter. The output of the counter are Q_0, Q_1, Q_2 and Q_3, where Q_0 is the LSB and Q_3 is the MSB.

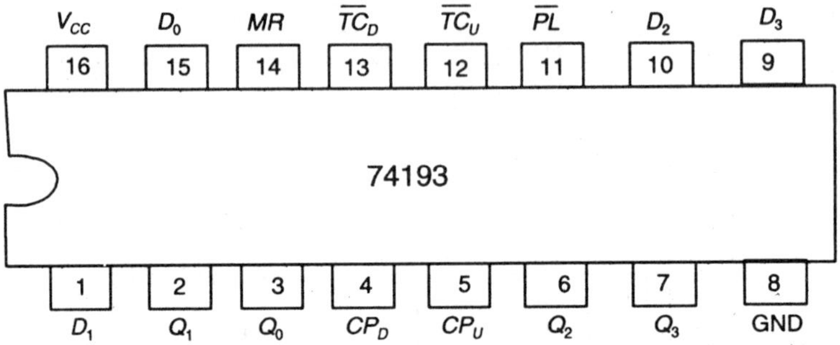

(a) Pinout of 74193

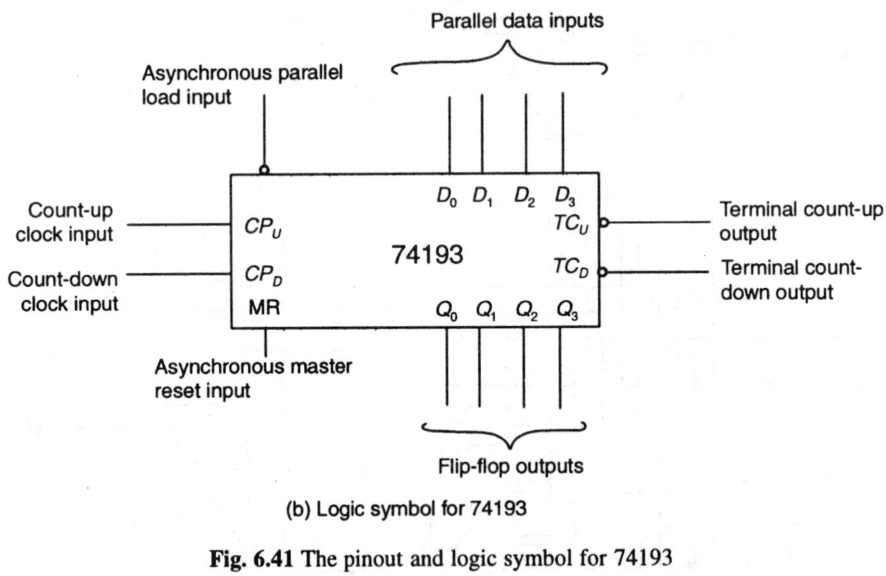

(b) Logic symbol for 74193

Fig. 6.41 The pinout and logic symbol for 74193

The mode select table and the state diagram for the counter are shown in Table 6.19 and Fig. 6.42, respectively.

Table 6.19 Mode select table

MR	$\overline{PL}$	CP_U	CP_D	Mode
1	×	×	×	Asynchronous reset
0	0	×	×	Asynchronous preset
0	1	1	1	No change
0	1	↑	1	Count up
0	1	1	↑	Count down

× = Don't care, ↑ = PGT

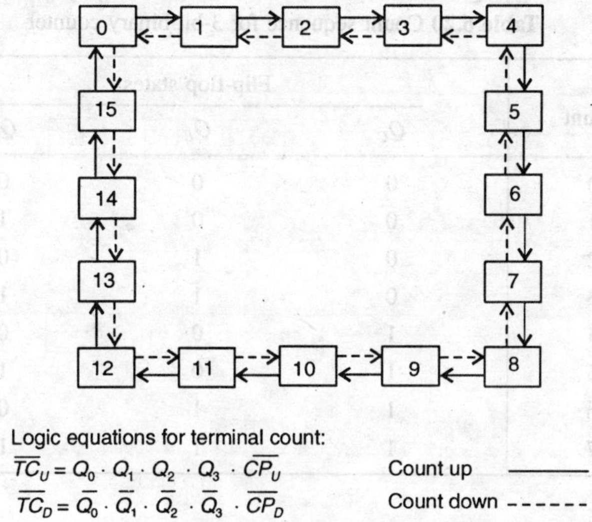

Fig. 6.42 State diagram for 74193

6.15 SYNCHRONOUS COUNTER DESIGN BY SYSTEMATIC PROCEDURE

Several methods exist for designing counters that follow arbitrary sequences. We will present the details for one common method that uses *J-K* flip-flops in a synchronous counter configuration. The same method can also be used while designing counters with the other flip-flops also.

Design procedure: Synchronous counters for any given count sequence and modulus can be designed in the following way.

1. Determine the number of flip-flops required and the desired count sequence. Choose the type of flip-flop to be used.
2. Draw the state diagram showing those states that are part of the desired count sequence.
3. Draw a table that lists all present states and next states by referring state diagram. Determine the flip-flop inputs for each present state in order to produce the transition to the next state using the excitation table of the flip-flops. Then enter these inputs in the above table.

4. Prepare K-map for each flip-flop input in terms of flip-flop outputs as the input variables. For the states that are not part of the desired count sequence, enter 'x' in the corresponding square of the K-map. Simplify the K-maps and obtain the minimized expressions.
5. Implement the expressions using flip-flops and other gates.

Let us apply the above procedure to the design of counters in the following examples.

EXAMPLE 6.1: Design a 3-bit synchronous binary counter using *J-K* flip-flops.

SOLUTION:

Step 1:

This counter requires atleast 3 flip-flops. The desired count sequence is shown in Table 6.20.

Table 6.20 Count sequence for 3-bit binary counter

Count	Flip-flop states		
	Q_C	Q_B	Q_A
0	0	0	0
1	0	0	1
2	0	1	0
3	0	1	1
4	1	0	0
5	1	0	1
6	1	1	0
7	1	1	1

Step 2:

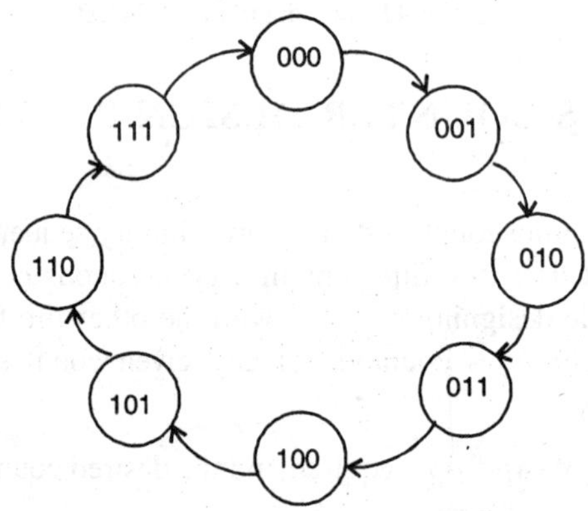

Fig. 6.43 State diagram of a 3-bit binary counter

Step 3:

Table 6.21 Circuit excitation table

Present state			Next state			Flip-flop inputs					
Q_C	Q_B	Q_A	Q_C	Q_B	Q_A	J_C	K_C	J_B	K_B	J_A	K_A
0	0	0	0	0	1	0	×	0	×	1	×
0	0	1	0	1	0	0	×	1	×	×	1
0	1	0	0	1	1	0	×	×	0	1	×
0	1	1	1	0	0	1	×	×	1	×	1
1	0	0	1	0	1	×	0	0	×	1	×
1	0	1	1	1	0	×	0	1	×	×	1
1	1	0	1	1	1	×	0	×	0	1	×
1	1	1	0	0	0	×	1	×	1	×	1

Step 4:

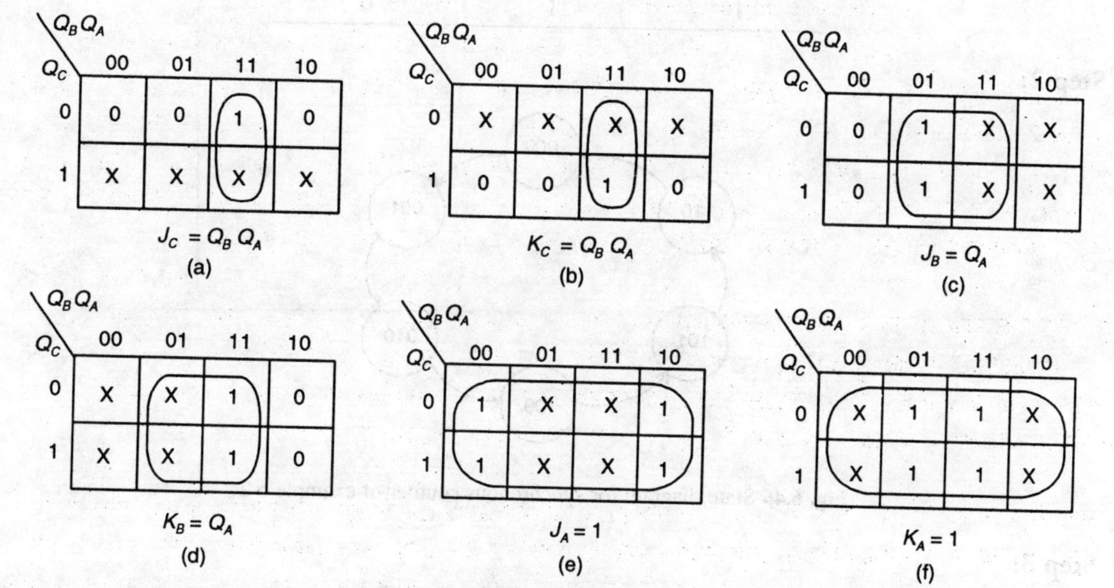

Fig. 6.44 K-maps

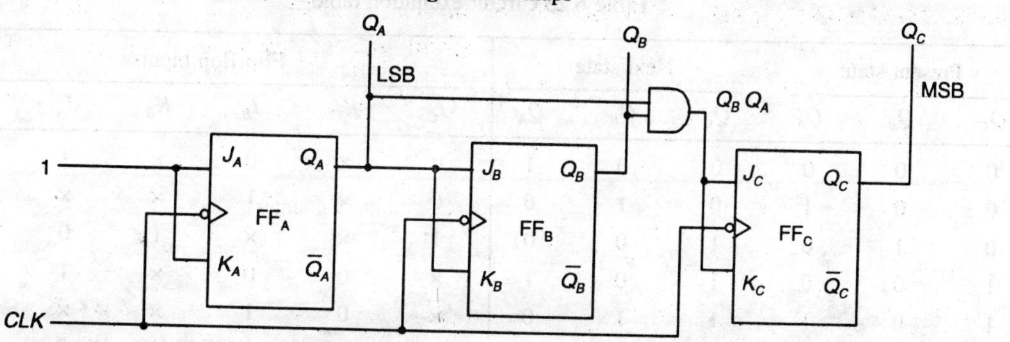

Fig. 6.45 3-bit synchronous counter

EXAMPLE 6.2: Design a counter which counts in the following sequence : 000, 001, 010, 100, 101, 110, 000 .... Use *J-K* flip-flops.

SOLUTION:

Step 1:

This counter requires 3 flip-flops. The desired count sequence is shown in Table 6.22.

Table 6.22 Count sequence

Q_C	Q_B	Q_A
0	0	0
0	0	1
0	1	0
1	0	0
1	0	1
1	1	0

Step 2:

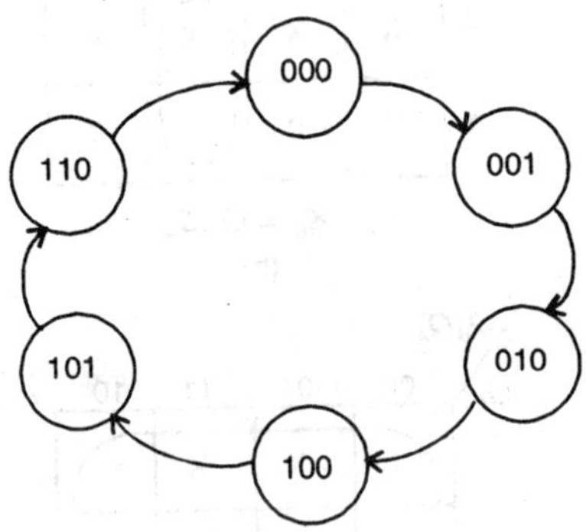

Fig. 6.46 State diagram for synchronous counter of example 6.2

Step 3:

Table 6.23 Circuit excitation table

Present state			Next state			Flip-flop inputs					
Q_C	Q_B	Q_A	Q_C	Q_B	Q_A	J_C	K_C	J_B	K_B	J_A	K_A
0	0	0	0	0	1	0	×	0	×	1	×
0	0	1	0	1	0	0	×	1	×	×	1
0	1	0	1	0	0	1	×	×	1	0	×
1	0	0	1	0	1	×	0	0	×	1	×
1	0	1	1	1	0	×	0	1	×	×	1
1	1	0	0	0	0	×	1	×	1	0	×

Step 4:

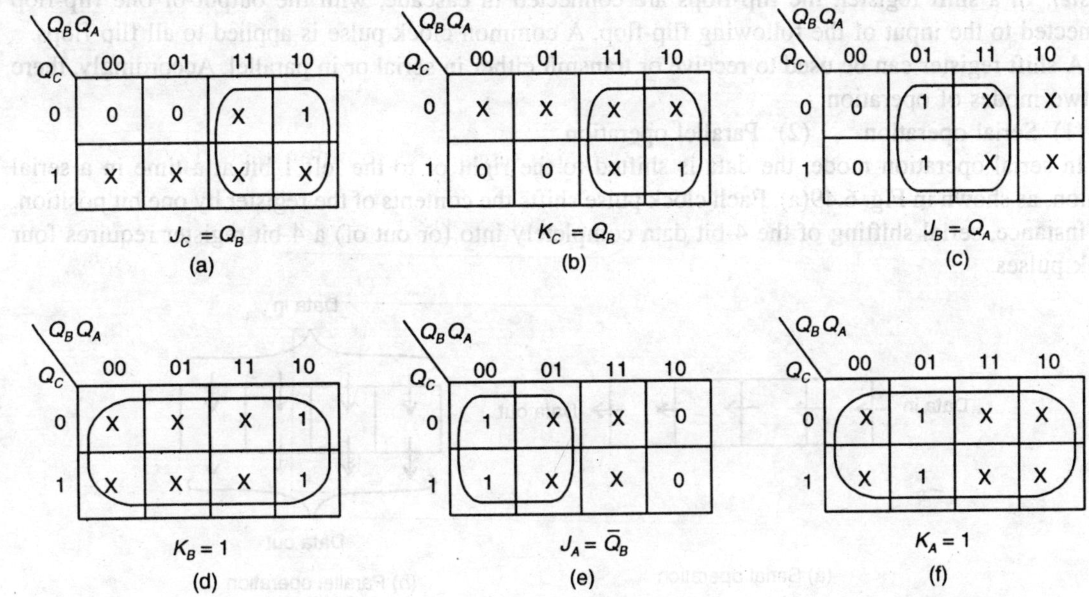

Fig. 6.47 K-maps

Step 5:

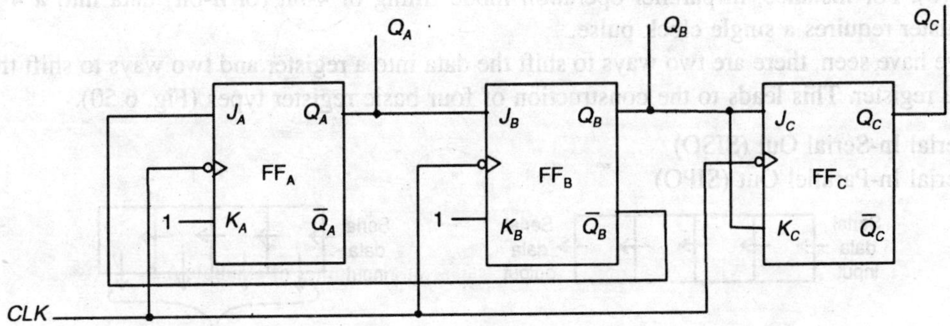

Fig. 6.48 Implementation of synchronous counter of example 6.2

Note: Sometimes the counter accidently gets into one of the unused (don't care) states upon power up or due to noise. For this reason, all of the don't care states in a counter can be designed to have a next state of some state contained in the desired sequence. If one of the unused states is entered, the system will recover to the desired sequence when the next clock pulse is applied. This type of system is referred to as a *self starting circuit.*

6.16 SHIFT REGISTERS

A *register* is a group of flip-flops that can be used for holding binary information. An n-bit register has a group of n flip-flops and is capable of storing any binary information containing n bits. D flip-flops are commonly used to construct registers.

A register capable of shifting its binary information either to the right or to the left is called a *shift register.* In a shift register, the flip-flops are connected in cascade, with the output of one flip-flop connected to the input of the following flip-flop. A common clock pulse is applied to all flip-flops.

A shift register can be used to receive or transmit either in serial or in parallel. Accordingly, there are two modes of operation:

(1) Serial operation (2) Parallel operation.

In serial operation mode, the data is shifted to the right or to the left 1 bit at a time in a serial fashion, as shown in Fig. 6.49(a). Each clock pulse shifts the contents of the register by one bit position. For instance, serial shifting of the 4-bit data completely into (or out of) a 4-bit register requires four clock pulses.

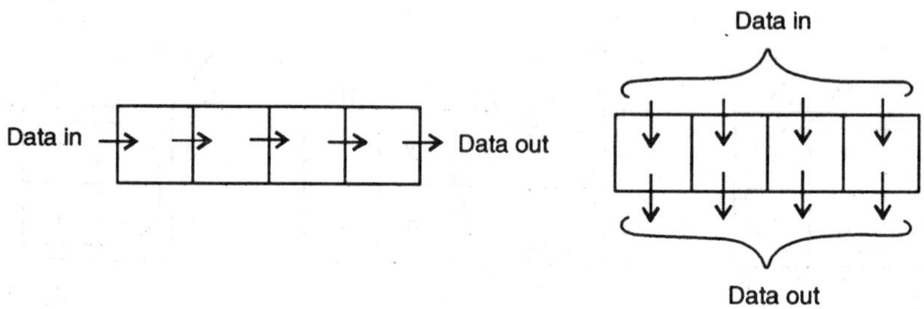

(a) Serial operation (b) Parallel operation

Fig. 6.49 Two modes of operation for shift registers

In parallel operation mode, the data is filled (or emptied) during a single clock pulse, as shown in Fig. 6.49(b). For instance, in parallel operation mode filling of 4-bit (or *n*-bit) data into a 4-bit (or *n*-bit) register requires a single clock pulse.

As we have seen, there are two ways to shift the data into a register and two ways to shift the data out of the register. This leads to the construction of four basic register types (Fig. 6.50).

1. Serial In-Serial Out (SISO)
2. Serial In-Parallel Out (SIPO)

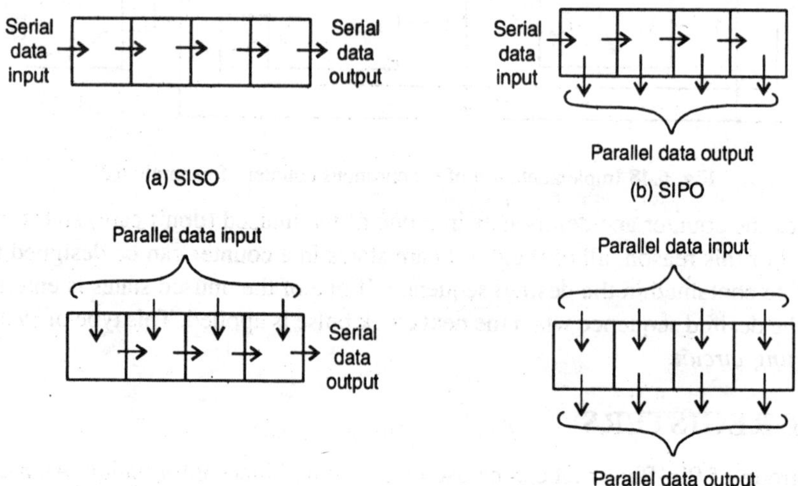

(a) SISO (b) SIPO (c) PISO (d) PIPO

Fig. 6.50 Shift register types

3. Parallel In-Serial Out (PISO)
4. Parallel In-Parallel Out (PIPO)

We will now discuss the four basic registers listed above.

1. Serial In-Serial Out (SISO) Shift Registers

This type of shift register accepts input data serially, one bit at a time on a single line and also produces the stored data serially, one bit at a time on its output.

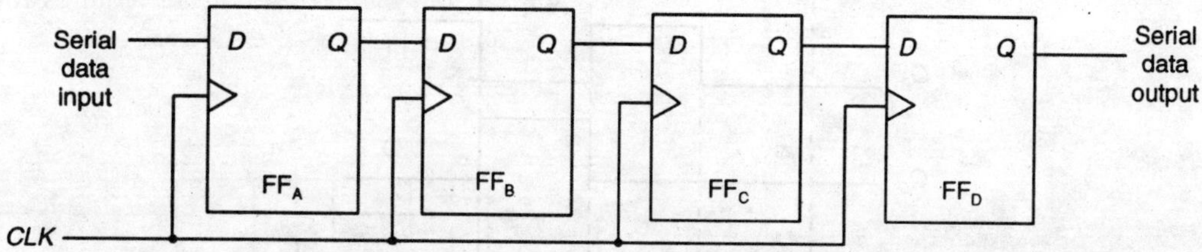

Fig. 6.51 4-bit SISO shift register

Figure 6.51 shows a 4-bit SISO shift register constructed with four D flip-flops and a common clock pulse input. Each clock pulse shifts the contents of the register one bit position to the right. Four consecutive clock pulses are required to store a 4-bit data into a 4-bit register in a serial fashion. This operation is clearly illustrated in the following example.

For getting the data out of the register, it must be shifted out serially and taken off the Q_D output.

EXAMPLE 6.3: Draw the waveforms to shift the binary number 1101 into the 4-bit register shown in Fig. 6.51. Also show the states of the register after each clock pulse. (Assume that the register is initially cleared.)

SOLUTION:

	Q_A	Q_B	Q_C	Q_D
Shift register with initial value	0	0	0	0
After PGT of CLK1	1	0	0	0
After PGT of CLK2	0	1	0	0
After PGT of CLK3	1	0	1	0
After PGT of CLK4	1	1	0	1

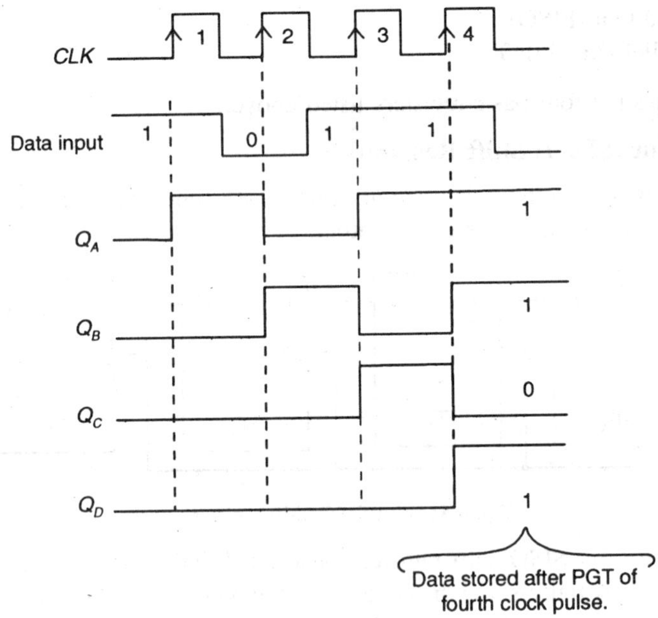

Fig. 6.52 Waveforms

2. Serial In-Parallel Out (SIPO) Shift Registers

This type of shift register accepts input data serially, but shifts the stored data in parallel form. In order to shift the data out in parallel form it is simply necessary to have all the data bits available as outputs at the same time. Figure 6.53 shows a 4-bit SIPO shift register.

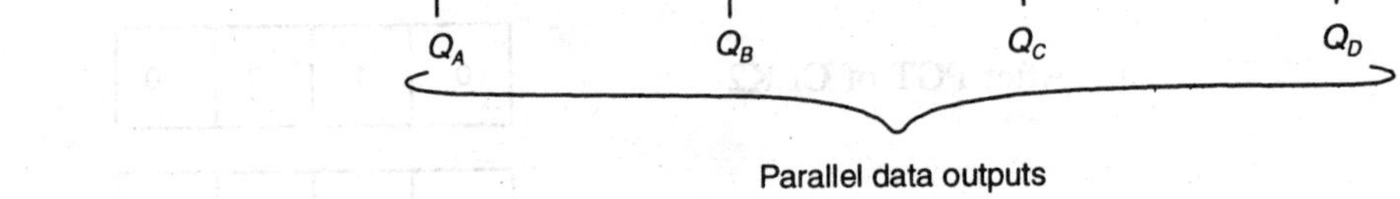

Fig. 6.53 4-bit SIPO shift register

3. Parallel In-Serial Out (PISO) Shift Registers

This type of shift register accepts data simultaneously on parallel lines but shifts the stored data serially on a single line as described previously.

Figure 6.54 shows a logic diagram of a 4-bit PISO shift register. Notice that there are four data input lines, *A*, *B*, *C* and *D*, and a control line labeled $SHIFT/\overline{LOAD}$. When $SHIFT/\overline{LOAD}$ is held LOW, gates G_1 through G_3 are enabled, allowing each data bit to be applied to the *D* input of its respective flip-flop. When a clock pulse is applied, 4-bit data is LOADED into the flip-flops. When $\overline{SHIFT/LOAD}$ is HIGH, gates G_1 through G_3 are disabled and gates G_4 through G_6 are enabled, allowing the data bits to shift through the register serially. The two-input OR gates allow either the serial data shifting operation or the parallel data-entry operation, depending on which AND gates are enabled by the logic level on the $\overline{SHIFT/LOAD}$ control line.

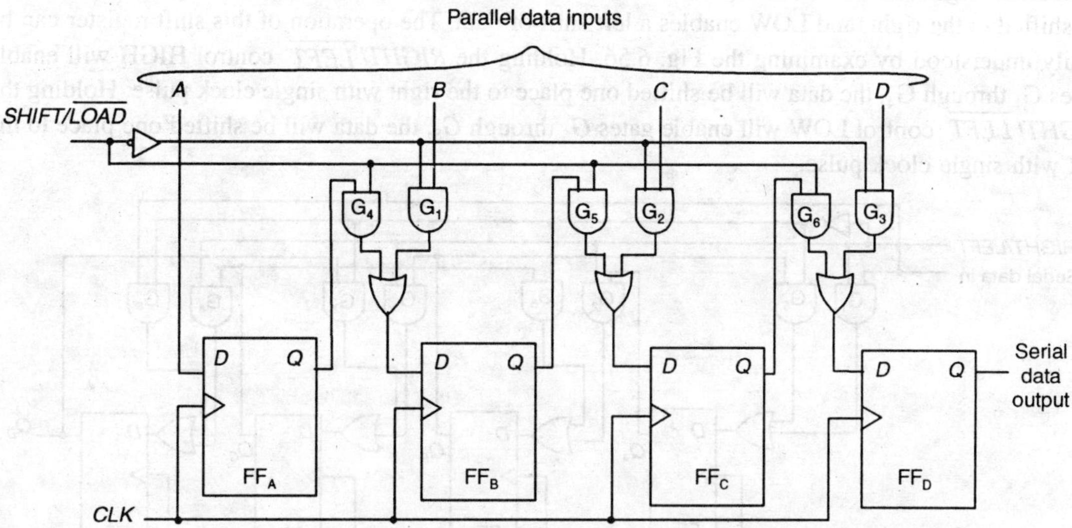

Fig. 6.54 4-bit PISO shift register

4. Parallel In-Parallel Out (PIPO) Shift Register

This type of shift register is designed such that data can be moved into or out of the register in parallel form. Figure 6.55 shows a 4-bit PIPO shift register.

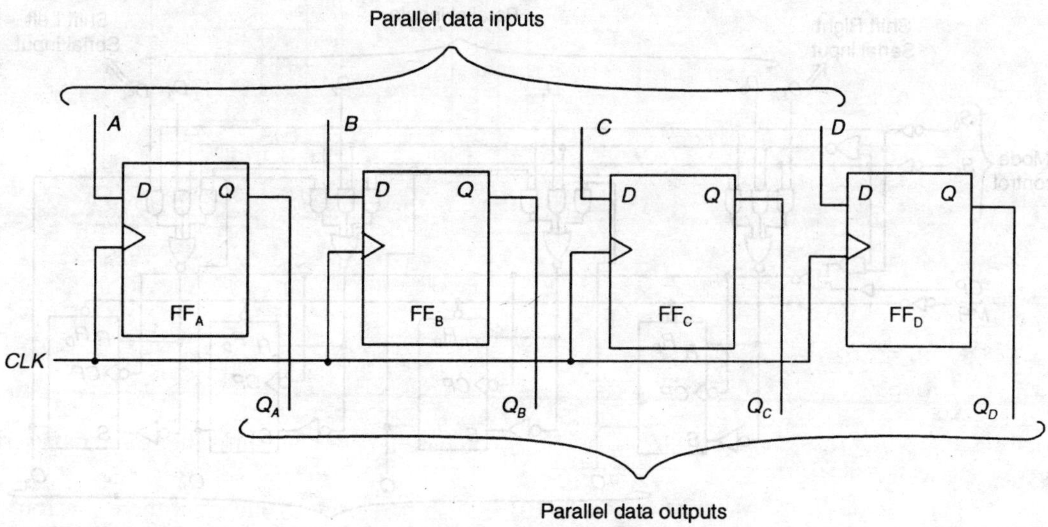

Fig. 6.55 4-bit PIPO shift register

6.17 BIDIRECTIONAL SHIFT REGISTERS

A *bidirectional shift register* is one which has both shift-right and shift-left capability. It can be implemented by using gating logic that enables the transfer of a data bit from one stage to the next stage, to the right or to the left, depending on the level of a control line. An implementation of a 4-bit bidirectional shift register is shown in Fig. 6.56. A HIGH on the $RIGHT/\overline{LEFT}$ control input allows data to be shifted to the right, and LOW enables a left shift of data. The operation of this shift register can be easily understood by examining the Fig. 6.56. Holding the $RIGHT/\overline{LEFT}$ control HIGH will enable gates G_1 through G_4, the data will be shifted one place to the right with single clock pulse. Holding the $RIGHT/\overline{LEFT}$ control LOW will enable gates G_5 through G_8, the data will be shifted one place to the left with single clock pulse.

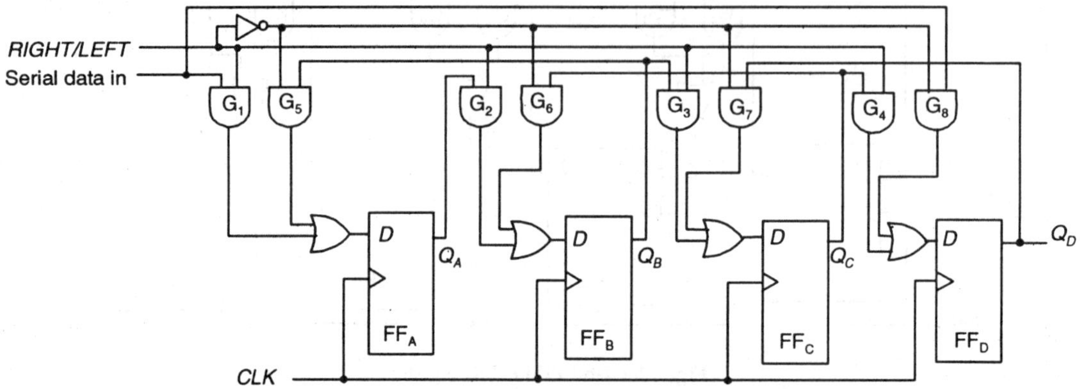

Fig. 6.56 4-bit bidirectional shift register

The 74194 4-Bit Bidirectional Universal Shift Register

The logic diagram for 74194 is shown in Fig. 6.57. The pinout and logic symbol are given in Fig. 6.58.

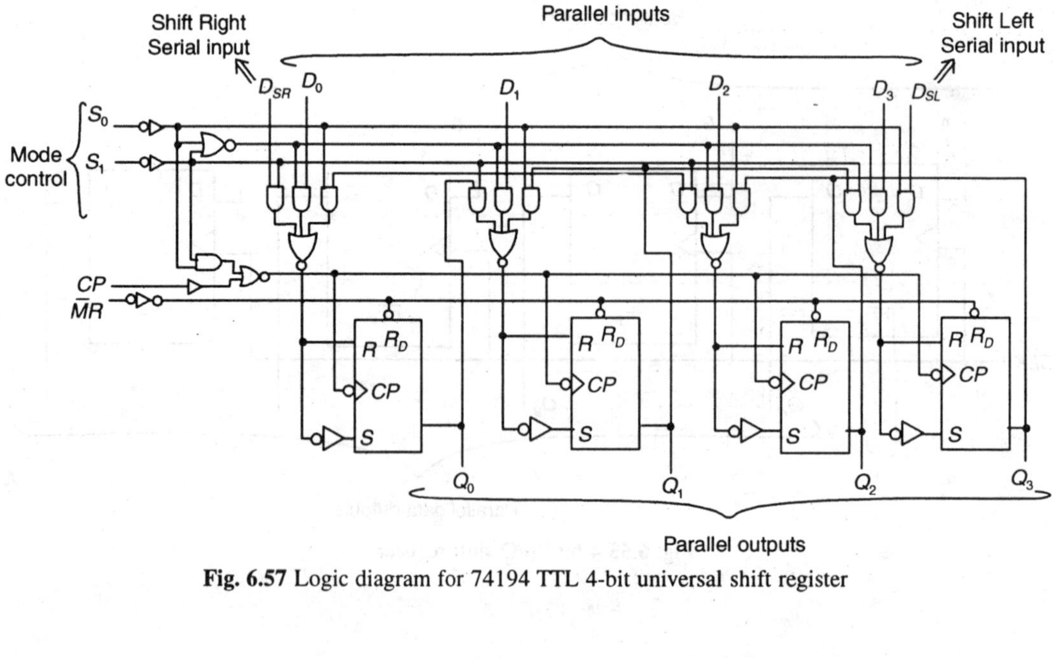

Fig. 6.57 Logic diagram for 74194 TTL 4-bit universal shift register

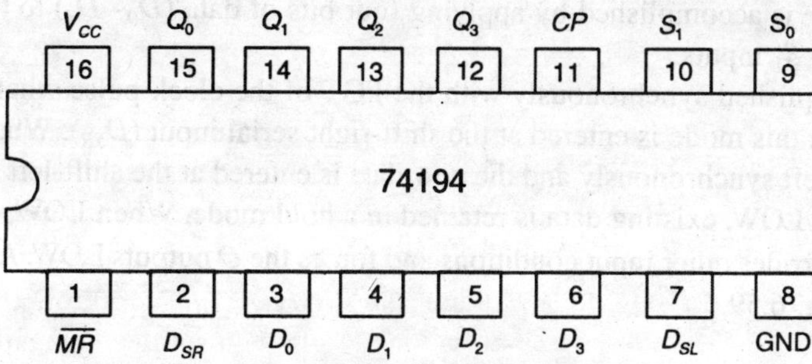

(a) Pinout of 74194

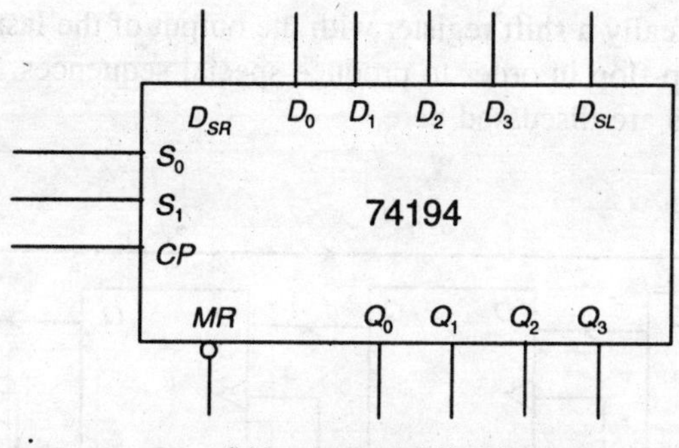

(b) Logic symbol for 74194

Fig. 6.58 The pinout and logic symbol for 74194

The 74194 has special features which increase the range of application. The synchronous operation of the device is determined by two mode select inputs S_0 and S_1. Parallel loading, which is synchronous

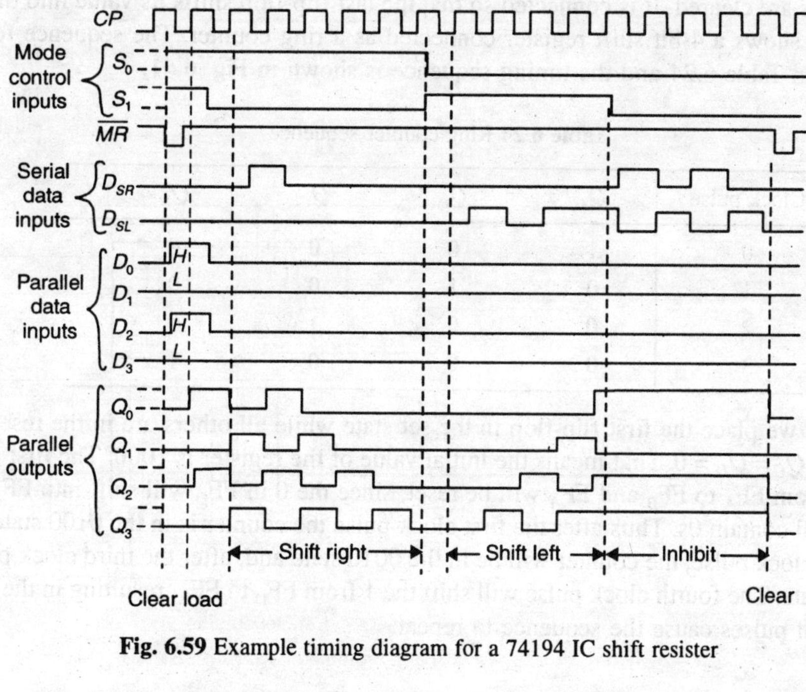

Fig. 6.59 Example timing diagram for a 74194 IC shift resister

with a PGT of the clock, is accomplished by applying four bits of data (D_0 - D_3) to the parallel inputs and HIGH to the S_0 and S_1 inputs.

Shift right is accomplished synchronously with the PGT of the clock pulse when S_0 is HIGH and S_1 is LOW. Serial data in this mode is entered at the shift-right serial input (D_{SR}). When S_0 is LOW and S_1 is HIGH, data shifts left synchronously and the new data is entered at the shift-left serial input (D_{SL}). When both S_0 and S_1 are LOW, existing data is retained in a hold mode. When LOW, the asynchronous Master Reset ($\overline{MR}$) overrides other input conditions and forces the Q outputs LOW. An example timing diagram is shown in Fig. 6.59.

6.18 SHIFT REGISTER COUNTERS

A shift register counter is basically a shift register with the output of the last flip-flop in the register is connected back to the first flip-flop in order to produce special sequences. Two of the most common types of shift register counters are discussed here.

The Ring Counter

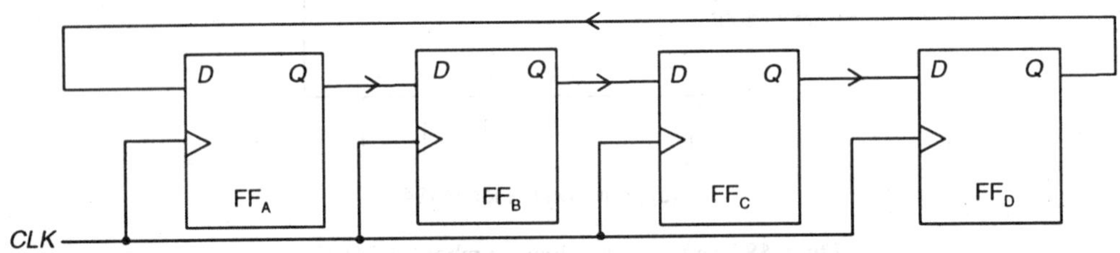

Fig. 6.60 4-bit ring counter

The *ring counter* is a circular shift register with only one flip-flop being set at any particular time; all other flip-flops are cleared. It is connected so that the last flip-flop shifts its value into the first flip-flop. Figure 6.60 shows a 4-bit shift register connected as a ring counter. The sequence for this ring counter is given in Table 6.24 and the timing sequence is shown in Fig. 6.61.

Table 6.24 Ring counter sequence

Clock pulse	Q_A	Q_B	Q_C	Q_D
0	1	0	0	0
1	0	1	0	0
2	0	0	1	0
3	0	0	0	1

Suppose that we place the first flip-flop in the set state while all others are in the reset state, i.e., $Q_A = 1$ and $Q_B = Q_C = Q_D = 0$. That means the initial value of the register is 1000. The first clock pulse will shift the 1 from FF_A to FF_B and FF_A will be reset, since the 0 in FF_D will shift into FF_A. All other flip-flops will still contain 0s. Thus after the first clock pulse the counter is in the 0100 state. Similarly after the second clock pulse, the counter will be in the 0010 state and, after the third clock pulse, it will be in the 0001 state. The fourth clock pulse will shift the 1 from FF_D to FF_A, resulting in the initial state 1000. Subsequent pulses cause the sequence to repeat.

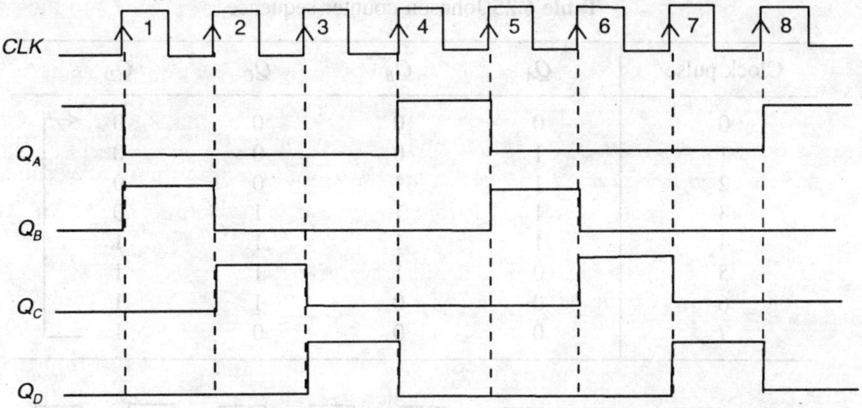

Fig. 6.61 Timing sequence for a 4 bit ring counter

Modified sequence can be achieved by having more than a single 1 in the counter.

The ring counter has the advantage of requiring no decoder, since we can read the count by simply noting which flip-flop is set.

Ring counters can be constructed for any desired MOD number. A MOD-*N* counter requires *N* flip-flops. In general, a ring counter will require more flip-flops than a binary counter for the same MOD number. For instance, a MOD-16 ring counter requires 16 flip-flops, while a MOD-16 binary counter requires only 4 flip-flops. Thus it has the disadvantage of being uneconomical of flip-flops.

The Johnson Counter

The *Johnson counter* is a modified form of a ring counter in which the complement of the output of the last flip-flop is connected back to the *D* input of the first flip-flop.

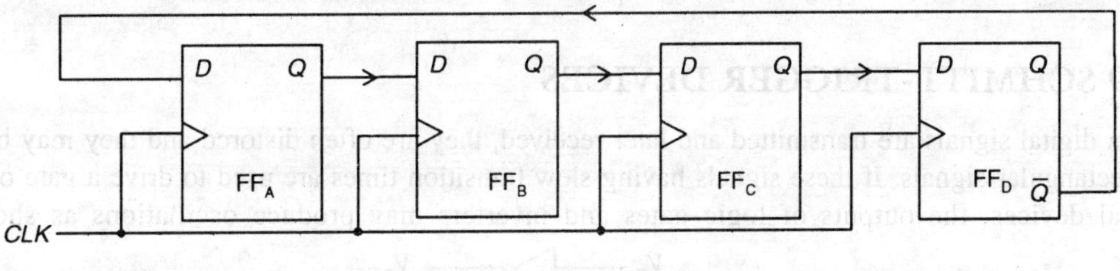

Fig. 6.62 4-bit Johnson counter

Figure 6.62 shows a 4-bit shift register connected as a Johnson counter. The sequence for this counter is given in Table 6.25 and the timing sequence is shown in Fig. 6.63.

The operation of the Johnson counter shown in Fig. 6.62 is very simple and easy to analyze if we realize that on each PGT of the clock pulse the content of FF_A shifts into FF_B, the content of FF_B shifts into FF_C, the content of FF_C shifts into FF_D, and the inverse of the content of the last flip-flop FF_D shifts into the first flip-flop FF_A. With these ideas if the sequence table is examined, we can easily understand the operation of the Johnson counter. The sequence table reveals that starting from the cleared state (i.e., 0000), the counter goes through a sequence of eight states. In general, an *n*-bit Johnson counter will go through a sequence of 2*n* states. One advantage of this counter is that it requires only 2-input gates to decode, regardless of the number of flip-flops in the counter.

Table 6.25 Johnson counter sequence

Clock pulse	Q_A	Q_B	Q_C	Q_D
0	0	0	0	0
1	1	0	0	0
2	1	1	0	0
3	1	1	1	0
4	1	1	1	1
5	0	1	1	1
6	0	0	1	1
7	0	0	0	1

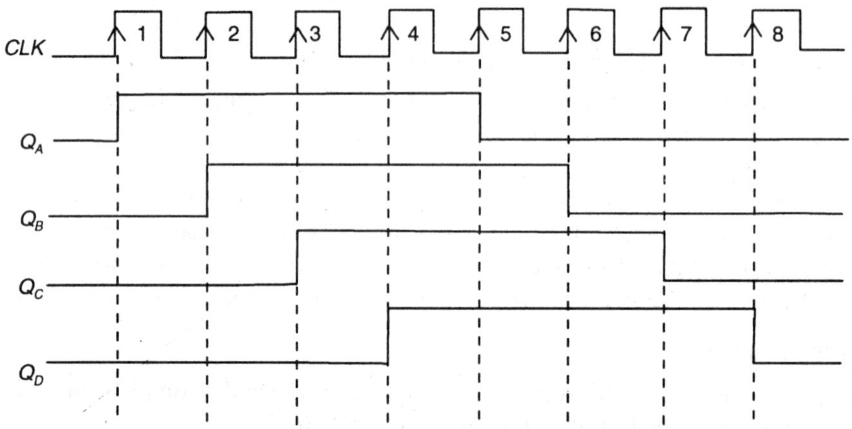

Fig. 6.63 Timing sequence for a 4-bit Johnson counter

6.19 SCHMITT-TRIGGER DEVICES

When digital signals are transmitted and later received, they are often distored and they may become nonrectangular signals. If these signals having slow transition times are used to drive a gate or other digital devices, the outputs of logic gates and inverters may produce oscillations as shown in

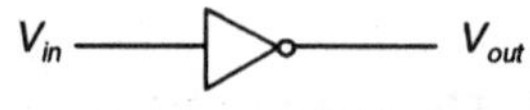

(a) Standard logic INVERTER

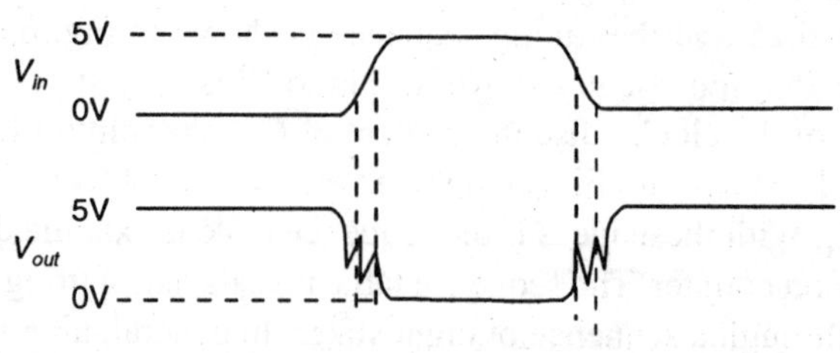

(b) Response to slow transition input signal

Fig. 6.64 Standard logic INVERTER and its response

Fig. 6.64(b). This may lead to unreliable operation. That is why a device called a Schmitt trigger comes in to take role.

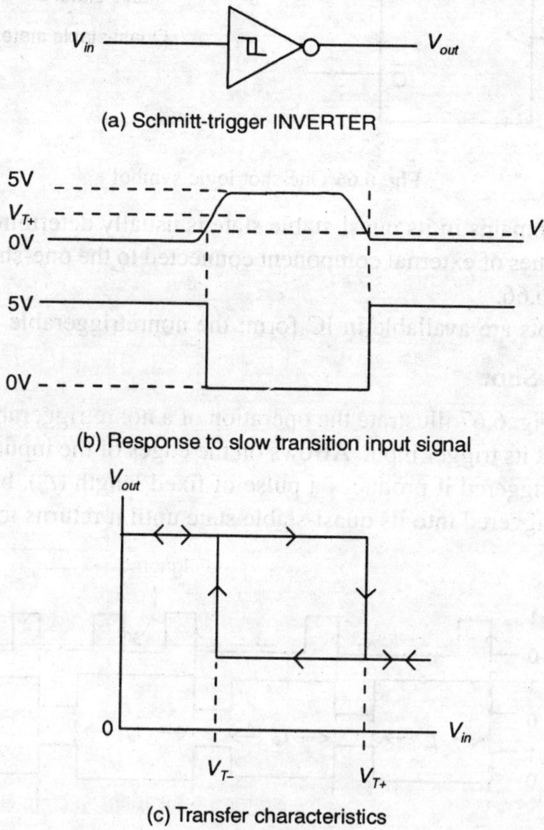

Fig. 6.65 Schmitt-trigger INVERTER and its response

A *Schmitt-trigger*, is an electronic circuit that is designed to accept slow transition signals and produce rectangular output that has oscillation-free transitions. The output will generally have clean and rapid transition times that are independent of input signal characteristics. Figure 6.65 shows a Schmitt-trigger INVERTER and its response to a slow-transition input.

From Fig. 6.65(c) we can observe that tie Schmitt-trigger operates with two threshold or trigger points. When an increasing input signal reaches the positive going threshold (V_{T+}), the circuit switches and the output goes to its LOW level. When the input signal decreases to the negative-going threshold voltage(V_{T-}), the circuit switches back and the output goes to its HIGH level.

There are several ICs available with Schmitt-trigger inputs. The 7414, 74LS14, and 74HC14 are hex INVERTER ICs with Schmitt-trigger inputs. The 7413, 74LS13, and 74HC13 are dual four-input NANDs with Schmitt-trigger inputs.

6.20 ONE-SHOT (MONOSTABLE MULTIVIBRATOR)

One-shot is a multivibrator circuit whose output has only one stable state. When externally triggered, the output goes to its quasi-stable for a predetermined amount of time and then returns to its stable state.

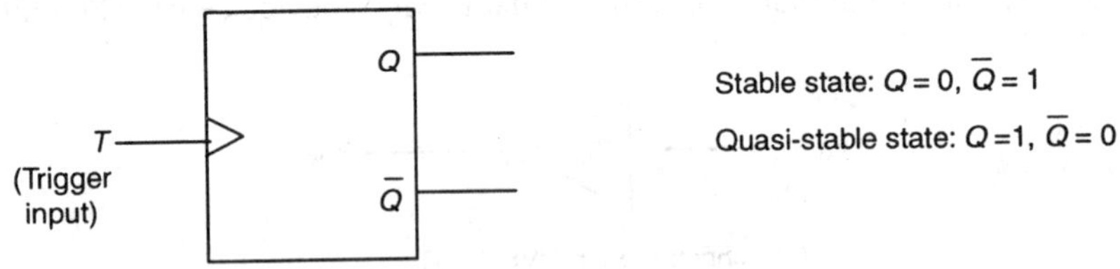

Fig. 6.66 One-shot logic symbol

The time that the output remains in its quasi-stable state is usually determined by an *RC* time constant which results from the values of external component connected to the one-shot. A typical one-shot logic symbol is shown in Fig. 6.66.

Two types of one-shots are available in IC form: the nonretriggerable and the retriggerable.

Nonretriggerable One-Shot

The waveforms given in Fig. 6.67 illustrate the operation of a nonretriggerable one-shot that triggers on positive-going transitior at its trigger input. Arrows on the edges of the input *T* signify triggering edges. Each time the device is triggered it produces a pulse of fixed length (t_w), but it ignores any additional trigger pulses once it is triggered into its quasi-stable state until it returns to its stable state (times out).

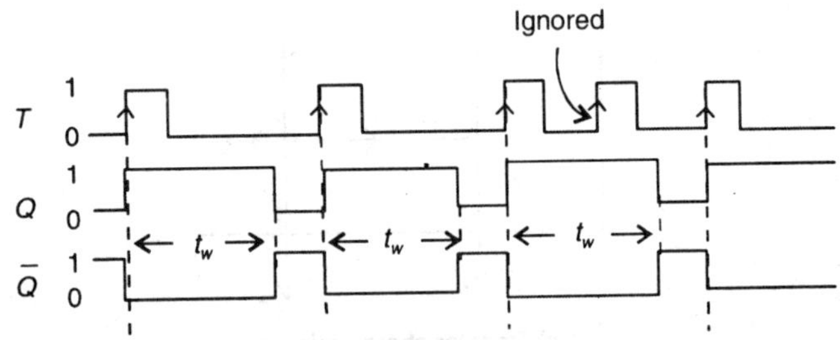

Fig. 6.67 Typical waveforms for nonretriggerable operation

Retriggerable One-Shot

The waveforms given in Fig. 6.68 illustrate the operation of a retriggerable one-shot. It can be observed from the waveforms that the device may be retriggered any number of times during its time-out period; it does not return to the reset condition until t_w after the final trigger pulse. Thus retriggering can be used as a means of extending the time-out.

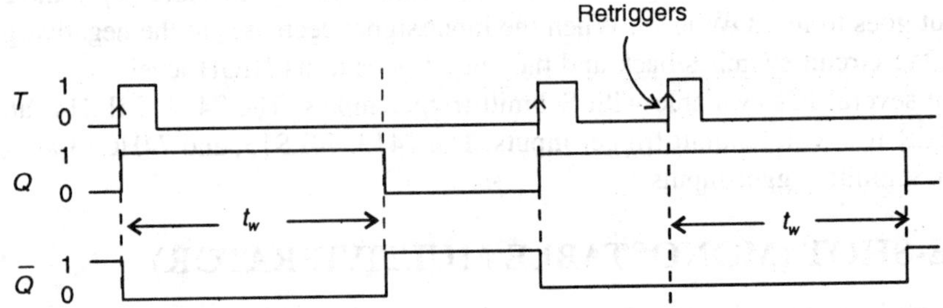

Fig. 6.68 Typical waveforms for retriggerable operation

There are several one-shot ICs available in both the retriggerable and nonretriggerable versions: The 74121 and 74L121 are single nonretriggerable one-shot ICs; the 74221, 74LS221, and 74HC221 are dual nonretriggerable one-shot ICs; the 74122 and 74LS122 are single retriggerable one-shot ICs, the 74123, 74LS123, and 74HC123 are dual retriggerable one-shot ICs.

6.21 CLOCK GENERATOR CIRCUITS

The CLOCK generator is the heart of every digital system. It provides clock signal, like heart beat, without which the system would cease to function. In this section we will present some circuits that can be used to generate the CLOCK for synchronous sequential circuits and systems.

Clock Circuit Using Schmitt-Trigger INVERTER

The clock circuit can be built using a Schmitt-trigger INVERTER, as shown in Fig. 6.69. The signal at the output is an approximate square wave with a frequency that depends on the *R* and *C* values. The expressions showing the relationship between the frequency and *R* and *C* values are given in Table 6.26 for different ICs. Notice the maximum resistance value given for each device. Note that the circuit will fail to oscillate if *R* exceeds these limits.

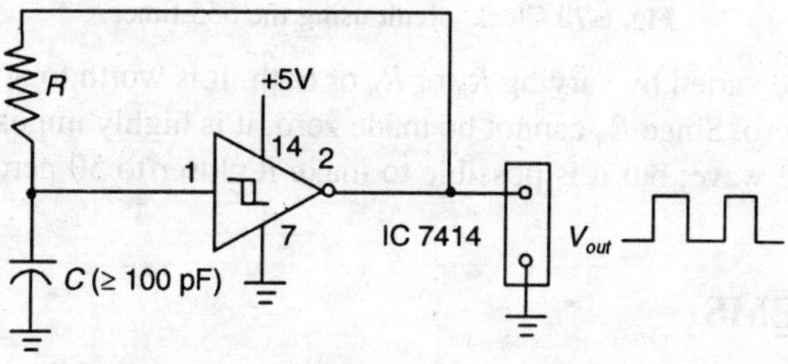

Fig. 6.69 Clock circuit using Schmitt-trigger INVERTER

Table 6.26

IC	Expression
7414	$f_0 =$ 0.8/ RC ($R \leq 500\Omega$)
74LS14	$f_0 =$ 0.8/RC ($R \leq 2k\Omega$)
74HC14	$f_0 =$ 1.2/RC ($R \leq 10M\Omega$)

Clock Circuit Using the 555 Timer

The 555 timer triggers itself and free runs as a multivibrator in the circuit configuration shown in Fig. 6.70. The output is a repetitive rectangular waveform that switches between two logic levels. The total time period (*T*), the frequency (*f*) and the duty cycle (*D*) of the output waveform are given by

$$T = T_1 + T_2$$

$$F = 1/T$$

$$D = T_1/T$$

where $T_1 = 0.693\ (R_A + R_B)\ C$

$$T_2 = 0.693\ R_A C$$

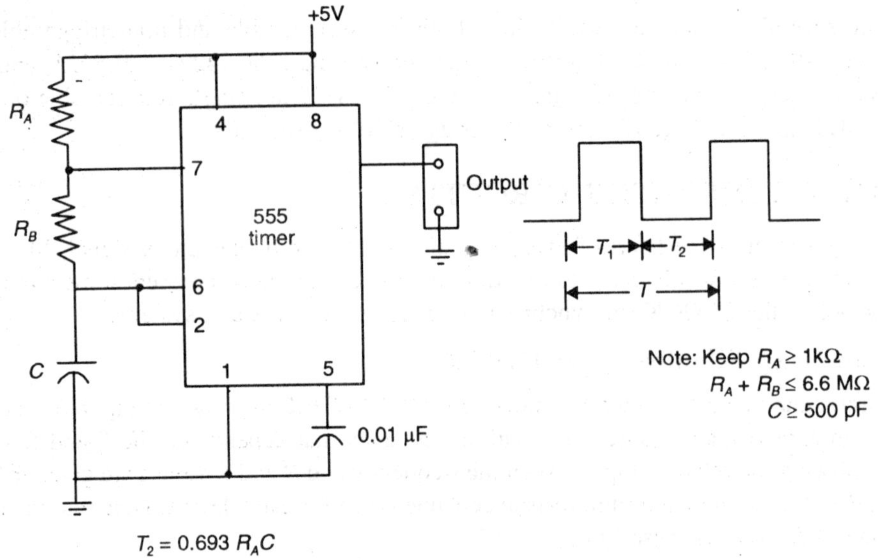

Fig. 6.70 Clock circuit using the 555 timer

The duty cycle can be varied by varying R_A or R_B or both. It is worth to note that T_1 cannot be equal to T_2 unless R_A is made zero. Since R_A cannot be made zero, it is highly impossible to get an exactly 50 percent duty cycle square wave; but it is possible to make it closer to 50 percent by making $R_B >> R_A$, so that $T_1 \approx T_2$.

SOLVED PROBLEMS

6.1 Convert a clocked *S-R* flip-flop to a clocked *J-K* flip-flop by adding external gates.

SOLUTION:

Step 1:

The circuit excitation table to convert *S-R* flip-flop to a *J-K* flip-flop is obtained by referring the excitation table of both the flip-flops.

Table P 6.1 Circuit excitation table

Present state	Flip-flops data inputs		Next state	*S-R* flip-flop inputs	
Q (*t*)	*J*	*K*	*Q* (*t*+1)	*S*	*R*
0	0	0	0	0	×
0	0	1	0	0	×
0	1	0	1	1	0
0	1	1	1	1	0
1	0	0	1	×	0
1	0	1	0	0	1
1	1	0	1	×	0
1	1	1	0	0	1

Step 2:

$S = \overline{Q}(t)\, J$ (a) $R = Q(t)\, K$ (b)

Fig. P6.1(i) K-maps

Step 3:

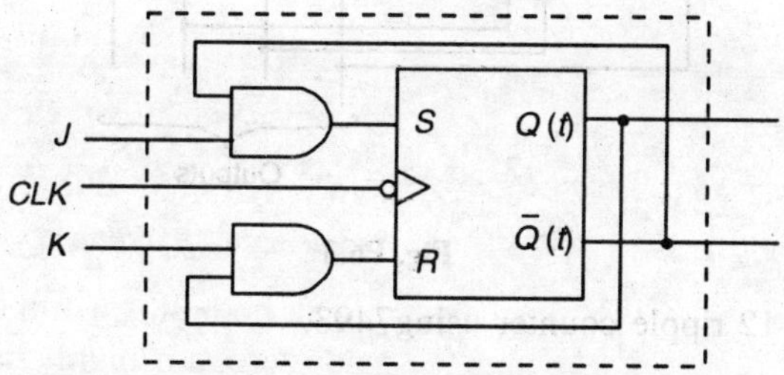

Fig. P6.1(ii) *J-K* flip-flop using *S-R* flip-flop

6.2 Design a divide-by-7 ripple counter using *T* flip-flops.

SOLUTION: We can find the number of flip-flops such that $2^n \geq$ MOD number, where n = Number of flip-flops. Thus the counter requires 3 flip-flops. For this counter, the resetting is required as soon as the counter state reaches 111. Hence all flip-flop outputs are connected as inputs to a 3-input NAND gate and the NAND gate output is connected to clear (*CLR*) inputs of all the flip-flops.

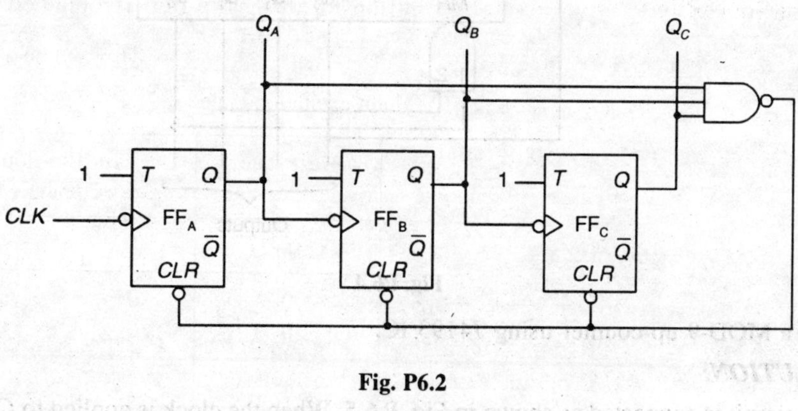

Fig. P6.2

6.3 Design a divide-by-6 ripple counter using 7490.

SOLUTION: The device is connected as a BCD decade counter. To obtain divide-by-6 counter, it is necessary to force the counter to recycle after the 0101 state. To achieve this, outputs Q_1

and Q_2 are connected to the *MR* inputs. Therefore as soon as the counter reaches the state 0110, the counter is reset to 0000.

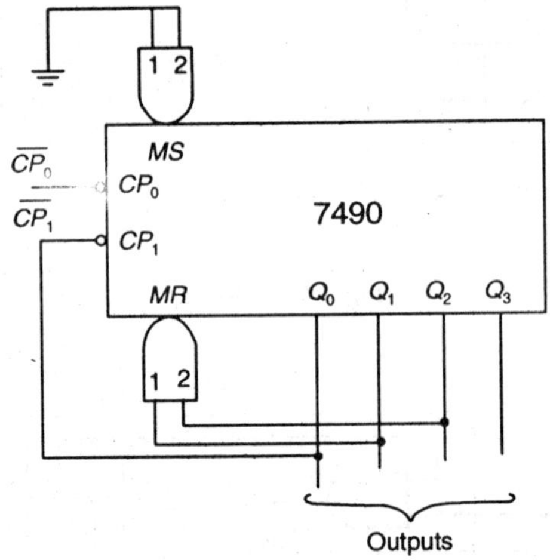

Fig. P6.3

6.4 Design a divide-by-12 ripple counter using7493.

SOLUTION:

The device is connected as a 4-bit counter. To obtain divide-by-12 counter, it is necessary to force the counter to recycle after the count 1011. This is accomplished by connecting Q_2 and Q_3 to the *MR* inputs. Immediately after the counter goes to count 1100, it is reset to 0000.

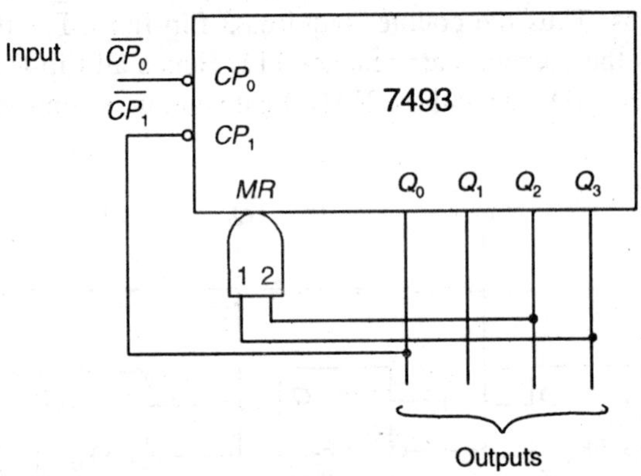

Fig. P6.4

6.5 Design a MOD-9 up-counter using 74193 IC.

SOLUTION:

The circuit is connected as shown in Fig. P 6.5. When the clock is applied to CP_U the counter will progress through 0, 1, 2, 3, 4, 5, 6, 7 and 8, and at count 9 (i.e. binary 1001) the counter is cleared.

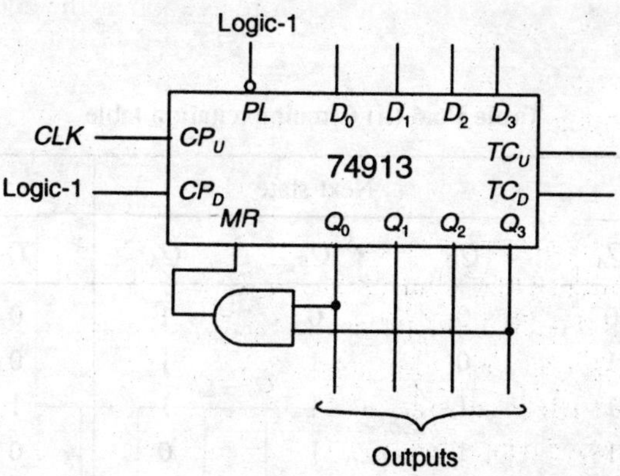

Fig. P6.5

6.6 Design a 3-bit counter with the following binary sequence: 0, 1, 3, 7, 6, 4 and repeat. Use *T* flip-flops.

SOLUTION:

Step 1:

This counter requires 3 flip-flops. The desired count sequence is shown in Table P6.6(i).

Table P 6.6(i) Count sequence for the counter of problem 6.6

Q_C	Q_B	Q_A
0	0	0
0	0	1
0	1	1
1	1	1
1	1	0
1	0	0

Step 2:

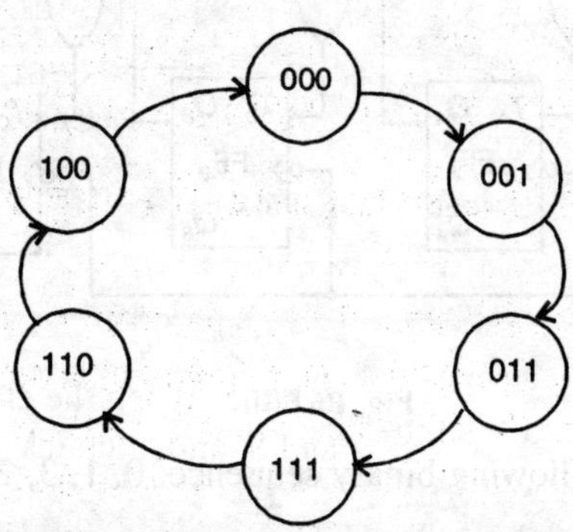

Fig. P6.6(i) State diagram for synchronous counter of problem 6.6

Step 3:

Table P6.6 (ii) Circuit excitation table

Present state			Next state			Flip-flop inputs		
Q_C	Q_B	Q_A	Q_C	Q_B	Q_A	T_C	T_B	T_A
0	0	0	0	0	1	0	0	1
0	0	1	0	1	1	0	1	0
0	1	1	1	1	1	1	0	0
1	1	1	1	1	0	0	0	1
1	1	0	1	0	0	0	1	0
1	0	0	0	0	0	1	0	0

Step 4:

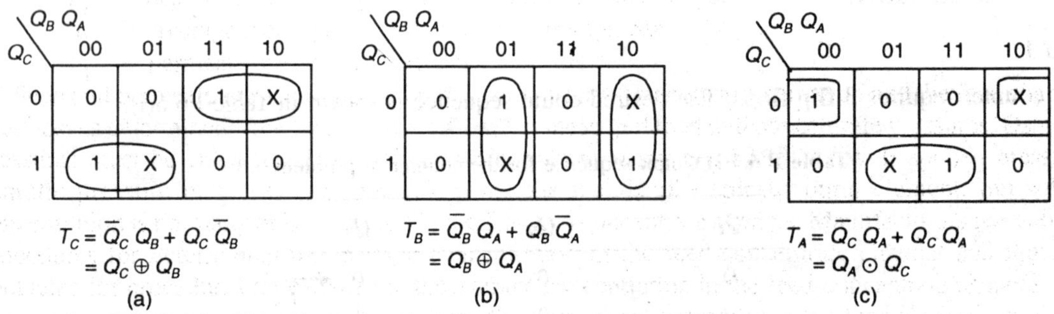

Fig. P6.6(ii) K-maps

Step 5:

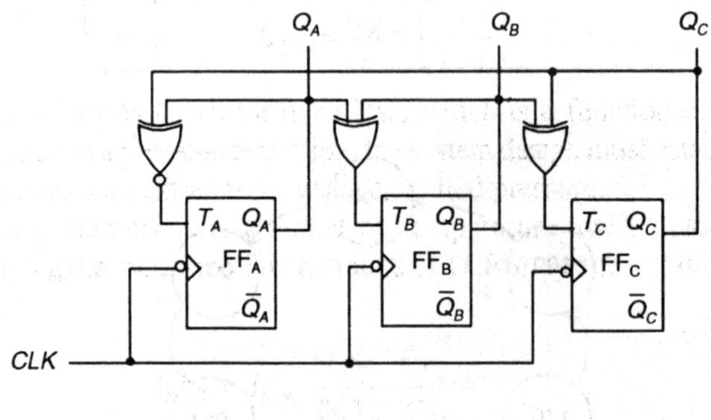

Fig. P6.6(iii)

6.7 Design a counter with the following binary sequence: 0, 1, 3, 2, 6, 4, 5, 7 and repeat. Use *S-R* flip-flops.

SOLUTION:

Step 1:

This counter requires 3 flip-flops. The desired count sequence is shown in Table 6.7 (i).

Table P6.7(i) Count sequence for the counter of problem 6.7

Q_c	Q_B	Q_A
0	0	0
0	0	1
0	1	1
0	1	0
1	1	0
1	0	0
1	0	1
1	1	1

Step 2:

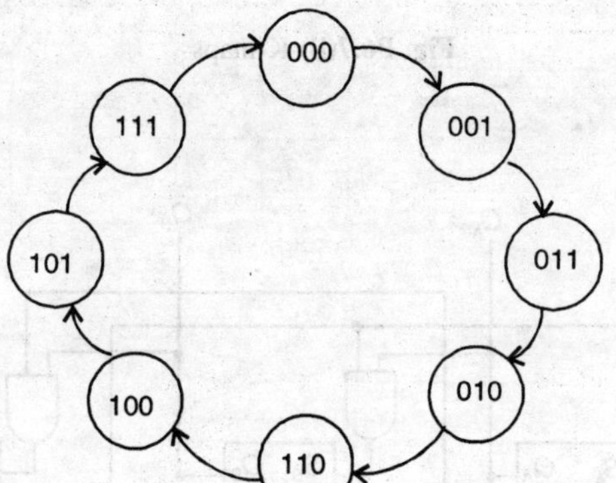

Fig. P6.7(i) State diagram for synchronous counter of problem 6.7

Step 3:

Table P6.7(ii) Circuit excitation table

Present state			Next state			Flip-flop inputs					
Q_C	Q_B	Q_A	Q_C	Q_B	Q_A	S_C	R_C	S_B	R_B	S_A	R_A
0	0	0	0	0	1	0	×	0	×	1	0
0	0	1	0	1	1	0	×	1	0	×	0
0	1	1	0	1	0	0	×	×	0	0	1
0	1	0	1	1	0	1	0	×	0	0	×
1	1	0	1	0	0	×	0	0	1	0	×
1	0	0	1	0	1	×	0	0	×	1	0
1	0	1	1	1	1	×	0	1	0	×	0
1	1	1	0	0	0	0	1	0	1	0	1

Step 4:

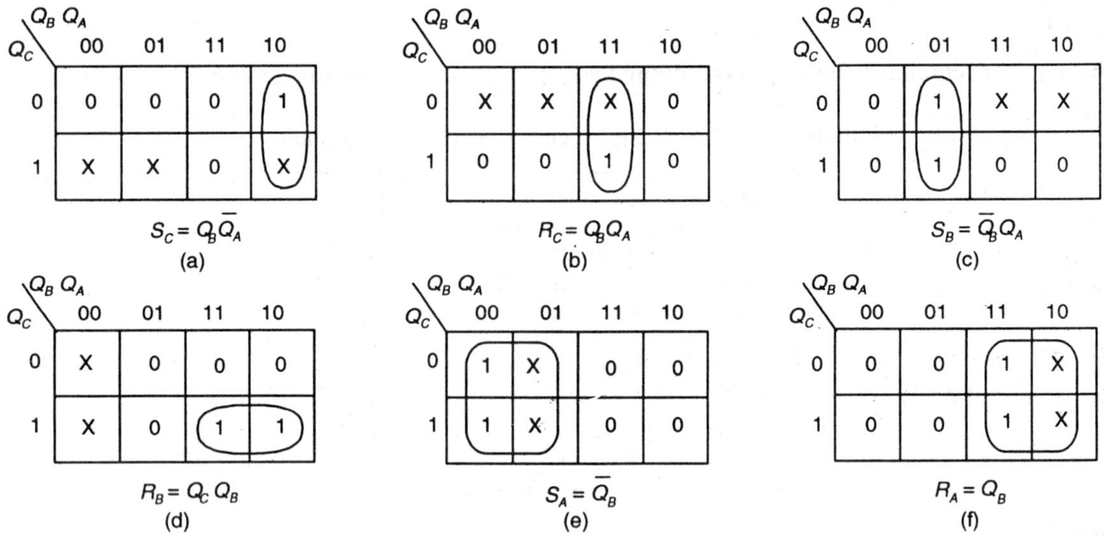

Fig. P6.7(ii) K-maps

Step 5:

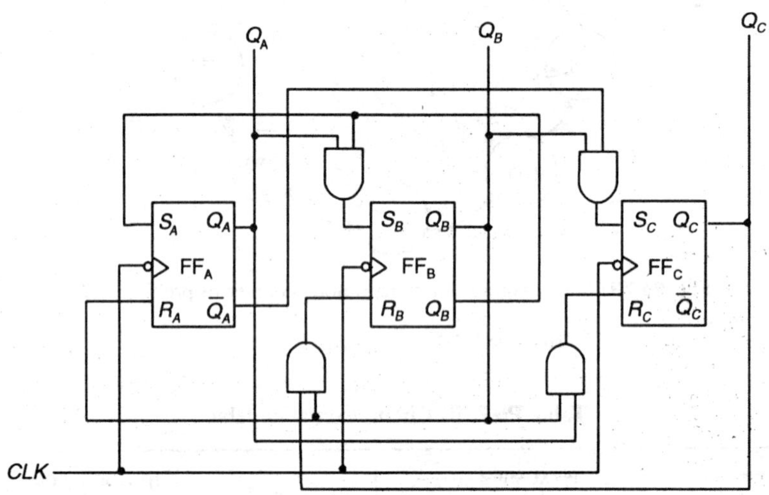

Fig. P6.7(iii)

6.8 Design a counter that counts according to the 2, 4, 2, 1 code. Use T flip-flops.

SOLUTION:

Step 1:

This counter requires 4 flip-flops. The desired count sequence is shown in Table P6.8(i).

Table P 6.8 (i) Count sequence for the counter of problem 6.8

Q_D	Q_C	Q_B	Q_A
0	0	0	0
0	0	0	1
0	0	1	0
0	0	1	1
0	1	0	0
1	0	1	1
1	1	0	0
1	1	0	1
1	1	1	0
1	1	1	1

Step 2:

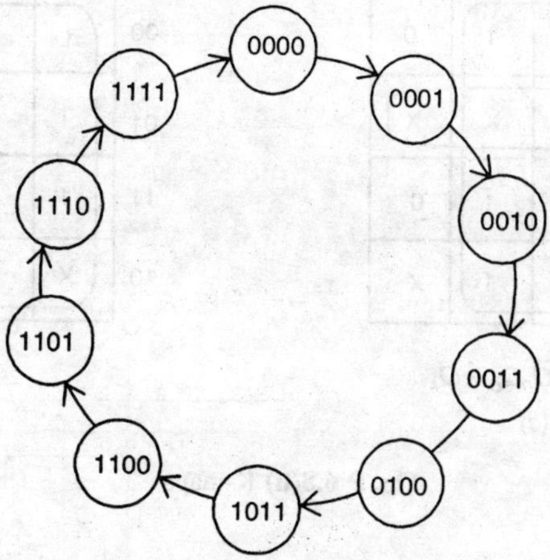

Fig. P6.8(i) State diagram for synchronous counter of problem 6.8

Step 3:

Table P6.8(ii) Circuit excitation table

Present state				Next state				Flip-flop inputs			
Q_D	Q_C	Q_B	Q_A	Q_D	Q_C	Q_B	Q_A	T_D	T_C	T_B	T_A
0	0	0	0	0	0	0	1	0	0	0	1
0	0	0	1	0	0	1	0	0	0	1	1
0	0	1	0	0	0	1	1	0	0	0	1
0	0	1	1	0	1	0	0	0	1	1	1
0	1	0	0	1	0	1	1	1	1	1	1
1	0	1	1	1	1	0	0	0	1	1	1
1	1	0	0	1	1	0	1	0	0	0	1
1	1	0	1	1	1	1	0	0	0	1	1
1	1	1	0	1	1	1	1	0	0	0	1
1	1	1	1	0	0	0	0	1	1	1	1

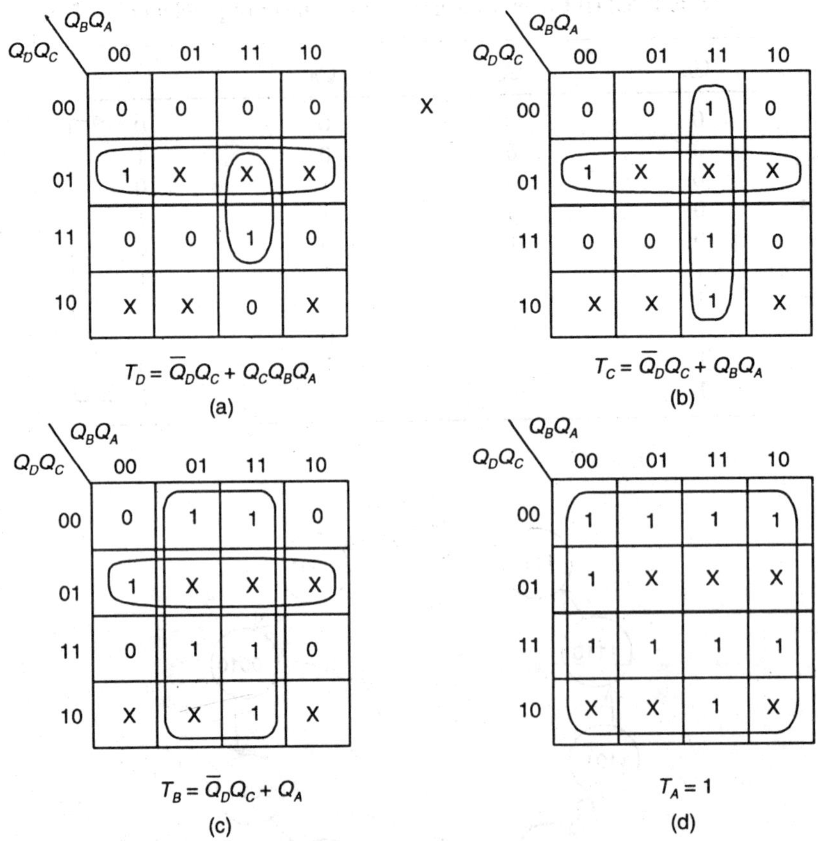

Fig. P 6.8(ii) K-maps

Step 5:

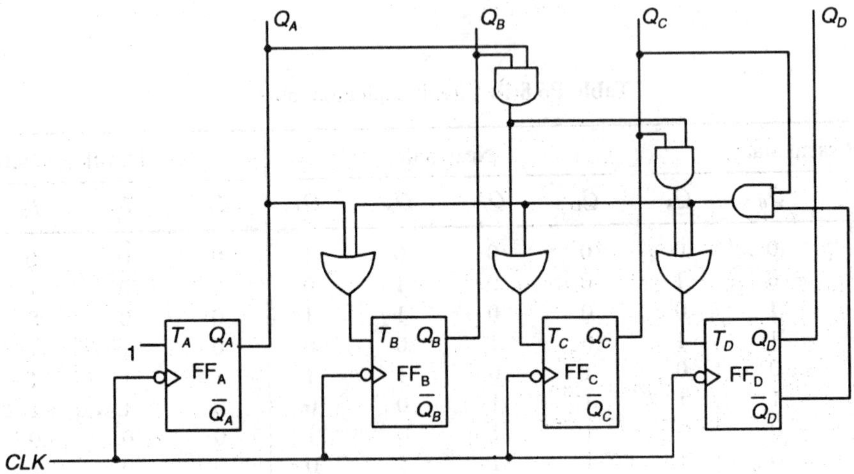

Fig. P6.8(iii)

6.9 Design a counter using *J-K* flip-flops to generate the following waveform.

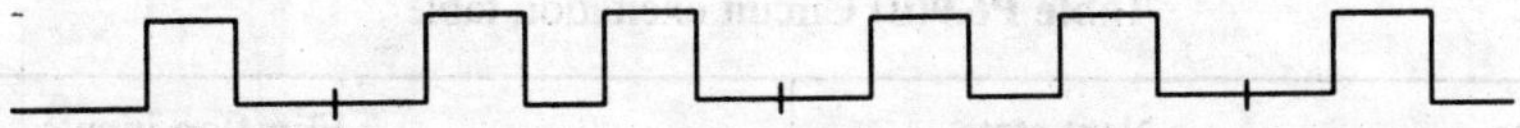

Fig. P6.9(i)

SOLUTION: Let the given waveform be the output Q_C of the FF_C. Knowing Q_C, let us assign Q_k and Q_b arbitrarily to obtain unique states. This results in the five unique states shown in Table P 6.9(i).

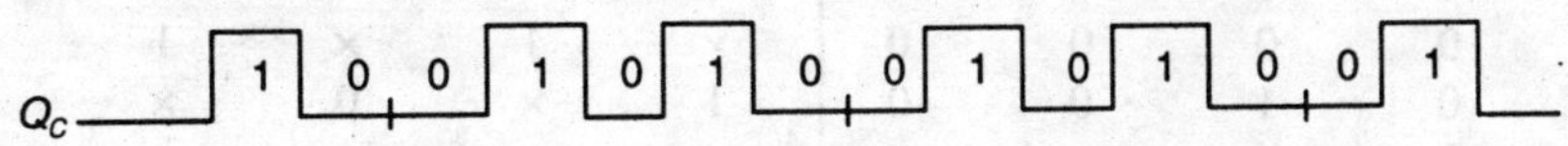

Fig. P6.9(ii)

Step 1:

Table P6.9(i)

Q_C	Q_B	Q_A
1	0	0
0	0	1
0	1	1
1	1	0
0	0	0

Step 2:

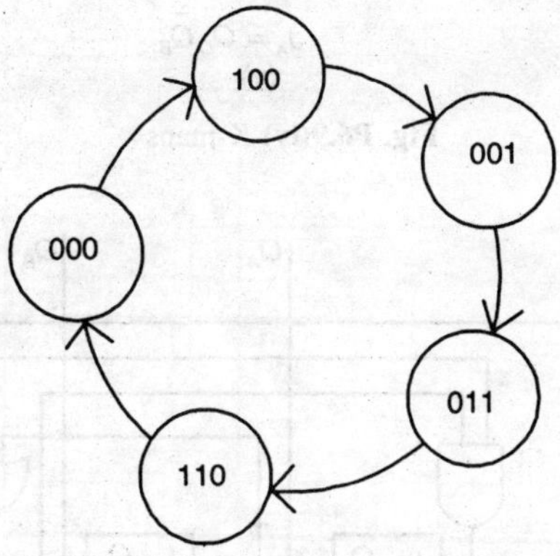

Fig. P6.9(iii) State diagram for synchronous counter of problem 6.9

Step 3:

Table P6.9(ii) Circuit excitation table

Present state			Next state			Flip-flop inputs					
Q_C	Q_B	Q_A	Q_C	Q_B	Q_A	J_C	K_C	J_B	K_B	J_A	K_A
1	0	0	0	0	1	×	1	0	×	1	×
0	0	1	0	1	1	0	×	1	×	×	0
0	1	1	1	1	0	1	×	×	0	×	1
1	1	0	0	0	0	×	1	×	1	0	×
0	0	0	1	0	0	1	×	0	×	0	×

Step 4:

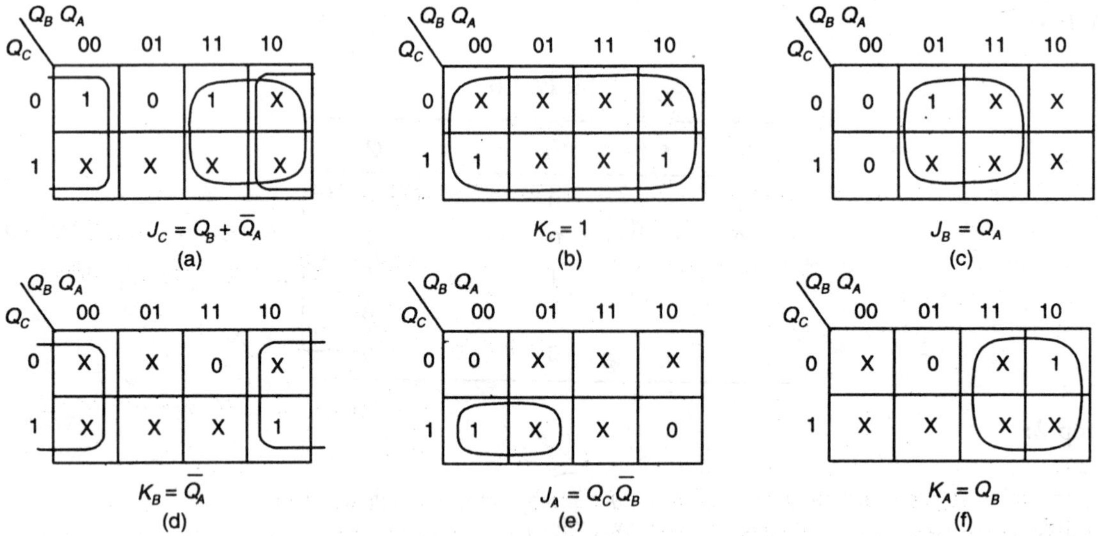

Fig. P6.9(iv) K-maps

Step 5:

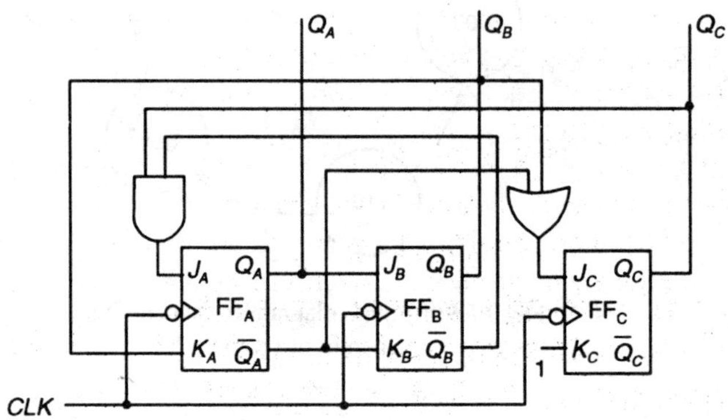

Fig. P6.9(v)

6.10 Design a self-starting counter using *D* flip-flops to generate the repetitive sequence 000, 001, 010, 100, 011, 110, 000, ...

SOLUTION:

Step 1:

This counter requires 3 flip-flops. The desired count sequence is shown in Table P6.10(i)

Table P6-10(i) Count sequence for the counter of problem 6.10

Q_C	Q_B	Q_A
0	0	0
0	0	1
0	1	0
1	0	0
0	1	1
1	1	0

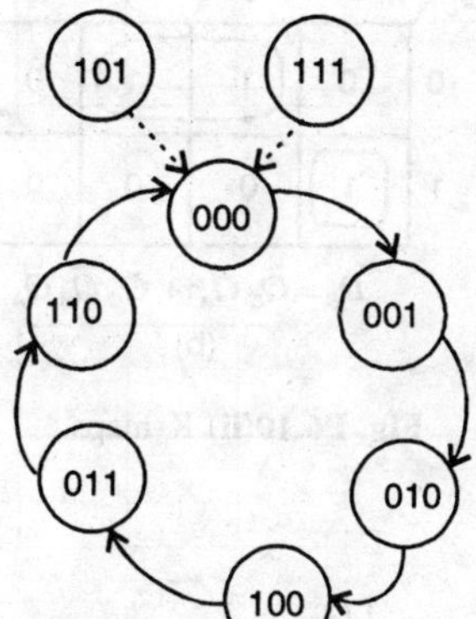

Fig. P6.10(i) State diagram for synchronous counter of problem 6.10

Step 2:

Since the counter to be designed is self-starting one, the state diagram should also include those states that are not part of the desired count sequence. We choose to have each of these undesired states go to the 000 state from where the correct sequence will be generated.

Step 3:

Table P6.10(ii) Circuit excitation table

	Present state			Next state			Flip-flop inputs		
	Q_C	Q_B	Q_A	Q_C	Q_B	Q_A	D_C	D_B	D_A
	0	0	0	0	0	1	0	0	1
	0	0	1	0	1	0	0	1	0
	0	1	0	1	0	0	1	0	0
	1	0	0	0	1	1	0	1	1
	0	1	1	1	1	0	1	1	0
	1	1	0	0	0	0	0	0	0
Undesired states	1	0	1	0	0	0	0	0	0
	1	1	1	0	0	0	0	0	0

Step 4:

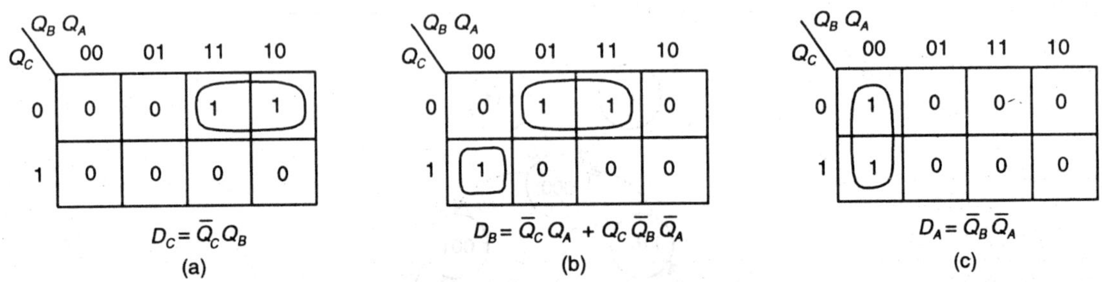

Fig. P6.10(ii) K-maps

Step 5:

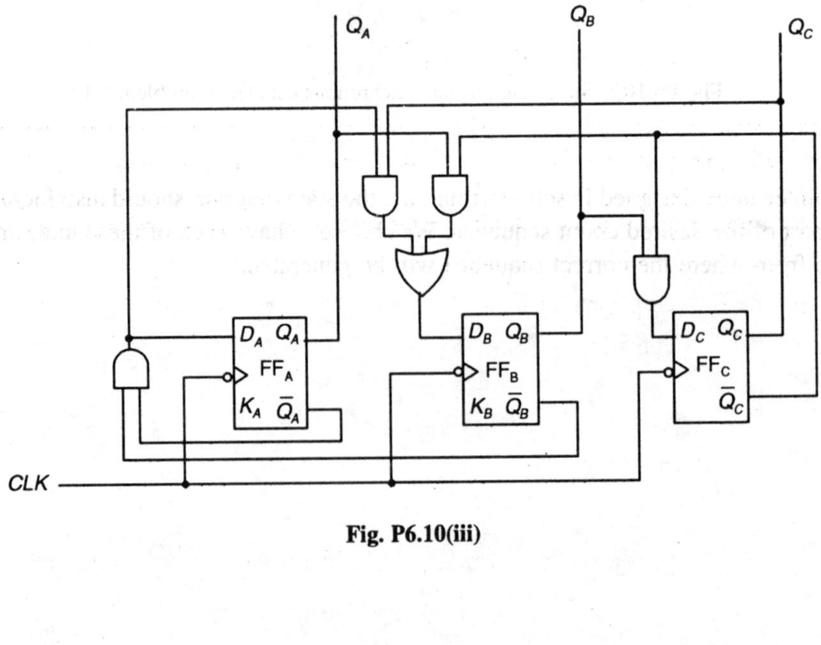

Fig. P6.10(iii)

6.11 Design a clock generator by using IC 74LS14 Schmitt-trigger INVERTER with output frequency of 2 kHz.

SOLUTION: We have the expression

$$f = \frac{0.8}{RC} \qquad \begin{array}{l} R \le \text{k}\Omega \\ C \ge 100\,\text{pF} \end{array}$$

It is given that $f = 2$ kHz.

Let $\qquad R = 1\text{k}\Omega$

Substituting these two values in the known expression to get C as follows:

$$C = \frac{0.8}{fR}$$

$$= \frac{0.8}{2000 \times 1000}$$

$$= 0.4\mu\text{F}$$

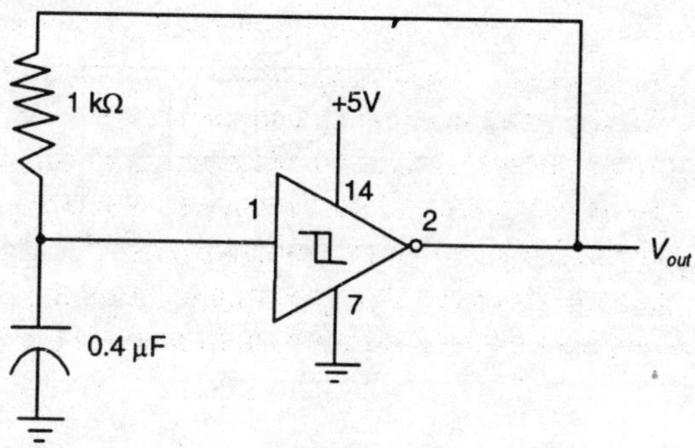

Fig. P6.11

EXERCISES

6.1 Convert a clocked *S-R* flip-flop to a clocked *T* flip-flop by adding external gates.

6.2 Design a divide-by-9 ripple counter using *T* flip-flops.

6.3 Design a divide-by-10 ripple counter using 7493 IC.

6.4 Design a divide-by-14 ripple counter using 7493 IC.

6.5 Design a MOD-12 up-counter using 74193 IC.

6.6 Design a 3-bit counter in the following sequence: 000, 100, 111, 010, 011 and repeat. Use *T* flip-flops.

6.7 Design a BCD counter with *J-K* flip-flops.

6.8 Describe a 2-bit counter that will count in two different modes (up or down), depending on the level of a control line (HIGH or LOW).

6.9 Design a counter using *S-R* flip-flops to generate the following waveform (Fig. E6.9).

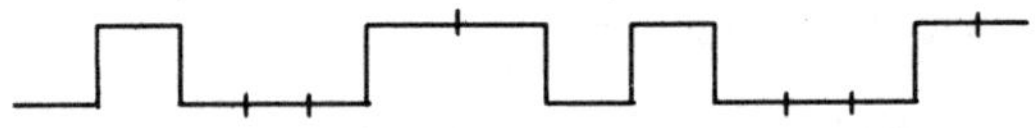

Fig. E6.9

6.10 Design a self-starting counter using *D* flip-flops to generate the repetitive binary sequence : 0, 3, 5, 7, 4, 0, ...

6.11 Design a clock generator by using IC 7414 Schmitt-trigger INVERTER to produce an approximate square wave with a frequency of 5 kHz.

6.12 Design a 555 free-running oscillator to produce an approximate square wave of 50 kHz.

Memory Devices

7

A digital processing system requires a facility to store digital information on permanent or semipermanent basis. The information usually consists of instructions coded in binary form, data to be processed, intermediate and final results, etc. We are already familiar with the flip-flops and registers that are used to store information. In this chapter we make an attempt to learn about such semiconductor memory devices that are used as the main memory of a computer.

The memory of a computer is divided into a main (primary or internal) memory and an auxiliary (secondary or storage) memory, as shown in Fig. 7.1. The main memory is composed of high-speed semiconductor devices: the RAM (random-access memory) and ROM (read-only memory). Auxiliary memory includes magnetic memories such as floppy disk, hard disk, etc.

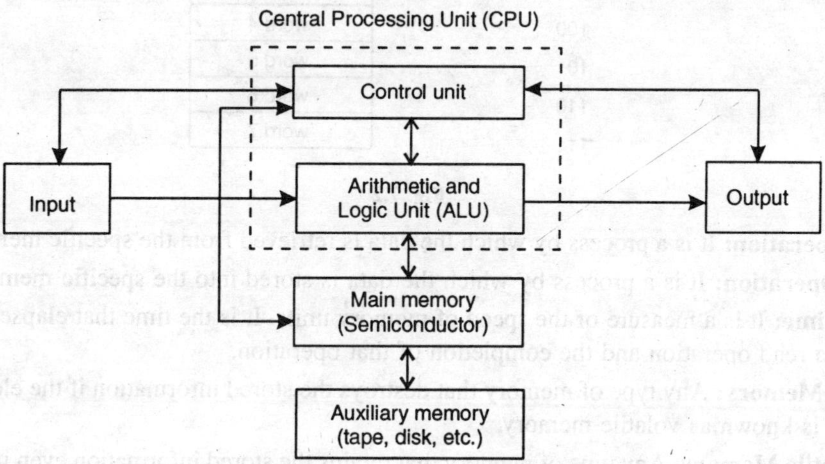

Fig. 7.1 Block diagram of a computer system

We also describe architecture of the basic types of programmable logic devices in this chapter.

7.1 MEMORY TERMINOLOGY

Let us define here some of the more basic terms associated with memory systems.

Memory Cell: It is a device or electrical circuit capable of storing one bit of information. The basic memory cell is typically a flip-flop, a circuit capable of storing charge or a single spot on magnetic tape or disk.

Memory Word: It is a group of bits (i.e., memory cells) the computer recognizes and processes at a time. For example, a register consisting of eight flip-flops can be considered to be a memory that is storing an 8-bit word.

Word Size: The number of bits in each word is referred to as the word size. Typical word sizes range from 4 to 64 bits.

Byte: A group of eight bits is known as byte. Word sizes can be expressed in bytes as well as in bits. Byte has become the basic unit of data used in computers.

Capacity: It is the amount of storage space in a memory specified in terms of bits or bytes.

Density: It is the measure of how many bits can be stored in some amount of space. When we say that one memory device has a greater density than another, we mean that it can store more bits in the same amount of space and it is more dense.

Address: An address is a binary number that identifies the location of a word in memory. Figure 7.2 illustrates a small memory consisting of eight words. Each of these eight words has a specific address represented as a 3-bit number ranging from 000 to 111.

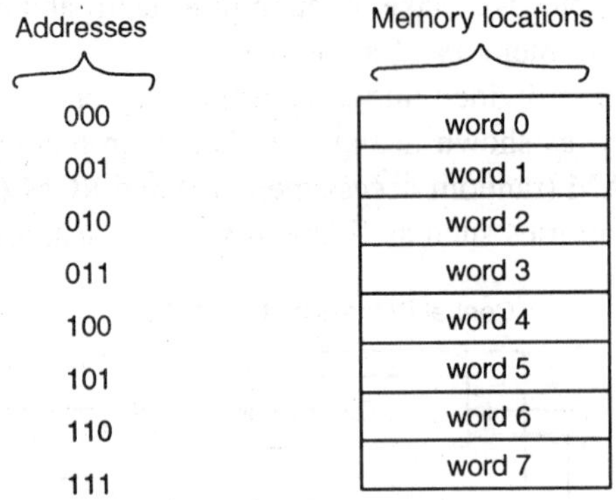

Fig. 7.2

Read Operation: It is a process by which the data is retrieved from the specific memory location.

Write Operation: It is a process by which the data is stored into the specific memory location.

Access time: It is a measure of the speed of memory units. It is the time that elapses between the initiation of a read operation and the completion of that operation.

Volatile Memory: Any type of memory that destroys the stored information if the electrical power is turned off is known as volatile memory.

Nonvolatile Memory: Any type of memory that retains the stored information even if the electrical power is turned off is known as nonvolatile memory.

Random-Access Memory (RAM): It is a memory in which the memory locations are assessed in any order to read or write data. Here, the access time is the same for any location.

Sequential-Access Memory: It is a memory in which the memory locations are accessed in a sequential order to read or write data. Therefore, the access time will vary depending on the storage location of the data.

Read/Write Memory (R/WM): It is a memory that stores binary information during the operation of the computer. The information stored in this memory can be read and altered easily. R/WM is a volatile memory.

Read-only Memory (ROM): It is a memory that stores binary information permanently. The information stored in this memory can only be read but cannot be altered. ROM is a nonvolatile memory.

Static Memory: It is a memory in which the stored data will remain permanently stored as long as power is applied, without the need for periodically rewriting the data into memory. Static memory stores a bit as a voltage.

Dynamic Memory: It is a memory in which the stored data will not remain permanently stored, even with power applied, unless the data is periodically rewritten into memory. Dynamic memory stores a bit as a charge.

Internal Memory (Main Memory): It is that part of a computer's memory that holds the program and data the computer is currently working on. It is the high-speed memory in the computer and is always a semiconductor memory.

Auxiliary Memory (Storage Memory): It is that part of a computer's memory that is separate from the computer's internal memory. It is slower in speed than internal memory and is always nonvolatile. Magnetic tape and disk are common auxiliary memory devices.

7.2 GENERAL MEMORY OPERATION

Each type of memory is different in its internal operation, but, certain basic operating principles are the same for all memory systems. Every memory system performs the following functions using several types of input and output lines:

1. Select the address in memory that is being accessed for a read or write operation.
2. Select either a read or a write operation to be performed.
3. Supply the input data to be stored in memory during a write operation.
4. Hold the output data coming from memory during a read operation.
5. Enable (or disable) the memory so that it will (or will not) respond to the address inputs and read/write command.

Figure 7.3 shows a memory chip of 32 registers with five address lines, four data input lines, four data output lines and two control lines: Read/ Write $(R/\overline{W})$ and chip select $(\overline{CS})$. The $\overline{CS}$ line is used to enable the chip, and the $R/\overline{W}$ line to control data flow. The registers are arranged sequentially and numbered in binary from 00000 to 11111. These numbers are nothing but memory addresses, identifying each register as a memory location.

To read from (or write into) a memory location, the address is placed on the address lines. The internal decoder decodes the address and identifies the register. The active high (or active low) $R/\overline{W}$ control signal enables the output buffer (or the input buffer) and the data is read from (or stored in) the memory location. The chip select $(\overline{CS})$ line, also known as chip enable $(\overline{CE})$, is necessary to select one particular memory chip from among several memory chips in a system.

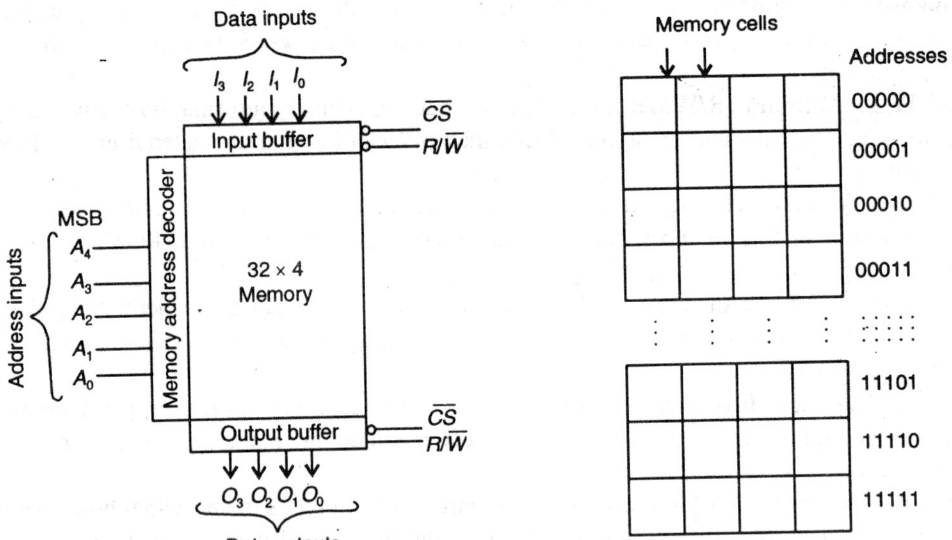

(a) Block diagram of a 32×4 memory chip

(b) Virtual arrangement of memory cells in 32×4 memory chip

Fig. 7.3 Memory chip

7.3 CPU-MEMORY CONNECTIONS

The connection between the CPU and the internal memory is shown in Fig. 7.4. The CPU needs three sets of communication lines called buses: the address bus, the data bus, and the control bus.

Address bus is a unidirectional bus that carries binary address outputs from the CPU to the memory chips to select one memory location.

Data bus is a bidirectional bus that carries data between CPU and the memory chips.

Control bus is comprised of various single lines that carry control signals from the CPU to the memory chips.

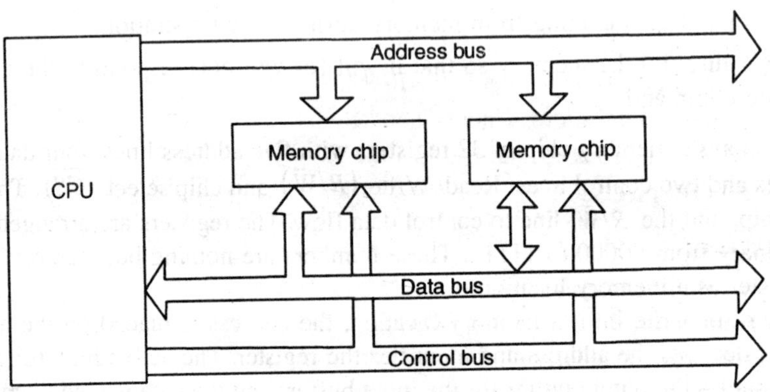

Fig. 7.4 Connection of the memory chips to the CPU

7.4 READ-ONLY MEMORIES (ROMs)

A ROM is a semiconductor memory device that stores binary information permanently. The information stored in this memory cannot be changed except through a special process that overwrites the data. ROMs are nonvolatile and they are widely used to store data that is used repeatedly in system applications, such as tables, conversions, or programmed instructions for system initialization and operation.

Figure 7.5 shows a typical block diagram for a 8 words × 4-bits ROM. Table 7.1 shows a table which relates the ROM inputs and outputs.

Table 7.1 Table showing binary data at each address location

A_2	A_1	A_0	O_3	O_2	O_1	O_0	
0	0	0	1	1	0	0	Typical data stored in ROM
0	0	1	1	1	1	1	
0	1	0	1	0	0	0	
0	1	1	0	1	1	1	
1	0	0	1	0	1	0	
1	0	1	1	0	1	0	
1	1	0	0	0	1	0	
1	1	1	1	0	1	1	

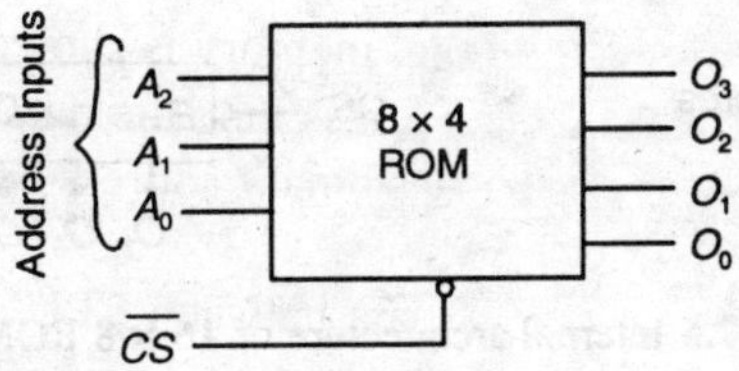

Fig. 7.5 Typical block diagram for a ROM

$\overline{CS}$ is an enable input that enables or disables the ROM outputs. $\overline{CS}$ is active LOW input. Therefore, it must be in the LOW state to enable the ROM. Any data stored in ROM can be read by applying the appropriate address to the address inputs, and keeping $\overline{CS}$ in active-LOW. For example, if we want to read the data (0111) stored at location 011 of the ROM, we have to apply 011 to the address inputs, and then apply a LOW to $\overline{CS}$.

ROM Architecture

ROMs have very complex internal structure. To illustrate how, ROM is structured a simplified diagram of the internal architecture of the 16 × 8 ROM (Fig. 7.6) is considered here. It consists of four basic parts: register array, row decoder, column decoder, output buffers.

The registers are arranged in a square matrix array so that we can easily specify the position of each register as being to specific row and specific column. The eight data outputs of each register are connected to an internal data bus. Each register has two active-HIGH enable inputs (E).

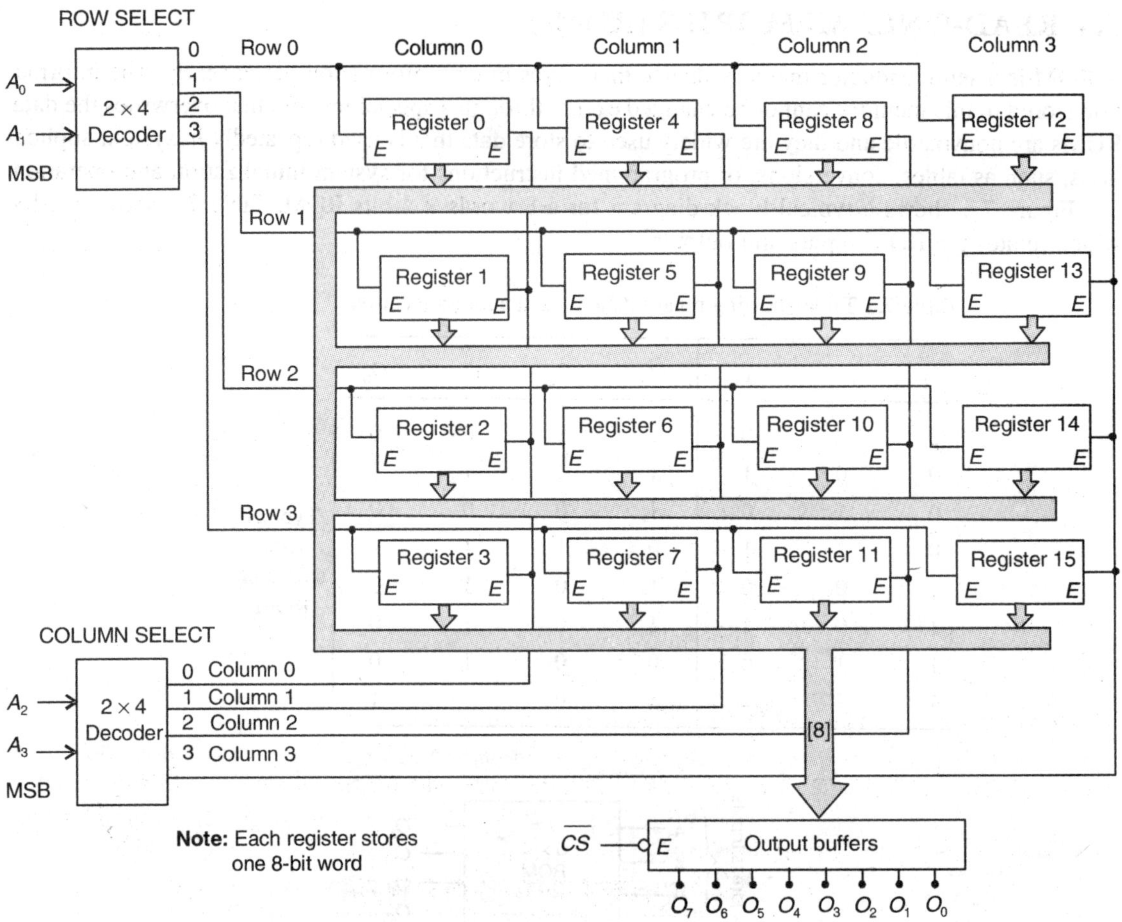

Fig. 7.6 Internal architecture of 16 × 8 ROM

The ROM works as follows: Two address lines A_0 and A_1 are decoded by the ROW decoder to select one of the 4 rows. The remaining two address lines A_2 and A_3 are decoded by the column decoder to select one of the 4 columns. When a 4-bit address code $A_3A_2A_1A_0$ is applied, the corresponding register is enabled and an 8-bit data word appears on the data outputs, provided that $\overline{CS}$ is LOW.

7.5 TYPES OF ROMS

The process of entering information into a ROM is referred to as programming the ROM. Depending on the way of programming, the ROMs are categorized as follows:

Masked ROM (MROM)

The masked ROM has its storage locations written into (programmed) by the manufacturer according to the customer's specifications. A photographic negative called a mask is used to control the electrical interconnections on the chip. Since the process is expensive, this type of ROM is economical only if we need a very large quantity of the same ROM. The disadvantage of MROM is that it cannot be erased and reprogrammed.

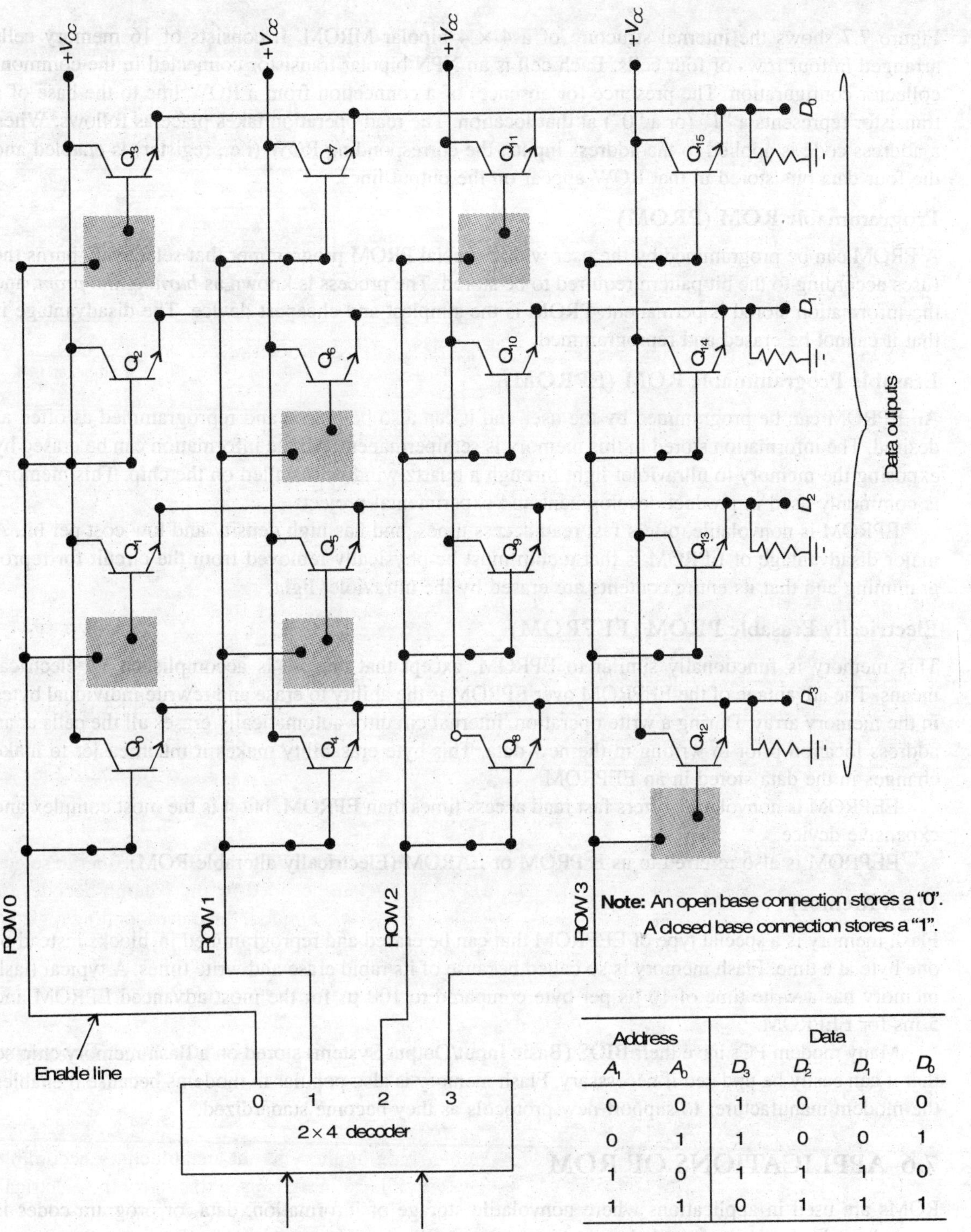

Address		Data			
A_1	A_0	D_3	D_2	D_1	D_0
0	0	1	0	1	0
0	1	1	0	0	1
1	0	1	1	1	0
1	1	0	1	1	0

Fig. 7.7 Internal structure of 4 × 4 bipolar MROM

Figure 7.7 shows the internal structure of a 4 × 4 bipolar MROM. It consists of 16 memory cells arranged in four rows of four cells. Each cell is an NPN bipolar transistor connected in the common-collector configuration. The presence (or absence) of a connection from a ROW line to the base of a transistor represents a "1" (or a "0") at that location. The read operation takes place as follows: When a address code is applied to the address inputs, the corresponding ROW (i.e., register) is enabled and the four data bits stored in that ROW appear on the output lines.

Programmable ROM (PROM)

A PROM can be programmed by the user with a special PROM programmer that selectively burns the fuses according to the bit pattern required to be stored. The process is known as *burning the prom*, and the information stored is permanent. PROM is the simplest and cheapest device. The disadvantage is that it cannot be erased and reprogrammed.

Erasable Programmable ROM (EPROM)

An EPROM can be programmed by the user and it can also be erased and reprogrammed as often as desired. The information stored in this memory is semipermanent. All the information can be erased by exposing the memory to ultraviolet light through a quartz window installed on the chip. This memory is commonly used in product development and experimental projects.

EPROM is nonvolatile, offers fast read access times, and has high density and low cost per bit. A major disadvantage of EPROM is that a chip must be physically removed from the circuit for reprogramming and that its entire contents are erased by the ultraviolet light.

Electrically Erasable PROM (EEPROM)

This memory is functionally similar to EPROM, except that erasure is accomplished by electrical means. The advantage of the EEPROM over EPROM is the ability to erase and rewrite individual bytes in the memory array. During a write operation, internal circuitry automatically erases all the cells at an address location prior to writing in the new data. This byte erasability makes it much easier to make changes in the data stored in an EEPROM.

EEPROM is nonvolatile, offers fast read access times than EPROM, but it is the most complex and expensive device.

EEPROM is also referred to as E^2PROM or EAROM (Electrically alterable ROM).

Flash Memory

Flash memory is a special type of EEPROM that can be erased and reprogrammed in blocks instead of one byte at a time. Flash memory is so called because of its rapid erase and write times. A typical flash memory has a write time of 10 μs per byte compared to 100 μs for the most advanced EPROM and 5 ms for EEPROM.

Many modem PCs have their BIOS (Basic Input/Output System) stored on a flash memory chip so that it can easily be updated if necesssary. Flash memory is also popular in modems because it enables the modem manufacturer to support new protocols as they become stadardized.

7.6 APPLICATIONS OF ROM

ROMs are used in applications where nonvolatile storage of information, data, or program codes is needed, and where the stored data rarely or never change. Here are some of the most common application areas.

Combinational Logic Implementation: ROMs are widely used to implement complex combinational circuits directly from their truth tables.

Firmware: ROMs are widely used to store data and program codes (software) that must be available on power-up in microprocesser based systems. Firmware is a combination of software and hardware. ROM chips that have data and program codes recorded on them are firmware. Some PCs and laptop computers have their operating system programs stored in ROM.

Bootstrap Memory: Most of the computers contain a small amount of ROM that stores critical program, called a bootstrap program that helps the computer get started.

Data tables: ROMs are widely used to store function tables (i.e., sine, cosine, square root, exponential, etc.) and code conversion tables.

Function Generator: A ROM look-up table can be used to make a function generator. Figure 7.8 shows how this can be achieved.

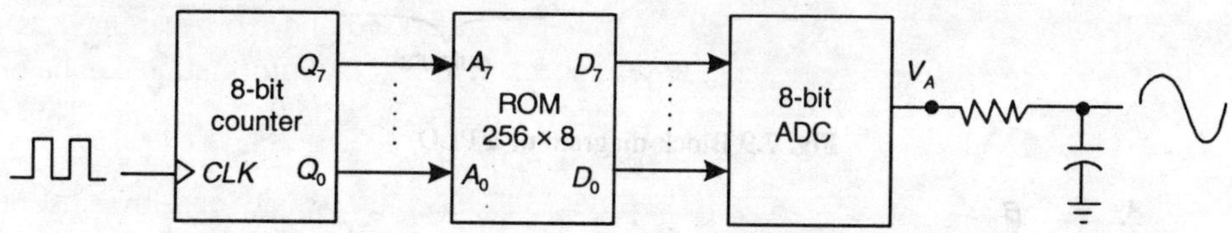

Fig. 7.8 Function generator using a ROM and a DAC

The ROM stores 256 different 8-bit values, each one corresponding to a different voltage point on the waveform. The 8-bit counter is continuously pulsed by a clock signal to provide sequential address inputs to the ROM. As the counter cycles through the 256 different addresses, the ROM outputs the 256 data points to DAC. The DAC output will be a waveform that steps through the 256 different analog voltage values corresponding to the data points. The low-pass filter smooths out the steps in the DAC output to produce a smooth waveform.

7.7 PROGRAMMABLE LOGIC DEVICES (PLDs)

A *programmable logic device* (or PLD) is an IC usually consists of array of logic gates and that is capable of being programmed to allow implementation of SOP expressions. The PLD simply allows a user to specify the connections among many of the logic gates. Many of the connections are fusible links that can be broken. The IC is said to be *programmable* because the specific function of the PLD for a given application is determined by the selective breaking of some of the interconnections while leaving other intact.

Figure 7.9 shows the block diagram of a PLD. It has n input variables and m output functions. Each output function is realized as a SOP terms that involve the input variables. The input variable $x_1 \ldots x_n$ are presented in uncomplemented and complemented form to the AND array, where up to K product terms are formed. These are then gated into the OR array where the output functions are formed.

Many different types of PLDs are presently available. They are the read-only memory (ROM) , the programmable array logic (PAL), the programmable logic array (PLA), the programmable logic sequencer (PLS), and the field-programmable gate array (FPGA). Two commonly used types of PLDs such as PALs and PLAs are discussed in the next two sections.

Let us demonstrate the basic idea used by PLD through an example shown in Fig. 7.10.

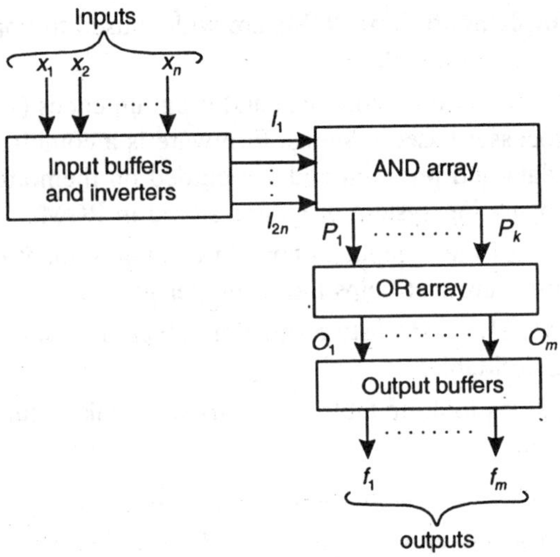

Fig. 7.9 Block diagram of a PLD

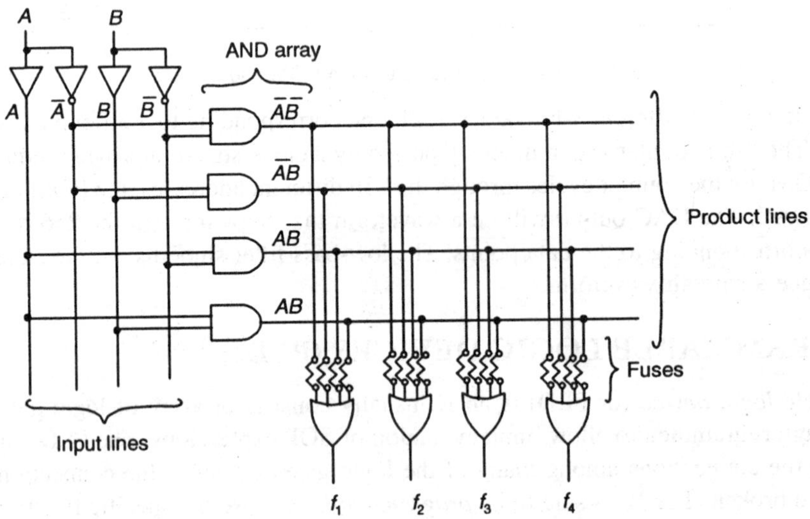

Fig. 7.10 Example of PLD

From Fig. 7.10 we can observe that each AND gate is connected to two different input lines so that the AND array produces all the fundamental products $\overline{A}\overline{B}$ to AB. These outputs of the AND array are called the product lines. Each of the product line is connected to one of the four inputs of each OR gate through a fusible link. Each of the four outputs (f_1 to f_4) can be programmed to be any function of A and B by selectively blowing the appropriate fuses. PLDs are designed so that a blown OR input acts as a logic-0. For example, if we blow the middle two fuses at the first OR gate, the output f_1 becomes: $f_1 = \overline{A}\overline{B} + AB$.

PLD Symbology

Although Fig. 7.10 depicts clearly the basic functionality of a PLD, this type of representation is very difficult in case of a larger PLDs. For this reason, a simplified symbology has been adopted in the technical literature to represent the internal circuitry of these devices.

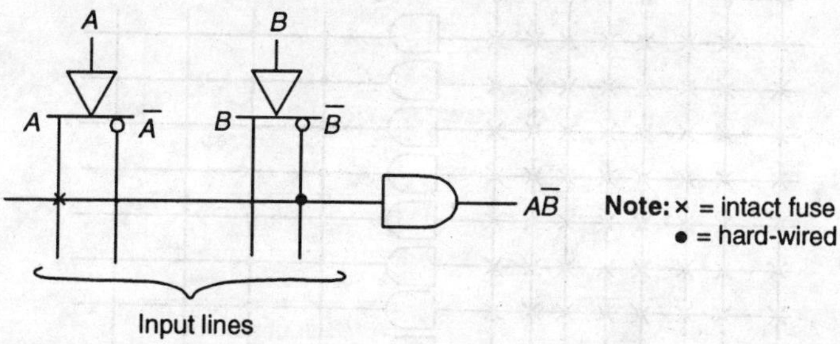

Fig. 7.11 Simplified symbology for PLDs

Figure 7.11 shows an example of the symbology for a 4-input AND gate. Note that the input buffers are represented as a single buffer with two outputs. Also note that a single line is shown going into the AND gate to represent the four inputs. The connection from the input variable lines to the AND gate are indicated as either a × or a dot. A × represents an intact fuse. A dot represents a hard-wired connection (i.e., one that cannot be changed). The absence of either of these indicates no connection. This symbology is used in Fig. 7.12 to represent the example of PLD from Fig. 7.10.

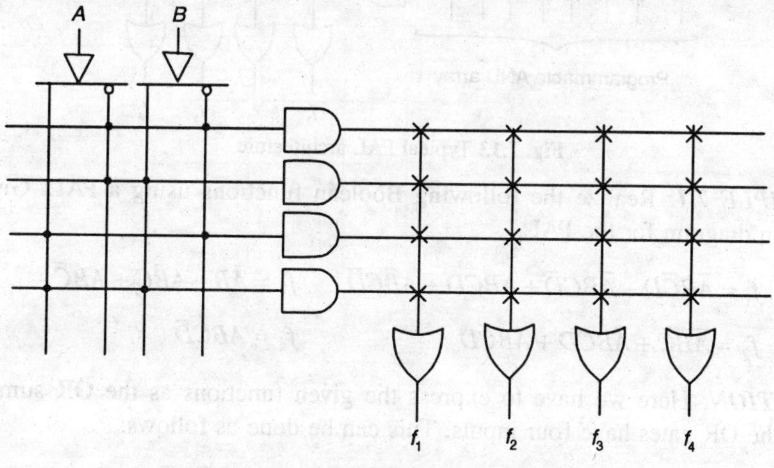

Fig. 7.12 A simplified sketch of the PLD in Fig. 7.10

7.8 PROGRAMMABLE ARRAY LOGIC (PAL)

The PAL is a class of PLD in which the AND array is programmable and the OR array is fixed. Figure 7.13 shows the internal architecture of a PAL with 4 inputs and 4 outputs.

The following example illustrates how the PAL would be programmed to realize the Boolean functions.

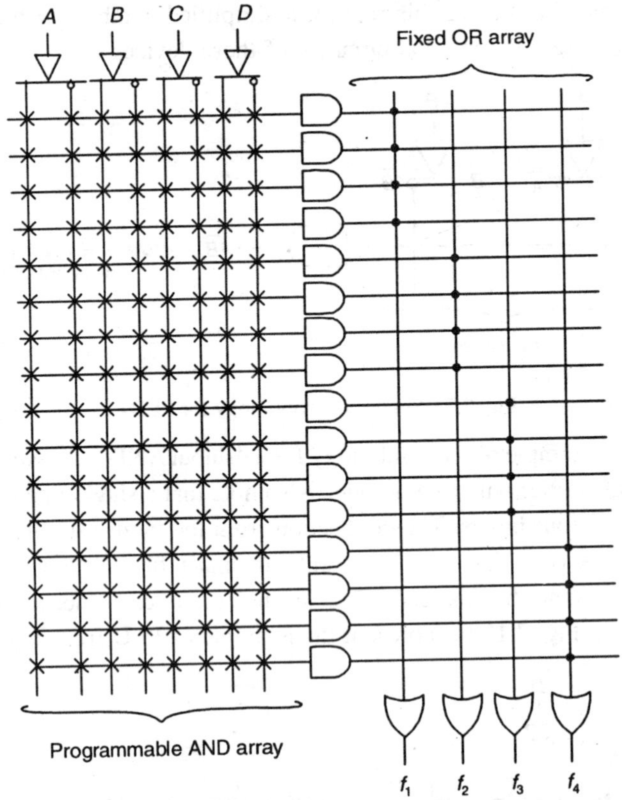

Fig. 7.13 Typical PAL architecture

EXAMPLE 7.1: Realize the following Boolean functions using a PAL. Give the internal connection diagram for the PAL.

$$f_1 = \bar{A}B\bar{C}D + \bar{A}BC\bar{D} + ABCD + A\bar{B}C\bar{D} \qquad f_3 = \bar{A}B + A\bar{B}C + AB\bar{C}$$

$$f_2 = \bar{A}\bar{B}\bar{C} + \bar{A}BCD + AB\bar{C}D \qquad f_4 = ABC\bar{D}$$

SOLUTION: Here we have to express the given functions as the OR sum of four terms because the OR gates have four inputs. This can be done as follows:

$$f_1 = \bar{A}B\bar{C}D + \bar{A}BC\bar{D} + ABCD + A\bar{B}C\bar{D}$$

$$f_2 = 0 + \bar{A}\bar{B}\bar{C} + \bar{A}BCD + AB\bar{C}D$$

$$f_3 = 0 + \bar{A}B + A\bar{B}C + AB\bar{C}$$

$$f_4 = 0 + 0 + 0 + ABC\bar{D}$$

Let us refer the PAL given in Fig 7.13 and start with function f_1. In this function the first desired product is $\bar{A}B\bar{C}D$. This term is obtained by leaving intact the fuses that connect $\bar{A}$, B, $\bar{C}$ and D to the top AND gate, and blowing all other fuses on that line. Likewise, the other terms are obtained. The fixed OR connection on the output side imply that the first OR gate produces an output of

$$f_1 = \bar{A}B\bar{C}D + \bar{A}BC\bar{D} + ABCD + A\bar{B}C\bar{D}$$

Similarly, the other Boolean functions are generated.

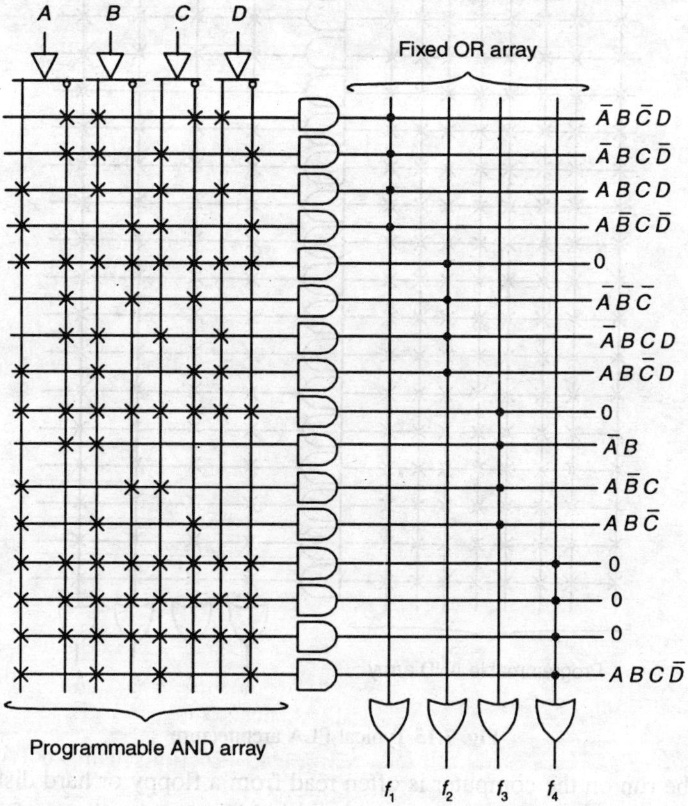

Fig. 7.14

The term 0 is produced at the out of an AND gate by leaving all its input fuses intact. This would produce an output of $A\bar{A}B\bar{B}C\bar{C}D\bar{D} = 0$. Note that many of the AND gates have all of their input fuses intact, since they need to generate 0s. A PAL programmed for the given functions is shown in Fig. 7.14.

7.9 PROGRAMMABLE LOGIC ARRAY (PLA)

The PLA is a class of PLD in which both the AND and the OR arrays are programmable. Figure 7.15 shows the internal architecture of PLA having 4 inputs and 4 outputs.

7.10 READ/WRITE RANDOM ACCESS MEMORIES (RAMs)

RAM stands for random-access memory. The term random access means that any storage location in the memory can be addressed (accessed) in any order to read or write data. Actually, many types of memory can be classified as having random access, but when the term RAM is used with semiconductor memories, it is unfortunately taken to mean read/write memory (*R/WM*) as opposed to ROM. Since it has become common practice to use the term RAM to mean semiconductor *R/WM*, we too use the term in the same sense throughout our discussion in this book.

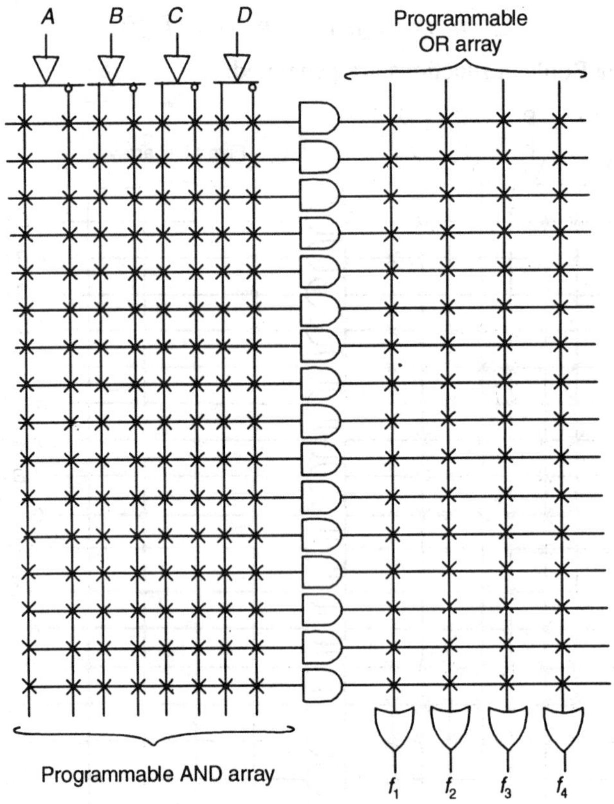

Fig. 7.15 Typical PLA architecture

A program to be run on the computer is often read from a floppy or hard disk to the RAM where instructions can be accessed more rapidly than they could if accessed directly from the disk.

There are two basic types of RAM : Static RAM (SRAM) and Dynamic RAM (DRAM). *Static RAM* will store data written into it for as long as the power supply is maintained without further attention. *Dynamic RAM,* on the other hand, is of the type of construction that requires constant refreshing in order to restore a fading charge.

RAM Architecture

To illustrate how RAM is structured a simplified diagram of the internal architecture of the 64 × 4 RAM (Fig. 7.16) is considered here. We can observe that many of the basic concepts are same as that of ROM.

The RAM works as follows: The address code is decoded by the decoder to select one of the 64 address locations for reading or writing. Since $64 = 2^6$, the decoder requires a 6-bit input code. When a 6-bit address code $A_5A_4A_3A_2A_1A_0$ is applied the corresponding register is enabled. In the read mode (i.e., when $R/\overline{W} = 1$), the output buffers are enabled (input buffers are disabled) and the four data bits from the selected address appear on the data outputs. In the write mode (i.e., when $R/\overline{W} = 0$), the input buffers are enabled (output buffers are disabled) and the four data bits that are applied to the data inputs are stored at the selected address. Note that the chip select $(\overline{CS})$ must be LOW during read and write.

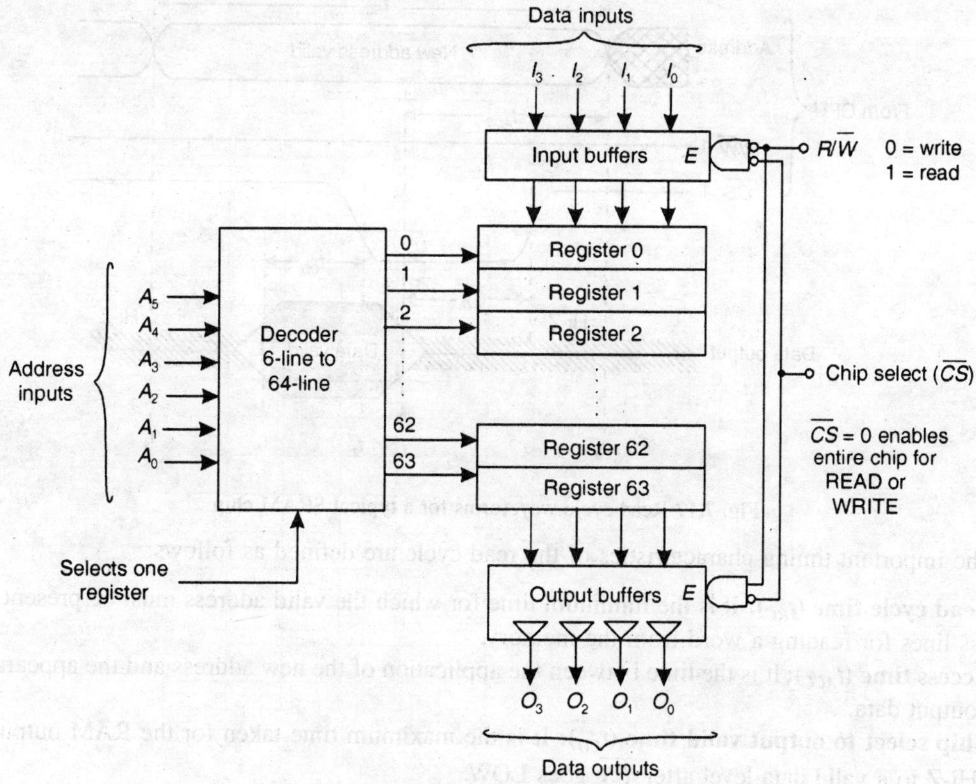

Fig. 7.16 Internal architecture of a 64 × 4 RAM

7.11 STATIC RAM (SRAM)

The RAM operation that we have discussed in the last section applies to a static RAM. A static RAM uses a flip-flop as the basic memory cell (either bipolar or MOS) , and once a bit is stored in a flip-flop, it will remain there as long as power is available to the chip.

Read Cycle

The waveforms in Fig. 7.17 shows how the address, $R/\overline{W}$, and $\overline{CS}$ inputs behave during a memory read cycle. Note that $R/\overline{W}$ line is HIGH prior to t_0 and stays HIGH throughout the read cycle. The RAM's data output is in its Hi-Z (i.e, high impedance) state since $\overline{CS}$ = 1. Let us give a step-by-step description of the events that occur at the times indicated on the diagram.

t_0 : The address of the location to be read is applied to the RAM inputs. After allowing time for the address signals to stabilize, the $\overline{CS}$ is activated.

t_1 : The RAM responds by placing data from the addressed location onto the data output line.

t_2 : The $\overline{CS}$ is returned HIGH.

t_3 : The RAM output returns to its high impedance state.

t_4 : The CPU supplies a new address to RAM for the read or write cycle.

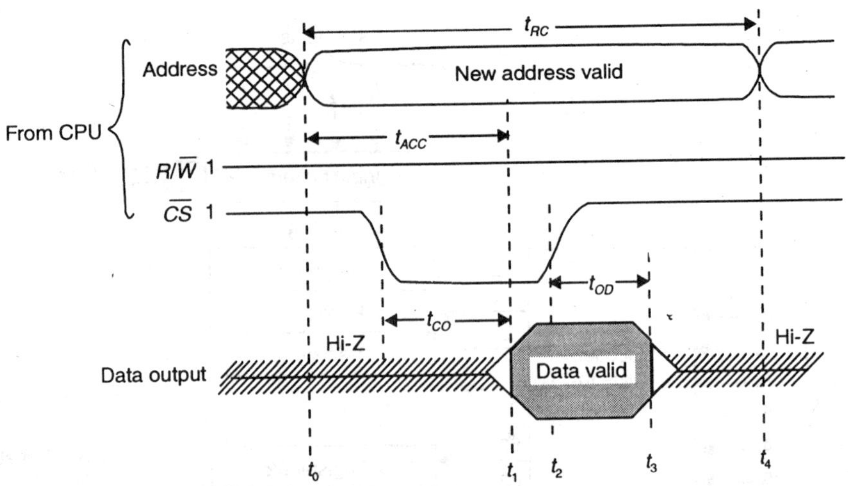

Fig. 7.17 Read cycle waveforms for a typical SRAM chip

The important timing characteristics of the read cycle are defined as follows:

Read cycle time (t_{RC}): It is the minimum time for which the valid address must be present on the address lines for reading a word from the memory.

Access time (t_{ACC}): It is the time between the application of the new address and the appearance of valid output data.

Chip select to output valid time (t_{CO}): It is the maximum time taken for the RAM output to go from Hi-Z to a valid data level after $\overline{CS}$ goes LOW.

Chip deselect to output in Hi-Z state (t_{OD}): It is the time taken for the RAM output to return to its Hi-Z state after $\overline{CS}$ goes HIGH.

Write Cycle

The waveforms in Fig. 7.18 shows how the address, $R/\overline{W}$, and $\overline{CS}$ inputs behave during a memory write cycle. The description of the sequence of events is as follows:

t_0 : The address of the location to be written is applied to the RAM inputs. After waiting for a time interval t_{AS}, the $R/\overline{W}$, and $\overline{CS}$ are pulsed LOW.

t_1 : Data to be written into the address location is placed an the data input line.

t_2 : The $\overline{CS}$ and $R/\overline{W}$ are returned HIGH.

t_3 : The RAM output returns to its high impedance state.

t_4 : The CPU supplies a new address to RAM for the read or write cycle:

The important timing characteristics of the write cycle are defined as follows:

Write cycle time (t_{WC}): It is the minimum time for which the valid address must be present on the address lines for writing a word in the memory.

Address setup time (t_{DS}): It is the time delay for which the CPU waits after applying the address to the address lines before it drives the $R/\overline{W}$ and $\overline{CS}$ lines LOW.

Write time interval (t_W): It is the time for which $R/\overline{W}$ goes LDW.

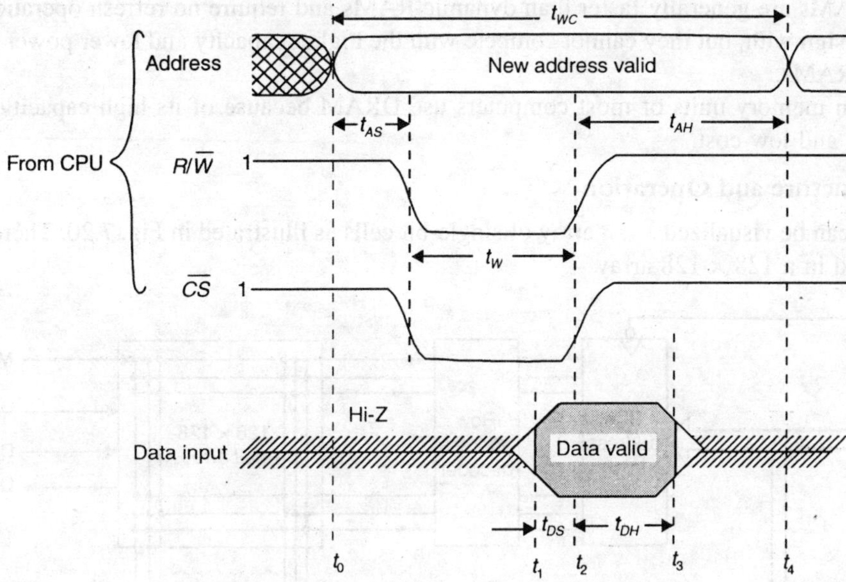

Fig. 7.18 Write cycle waveforms for a typical SRAM chip

Data setup time (t_{DS}): It is the minimum time for which the data must be valid on the data input lines before $R/\overline{W}$ goes HIGH.

Data hold time (t_{DH}): It is the minimum time for which the data must be valid on the data input lines after $R/\overline{W}$ goes HIGH.

Address hold time (t_{AH}): It is the time for which address will remain on address lines after $R/\overline{W}$ goes HIGH.

7.12 DYNAMIC RAM (DRAM)

A dynamic RAM uses a single MOS transistor and a capacitor as the basic memory cell. The bit is stored as charge on the capacitor. Typically, the 1 bit is stored by charging the capacitor while 0 bit is represented by an uncharged capacitor. Because of the tendency of the stored charge to leak off after a period of time, dynamic RAMs require periodic recharging of the memory cells; this is called *refreshing* the dynamic RAM. This process of refreshing requires additional memory circuitry and complicates the operation of the dynamic RAM. Some memory chips incorporate a refresh facility within the chips themselves. Figure 7.19 shows a typical memory cell of a dynamic RAM.

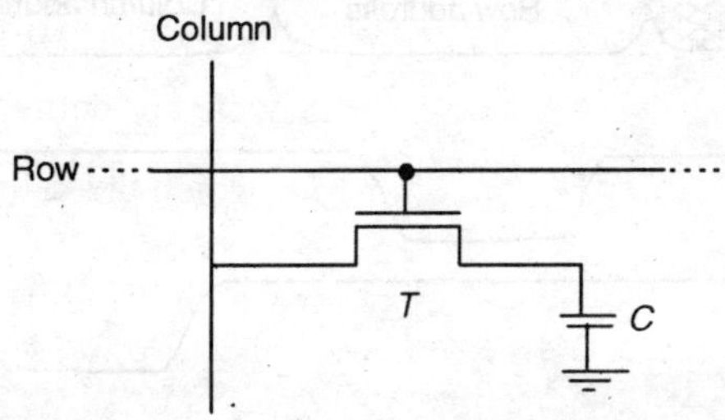

Fig. 7.19 A dynamic MOS RAM ce

Static RAMs are generally faster than dynamic RAMs and require no refresh operation. They are simpler to design with, but they cannot compete with the higher capacity and lower power requirement of dynamic RAMs.

The main memory units of most computers use DRAM because of its high capacity, low power consumption and low cost.

DRAM Structure and Operation

The DRAM can be visualized as an array of single-bit cells as illustrated in Fig. 7.20. There are 16,384 cells arranged in a 128 × 128 array.

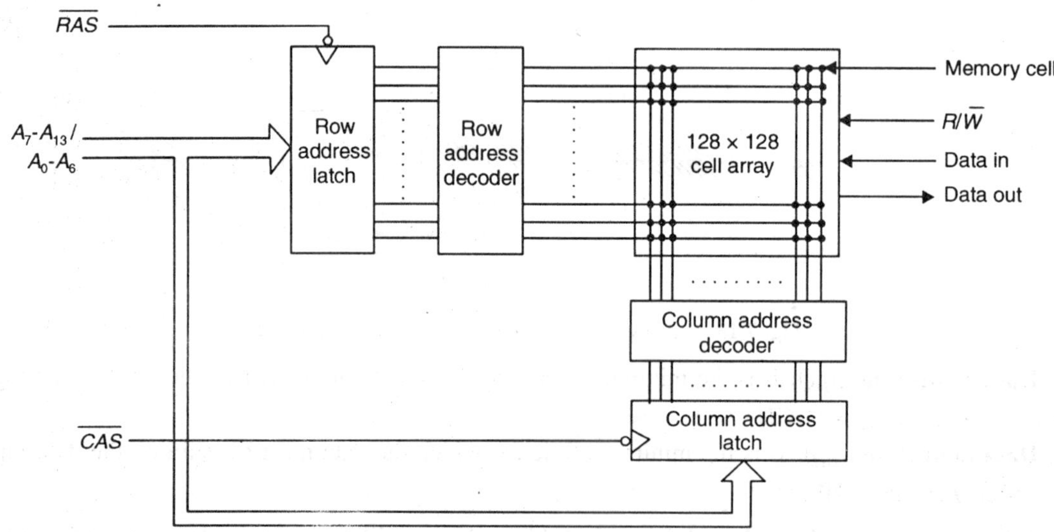

Fig. 7.20 Internal architecture of 16K × 1 DRAM

Fourteen address inputs are needed to select one of the cells (2^{14} = 16,384). The chip considered here requires 14 pins if each address input required a seperate pin. In order to minimize the number of pins to the chip, the row and column addresses are multiplexed on 7 pins; this technique is called *address multiplexing.*

Now let us see how we can address 16, 384 cells using only 7address lines employing multiplexing technique.

The 14-bit address is applied 7 bits at a time to the address inputs. To select a particular memory cell, first, the 7-bit row address (A_0-A_6) is applied to the address inputs, and the $\overline{RAS}$ (Row Address

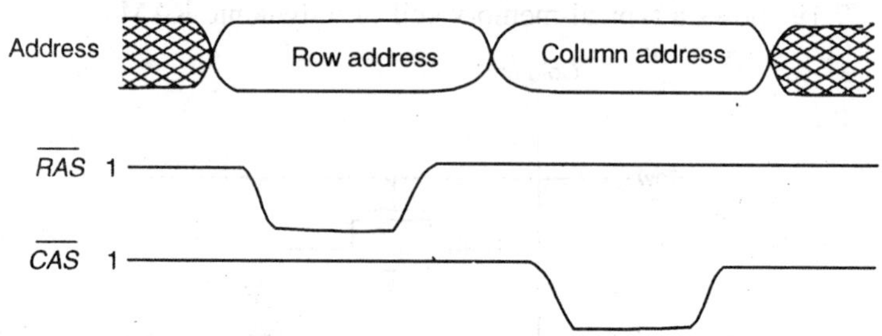

Fig. 7.21 Timing for address multiplexing

Strobe) input is driven LOW. This latches the 7 bits of address into the row address latch, selecting a particular row. Next, the 7-bit column address (A_7-A_{13}) is applied to the address inputs, and $\overline{CAS}$ (Column Address Strobe) is driven LOW. This latches the 7 bits of address into the column address latch, selecting a particular column. The 7-bit row address and the 7-bit column address are then decoded to select the appropriate memory cell for a read or write operation. The basic timing for this address multiplexing operation is shown in Fig. 7.21.

Figure 7.22 Illustrates how this addressing can be done using a multiplexer.

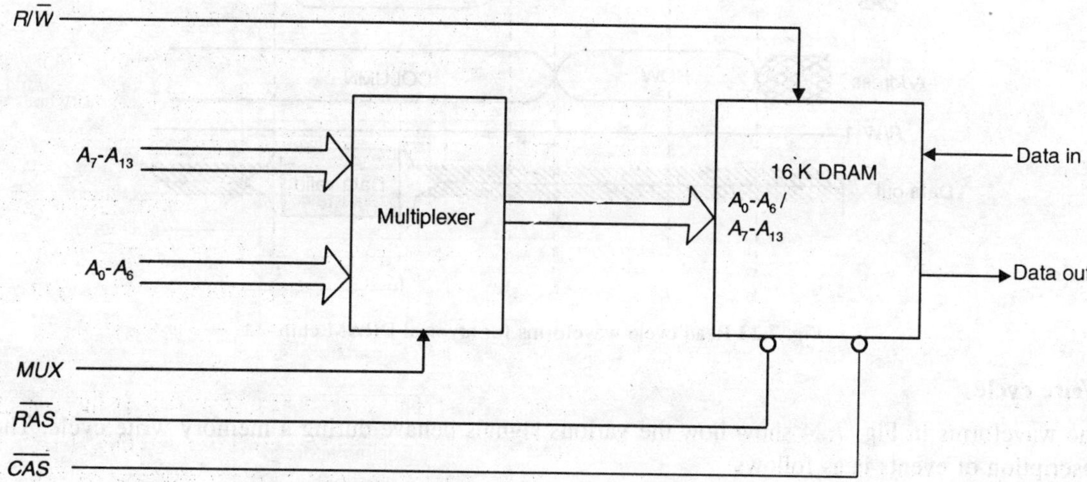

Fig. 7.22 Addressing using multiplexer

Note: *MUX* = 0 transmits A_0 - A_6 to DRAM

MUX =1 transmits A_7 - A_{13} to DRAM

The timing diagram of read and write cycles for a DRAM is much more complex than for a static RAM, and there are many critical timing requirements to consider. In order to avoid confusion, we will concentrate on the basic timing sequence for the read and write cycles for a typical DRAM like that of Fig. 7.22.

Read Cycle

The waveforms in Fig. 7.23 show how the various signals behave during memory read cycle. Here we can notice that $R/\overline{W}$ line is HIGH prior to t_0 and stays HIGH throughout the read cycle.

Let us give a step-by-step description of the events that occur at the times indicated on the diagram.

t_0 : MUX goes LOW to place the row address (A_0 to A_6) at the DRAM address inputs.

t_1 : $\overline{RAS}$ is driven LOW to load the row address into the DRAM.

t_2 : MUX goes HIGH to place the column address (A_7-A_{13}) at the DRAM address inputs.

t_3 : $\overline{CAS}$ is driven LOW to load the column address into the DRAM.

t_4 : The DRAM responds by placing data from the addressed cell on to the data output line.

t_5 : MUX, $\overline{RAS}$, $\overline{CAS}$, and data output are returned to their initial states.

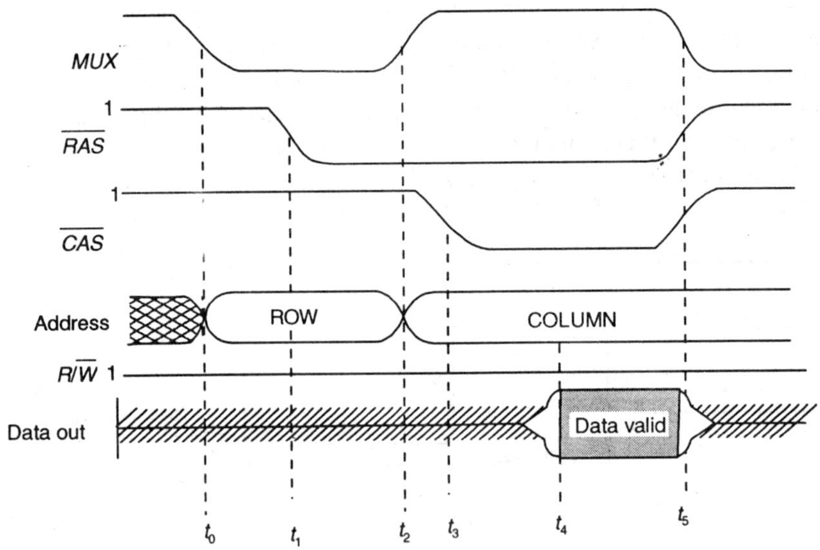

Fig. 7.23 Read cycle waveforms for atypical DRAM chip

Write cycle

The waveforms in Fig. 7.24 show how the various signals behave during a memory write cycle. The description of events is as follows:

t_0 : *MUX* goes LOW to place the row address (A_0 to A_6) at the DRAM address inputs.

t_1 : $\overline{RAS}$ is driven LOW to load the row address into the DRAM.

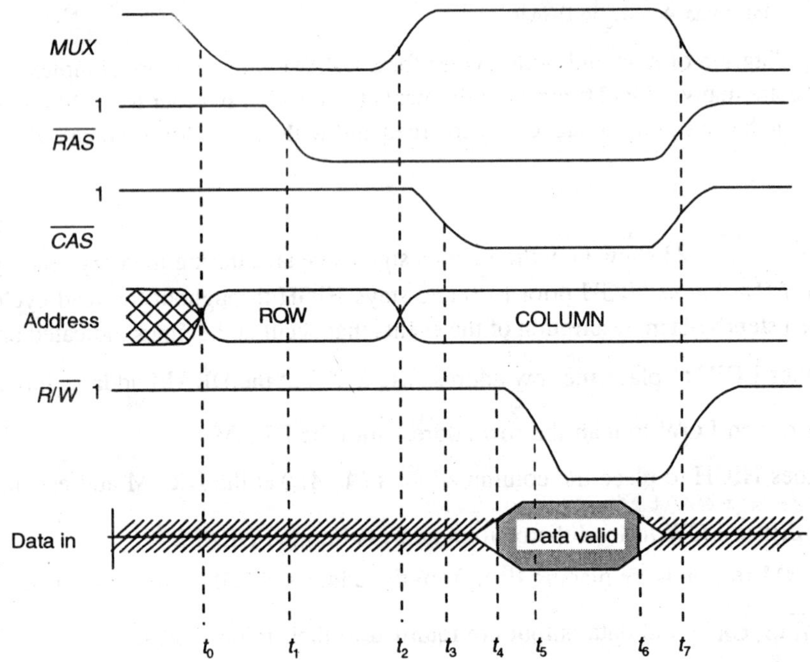

Fig. 7.24 Write cycle waveforms for a typical DRAM chip

t_2 : *MUX* goes HIGH to place the column address (A_7 to A_{13}) at the DRAM address inputs.

t_3 : $\overline{CAS}$ is driven LOW to load the column address into the DRAM.

t_4 : Data to be written is placed on the data input line.

t_5 : $R/\overline{W}$ is driven LOW to write the data into the addressed cell.

t_6 : Input data is removed from data input line.

t_7 : *MUX*, $\overline{RAS}$, $\overline{CAS}$ and $R/\overline{W}$ are returned to their initial states.

7.13 EXPANDING WORD SIZE AND CAPACITY

In some instances of memory applications, the capacity or word size of a single available memory chip (RAM or ROM) is not sufficient. Therefore we need to go for expanding the capacity and/or word size to achieve the requirement, by connecting several memory chips in a suitable manner.

Expanding Word Size

Suppose it is required to have memory of word size n_m from the available memory chips of word size n_c ($n_m > n_C$), then a number of similar chips can be combined together to achieve the desired word size. The number of memory chips (N_C) required to implement a given memory size is given by

$$N_C = \frac{NB_m}{NB_C}$$

where NB_m is the bit capacity of the overall memory, and NB_C is the number of bits per chip. This equation is appropriate only if the word size of the memory (n_m) is an integral multiple of the word size (n_C) of the chip, which is generally the case.

In order to expand the word size, the chips are to be connected in the following way:

1. Connect the corresponding address lines of each chip. For example, A_0 of each chip is connected together so that it becomes A_0 of the overall memory. The same is done for each address line.

2. Connect $R/\overline{W}$ (in case of RAM) and $\overline{CS}$ inputs of each chip together to have $R/\overline{W}$ and $\overline{CS}$ inputs for the overall memory.

The following example will demonstrate the above procedure.

EXAMPLE 7.2: Obtain a 16 × 8 RAM using 16 × 4 RAM chips.

SOLUTION: Here we need to increase the word size from 4 bits to 8 bits. For this the number of chips (16 × 4 RAMs) required is

$$N_C = \frac{NB_m}{NB_C} = \frac{16 \times 8}{16 \times 4} = 2 \text{ chips.}$$

The two 16 × 4 RAM chips are connected to obtain a 16 × 8 RAM as shown in Fig. 7.25 in accordance with the procedure given. Since each chip can store sixteen 4-bit words and we want to store sixteen 8-bit words, each chip is required to store half of each word. In other words, RAM-1 store the four higher order bits of each 8-bit word, and RAM-2 stores the four lower order bits. A full 8-bit word is available at the RAM outputs connected to the data bus.

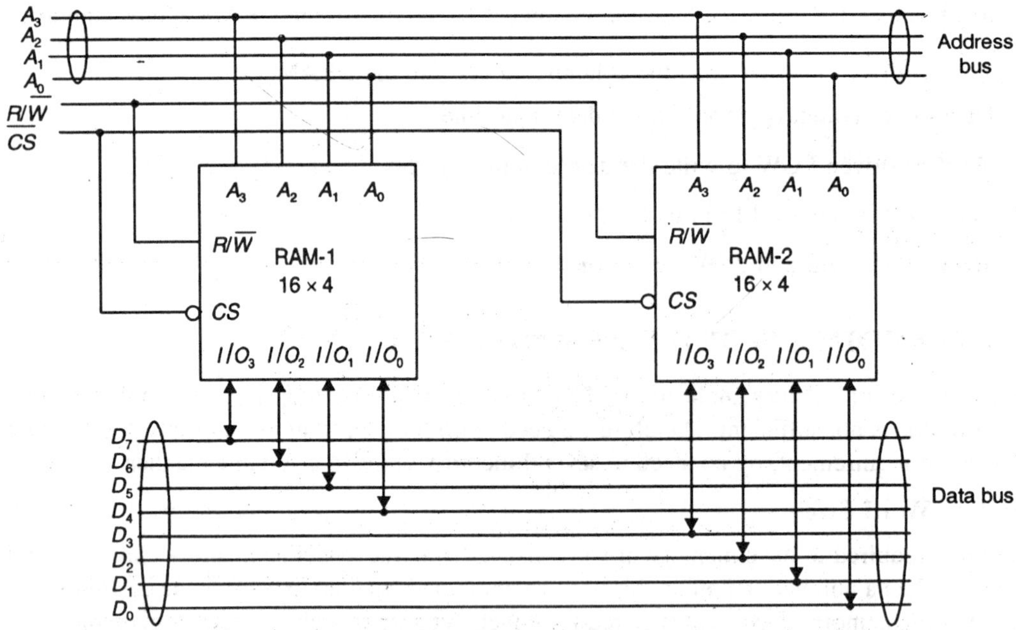

Fig. 7.25 A 16 × 8 RAM obtained by combining two 16 × 4 RAM chips

Expanding Word Capacity

Memories can also be expanded to increase word capacity. In order to obtain a word capacity of m_m words from the available memory chips with m_C words each, a number of similar chips can be combined together in a suitable way. The number of memory chips (N_C) required to implement a given memory is again given by the equation which we have discussed previously. That is,

$$N_C = \frac{NB_m}{NB_C}$$

In order to expand the word capacity, the chips are to be connected in the following way.

1. Connect the corresponding address lines of each chip individually.
2. Connect $R/\overline{W}$ (in case of RAM) input of each chip together to have $R/\overline{W}$ input for the overall memory.
3. Use a suitable decoder and connect each of its outputs to one of the $\overline{CS}$ terminals of memory chips. For example, if eight chips are to be connected, a 3 × 8 decoder is used to select one out of eight chips at any one time.

The following example ilustrates the above procedure.

EXAMPLE 7.3: Obtain a 1024 × 8 RAM using 256 × 8 RAM chips.

SOLUTION: Here we need to increase the word capacity from 256 words to 1024 words. For this the number of chips (256 × 8 RAMS) required is

$$N_C = \frac{NB_m}{NB_C} = \frac{1024 \times 8}{256 \times 8} = 4$$

At any instant, only one of the 1024 locations is to be accessed, which will be in one of the four chips. That means only one of the four chips must get selected at a time.

To select one of the 1024 locations (i.e., words), the number of address lines required is 10 ($2^{10} = 1024$). The higher order two bits (A_9 and A_8) of the address code are used to select one out of four chips and lower order eight bits (A_7 to A_0) are used to select one of the 256 memory locations in the selected chip. For this purpose, a 2 × 4 decoder is required. Figure 7.26 shows the relevant connections of the 4 chips to obtain the desired capacity of RAM.

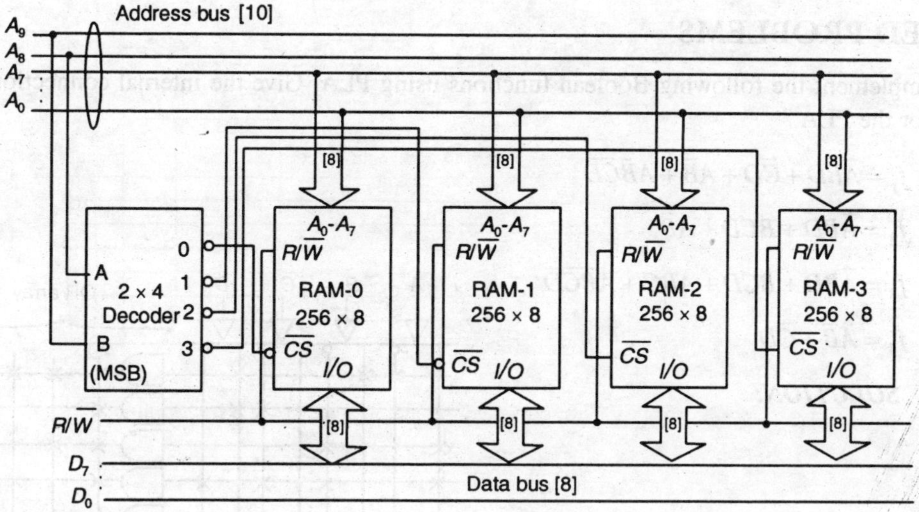

Fig. 7.26 A 1024 × 8 RAM obtained by combining four 256 × 8 RAM chips

7.14 SPECIAL MEMORY FUNCTIONS

In this section, we briefly describe some of the special functions that semiconductor memory devices perform in computers and other digital equipment and systems.

Power-Down Storage: In many applications, the volatility of semiconductor RAM can mean the loss of critical data when power to the memory is lost. There are many approaches to provide storage of critical data in power-down situations:

- All critical data during normal system operation are stored in RAM that can be powered from backup batteries whenever power is interrupted. Some CMOS RAM chips have very low standby power requirements (as low as 0.5 mW) and are particularly well suited for this task. Some CMOS SRAMs actually include a small lithium battery right on the chip.
- All critical data are stored in nonvolatile flash memory.
- On power-down, the CPU executes a short power-down program (from ROM) that transfers critical data from the system RAM into ether battery-backup CMOS RAM or non-volatile flash memory.

Cache Memory: Cache memory is a portion of memory made of high-speed static RAM instead of the slower and cheaper dynamic RAM used for main memory. Use of cache memory is effective because most programs access the same data or instructions over and over. By keeping as much of this information as possible in cache memory, the computer avoids accessing the slower DRAM.

First-In, First-Out memory (FIFO): FIFO memory is formed by an arrangement of shift registers. The term FIFO refers to the operation of this type of memory, in which the first data written into the memory is the first to be read out.

One important application area of the FIFO is the case in which two systems of differing data rates must communicate. Data can be entered into a FIFO at one rate and be put out at another rate.

SOLVED PROBLEMS

7.1 Implement the following Boolean functions using PLA. Give the internal connection diagram for the PLA.

$$f_1 = \bar{A}BD + \bar{C}D + A\bar{B} + AB\bar{C}\bar{D}$$

$$f_2 = \bar{A}BD + BCD + A\bar{B}$$

$$f_3 = \bar{A}BD + BCD + ABC + AB\bar{C}\bar{D}$$

$$f_4 = A\bar{B} + \bar{C}D$$

SOLUTION:

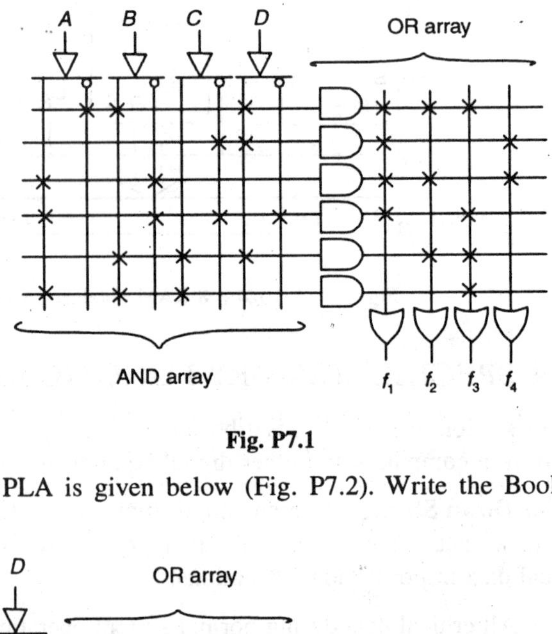

Fig. P7.1

7.2 The internal connection diagram for a PLA is given below (Fig. P7.2). Write the Boolean functions realized by the PLA.

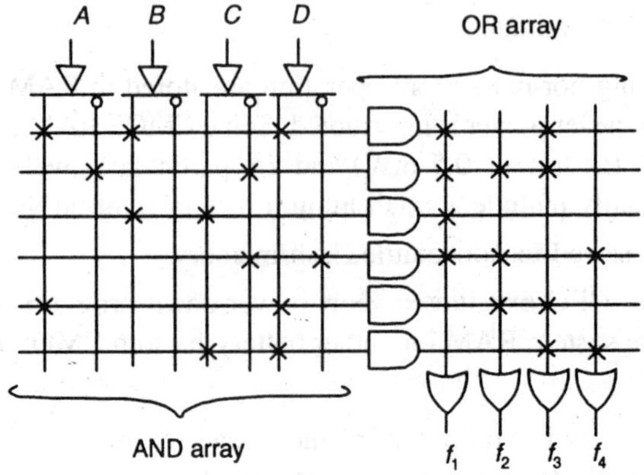

Fig. P7.2

SOLUTION:

$$f_1 = ABD + \overline{A}\overline{C} + BC + \overline{C}\overline{D}$$

$$f_2 = \overline{A}\overline{C} + \overline{C}\overline{D} + AD$$

$$f_3 = ABD + \overline{A}\overline{C} + AD + CD$$

$$f_4 = \overline{C}\overline{D} + CD$$

7.3 A 2K × 4 chip is used to realize a 32K × 8 memory. How many chips are required?

SOLUTION: The number of memory chips (N_C) required to realize a given memory is given by

$$N_C = \frac{NB_m}{NB_C} = \frac{\text{Number of bits in the overall memory}}{\text{Number of bits per chip}}$$

$$NB_m = 32\text{K} \times 8 = 256 \text{ Kbits}, \quad NB_C = 2\text{K} \times 4 = 8 \text{ Kbits}$$

The number of chips is then $N_C = \dfrac{256}{8} = 32.$

7.4 It is desired to combine several 2K × 8 chips to realize a 32K × 8 memory. How many chips are needed? How many address lines are required?

SOLUTION: The number of chips required, $N_C = \dfrac{NB_m}{NB_C} = \dfrac{32K \times 8}{2K \times 8} = 16$

$$32K \times 8 = 32 \times 1024 \text{ bytes} = 2^{15} \text{ bytes}.$$

Hence, a total of 15 address lines are required.

7.5 (a) How many 128 × 8 RAM chips are needed to provide a memory capacity of 2048 bytes?
(b) How many lines of the address bus must be used to access 2048 bytes of memory? How many of these lines will be common to all chips?
(c) How many lines must be decoded for chip select? Specify the size of the decoder.

SOLUTION:

(a) The number of 128 × 8 RAM chips required to provide a memory capacity of 2048 bytes is given by:

$$N_C = \frac{NB_m}{NB_C} = \frac{2048 \times 8}{128 \times 3} = 16$$

(b) 2048 = 2^{11}. Hence, eleven lines of the address bus are used to access 2048 bytes. Since 128 = 2^7, seven lines will be common to all chips.

(c) Since there are 16 chips and 16 = 2^4, four lines must be decoded for chip select. The required size of the decoder is 4 × 16.

7.6 Design the following by using the memory chips, decoders and logic gates. Available memory chips are: 2K × 8 ROM and 2K × 4 RAM.

(i) 8K × 8 ROM with starting address 0000H.
(ii) 8K × 8 RAM with starting address 2000H.

SOLUTION:

(i) Design of 8K × 8 ROM

The number of ROM chips required, $N_C = \frac{NB_m}{NB_C} = \frac{8\text{K}\times 8}{2\text{K}\times 8} = 4$

Let us draw a memory address map (Table 7.6(a)) which is a pictorial representation of assigned address space for each chip in the system.

Table P7.6(a) Memory address map of 8K × 8 ROM

Memory chip	Hexadecimal	A_{15}	A_{14}	A_{13}	A_{12}	A_{11}	A_{10}	A_9	A_8	A_7	A_6	A_5	A_4	A_3	A_2	A_1	A_0
		Address															
		Binary															
ROM-0	Start : 0000	0	0	0	0	0	0	0	0	0	0	0	0	0	0	0	0
	End : 07FF	0	0	0	0	0	1	1	1	1	1	1	1	1	1	1	1
ROM-1	Start : 0800	0	0	0	0	1	0	0	0	0	0	0	0	0	0	0	0
	End : 0FFF	0	0	0	0	1	1	1	1	1	1	1	1	1	1	1	1
ROM-2	Start : 1000	0	0	0	1	0	0	0	0	0	0	0	0	0	0	0	0
	End : 17FF	0	0	0	1	0	1	1	1	1	1	1	1	1	1	1	1
ROM-3	Start : 1800	0	0	0	1	1	0	0	0	0	0	0	0	0	0	0	0
	End : 1FFF	0	0	0	1	1	1	1	1	1	1	1	1	1	1	1	1

Referring to the memory address map given in Table P 7.6(a), we can draw ROM system shown in Fig. P 7.6(a). The ROM chip has 2K bytes and needs eleven address lines ($2\text{K} = 2 \times 1024 = 2^1 \times 2^{10} = 2^{11}$), A_{10} to A_0, to identify 2048 memory locations (2K = 2 × 1024 = 2048). The address lines A_{15} to A_{11} are used to select the memory chip through 2 × 4 decoder and logic gates.

(ii) Design of 8K × 8 RAM

The number of RAM chips required, $N_C = \frac{NB_m}{NB_C} = \frac{8\text{K}\times 8}{2\text{K}\times 4} = 8$

Here we need to increase the word size from 4 bits to 8 bits and the word capacity from 2K bytes to 8K bytes. Keeping this in mind let us draw a memory address map (Table P 7.6(b)). Referring the memory address map given in Table P 7.6(b), we can draw RAM system shown in Fig. P 7.6(b). The RAM chip has 2K bytes and needs eleven lines, A_{10} to A_0, to identify 2048 memory locations. The address lines A_{15} to A_{11} are used to select the memory chip through 2 × 4 decoder and logic gates.

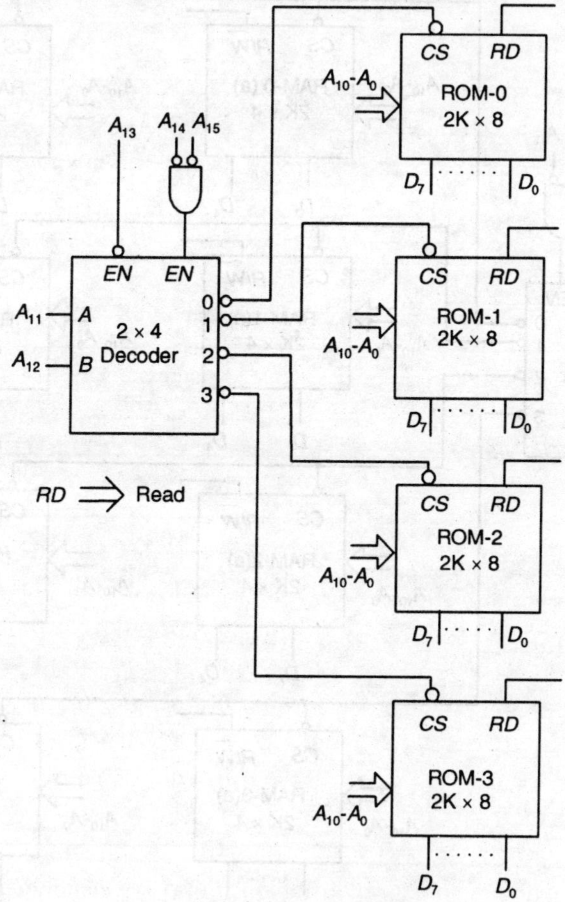

Fig. P7.6(a) 8K × 8 ROM

Table P7.6(b) Memory address map of 8K × 8 RAM

Memory chip	Address																
	Hexadecimal	Binary															
		A_{15}	A_{14}	A_{13}	A_{12}	A_{11}	A_{10}	A_9	A_8	A_7	A_6	A_5	A_4	A_3	A_2	A_1	A_0
RAM-0 (a)	Start : 2000	0	0	1	0	0	0	0	0	0	0	0	0	0	0	0	0
RAM-0 (b)	End : 27FF	0	0	1	0	0	1	1	1	1	1	1	1	1	1	1	1
RAM-1 (a)	Start : 2800	0	0	1	0	1	0	0	0	0	0	0	0	0	0	0	0
RAM-1 (b)	End : 2FFF	0	0	1	0	1	1	1	1	1	1	1	1	1	1	1	1
RAM-2 (a)	Start : 3000	0	0	1	1	0	0	0	0	0	0	0	0	0	0	0	0
RAM-2 (b)	End : 37FF	0	0	1	1	0	1	1	1	1	1	1	1	1	1	1	1
RAM-3 (a)	Start : 3800	0	0	1	1	1	0	0	0	0	0	0	0	0	0	0	0
RAM-3 (b)	End : 3FFF	0	0	1	1	1	1	1	1	1	1	1	1	1	1	1	1

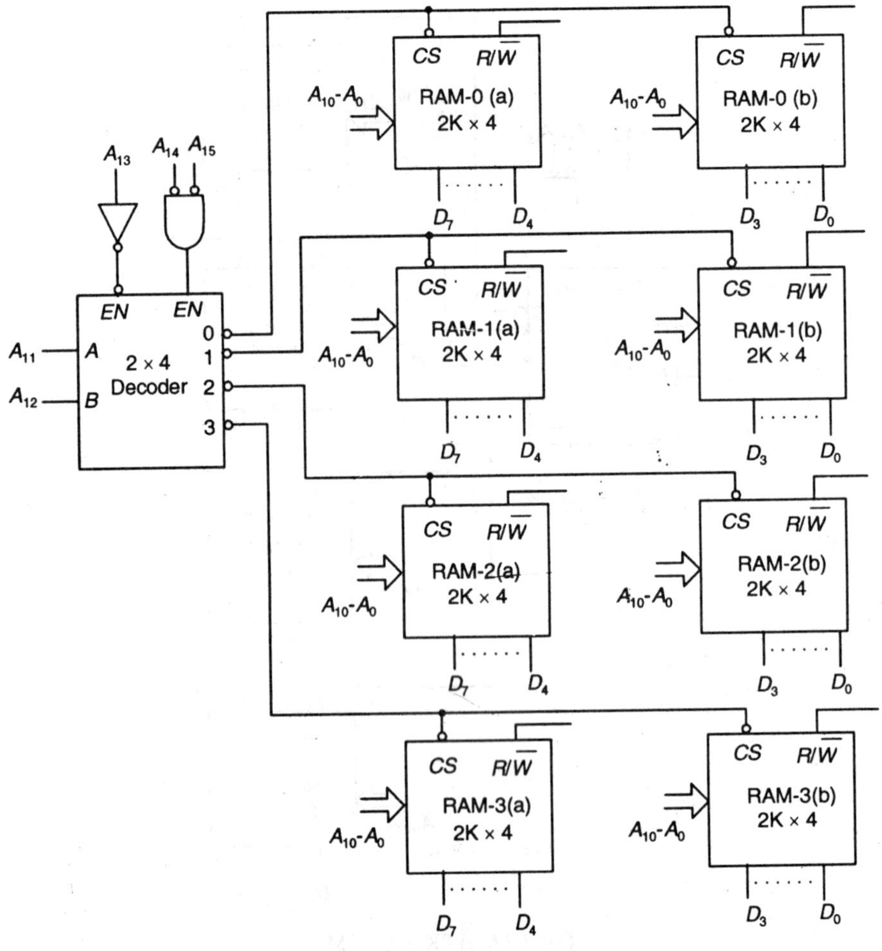

Fig. P7.6(b) 8K × 8 RAM

EXERCISES

7.1 Implement the following Boolean functions using PLA. Give the internal connection diagram for the PLA.

$$f_1 = AB + A\overline{C} + \overline{A}\overline{B}C$$

$$f_2 = AB + AC + \overline{A}\overline{B}C$$

7.2 The internal connection diagram for a PLA is given below. Write the Boolean functions realized by the PLA.

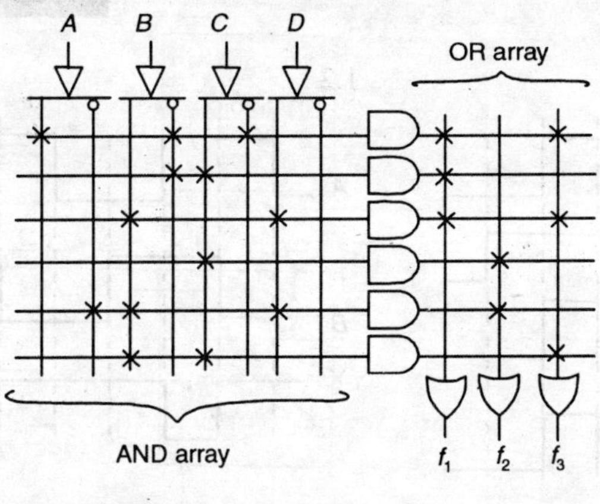

Fig. E7.2

7.3 A 2K × 4 chip is used to realize 16K × 6 memory. How many chips are required?

7.4 It is desired to combine several 2K × 8 chips to realize a 16K × 8 memory. How many chips are needed? How many address lines are required?

7.5 (a) How many 256 × 8 RAM chips are needed to provide a memory of 2K bytes?

(b) How many lines of the address bus must be used to access 2K bytes of memory? How many of these lines will be common to all chips?

(c) How many lines must be decoded for chip select? Specify the size of the decoder.

7.6 You are provided with 4K × 8 ROM chips, 4K × 4 RAM chips, decoders and logic gates. Using these items design the following:

(i) 8K × 8 ROM with starting address 0000H

(ii) 16K × 8 RAM with starting address 8000H

Chapter 1

1.1

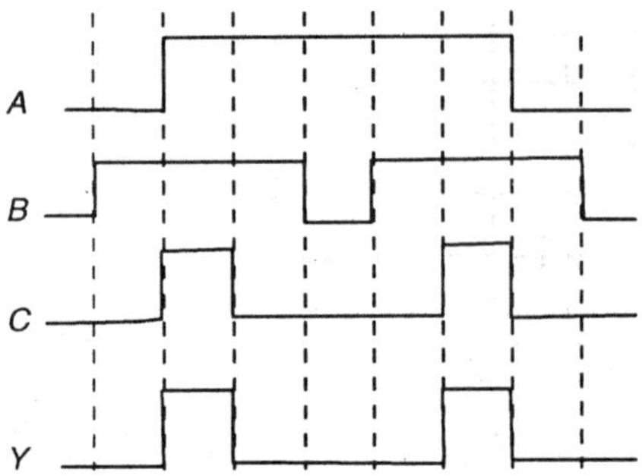

1.2

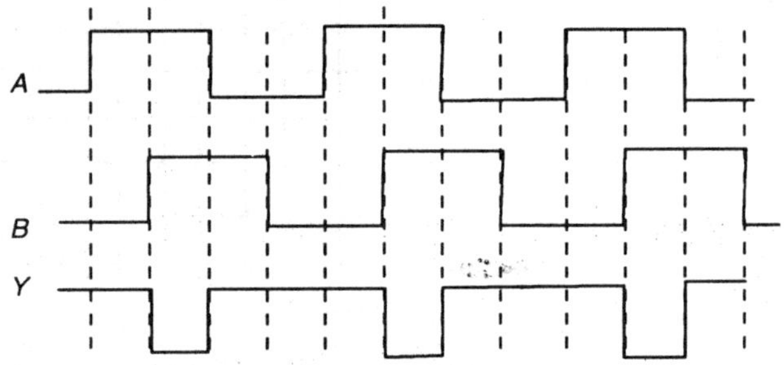

1.3

A	B	Y
0	0	0
0	1	0
1	0	1
1	1	0

1.4 AND gate

Chapter 2

2.1 (a) $F = Q\bar{R}$ (b) $F = A + CD$ (c) $F = AB + CD$

2.3 $F = A + B + C + D$

2.4

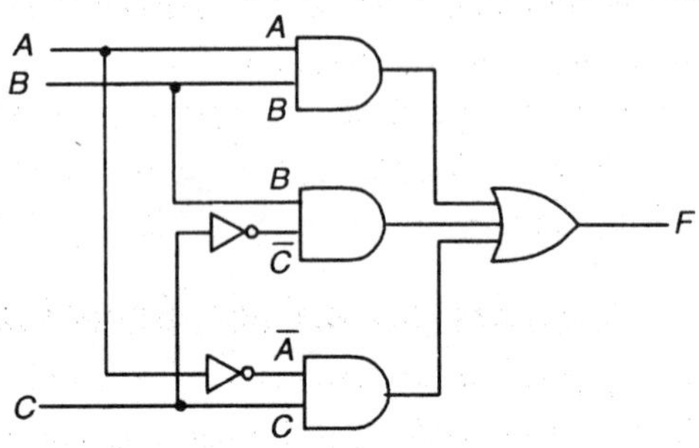

A	B	C	F
0	0	0	0
0	0	1	1
0	1	0	1
0	1	1	1
1	0	0	0
1	0	1	0
1	1	0	1
1	1	1	1

2.5

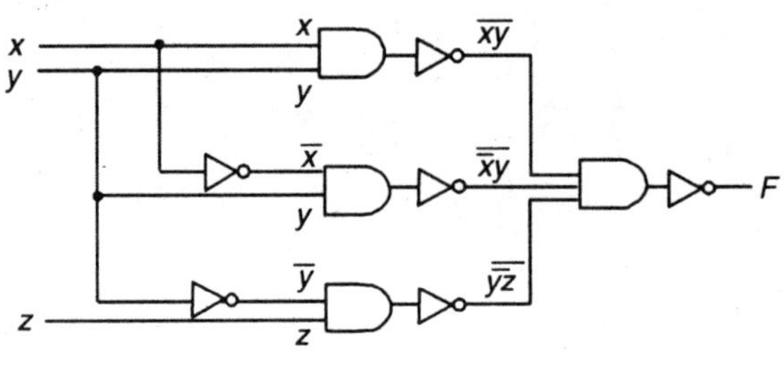

$$F = \overline{(\overline{xy})\,(\overline{\bar{x}y})\,(\overline{\bar{y}z})}$$
$$= xy + \bar{x}y + \bar{y}z$$

2.6 (a) Σ (1, 3, 5, 7), π (0, 2, 4, 6)

(b) Σ (1, 3, 5, 7, 9, 11, 13, 15), π (0, 2, 4, 6, 8, 10, 12, 14)

2.7 Σ (3, 5, 6, 7)

2.8 π (0, 2, 3, 6)

Chapter 3

3.1 (a) $F = B\bar{C} + \bar{B}D + A\bar{B}C$

(b) $F = \bar{B} + \bar{D}$

3.2 (a) $F = \bar{B}\bar{D} + \bar{A}BD + AB\bar{C}$

(b) $F = \bar{P}R + QS + PS + \bar{Q}\bar{R}\bar{S}$

3.3 $f = (w + x)(x + \bar{y})(x + y + z)$

3.4 $Y = (\bar{A} + B)(\bar{A} + D)(B + \bar{C} + D)$

3.5 SOP : $F = \bar{A}\bar{B} + \bar{C}\bar{D} + \bar{B}\bar{C}$

POS : $F = (\bar{A} + \bar{C})(\bar{B} + \bar{C})(\bar{B} + \bar{D})$

3.6 SOP : $F = AC + \bar{B}C + \bar{A}D$

POS: $F = (C + D)(\bar{A} + C)(A + \bar{B} + D)$

3.7 $f = \bar{A}\bar{B} + \bar{C}\bar{D} + \bar{A}\bar{D}$

3.8 Minimal set of prime-implicants :

$A\bar{B}\bar{C}\bar{E}$, $\bar{A}B\bar{D}E$, $\bar{A}\bar{B}D$, $\bar{A}\bar{B}D$ and $D\bar{E}$

3.9 $F = \bar{A}\bar{C} + \bar{B}\bar{D} + ABC$

3.10 $f = \bar{v}w + \bar{w}\bar{z}$

Chapter 4

4.1 Inputs: A, B, C, D

Outputs : w, x, y, z

$$w = AB + A\bar{C}\bar{D} = A\left[B + \left(\overline{C + D}\right)\right]$$

$$x = \bar{B}C + \bar{B}D + B\bar{C}\bar{D} = B \oplus (C + D)$$

$$y = C\bar{D} + \bar{C}D = C \oplus D$$

$$z = D$$

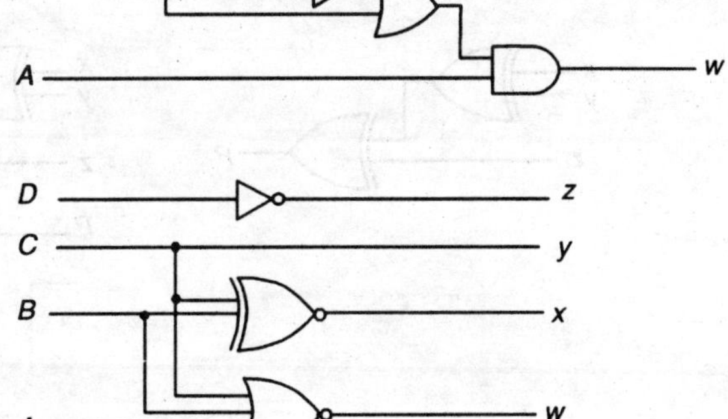

4.2 Inputs : A, B, C, D

Outputs : w, x, y, z

$$w = \bar{A}\bar{B}\bar{C} = \overline{(A + B + C)}$$

$$x = B\bar{C} + \bar{B}C = B \oplus C$$

$$y = C$$

$$z = \bar{D}$$

4.3

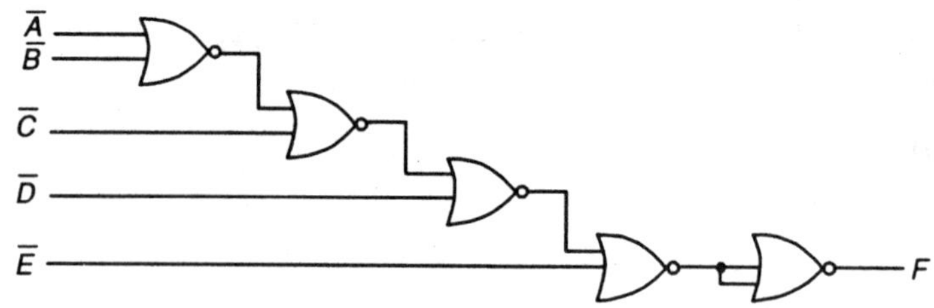

4.4

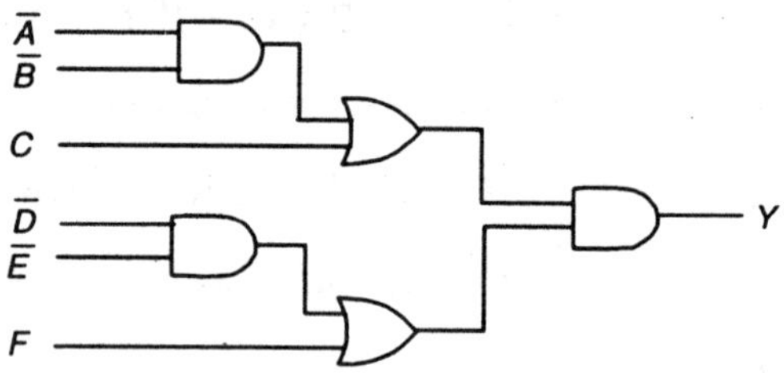

4.5

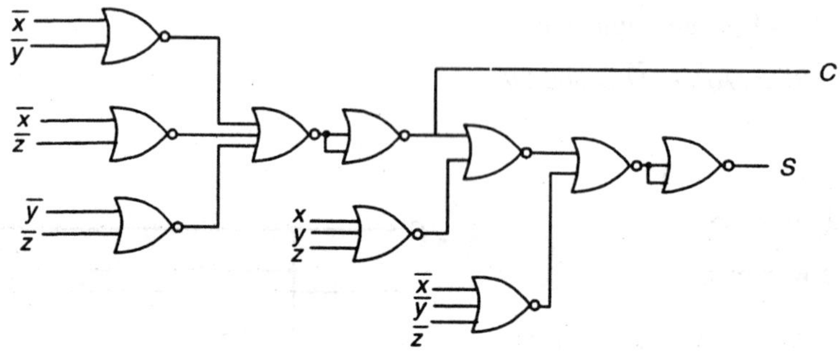

4.6 $P = x \oplus y \oplus z \qquad C = x \oplus y \oplus z \oplus P$

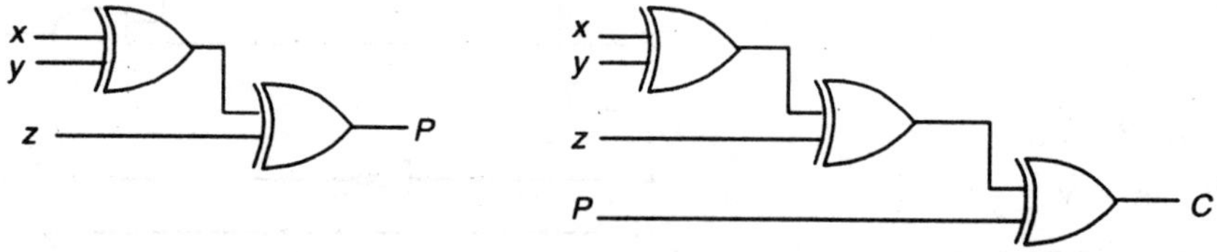

Chapter 5

5.1

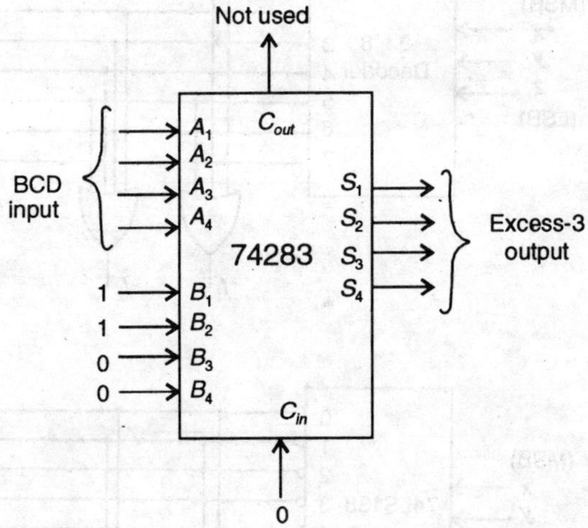

5.2 Similar to solved problem 5.2.

5.3

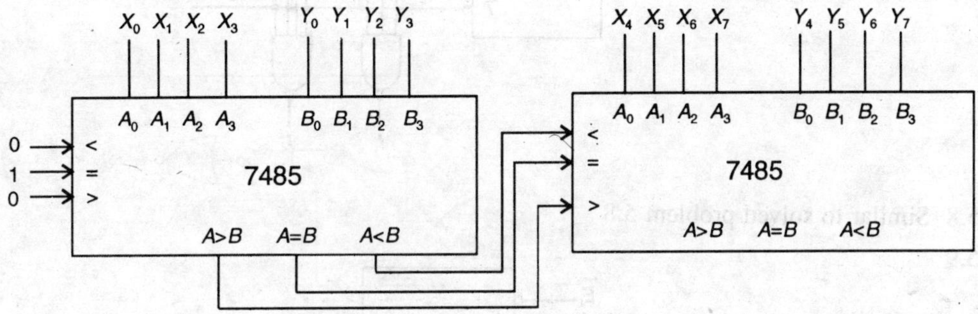

5.4 Similar to solved problem 5.6.

5.5

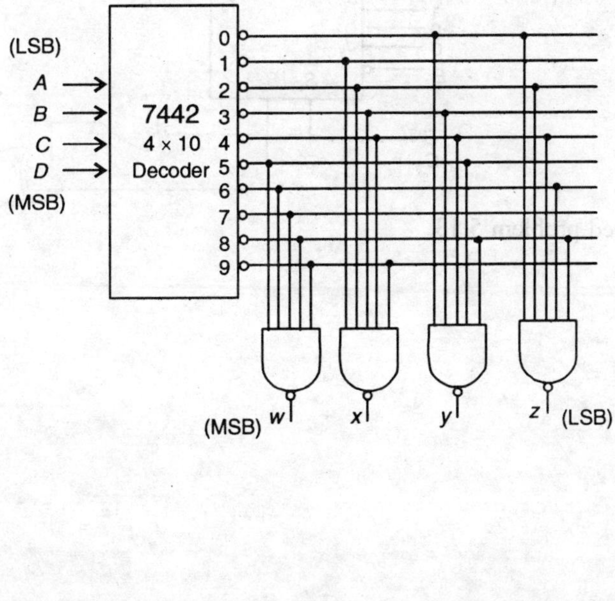

5.6

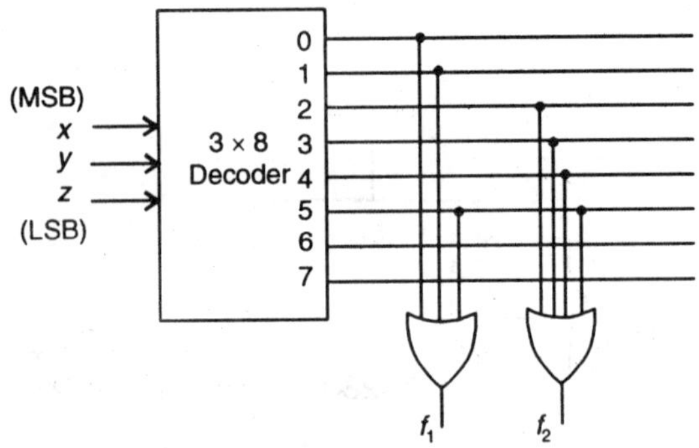

5.7

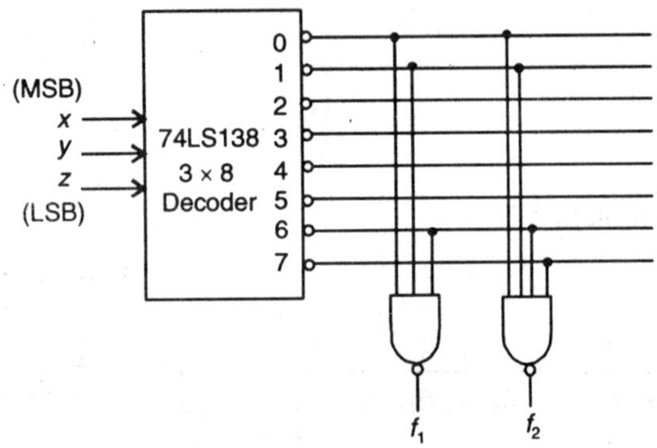

5.8 Similar to solved problem 5.8

5.9

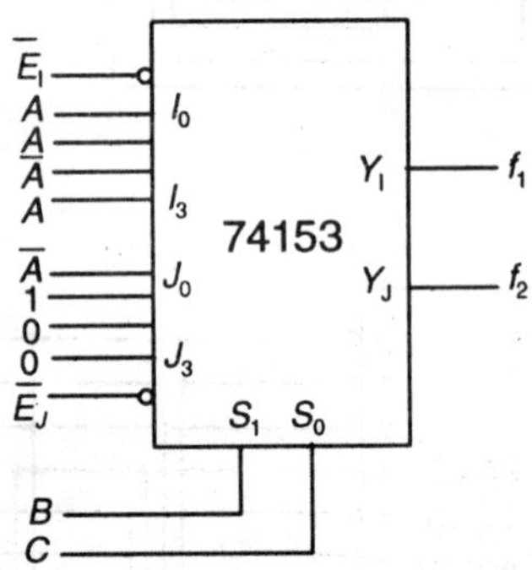

5.10 Similar to solved problem 5.13.

Chapter 6

6.1

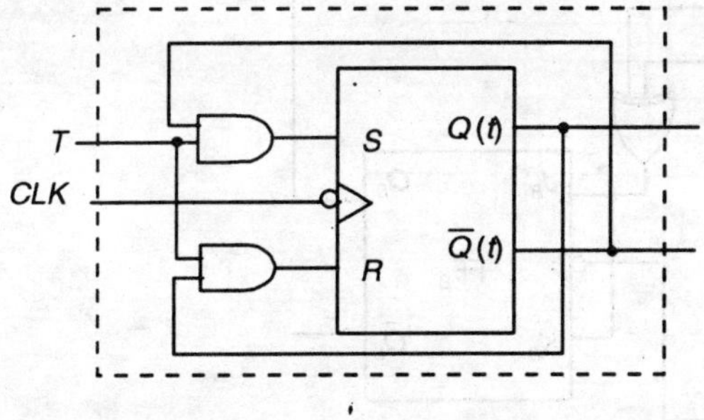

6.3

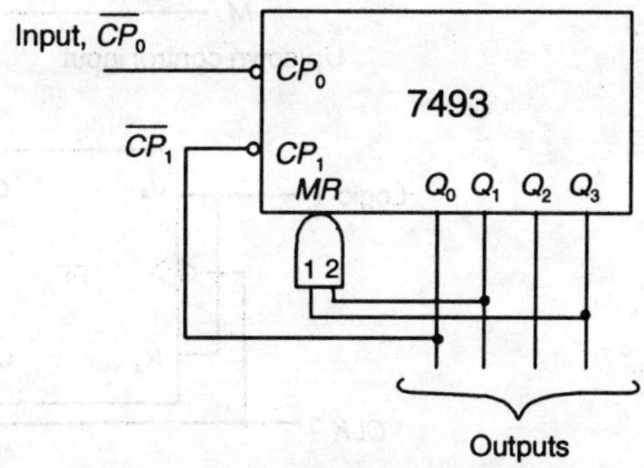

6.2 Similar to solved problem 6.2.

6.4

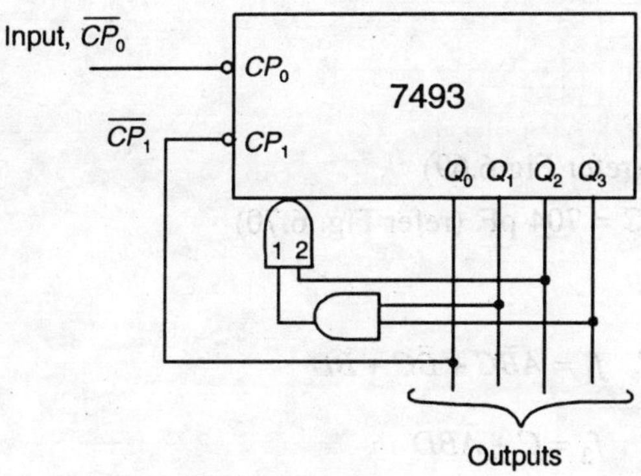

6.5

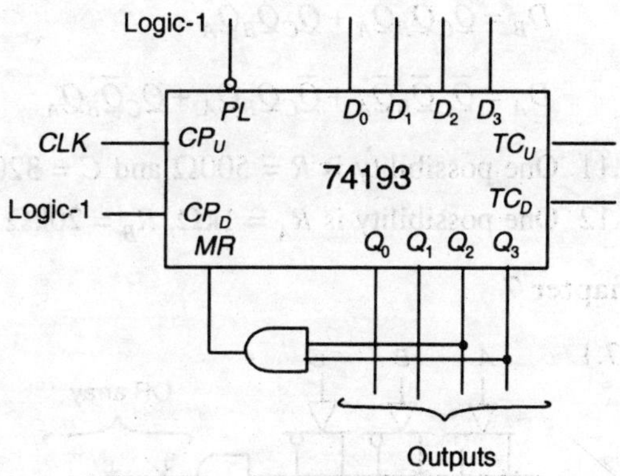

6.6 $T_C = Q_C \odot Q_B$

$T_B = Q_C \oplus Q_A$

$T_A = Q_C + Q_B$

6.7 $J_D = Q_C Q_B Q_A$; $K_D = Q_A$

$J_C = Q_B Q_A$; $K_C = Q_B Q_A$

$J_B = \overline{Q}_D Q_A$; $K_B = Q_A$

$J_A = 1$; $K_A = 1$

6.8

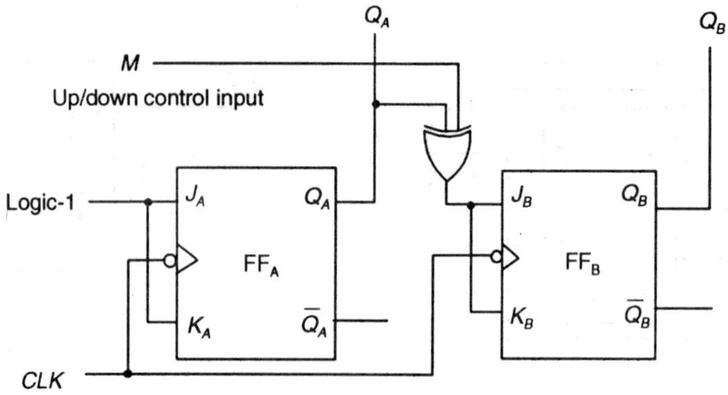

6.9 Similar to solved problem 6.9.

6.10 $D_C = Q_BQ_A + Q_CQ_A$

$D_B = \overline{Q}_C\overline{Q}_B\overline{Q}_A + Q_C\overline{Q}_BQ_A$

$D_A = \overline{Q}_C\overline{Q}_B\overline{Q}_A + \overline{Q}_CQ_BQ_A + Q_C\overline{Q}_BQ_A$

6.11 One possibility is $R = 500\Omega$ and $C = 320$ nF (refer Fig 6.69)

6.12 One possibility is $R_A = 1\text{k}\Omega$, $R_B = 20\text{k}\Omega$ and C = 704 pF. (refer Fig. 6.70)

Chapter 7

7.1

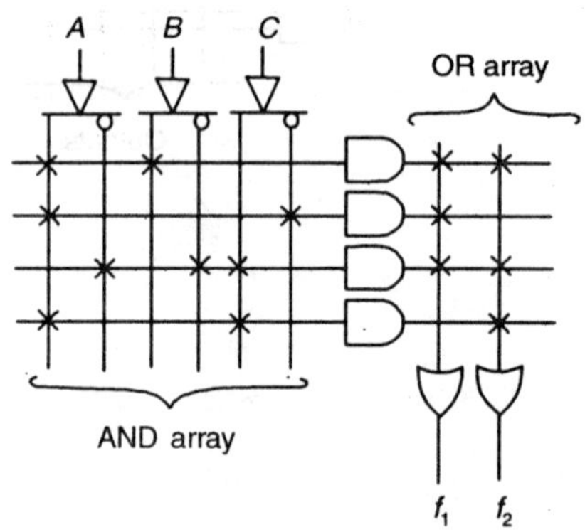

7.2 $f_1 = A\overline{B}C + \overline{B}C + BD$

$f_2 = C + \overline{A}BD$

$f_3 = A\overline{B}\overline{C} + BC + BD$

7.3 32 chips

7.4 8 chips, 14 address lines

7.5 (a) 8 chips, (b) 11, 8, (c) 4, 3 × 8

7.6 Similar to solved problem 7.6

REFERENCES

1. M. Morris Mano, *Digital Logic and Computer Design*, Prentice-Hall, 1999.
2. Ronald J. Tocci, *Digital Systems: Principles and Applications*, 6th Ed., Prentice-Hall, 1999.
3. Floyd, *Digital Fundamentals*, UBS, 1999.
4. Malvino and Leach, *Digital Principles and Applications*, 4th Ed., McGraw-Hill, 1986.
5. Charles H. Roth, Jr., *Fundamentals of Logic Design*, 4th Ed., Jaico Publishing House, 1994.
6. William I. Fletcher, *An Engineering Approach to Digital Design*, Prentice-Hall, 2001.
7. David J. Comer, *Digital Logic and State Machine Design*, 3rd Ed., Saunders College Publishing, 1995.
8. R.P. Jain, *Modern Digital Electronics*, 2nd Ed., Tata McGraw-Hill, 1999.
9. The IC Application Staff of Texas Instruments Incorporated, *Designing with TTL Integrated Circuits*, McGraw-Hill, 1989.
10. Semiconductor Manufacturers' Data Book: (a) *The TTL Data Book*: Texas Instruments Incorporated. (b) *TTL Logic Data Manual 1982*: Signetics.

DIGITAL ICs

TTL Devices

IC Number	*Function*
7400	Quad 2-input NAND gates
7401	Quad 2-input NAND gates (open collector)
7402	Quad 2-input NOR gates
7403	Quad 2-input NOR gates (open collector)
7404	Hex inverters
7405	Hex inverters (open collector)
7406	Hex inverter buffer-driver
7407	Hex buffer-drivers
7408	Quad 2-input AND gates
7409	Quad 2-input AND gates (open collector)
7410	Triple 3-input NAND gates
7411	Triple 3-input AND gates
7412	Triple 3-input NAND gates (open collector)
7413	Dual Schmitt triggers
7414	Hex Schmitt triggers
7416	Hex inverter buffer-drivers
7417	Hex buffer-drivers
7420	Dual 4-input NAND gates
7421	Dual 4-input AND gates
7422	Dual 4-input NAND gates (open collector)
7423	Expandable dual 4-input NOR gates
7425	Dual 4-input NOR gates
7426	Quad 2-input TTL-MOS interface NAND gates
7427	Triple 3-input NOR gates
7428	Quad 2-input NOR buffer
7430	8-input NAND gate
7432	Quad 2-input OR gates
7437	Quad 2-input NAND buffers
7438	Quad 2-input NAND buffers (open collector)
7439	Quad 2-input NAND buffers (open collector)
7440	Dual 4-input NAND buffers
7441	BCD-to-decimal decoder-Nixie driver
7442	BCD-to-decimal decoder
7443	Excess 3-to-decimal decoder
7444	Excess Gray-to-decimal
7445	BCD-to-decimal decoder-driver

IC Number	*Function*
7446	BCD-to-seven segment decoder-drivers (30-V output)
7447	BCD-to-seven segment decoder-drivers (15-V output)
7448	BCD-to-seven segment decoder-drivers
7450	Expandable dual 2-input 2-wide AND-OR-INVERT gates
7451	Dual 2-input 2-wide AND-OR-INVERT gates
7452	Expandable 2-input 4-wide AND-OR gates
7453	Expandable 2-input 4-wide AND-OR-1NVERT-gates
7454	2-input 4-wide AND-OR-INVERT gates
7455	Expandable 4-input 2-wide AND-OR-INVERT gates
7459	Dual 2-3 input 2-wide AND-OR-INVERT gates
7460	Dual 4-input expanders
7461	Triple 3-input expanders
7462	2-2-3-3 input 4-wide expanders
7464	2-2-3-4 input 4-wide AND-OR-INVERT gates
7465	4-wide AND-OR-INVERT gates (open-collector)
7470	Edge-triggered *JK* flip-flop
7472	*JK* master-slave flip-flop
7473	Dual *JK* master-slave flip-flop
7474	Dual *D* flip-flop
7475	Quad latch
7476	Dual *JK* master-slave flip-flop
7480	Gates full adder
7482	2-bit binary full adder
7483	4-bit binary full adder
7485	4-bit magnitude comparator
7486	Quad EXCLUSIVE-OR gate
7489	64-bit random-access read-write memory
7490	Decade counter
7491	8-bit shift register
7492	Divide-by-12 counter
7493	4-bit binary counter
7494	4-bit shift register
7495	4-bit right-shift–left-shift register
7496	5-bit parallel-in–parallel-out shift register
74100	4-bit bistable latch
74104	*JK* master-slave flip-flop
74105	*JK* master-slave flip-flop
74107	Dual *JK* master-slave flip-flop
74109	Dual *JK* positive-edge-triggered flip-flop
74116	Dual 4-bit latches with clear
74121	Monostable multivibrator
74122	Monostable multivibrator with clear
74123	Monostable multivibrator

IC Number	*Function*
74125	Three-state quad bus buffer
74126	Three-state quad bus buffer
74132	Quad Schmitt trigger
74136	Quad 2-input EXCLUSIVE-OR gate
74141	BCD-to-decimal decoder-driver
74142	BCD counter-latch-driver
74145	BCD-to-decimal decoder-driver
74147	10/4 priority encoder
74148	Priority encoder
74150	16-line-to-l-line multiplexer
74151	8-Channel digital multiplexer
74152	8-Channel data selector-multiplexer
74153	Dual 4/1 multiplexer
74154	4-line-to-l6-line decoder-demultiplexer
74155	Dual 2/4 demultiplexer
74156	Dual 2/4 demultiplexer
74157	Quad 2/1 data selector
74160	Decade counter with asynchronous clear
74161	Synchronous 4-bit counter
74162	Synchronous 4-bit counter
74163	Synchronous 4-bit counter
74164	8-bit serial shift register
74165	Parallel-load 8-bit serial shift register
74166	8-bit shift register
74173	4-bit three-state register
74174	Hex *F* flip-flop with clear
74175	Quad *D* flip-flop with clear
74176	35-MHz presettable decade counter
74177	35-MHz presettable binary counter
74179	4-bit parallel-access shift register
74180	8-bit odd-even parity generator-checker
74181	Arithmetic-logic unit
74182	Look-ahead carry generator
74184	BCD-to-binary converter
74185	Binary-to-BCD converter
74189	Three-state 64-bit random-access memory
74190	Up-down decade counter
74191	Synchronous binary up-down counter
74192	Binary up-down counter
74193	Binary up-down counter
74194	4-bit directional shift register
74195	4-bit parallel-access shift register
74196	Presettable decade counter

IC Number	Function
74197	Presettable binary counter
74198	8-bit shift register
74199	8-bit shift register
74221	Dual one-shot Schmitt trigger
74251	Three-state 8-channel multiplexer
74259	8-bit addressable latch
74276	Quad *JK* flip-flop
74279	Quad debouncer
74283	4-bit binary full adder with fast carry
74284	Three-state 4-bit multiplexer
74285	Three state 4-bit multiplexer
74365	Three-state hex buffers
74366	Three state hex buffers
74367	Three-state hex buffers
74368	Three-state hex buffers
74390	Individual clocks with flip-flops
74393	Dual 4-bit binary counter

CMOS Devices

IC Number	Function
74HC00	Quad 2-input NAND gate
74HC02	Quad 2-input NOR gate
74HC04	Hex inverter (buffered)
74HC08	Quad 2-input AND gate
74HC14	Hex inverting Schmitt trigger
74HC20	Dual 4-input NAND gate
74HC30	8-input NAND gate
74HC32	Quad 2-input OR gate
74HC42	BCD-to-decimal decoder
74HC74	Dual D flip-flop with preset and clear
74HC85	4-bit magnitude comparator
74HC123	Dual monostable multivibrator
74HC132	Quad 2-input NAND Schmitt trigger
74HC138	3- to 8-line decoder
74HC139	Expandable dual 2- to 4-line decoder
74HC154	4- to 16-line decoder (use 24SLP socket)
74HC161	Synchronous binary counter
74HC163	Synchronous binary counter
74HC164	8-bit serial in-parallel out shift register
74HC165	8-bit parallel in-serial out shift register

IC Number	*Function*
74HC174	Hex *D* Flip-Flop with clear
74HC175	Quad *D* type flip-flop with clear
74HC191	Up-down binary counter
74HC192	Synchronous decade up-down counter
74HC193	Synchronous binary up-down counter
74HC221	Dual monostable multivibrator
74HC240	Inverting octal tri-state buffer
74HC244	Octal tri-state buffer
74HC245	Octal tri-state transceiver
74HC257	Quad 2-channel tri-state multiplexer
74HC273	Octal *D* flip-flop
74HC367	Tri-state hex buffer
74HC373	Tri-state octal *D*-type latch
74HC374	Tri-state octal *D*-type flip-flop
74HC390	Dual 4-bit decade counter
74HC393	Dual 4-bit binary counter
74HC541	Octal buffer-line driver (tri-state)
74HC573	Tri-state octal *D*-type latch
74HC574	Tri-state octal *D*-type flip-flop
74HC595	8-bit serial to-parellel shift register latch
74HC688	8-bit magnitude comparator (equality detector)
74HC942	Full duplex low-speed 300-baud modem chip
74HC943	Full duplex 300-baud modem chip
74HC4017	Decade counter-divider with 10 decoded outputs
74HC4020	14-stage binary counter
74HC4040	12-stage binary counter
74HC4046	CMOS phase-lock loop
74HC4060	14-stage binary counter
74HC4066	Quad analog switch
74HC4514	4- to 16-line decoder with latch (use 24SLP socket)
74HC4538	Dual retriggerable monostable multivibrator

Index

126